The Corporatization of American Health Care

J. Warren Salmon • Stephen L. Thompson

The Corporatization of American Health Care

The Rise of Corporate Hegemony
and the Loss of Professional Autonomy

 Springer

J. Warren Salmon
School of Public Health
University of Illinois
Chicago, IL
USA

Stephen L. Thompson
College of Professional Studies
and Advancement
National Louis University
Chicago, IL
USA

ISBN 978-3-030-60669-5   ISBN 978-3-030-60667-1   (eBook)
https://doi.org/10.1007/978-3-030-60667-1

This Springer imprint is published by the registered company Springer Nature Switzerland AG
The registered company address is: Gewerbestrasse 11, 6330 Cham, Switzerland

This book is dedicated to the memory of Karen H. Thompson (1947–2016) and Dr. Bernard H. Baum (1926–2008).

Preface

The American healthcare system frequently has been called a "non-system"; yet we clearly interpret it very much as a *coherent system*—it is a system designed, much the same way as other businesses in America are organized, for private profit-making and return on investment.

We have relied heavily upon news sources as academic writing lags on current topics of concern. At times, we may generalize, or seem abstract, in presenting points, since we have absorbed an immense amount of knowledge to be sorted out, synthesized, and presented over the past history of 150 years. Much of what we focus upon contains numerous moving targets, changing weekly, often hidden or obscured from the public's attention. With the onset of the global pandemic caused by the COVID-19 virus, the blatant weaknesses in our healthcare structure and with the populations, not historically well served by the current system, have been laid bare. The power structure and its tendencies for greed have been exposed with lower socioeconomic communities and confined populations in nursing homes, prisons, and detention camps particularly hard hit by this virus. The resultant economic calamities caused by the preventive "stay-at-home orders" imposed by state governments also have created much harm (Nicola et al., 2020).

The approach of our book has been somewhat selective. There is admittedly much more to make it complete, despite our extensive referencing. In the healthcare system and outside of it, there needs much more detailed analysis of what we have attempted to focus upon. Trump exclaimed, "Nobody knew healthcare could be so complicated." Well, we did understand how complicated our system is and still do marvel at its complexity, even as we only begin to ponder the difficult reform road ahead.

In our opinion, doctors are so key in the direction for reforming our healthcare system, surely along with other health practitioners and scientists. Physicians often determine the course of treatment and still have relative power in the system if they choose to exert it in new and different ways for progressive directions. The roles and relationships among health professionals can mediate in both the clinical realm as well as for political action for the public's health. Gaining renewed trust in the professions by the public will be necessary to give them authority to perform and to maintain a relatively decent degree of professional autonomy and respect. First and foremost, this comes with competent technical performance and a dedication to both patients and populations. New resource allocations will hopefully not be too abrupt; progress may go slowly even as difficulties are delineated and confronted. An analogy may be that the protests in the summer of 2020 asking for changes in policing are quite challenging, but clearly very needed. Popular sentiments on both sets of issues must be listened to and understood so that the health system evolves new responsibilities for the profession. We encourage the profession to live up to its capacity and potentials.

So much confusion remains within the medical profession to interpret the ongoing changes in medical practice. Much has been brought on by increasing administrative control and reductions in professional prerogatives. In the 1850s, Marx made the point that today remains critical: Production thus produces consumption (Marx, 1857). When we examine modern medicine, it is important to note that true public health needs are hidden by mere medical care utilization, which in the United States has historically been individually centered, episodic, end-staged, highly tertiary care-based, technologically reliant, curative-oriented, with little prevention, and very, very costly, so thus profitable.

The lack of a public health focus is quite sad in that modern social epidemiology demonstrates that people do get sick in predictable and preventable ways depending on what socioeconomic status they possess. The waste of financial resources as well as years of productive lives lost due to a shortsighted market-based approach to healthcare is beyond tragic. We attempt to explain how and why this is happening to address the policy question of who benefits by continuing to increase the reach of such a flawed profit-based system.

What has evolved with the offered commodified form of services does not truly reflect a patient's, nor a population's, health and well-being. The definition of health has been argued and debated over time as modern medicine has been significantly critiqued. We wish readers to ponder a newer broader concept of the public's health as they examine our writing: the sustenance of well-being of the entire population apart from the clinical condition of a single individual patient's designated utilization of services. In the recent past, healthcare organizations have engaged in increased efforts in population health, but what that often means is extending the current system out into the ambulatory sphere for purposes of extending their brand and creating greater opportunities for profit-making in the face of declining inpatient revenues. Very few of these efforts are intended to actually do much about the population's well-being as it relates to the environments people live in, the endemic health conditions in their neighborhoods, poor infrastructure, schools and services, and general hopelessness.

Since the 1970s, corporate healthcare has been reorganizing the production of health services, yielding new production techniques, producing many new products and services, and reaping bountiful operating margins. While most of these entities operate as so-called not-for-profit due to their historic origins, many operate as though their prime directive is to generate surplus value rather than objective improvements in community health. All of this is changing the relationships between patients and health professionals. Through these processes, different expectations and new *needs* have arisen so that these processes also create additional services that production attempts to satisfy; nevertheless, these new services may not be what is necessary to advance true public health. In short, the market attempts to satisfy patients' needs of those who can afford to pursue such perceived enhancements by providing them with whatever service they may require while neglecting those who actually need medical oversight of more mundane and lesser profitable problems and who also possess limited ability to pay for much of anything.

Clearly, the means to satisfy health needs are constantly changing. Availability of new technologies multiplies medical production possibilities and further offers commoditized versions of what is to be consumed, usually with explosive costs. For example, the pharmaceutical industry has come up with a plethora of drugs to address adverse drug reactions created by other drugs. They advertise them directly to consumers to have them create demands upon their physicians to prescribe them with the latest medication for whatever they perceive ails them. Production requires many people to buy into the system without questioning what we as a population are getting out of the deal in terms of improved health status (O'Connor, 1974).

If we are to journey as a nation toward a more rational, effective, and humane system of healthcare that sustains and improves the *health of the entire population*, we need positive contributions to the development of health professional awareness to resist the very corporate financial relationships being foisted upon them. Most analyses of modern medicine have taken narrow, specialist, and mechanical views, uncritical of the existing social order: the very social order that the COVID-19 pandemic has exploited and laid bare. Tendencies to alter such perspectives require human efforts against the dominant interests that constrain varying professional and consumer behaviors. There are connections between economic, social, cultural, and political life that make it difficult for the average health professional to grasp. Traditional health professional education fails miserably in preparing practitioners for practice under the emerging conditions. Coupled with our nation's limited sense of history, this creates little clarity in health policy and its implementation.

One of us (Salmon) taught medical students as a community medicine faculty member in the 1970s, when the organization, financing, and delivery of care was being introduced into curricula. Rapid advances in science and technology squeezed out such non-clinical courses in most medical colleges. Today, few curricula adequately prepare most health professional graduates for the complexity of the emerging healthcare delivery system, though admonition for utilization management and cost control lectures have worked their way into becoming common.

Fifty years ago, liberal faculty efforts sought to reduce "medical mystification" over patients' bodies, disease processes, and treatments chiefly to aid patients' understanding for getting better. Inklings of such educational efforts are here again today, but under the guise of patient engagement for containment of utilization and cost reduction. More academicians are calling for new emphases on population health, spurred forward by the COVID-19 awareness (Nash, 2020).

Today, consumers and professionals both face a highly complicated, constantly changing healthcare system. A growing "administrative obfuscation" makes it difficult to grasp insurance concepts, making it far more difficult to ascertain federal policy and rapid marketplace changes, and to comprehend the bases in most managerial decision-making over directions. The rapidly evolving system is manifested most profoundly in the loss of professional autonomy; its effects are seen every day in terms of physicians and nurses adhering to corporate treatment protocols, while at the same time losing the ability to utilize the professional judgment and expertise gained through their education and training. The growing burnout has much to do with these changes and the internal conflicts, which are inherent.

This book's chapters represent our ongoing assessment from different angles, so what may appear to be redundancy is actually designed to reinforce the points. We have reviewed and assembled a massive bibliography of literature relying upon academic experts who came before us as mentors in public health. We have also followed many journalists who have become authorities on various topics, particularly in the information technology sector. Publishing guidelines have restricted the use of their insights using their own words as quotes, so we paraphrase and reference with respect and appreciation as we strive to synthesize their contributions into our analysis here. It makes for much to take in by the readers. We often delve into higher levels of generalization in places to draw analogies to reveal how the healthcare system reflects the larger American political economy.

One example is the concept of "development and underdevelopment," where growth gets fetishized in corporate advancement. Yet, such a process is always accompanied by underdevelopment of a segment: one side grows, the other side diminishes usually in terms of what procedures have the best payer reimbursement. Whiteis and Salmon (1990) utilized this contribution by the economist Andre Gunder Frank (1967) in establishing this dynamic of development/underdevelopment of the proprietary health system growth across the 1970s and 1980s, amidst the neglect and decline of public sector providers and certain "not-for-profit" hospitals. Much of this wide disparity resulted from dynamics in the medical marketplace, but it was promulgated by the then health policy decisions—and still continues to be!

The role of large corporations and powerful interests behind US healthcare and its distortion of the healthcare system are a unifying focus of this book. We maintain there is a clear relationship between production growth and the development of new kinds of social organization in the health sector (Dreitzel, 1968). Now, most mainstream observers rarely stray from the conventional and dominant perspective that tends to support existing relations and hovers at micro levels of analysis. Thus, the overall system gets little critique except for managerial rationalist tinkering in terms of minor incremental corrections, usually for its legitimation; the overall structure is assumed to stay intact, its directions and priorities are assumed to be immutable.

Nevertheless, the apparent contradictions in American healthcare are becoming so evident to many more Americans these days: profits over people with widening inequalities persisting and with the coronavirus exacerbating. This social reality is increasing a fresh pondering of *why things are the way they are, how they got that way, and what should be done* to avoid a continuation of decline.

We encourage other scholars and analysts to probe the downsides of corporate health and help propose routes to find reasonable resolutions in a reform direction. In short, there needs to be a re-examination of the American healthcare system that has been created and ask the questions, "Is this the best we can do?" and "Is this what the American public really wants and needs?"

Health policy academics have little to say to engage the broader American public, many of whom seem to "get it" with their own personal critiques given their mounting dissatisfaction long before the academic journals delineate problems. Businesspersons, politicians, bureaucrats, and many professionals too often fail to perceive the consumer/patient perspective, though efforts by healthcare marketers are surely trying of late. Of course, these groups have a greater ability to control and regulate health policies, but rarely do you see them choosing to compromise their position when it runs counter to their vested interests.

As public health professionals, we seek a different and more holistic assessment of human beings and their health in their daily, family, community, and work lives. We see this at the collective level of groups of people; in fact, the entire population in the social and ecological environments in which we all function. The experts, specialists, and researchers usually work on individuals as separate unrelated entities in bits and pieces, not globally in their assessments of health. Notwithstanding, the pandemic may be leading to a paradigm shift in public health as a younger generation of basic and clinical scientists forge a new outlook for addressing disease patterns.

Chicago, IL, USA   J. Warren Salmon
Chicago, IL, USA   Stephen L. Thompson

References

Dreitzel, H. P. (1968). Die *Gesellshcaftlichen Leiden und das Leiden and der Gesellschaft*. Eine Pathologie des Alltagslebens, Stuttgart, Perfect Paperback.

Frank, A. G. (1967). *Capitalism and underdevelopment in Latin America: Historical studies in Chile and Brazil*. Monthly Review Press. Available via DIALOG. https://monthlyreview.org/product/capitalism_and_underdevelopment_in_latin_america/. Accessed 12 June 2020.

Marx, K. (1857). Introduction to a contribution to the critique of political economy. *Marxists*. Available via DIALOG. https://www.marxists.org/archive/marx/works/1857/grundrisse/ch01.htm. Accessed 12 June 2020.

Nash, D. (2020). We need a retooled post-COVID-19 curriculum to emphasize the role of population health. *Modern Healthcare*. Available via DIALOG. https://www.modernhealthcare.com/opinion-editorial/medical-schools-should-emphasize-population-health-post-covid. Accessed 3 June 2020.

Nicola, M., Alsafi, Z., Sohrabi, C., Kerwan, A., Al-Jabir, A., Iosifidis, C., & Agha, R. (2020). *The socio-economic implications of the Coronavirus and COVID-19 pandemic: A review*. NCBI. Available via DIALOG. https://www.ncbi.nlm.nih.gov/pmc/articles/PMC7162753/. Accessed 12 June 2020.

O'Connor, J. (1974). *The corporations and the state: Essays in the theory of capitalism and imperialism*. New York, NY: Harper.
Whiteis, D. G., & Salmon, J. W. (Eds.). (1990). The proprietarization of healthcare and the underdevelopment of the public sector. In *The corporate transformation of health care: Issues & directions* (pp. 117–131). New York, NY: Baywood.

Acknowledgments

Undertaking a journey for this book engaged us with a number of progressive scholars to whom we are most grateful. We count among our teachers several progressive professionals who have illuminated much of the American healthcare system. They are frequently referenced throughout the book.

We have enjoyed a long-standing friendship and collaboration on several research publications. Stephen Thompson was a delight to work with in all aspects of the research and writing. His perspective from his clinical and industrial relations studies gave him insights into the sociology of the medical profession, which enriched that of Jack Salmon. Over the 2 years of research, we had many worthwhile discussions over glasses produced by the Sixteen Men of Tain. Salmon's pioneering work on the corporatization of medicine has been strengthened by collaborators on his previous books and several publications.

Professor Salmon needs to personally thank two women who provided him with superior support: Patricia Soriano, who someday will become a fine attorney, became my research assistant near the beginning of this project. She tirelessly typed over a thousand references besides many other helpful tasks. And then Naimah Malik was always available for transcribing my dictated sections that I plugged into chapters along the way. The dedication of both individuals to the project deserves my deep gratitude. Then, our Editor, Janet Kim, was always understanding of our predicaments and the delay of getting this manuscript completed. We have surely enjoyed this professional relationship and many conversations.

Our respective families, Kim and Agatha, both deserve our thanks for their support, along with our children, who may have asked at times about our progress, read sections, and were always ready to say, "Just get it done."

Lastly, we appreciate our designated outside reviewers, past graduate students who read earlier drafts and offered detailed commentaries: Doctors Gina Gilomen Study, Joseph Feinglass, Meghana Aruru, and Thomas Blackman, plus Chris Salmon and daughter Bethany Salmon, who were dearly supportive.

For our readers, it will be gratifying that our analysis may provoke new thinking to instill further observation of American healthcare through a critical lens. May more of us unite in struggles for future social justice and equity in healthcare for our citizenry.

As public health professionals, we truly believe health is a fundamental human right and ask for all to join us in this declaration.

Contents

About the Authors

J. Warren Salmon, PhD is an author, researcher, and lecturer. Previously, he was Professor of Health Policy and Administration, School of Public Health, at the University of Illinois at Chicago (UIC). He was formerly Professor and Head of the Department of Pharmacy Administration, College of Pharmacy; Professor of Public Policy Analysis, College of Urban Planning and Public Affairs; and Adjunct Professor of Medical Education, College of Medicine at UIC. Prior to coming to UIC, Professor Salmon held faculty appointments at Thomas Jefferson Medical College and Drexel/Hahnemann Medical College, both in Philadelphia, Pennsylvania. Professor Salmon's research interests have focused on the corporatization of medicine and pharmacy, managed care pharmacy, urban healthcare delivery, comparative healthcare systems, global pharmaceutical industry developments, and alternative and complementary medicines, among selected health policy issues. He edited *Alternative Medicines: Popular and Policy Perspectives* (Tavistock/Methuen/Routledge, 1984); (with Jeffrey W. Todd) *The Corporatization of Health Care: A Two Day Symposium and Public Hearing* (Illinois Public Health Association, 1988); (with Eberhard Goepel) *Community Participation and Empowerment Strategies in Health Promotion*, 7 volumes (Zentrum fuer Interdisziplinare Forschung, 1990); *The Corporate Transformation of Health Care, Part I: Issues and Directions* (Baywood, 1990); *The Corporate Transformation of Health Care, Part II: Reflections and Implications* (Baywood, 1994); and (with Linda Shapiro) *Health Care for Chicagoans: How Will Health System Integration Affect the Health of the Public?* (Health & Medicine Policy Research Group, 1995). Professor Salmon resides in River Forest, Illinois, as a still-active independent researcher, writer, mentor, and frequent lecturer.

Stephen L. Thompson, PhD is Associate Professor in the Health Studies Department, College of Professional Studies and Advancement, at National Louis University (NLU) in Chicago, Illinois. He is the former Associate Dean and former Interim Dean of the College of Arts and Sciences at National Louis University. He received his PhD in Health Policy and Administration from the University of Illinois at Chicago in 2000, his Master of Science in Industrial Relations from Loyola

University Chicago in 1984, and a Bachelor of Arts in Biology from Drake University in Des Moines, Iowa, in 1975. He also completed a program in respiratory therapy at Northwestern University Affiliated Programs in 1975 and is a Registered Respiratory Therapist (RRT) and a Neonatal/Pediatric Specialist (NPS). He teaches in the Master of Business Administration, Master of Health Administration, and the Bachelor of Health Care Leadership programs at NLU. His major interests are in health policy, research methodology, and unions and collective bargaining and organizational theory. He has published in the areas of Collective Bargaining and Physicians, Health Reform, and Privatization of Public Education.

Chapter 1
History of the Corporatization of American Medicine: The Market Paradigm Reigns

Introduction

Economic systems have been analyzed and debated by economists and governmental leaders for centuries. Historically, economic systems have been assessed by the products and techniques of production and how they are distributed, today with capitalism predominant and with mounting inequality within every society (Piketty, 2016). Under global capitalism, ownership of land and productive capital is chiefly in private hands, with the role of the state fiercely debated with continual attempts seeking to restrain its oversight (O'Connor, 1973). Social justice in more liberal advanced societies has been championed over time, but the rise of finance capital and its presence in corporate-dominated economies has emerged with a massive concentration of ownership in almost every sector of the American economy. With its tendency toward managerial and administrative quantifications to fix existing flaws in the system, neoclassical economics has prevailed; few alternative or opposing perspectives rarely get debated. Thus, the overall structure is taken as a given and immutable (Hunt & Schwartz, 1972). Global efforts toward privatization and monopolization mark the current stage of development.

When analyzing the United States, one observes that almost every sector of the economy—industrial, financial, construction, agriculture, communications and media, and even services—is dominated by just a few large national, if not multinational, firms (Baran & Sweezy, 1966; O'Connor, 1973, 1974; Barnet & Muller, 1974; Hermann, 1981). This monopolization has been ongoing over the last century. However, today there is an incredible degree of concentration and centralization of capital, which is an indicator of the strong political influence that large corporations exert on public policy at all levels of government: federal, state, and local.

Therefore, it is *not* difficult to realize that the American healthcare system would eventually reflect this larger concentrated economy. Health care is not alone, as this phenomenon is also seen in higher education, private prison management, and, under President Donald J. Trump, immigration detention camps. Given current

© Springer Nature Switzerland AG 2021
J. W. Salmon, S. L. Thompson, *The Corporatization of American Health Care*,
https://doi.org/10.1007/978-3-030-60667-1_1

political trends, we may see upswings among other public and "not-for-profit" services becoming targets for further privatization, usually masked as being for increased "cost control" and "efficiency" and always with the epitaph that "the private sector can do it better."

This book's analytic perspective is broad, seeking to define the overall structure to delineate the changing context of medical practice under which costly medical malpractice reigns within a profit-based medical-industrial complex functions. Grasping the dominant social relationships that compose the healthcare system requires a political economic lens to reduce the overriding ideology of the marketplace and to discern its underlying dynamics.

Ushered in during the Reagan Administration, the heightened fetish for cost containment in health care reflects the Republican disdain over the distribution of healthcare expenditures, not just by the federal government, but within the entire economy. It was the time when economists rose to prominence in health policy discussions (Fox, 1979), the majority of whom seemed much less focused on access to care and more on providing improving amenities to their well-heeled clients. It is not a surprise that cost containment often went together with disenfranchisement of the poor, disabled, and minorities, who had previously secured some access through federal programs, but basically excluded many other vulnerable population groups in need.

Nelson (2018, p.2) critiques the economics profession as vulnerable to groupthink, along with its lack of diversity, especially at the highest echelons of economic *policymaking*. Such is the case that provides the lack of attention to issues that address minorities in economic research to macroeconomic models used in public policy decisions. In effect, the profession has less chance to serve the public effectively and remains a tool of those in power; this became obvious from the 1980s on with health policy. Critics have chimed in on the dismal cost of economics' lack of racial diversity that surely has affected *what questions get asked* and *what issues get readily dismissed for lack of "scientific study."*

Privatization has been rampant across the developed capitalist world for decades as many governments divest themselves. Prime Minister Margaret Thatcher privatized public utilities, healthcare facilities, and much more without necessary oversight to prevent thereafter exploitation (Ford & Plimmer, 2018). President Emmanuel Macron in France has sought privatization schemes to fund infrastructure projects; many transactions are complicated with murky implications (Kegshae, 2018). Even space exploration is being privatized (Pasztor, 2020).

Since President Ronald Reagan's first inaugural address in 1981 when he proclaimed, "Government is not the solution, it is the problem," the very thought of reforming the public sector has faded from the general consciousness. Consider, after a number of veterans Administration (VA) hospital scandals over access and quality from the George W. Bush years through Trump, the federal budget was seen as bountiful for subsidizing private entities for care of our veterans and military, and perhaps to entirely transition to private insurance coverage. While local news media had reported extensively on the VA for years to enumerate multiple issues, many Democrats and most veterans groups oppose such a move to privatize care

(Bhagwati, 2019). ProPublica reported that Trump's "private care program gave companies billions and Vets longer waits" including higher overhead (Arnsdorf and Greenberg, 2018).

Opening access may shorten waits, provide more choices, and perhaps lessen co-pays, although switching vast numbers of veterans to private hospitals (a massive endeavor itself) may actually strain care in parts of the private sector (Steinhauser & Philipps, 2019; Meyer, 2019). Even before this dramatic policy change, the Government Accountability Office (GAO) examination of one of the nation's largest health systems found a crucial need for improved oversight and greater clarity over roles and responsibilities (GAO, 2019b)—the operative word is oversight! The VA was previously charged with grievously *not* reviewing credentialing of practitioners (GAO, 2019a), keeping on doctors despite misconduct allegations (Luthi, 2019).

At the same time, the VA and the US Department of Defense (DoD) are together attempting to create a new electronic health record (EHR) system, which could transition active duty servicemen to local VA care. A huge government contract will be awarded to a private firm (likely, Cerner) for its development. In 2019 McKesson Technologies was awarded a $400 million contract for the Department of Defense digital imaging network picture archiving and communications health IT system. In many cases, governments lack the expertise to carry out functions to greatly advance their agency; the issue then becomes assuring performance-based contracting and avoiding the typical cost overruns, where excess private profit can be gained—particularly given the outlandish history of DoD military outsourcing.

Thus, privatization is widely overtaking multiple aspects of the American healthcare system, as the corporate for-profit basis of reorganizing our citizenry's health care seems substantially entrenched at huge taxpayer costs. The Trump Administration is also planning to privatize Fannie Mae and Freddie Mac, the core of American housing finance; they hold nearly half the total outstanding in America (The Economist, 2019b). More such moves will likely spread under the Trump Administration, since awards of taxpayer's money to private firms—like huge corporate tax cuts—provide the cycle of reelection campaign donations. This direction goes hand in hand with his massive deregulation efforts.

There are surely better ways to proceed. Lessons can be learned from abroad, as noted by the political and cultural differences seen in Japan's privatizing its railways versus the slack, highly unpopular British railway privatization under Thatcher. The much-criticized franchise system in Britain has endured a catastrophically botched timetable change, major delays and cancellations at the worst level in a decade, and a passenger usage decline; ticket prices have risen twice as fast as wages since 2010 (How rising rail fares and falling punctuality, 2019). Unreliable service due to poor performance by the British rails became symbolic of the broader discontent with privatization and neoliberal economics since Thatcher. In contrast, Harding (2019, p. 7) reports in the *Financial Times* that Japan's private enterprise has a robust system of regulation, and rail companies feel a responsibility to society; they also operate on consumer payments *without public subsidy*.

Reich (2018) points out that privatization boosting efficiency and reducing taxes is a myth; rather privatization often only boosts corporate bottom lines. He warns "don't privatize when the purpose of the service is to bring us together—reinforcing our communities" to connect across class and race, "linking up Americans who'd otherwise be isolated or marginalized… don't privatize when the people who are supposed to get the services have no power to complain when services are poor" or maybe cannot recognize their poor quality (2018, p. 2). These are surely apropos to health care for Americans.

Chapter Purpose

This chapter will provide an overview of the historical development of American health care from its nineteenth-century cottage system to the onset of its now dominant corporate for-profit form. The main characteristic of private ownership with public subsidy reveals the lack of moral national commitment to health care for all citizens. Interventions by powerful economic forces have been key from reorganizing medical education through business sources arranging for financing strategies for the hospital industry to the current encroachment by the IT industry firms. The chapter traces the beginning concentration of capital in the medical-industrial complex (MIC) through various social interventions that allowed profit-making to emerge. Actions by capitalist philanthropic foundations at the turn of the twentieth century reorganized medical education to promote scientific medicine which greatly advanced productive health resources. As the delivery system started to industrialize, the Committee on the Costs of Medical Care (CCMC) in the late 1920s proposed hospitals to become the employment center for physicians and other professionals to deliver *organized care for populations*, but its ideas were staunchly defeated by the medical profession.

As an alternative, solo fee-for-service medical practice was preserved so hospitals sought their own cost-plus reimbursement through employment-based voluntary insurance. This model supported by Blue Cross persisted with broad support until the 1960s when the federal government grafted on Medicare and Medicaid with a similar payment mechanism. As a result, costs exploded to warrant President Richard M. Nixon's healthcare crisis declaration in 1968. The genesis of corporatization came with his health maintenance organization strategy, which in effect unleashed market forces for the advancement of profit-making in multiple segments of the healthcare industry. This chapter spells out the rise to supremacy of marketplace medicine with the emergence of the proprietary hospital chains, the growth of the medical-industrial complex, and the societal confrontation over access, cost, quality, and accountability issues up against progressive calls for universal coverage for all Americans. The chapter will reveal that historically the private sector's pursuit of profit in health care with heavy public subsidization leaves less than desirable outcomes for the public's health. The commoditization of health needs runs opposite to consideration of a collective public health.

Historical Background

The corporate consolidation of American medicine came rapidly (Gray, 1983; Institute of Medicine, 1986; Brown & McCool, 1986). Today several giants dominate the production of health services (Light, 1986) with a handful of nationwide insurance firms continually passing through a merger and acquisition (M&A) activity of their own. The mighty Anthem-Cigna and Aetna-Humana horizontal combinations were defeated in 2015–2017 by the Federal Trade Commission (Dranove, 2017), but a new stage witnesses these players, among many others, seeking out partners in vertically integrated lines of business, as well as with pharmacy benefit managers, chain drug stores, and now information technology firms (see Chaps. 2 and 5). Greater permeations of smaller insurance mergers are likely under Trump's executive order for cross-border insurance (Jopson & Sevastropulo, 2017). Republican tax-cutting actions and support for repatriation of overseas profits are spurring stock buybacks and a much larger M&A furor among all parties in the "medical-industrial complex" (MIC).

Box 1.1 $3.8 Trillion Fuels the Medical-Industrial Complex

Profit margins for health providers and the corporate supply firms have become huge, including pharmaceutical biotechnology, medical diagnostics, and biomedical research and development; medical, dental, and optical hardware or services; construction of facilities; real estate investment trusts for health facility holdings; provision of legal, accounting and consulting services; computers, software, and information technology; analytics firms, among other products to assist providers in their treating patients. Entities in the medical-industrial complex have been the motor force of development and chiefly responsible for the cost spiral.

Phenomenal inappropriate services, rampant administrative overhead, excessive executive salaries, "drug misadventuring," and more fraud and waste are characteristic, which do not promote the public health.

New England Journal of Medicine editor Arnold Relman (1980) decried the *new medical-industrial complex*: investor-owned hospital and nursing home chains, home care, dialysis centers, health maintenance organizations (HMOs), and now pharmacy benefit managers (PBMs), Accountable Care Organizations (ACOs), and drug store retail clinics. All of these segments have reaped bountiful returns on their investments by stiffly challenging traditional "not-for-profit" and public providers, who are left to primarily serve the less fortunate populations, including the uninsured and many Medicaid patients. For-profit corporate drug store clinics also now compete against practicing physicians in many communities. The ongoing consolidation of PBM/insurers portends an even greater threat to the playing field of existing providers.

Of note, mergers and acquisitions (M&As) are almost always disruptive; they lead to layoffs, which may provoke union unrest—as with the 2018 Dignity and Catholic Health Initiatives (CHI) example below (Gooch, 2018), closing of offices and plants, significant community impacts, and geographical dislocations, even while stockholders don't always benefit, but the top executives, including those in the so-called not-for profits, who manage the process, clearly do!

Merging the Dignity-CHI "not-for-profit" systems faced an unfavorable "moral analysis" from the National Catholic Bioethics Center. Later organized reviews by the local archbishops, other bioethicists, respective state attorney generals, and the Vatican then pushed this Catholic/secular merger forward as CommonSpirit with 150,000 employees (AnyDay: nearly 2 years in the making, 2018). The combined system of 139 hospitals and 25,000 physicians in 21 states will reap almost $30 billion in revenues annually (Meyer & Bannow, 2018), but it's no overlap in service areas presents obstacles to coordinating and standardizing care (Kacik & Bannow, 2017). Its co-CEO leadership structure (Kacik & Bannow, 2017) may face a few financial challenges, while they figure out integration, people, and cultures. Both systems had huge operating losses in 2017, but Dignity bounced back in 2018, with the new CommonSpirit Health rivaling its Catholic competitor, Ascension, in total hospitals, and with revenue just below Kaiser Permanente's $72.7 billion in 2017.

Kaiser Health News asked if Catholic-run systems will tie doctors' hands by prohibiting previous policies on contraception services, abortions, in vitro fertilizations, and physician-assisted death (Gold, 2019). Advocates for women's health and the LGBTQ community fear their concerns could be a casualty of Dignity taking over the University of California San Francisco Hospital, a public entity with a long-standing commitment on liberal health issues. One in six acute care hospital beds in the United States are in Catholic systems, with such hospital ownership increasing 22% from 2001 to 2016 (Gold, 2019).

This trend of rapid consolidation in both horizontal and vertical mergers is based on the assumption that large scale is needed to lower costs, although the evidence points to a different reality of higher prices for consumers (Kacik & Bannow, 2017, p. 5). The year 2015 was record-breaking for M&As, with the following year seeing continued adaptations to the evolving financial landscape.

With M&As that climbed from 38 in 2003 to 115 in 2017, economists and the American Hospital Association debated whether consolidation typically raises prices, often does not produce expected savings, and can diminish quality (Kacik, 2019a, 2019b). Owens has commented on an American Hospital Association (AHA) report which claimed that mergers resulted in better care and savings, but all other studies point to the outcomes of less competition and higher prices for patients (Owens, 2019, p. 1).

Analyses that focus on costs and not prices skew all conclusions. Mergers can beget greater capital and clinical expertise, which may mean wider use of "best practices." Yet hospitals joining together seems in part to be a response to rising information technology (IT) costs, among other cost trends (see Chaps. 2 and 5). The cost burden in the executive suite usually becomes an issue in that already high salaries tend to balloon. It is important to point out that consolidation is *not* the same as integration of services (Owens, 2019). For example, a local hospital chain here in Chicago, almost a decade after merging, still cannot transfer medical records from the flagship to an affiliate in the suburbs. Knowles reports that when institutions merge and competition declines, mortality rates and adverse health outcomes increase (2019, p. 91).

Beyond changing historic hospital names, local disruptions occur, which altered the range of services residents have been used to providing, e.g., women's health when Catholics chains absorb, HIV/AIDS care cuts, closing ERs and OPDs, and elimination of other not-so-profitable services. Research has shown that closures take a huge toll on a local economy, besides the surrounding community (McLafferty, 1986; Whiteis, 2000; Rich, 1982; Sager, 1983; Oloroso, 1988, 1989; Friedman, 1978; Dranove & White, 1997). Community characteristics often determine payor mix and thus financial stability; overtime viability of the hospital puts poorer folks most at risk. Hospital competition under the uneven playing field and M&As are both chiefly responsible for the decimation of many local community hospitals from the 1980s through today. The marketplace for hospitals has been highly unstable for decades, where today 1 in 5 rural hospitals remain at high risk for closing (Gooch, 2019).

Modern Healthcare annually publishes its *Resource Guide*, a listing of the firms in each line of health business, from management consulting, law, electronic health records (EHRs), investment banks, outsourcing vendors, to professional membership organizations, among others (*Modern Healthcare*, 2018a, 2018b, 2018c). This is a valuable tool for recognizing the concentration that parallels every segment of the healthcare industry. The larger proprietary and "not-for-profit" chains are delineated (see Chap. 2).

In recent years, the wide range of corporate health entities has been caught up in a frenzy of amalgamations, including the so-called "not-for-profit" hospital systems, the pharmaceutical industry, managed health care, pharmacy benefit managers, specialty pharmacy groups, health information technology firms, and chain drug stores and retail clinics. This has resulted in a few firms dominating in most of these arenas, also including facility construction, consulting, and legal and accountancy firms, and other firms specializing in the health sector. Marketplace medicine yields a plethora of entrepreneurial startups in multiple areas to grab what they can get with innovative spins (just witness exhibitors at any health professional meeting and trade show). Ideological support can be garnered from the powerful charitable foundations that have long been influential across the healthcare system.

Making a Business off of Sick Folks

With handsome returns on investment to be made, achieving greater market size has become the modus operandi. A prominent example of health sector transformation is the distorted growth of health expenditures directed toward medical marketing reaching $30 billion in 2016 (Tanner, 2019). Among the top 20 firms grossing over $40 million listed by *Modern Healthcare* (2018a, 2018b, 2018c, p. 42) was Omnicom Health Group with $739 million in revenues in 2017. Such "health" expenditures add to the per capita *cost of care* (sic) for every American.

Often in response to the strengthened market power they must confront, physician groups have gotten larger as well. IQVIA's review finds 50 largest medical group parents that own and manage about 20,757 medical group locations, employing an estimated 102,600 physicians (Schember, 2018).

Likewise, there will be no letup in M&As across all segments of health care given Republican policies for healthcare market "reform." Of late, vertical integration appears to be more prevalent than horizontal mergers—combining separate business lines, as in the CVS-Aetna and other pharmacy benefit management arrangements (Japsen, 2018). Such amalgamations challenge organizational theorists for conceptualizing sets of complex functions across the rapidly changing field (Etzioni, 1961).

In addition, the host of large corporate firms, long constituting the medical-industrial complex (MIC) to supply providers for services provision (Box 1.1), has substantially grown given generous pass-through providers from employer and federal/state funding. Several of the economy's largest corporate giants (including Amazon, Buffett's Berkshire Hathaway, Morgan Stanley, Apple, Google, Microsoft, IBM, and General Electric, among numerous other Fortune 500 firms) are staking out new much larger investments in health care. Their strategies in health appear to be ripe for both innovations and exploitation. Is a new wave of corporate transformation of American health care underway as the technology-driven invasion by behemoth IT entities swoops into the health sector? (see Chap. 5).

McKinlay (1984) offers an excellent class analysis of what has been happening in the structural development of our American health care as it has spread across the globe. His main point is that the US medical-industrial complex (MIC) tied in with other Northern global powers, yielding a worldwide MIC. This is properly understood mainly by seeing how multinational corporations in general *as a class* develop and preside over new markets much as they wield their power inside the United States. It is believed that innovation drives deep changes in the structure of economies. This predicted larger corporate involvement follows the pattern that truly transformative effects are still mostly concentrated in specific sectors (Donay, 2018). But is this a prelude to "better things to come," as techno-optimists may have us believe?

McKinlay points out that the "types of health services research that dominate the health field around the world" are "much atheoretical, frequently ahistorical, usually apolitical, and usually defensive of the status quo, and normally dominated by managerialism." To understand the true dynamics, he suggests a structural analysis of political economic forces that influence the shape and the content of medicine and its institutions to evidence the broad corporate involvements. It is much broader than interactions of merely professionals and provider institutions (Navarro, 1976). The actual MIC expansion in size and power over several decades is reflective of the larger capitalist society. McKinlay states:

> The phenomenal and uncontrolled expansion of the Medical Industrial Complex over the last 50 years has paralleled the now uncontrollable requirements of advanced capitalism. ... In order to explain why the ideologies and institutions comprising the health care complex have developed as they have, we require first, some understanding of the logic, pressures, and contradictions with which capitalism is beset; and second, an awareness of the reasons why predatory corporations had penetrated and now dominate health-related activities around the world. ... The term "predatory" is employed here to characterize the rapinous activities of large-scale capitalist institutions (mainly banks, insurance companies, and industrial corporations): the act of invading, exploiting, and ultimately despoiling a field of endeavor -- with no necessary humane commitment to it -- in order to seize and carry away an acceptable level of profit. (McKinlay, p. 2)

In McKinlay's same volume, Bodenheimer (1984) examines transnational corporate plans to operate on a global scale, particularly given the pharmaceutical industry's near 20-year patents where they hold a monopoly on each compound. This monopoly allows the shifting of product lines to other industrial activities, as well as many developing economies, to gain footholds to guarantee profit flows transnationally. Through our book here, the authors will lay out numerous data points to demonstrate how this structural approach is preferable to other examinations of American medicine that ignore or discount power and wealth (Navarro, 1976).

Borrowing heavily from McKinlay, the logic of this expansionary activity can be applied to the corporate provider entry into healthcare provision and the subsequent changes wrought since the mid-1960s. Some forms of competition led to expansion of the total productive services output, yet questions may be raised over the "use value" of what was, and is being, produced, i.e., inappropriate care, huge administrative waste, plus fraud and abuse—estimated to reach $272 billion in 2014 (The $272 billion swindle, 2014). Trump's preoccupied Department of Justice is reported to have recovered only $2.5 billion in fraud and false claims in 2018 (Boggs, 2019).

All of these production downsides tend to characterize the recent functioning of providers. If the aim of production is to primarily result in expanded profits, which are then reinvested in more enterprises and more technologically efficient production this might conceivably improve delivery of health services. However, this has led to creation of a commodity fetish promulgated by deceptive advertising for even higher utilization. Kennedy examined the significant impact of for-profit organizations on voluntary and public hospitals by the mid-1980s to find reduced overall access and rising costs resulted while professional standards were lessened (Kennedy, 1985).

More attention becomes directed at foreign markets when regulatory constraints develop domestically (Bell, 1996); multinational expansions seek even higher returns on their investment (ROI) amidst likely less regulation abroad, though social and cultural barriers can be challenging (Perez-Stable, 1999). The ideological sales program for US health care has been that it is far superior to any other nations and that American medicine and technology (and its capital sponsors) are unsurpassed (Human Development Network, 1997). Multinational health corporations sped into other nations' markets (Berliner & Burlage, 1990; Maier & Engelberts, 1986; Berliner & Regan, 1987). Witness American proprietary hospitals in Latin America, Asia, England, and Europe (Euro-Fiet, 1987; Milmo, 1987; Hagland, 1998; Berliner & Regan, 1990; Salmon, 1984); HMOs across Latin America and elsewhere (Snow, 1996; Ham, 1995; Hensley, 1999; Bosch, 2000); academic medical centers in the Middle East and Asia (Marquee Brand, 2016); clinical trials outsourcing across Asia and the Caribbean; and a variety of PBMs all over (Navarro, 1995a, 1995b, 1998; Hotchkiss & Jacobalis, 1999; Stocker, Iriart, & Waitzkin, 1999). Some of this overseas investment is tied into the widespread private profit-based medical tourism industry (Medical Tourism, 2013; Salmon & Aruru, 2019).

In several national healthcare systems, these advanced for-profit organizational forms may make some innovative contributions in addressing their current cost, access, and quality problems (Meyer, 1997). Unfortunately, innovative and/or advanced services usually stay confined to multinational employees, well-insured upper-class residents, and medical tourists—not the bulk of ordinary citizens. More lately, a McKinsey executive, among other corporate spokesmen, report American systems and Big Pharma lie in wait while building sales and R&D infrastructures to move into developing private insurance markets in places like India and China (Carroll, 2012). Ongoing and longer-term effects are diminishing existing public health sectors through privatization schemes that open foreign markets to American multinationals (COM, 2002; DeGroote et al., 2008; Alvarez, Salmon, & Swartzman, 2011).

Writing in *Modern Healthcare*, about corporate managed care making money off the state Medicaid, Terhune in a piece "As billions in tax dollars flow to private Medicaid plans, who's minding the store?" notes that these privately managed Medicaid plans do not provide sufficient oversight of patient care and the quality of that care to the 54 million people now on Medicaid managed care. The expansion of Medicaid managed care now consumes $300 billion annually, and yet we have little information as to what we are getting for the money (Terhune, 2018, p. 14).

In another *Modern Healthcare* article, Terhune (2019, p. 1) explores how the legion of private subcontractors control crucial decisions over care denials of services for the millions of low-income Americans on Medicaid managed care.

Dr. Arnold Relman clearly saw mounting consequences arising from unfettered marketplace medicine (Relman in Salmon & Todd, 1988). It is important to reiterate that Relman (1980) noted the emergence of a "new medical-industrial complex" that arose from the late 1960s to capture a part of the influx of federal largess; it was also positioned to capture benefits from the Democratic-constructed Affordable Care Act of 2018, which failed to safeguard against such practices.

For-profit care is subjected to management control from distant centers accountable to stockholders, not communities, nor in fact to patients themselves when safeguards against such practices interfere with care patterns. The growing variety of corporate entities today reap handsome returns on their investments, by selectively choosing locations and patient groups, still highly subsidized from the public trough.

In conclusion, public policymaking remains largely shaped by powerful firms to satisfy their vested interests, which are often at odds with the overall public's health. Regulatory constraints imposed by government to redirect efforts to address the public's health are stiffly resisted in this medical marketplace. Thus, the quest for financial gain underlies the passion to forge larger more powerful, diversified, and integrated entities to gain, and try to dominate, market share. Their grip on policymaking comes from their lobbying strength, and the widespread acceptance that this corporate healthcare system seems to be the one the American people supposedly want. The populous remains uniformed of the most crucial issues and unfortunately can be easily manipulated by prevailing ideology.

Background to Corporate Involvement

Following business support for urban sanitation measures in the 1890s, interventions by the Carnegie and Rockefeller Foundations post Flexner Report in 1910 marked the first major phase of business involvement in American health care (Salmon, 1978). The Rockefeller Foundation's huge funding of scientific medical schools, and its infectious disease programs through 1914, in effect reshaped medical education (Ludmerer, 1985) and transformed the entire healthcare delivery system by changing the nature of doctoring (Salmon, 1990, 1994). The medical profession became principally upper middle-class white males thereafter (Brown, 1976; Berliner, 1984). In the 1960s a beginning feminization of medicine began with more women admitted to medical schools, with sporadic minority physician numbers up too, many being foreign medical graduates, growing now to about 20% today (see Chap. 3).

Ironically, for-profit medical schools lost out with the Flexnerian reforms after 1910 after the Carnegie and Rockefeller Foundations reorganized medical education to a 4-year, university-based curricula to professionalize medicine. The advent of *scientific medicine* eventually improved the quality of doctoring, the specialties emerged in academic medical centers, and hospitals modernized to no longer be "places to die" (LeFanu, 1999). Most US hospitals then were religiously sponsored, traditionally non-profit, and charitable to serve their communities. In the late 1920s, the privately funded Committee on the Cost of Medical Care sought to set in place the concept of an industrialized hospital system. Government had established urban public health facilities to control epidemic diseases; the need for public hospitals during the Great Depression led to widespread building under the federal Works

Progress Administration (WPA) to open access to poorer areas and for the unemployed across the nation. This public effort continued with subsidization of private non-profits with the Hill-Burton Hospital Construction Act of 1947 (Stevens, 1999; Starr, 1982). By the 1960s overbedding (the high ratio of beds to community residents) was established, so hospital costs zoomed since a "bed built was a bed filled" (Roemer's Law) (Roemer & Shain, 1959).

Thus, the predominant configuration of the delivery system and its reimbursement increased access while ballooning costs primarily within inpatient care, generally disregarding ambulatory care until higher profit margins began to be mined in later decades. With care centered in hospitals, the MIC found a growing market for medical supplies and technology, etc. Undertaken without proper population-based health planning, the necessity for better outcomes now for Americans has led marketplace medicine to begin to craft its "new solutions" to cost control (e.g., prospective payment, health savings accounts, vertical integration, narrower networks, value-based care, outright disenfranchisement of certain population segments, etc.), but unfortunately such solutions come under the auspice of private gain.

These early interventions occurred against the backdrop of successive stages in the organizational and technological transformation of American healthcare delivery. It is important to grasp the transitions from cottage industry through small-scale competitive entrepreneurship to the now emerging corporate monopolization stages (Kelman, 1971). Each stage can be demarcated by imbalances between larger societal productive forces and the existing social organization of health services (Dreitzel, 1971). The nineteenth-century guild-like petty commodity production under the cottage system gave way to the beginning of the modern hospital as medical education was substantially upgraded to 4-year laboratory-based university training. A new division of labor under the hospital administrator was established with physicians over other health worker categories, as well as with the specialization of medicine (Stevens, 1971). Each health worker category, in its self-interest, sought a respective professionalization on its own to help advance the productive health forces.

With modernization, the hospital's earlier role changed as an institution of social control, particularly in urban areas to house the deviant and undesirable: the insane, criminal, handicapped, and orphaned, including the sick (Goffman, 1961). Scientific discoveries and new medical breakthroughs greatly improved hospital care and altered its purpose and organization. Anesthesia, the contributions of Pasteur and Lister in antisepsis, and pharmaceutical advancement contributed to more sophisticated care and efficacious surgery and more. The germ theory of disease amidst Rudolf Virchow's laboratory discoveries on cellular structure, along with improvements in laboratory medicine and pathology techniques, led to refinements for more effective patient and population interventions (Rosen, 1958). Along with radiology, such advances massively changed diagnostic and treatment procedures.

The glamour of rapid change in hospital care left behind the image of the "place to die." These advances attracted greater religious group sponsorship and upper-class charity to build more and larger hospitals, as well as upgrade existing ones.

Public institutions advanced as well, with federal public health service hospitals at ports and municipal-sponsored hospitals, addressing infectious outbreaks.

Medicine as a social institution thus legitimized itself, which in turn provided the material basis for industry growth through the vast funding that subsequently followed. Medical specialties came to dominate the larger urban hospitals, mainly in a non-wage-contract relationship as they were outside private practitioners. In addition to practicing in homes and community agencies, nurses made up almost the entire waged hospital workforce, some of whom began to resist their "handmaiden" status to the doctor (Moccia, 1994). Hospitals had established formal schools of nursing to exploit the unpaid labor of students, as well as to secure their employment upon graduation for their increasing technical labor needs. Nurses were almost exclusively female and white working class, while medical school entrants post-Flexnerian reforms increasingly came from white wealthier ranks (Berliner, 1984). Professional nursing began with the advancement of the hospital, with its nursing elite attempting to upgrade the discipline by establishing RN registration upon completion of accredited schooling and passing state boards (Reverby, 1994). As with medicine, adherence to nursing practice standards was to raise quality of care.

Other health professional categories followed similar paths to attempt semiprofessional identity and some self-regulation, e.g., social workers, physical therapists, laboratory and radiological technicians, nutritionists, etc. (Friedson, 1973, 1974). Professionalization among these various "semiprofessions" under medicine (Friedson, 1971) at times led to challenges to the white male-dominated upper middle-class status of the doctor, but such challenges have yet to break down the class, gender, and racial hierarchy that prevails in American health care through today (Navarro, 2017). Even with rising demands for women's rights across society, doctors continue to rule over the generally female nursing ranks and still mostly dominate in clinical decision-making (Donbek, 2003). The role of nurses being the so-called handmaiden to the physician was altered over time as middle-class women chose nursing careers with their professional rank forging new avenues of expertise in *credentialed advanced practice roles* (Price, 2013). Masters and doctoral-prepared nurses came from upgraded curricula, with greater independence sought. Nurses had been at the forefront of public health in the community in public health departments, visiting nurse associations, and community health centers in the 1960s. Many gains coincided with the societal women's movement evolving as medicine itself became feminized with greater medical school enrollments of women. More collaborative team functioning has been sought that blurred traditional roles too.

Recently, the Institute of Medicine (IOM) has recognized the valuable role of the three million nurses in the frontlines of patient care (Institute of Medicine, 2011). Advances in nursing education and everyday practice eroded past images of the nurse, all feeding into improved interprofessional relations. As perceptions and expectations of work life altered, stereotypes among the public changed as patients came to appreciate and rely upon nurses for clinical care and guidance.

Nurses became respected in and out of the hospital setting for their knowledge, skills, as well as greater time spent with patients. Similarly, this response has been fueling the rise of the chain drug store clinics where nurse practitioners handle primary care, and now chronic care conditions, among the populace. The IOM urges bachelor's degree BSN curriculum to prepare more technically competent graduates and urges the preparation of more nursing doctorates, as colleges of nursing are doing along with residencies for more students. While remuneration of advanced nurses has climbed, their pay has never come close to physicians and especially well behind administrators.

It is interesting to note how the ideas of industrial capitalism did come to permeate medicine in not so subtle ways. While the delivery system moved rather haphazardly, an industrial model influenced doctors who relayed to the public an explanation of the human body in mechanistic terms: the heart was a pump; the lungs were bellows; the kidneys were filters; and later the brain became conceived as a computer.

Such a mechanistic and materialist representation of the body and one's health neglects or downplays a broader sense of self that includes the human mind and spirit (Frank, 1963; Frankl, 1955; Hastings, Fadiman, & Gordon, 1980; Ferguson, 1978; Krippner & Villoldo, 1976; Pelletier, 1976). From the 1970s onward, the rise of the holistic health movement (Berliner & Salmon, 1980; Salmon & Berliner, 1980) and its entrepreneurial practitioners have capitalized on the limitations of modern medicine with an expanded notion of human existence and healing (Salmon, 1984). More among the world's populations exclaim, as the German alternative health movement has, that "Gesundheit ist mehr," which translates to "health is more" than just medical care (Salmon & Gallo, 1985; Salmon & Goepel, 1990). On a sadder note, social media has fueled diverse notions of alternative medicines in a generally unregulated marketplace (Liu & Salmon, 2010) of nostrums with dubious value that tend to confuse peoples' minds. Despite reasonable due skepticism, the anti-vaccine movement has eroded needed institutional trust for addressing twenty-first-century global health problems.

The larger context of the health sector development was the society's rapid industrialization in most spheres across the twentieth century's economy, particularly in the urbanized Northeast and Midwest. Both industrialization and urbanization brought migration and sped up the economy, which eventually demanded a more highly trained, specialized workforce for its expanding division of labor. This reality edged in becoming recognized as needed for more rapid capitalist development. In 1890 Germany, Chancellor Otto von Bismarck enacted national health insurance for workers to essentially prepare for Germany's industrialization and later European armed aggression.

In modern societies, formal education has taught necessary skills, as well as how to get up and go to work, properly behave, and relate to authority and competition (Aronowitz & Giroux, 1985; DiLeo, Giroux, McClennan, & Saltman, 2013). Certain segments of US industrial capital came to realize that their labor force also required greater protection from infectious diseases, as well as the ravages of the production processes themselves; issues of frail population health began to be seen as delimiting the rate of capital accumulation and fomenting underlying social unrest, as Bismarck had understood: replacement of valued skilled, professional, and managerial workers due to disease was disruptive to production and very costly. European capital amidst the relative strength of their labor unions seems to have made note that government and their own investments in population health is integral to economic development; thus universal health coverage was implemented earlier in Europe, unlike no path chosen by US corporations (Navarro, 1975).

In the United States, business interests started to see that improvements beyond the workplace might also be necessary for social development. George Rosen (1975, p. 10) reported:

> Concern with the relation of environmental conditions to ill health was not limited to industrial workers. It was recognized that the health of the worker in the plants could not be compartmentalized. Conditions of life in the home, as well as conditions in the factory, could deleteriously affect the worker's health so that effective prevention required action along several interrelated lines.

The Federal Commission on the Conservation of Natural Resources, established by President Theodore Roosevelt, recognized the value of a healthier labor force to production and for overall economic development. Federal, state, and municipal governments were urged to protect people from diseases and conserve this "basic natural resource." The elites of the society were more mindful that interventions into the social sphere of the individual and community life accrued benefits to the business class as a whole (Fisher, I., Committee of One Hundred on National Health., United States. National Conservation Commission, 1909).

Roosevelt faced what historian Gabriel Kolko (1963) describes as a dominant tendency in the American economy toward growing competition with economic decentralization rather than increasing monopolization of industry and finance. Therefore, "many leaders of big business became the chief imitators of progressive legislation to maintain existing social and power relations in a new economic context." This was a time when banking regulation, a Federal Trade Commission, meat inspection, and other vital aspects of "progressivism" came as a surprise to many, but the regulatory agencies became essentially captured by powerful economic interests, which we observe continuing to this day (Kolko, 1963, book cover).

O'Toole, a biographer of Theodore Roosevelt, claims that TR was able to persuade Congress to pass the Meat Inspection Act and the Pure Food and Drug Act. He succeeded by seizing on public outrage over the putrid disease-causing conditions described in Upton Sinclair's bestselling novel, *The Jungle*, which exposed the stomach-turning conditions in Chicago's meatpacking plants. Both laws, enacted on the same day in 1906, were considered huge achievements in improving the health and well-being of Americans (O'Toole, 2019, A23).

The ideas behind the Roosevelt agenda or "ostensible goals" were economic, but its mandate also called for flood control, soil reclamation, and pollution abatement, all boons to the public health regarding his Natural Parks and Waterways Commission. When Roosevelt later ran for the national Progressive Party's ticket, his platform called for universal health insurance; a national public health service; insurance for the elderly, the unemployed, and the disabled; the end of child labor; the abolition of the 7-day work week; and a living wage.

The point to be realized from these past times in America is that government leaders, with tacit going along by the business sector, reflected views long gone as part of the Trump era policymaking. TR's perspective, as well as later his relative President Franklin Delano Roosevelt, offered a different political economic vision for America than that we find expressed today.

Significantly, the Carnegie and Rockefeller Foundations' interventions in the beginning of the twentieth century had virtually rebuilt the entire medical care system by endowing research institutes and select medical schools (Brown, 1976). This funding cleaned up the inadequate situation of poor-quality medical education, leading many private for-profit schools to close (Berliner, 1977). It can be interpreted that the organization of medical practice under the previous cottage industry had then come into conflict with the aims of industrial capitalists. The developing delivery system was ripening for change, and groups began a process of reimaging health services, much as we may be witnessing this decade.

The Committee on the Costs of Medical Care

By the 1920s, the Committee on the Costs of Medical Care (CCMC) became perhaps the most significant historical attempt to mold a new organization form for American health services delivery (Salmon, 1978). Funded by eight philanthropic foundations, the CCMC assembled a host of health providers with insurance and banking representatives from the private sector. Staff issued 28 major reports from extensive investigation into the "economics of medical care and prevention of illness." In 1929, health expenditures were at $3.5 billion, merely 4% of the gross national product (GNP). Approximately 30% of this amount, however, was allocated directly to private physicians, which was then considered exorbitant for the perceived safety and quality of care. Consumers paid 79% of their healthcare costs directly out of pocket. Philanthropy and local government operations were present, but these would be quelled with the oncoming Great Depression.

The suggested major restructuring was to create large-scale production to reduce the cost of its "unit product," the worker (Salmon, 1978). The final volume of the CCMC published in 1933 recommended that:

> …medical service should be furnished largely by organized groups of physicians, dentists, nurses, and pharmacists and other associated personnel. Such groups should be organized around a hospital for rendering complete home, office, and hospital care. The form of organization should encourage the maintenance of high standards and the development of preservation of a personal relationship between patient and physicians. (Committee on the Costs of Medical Care, 1932, p. 109)

Thus, the CCMC endorsed an industrial model of group medical practices under the control of the hospital factory to be financed by prepaid group insurance for defined enrolled populations. This proposal aimed to consolidate a more rational division of medical labor to maximize productivity with voluntary insurance to cover costs equally distributed over the enrollee group and over periods of time.

Doctors and hospitals would be assured more stable financing, while consumers would be required to pay for their medical care through fixed prepayment, supplemented by employers. This required insertion of middlemen, which adds to the administrative overhead.

It is not difficult to grasp why the medical profession, full of rugged individualists, opposed the design espoused by the Committee. Traditionally, doctors were supposed to "hang out a shingle" and mostly practice from their homes or a small office; this ethos continued for the next forty-some years. By the time the work of the Committee ended, general practitioners in private practice had been hit hard by the Depression. They organized to combat most of the ideas expressed in the reports; this reform was labeled erroneously as "socialized medicine."

The power of hospitals in no way matched that of organized medicine; the outcome was that essentially doctors resisted their losing private practice status to become hospital captured employees, i.e., proletarians. Organized medicine would keep up the mantra "no interference to the private practice of medicine," preserving the sanctity of the "doctor-patient relationship." Later the American Medical Association (AMA) opposed the Franklin Roosevelt Administration leading to the elimination of health insurance from the Social Security Act in 1935. Yet, the medical profession was not really united as a whole, for some physicians in certain locales chose group practices of the prepayment sort, for example, Ross-Loos in Los Angeles, among several union-sponsored plans in major cities; physicians also joined group practices based on the fee-for-service model as seen in Mayo, Cleveland, and Guthrie Clinics (Rorem, 1931). Besides regional divisions, the varying medical sects of homeopathy, naturopathy, osteopathy, and eclecticism separated from the allopathic membership of the AMA and eventually lost importance (Shryock, 1936).

Nevertheless, the general instability and insecurity endured by all of society during the Great Depression hindered the implementation of all the Committee's recommendations. Financing group practices remained tenuous, but certain models in different locales found physicians who preferred group practice over solo practice. In addition, a wide variety of payers (unions certain employers, coops), along with consumers, preferred the advantages from this type of medical practice (MacColl, 1966).

The most noteworthy prepaid group practice began with the Kaiser Permanente medical care program, a corporate initiative by the mining, aluminum, and shipbuilding magnate Henry J. Kaiser. In the early 1930s, Kaiser workers at isolated construction sites had no access to doctors and hospitals until the company leadership brought services to places where the employees lived and worked (Saward & Fleming, 1980). Industrial and family medicine integration was then seen worthwhile for assuring labor productivity (Spencer, 1973). Other sites across the West were built on this model in competition to fee-for-service practice.

During the Great Depression, hospitals saw charity donations wither, with unemployed and poor patients having no money for their care. In the absence of financing for health care, the voluntary hospital insurance movement arose on a number of local fronts, bringing about self-interested hospital insurance-only plans that eventually united under the Blue Cross Association in Chicago in the late 1930s

(Anderson, 2005). The structural arrangement of solo fee-for-service physician practice and the cost reimbursement of hospital care then became entrenched with the advent of provider-controlled Blue Cross and subsequently Blue Shield payments.

The prepaid group practice (PPGP) model had been conceptualized, advocated, and operationalized under traditional not-for-profit designations (Saward, 1980). Yet it did not take widespread root across the country, but only established in isolated locations. Just as hospitals became aware of their key role in the advancement of scientific medicine, many institutions faced bankruptcy due to occupancy declines and an inability to collect from patients with little or no income. Most hospitals barely staved off bankruptcy through local charity support since income-depleted upper-class patrons and religious groups no longer could subsidize their communities' care.

Blue Cross Blue Shield Plans Take Off Nationwide

Blue Cross plans began to sell hospital coverage for select employer groups usually under community-rated (i.e., one price for everyone, collectively sharing costs of care). The plans secured their financial base as the *major player*; employment-based voluntary insurance became the alternative that ruled out consideration of national health insurance. Of note, most hospitals were "not-for-profit," and the Blue Cross Blue Shield plans were established in this same vein. Hospital administrators and local employers (who were usually hospital board members) ran the Blue Cross plans (Anderson, 2005; Miller, 1992). With cost reimbursement, hospitals were able to expand their services and facilities, to increase their workforces, and to cover any overhead from research and teaching activities, plus some bad debt expenses or charity care. By 1938, the American Hospital Association (AHA) was officially approving Blue Cross plans; this incestuous relationship between the national Blue Cross of America and the AHA would last through the 1970s when conflicts over cost containment between insurers and hospitals were exacerbated.

Likewise, state and county medical associations initiated Blue Shield organizations to remunerate certain medical services by, at first, hospital-based physicians, such as radiologists and pathologists, and for doctors who practiced on hospitalized patients under fee-for-service. Blue Shield plans provided an alternative to any federal proposals for national health insurance. The doctor-patient relationship, ideologically considered sacrosanct, had resisted "third-party" interference until medical society-controlled Blue Shield plans set up a suitable payment program to pay themselves well—but at least it was *not* government money!

When industrial unions under John L. Lewis won medical coverage as a fringe benefit during the Roosevelt Administration wage-frozen war years (Alinsky, 1950), the dominant position of Blue Cross Blue Shield in the insurance market chiefly became secured during the 1940s. The removal of the patient from this equation created a moral hazard for insured groups who were insulated from the full cost of care; thus they tended not to be concerned with what was being charged by providers. The strong belief in health insurance has, however, begun to erode across the past few decades with increased burden from ever-rising premiums, deductibles, co-pays, and exclusions. Both consumers and some payers have differing perspectives on provider behavior today. Consumers were not aware of the true care costs, except their out-of-pocket spending, which today has become fully understood due to very high co-pays. The resultant burgeoning cost dilemma and the parties who benefit will be addressed in Chap. 2.

To sum up this earlier history, healthcare providers established a financing mechanism that separated physician practice and hospital care. Medical professionals and hospital interests maintained complete control over their respective activities, that is, the physician stayed independent and *not* employed by the hospital itself. With costs covered, hospital worker categories were elaborated to include pharmacists, medical social workers, physiotherapists, occupational therapists, laboratory technicians, dieticians, as well as a stratified hierarchy of nursing personnel. Services became commoditized and billable. The hospital workers in these roles— while not paid by physicians—served their admitted patients under physicians' supervision.

Outside of the hospital setting, dentists, optometrists, podiatrists, chiropractors, and a few other categories remained independent, like physicians, as fee-for-service private practitioners. They usually collected from self-pay patients until commercial insurance companies broadened benefit coverage to undercut the local Blue Cross monopolies. The desire of the CCMC to industrialize the entire medical care operation was never achieved. The corporate vision of business rationality through the prepaid group practice model attached to the hospital factory was yet to be realized.

Financing medical care in United States was thus imbedded with solo fee-for-service medicine and cost-plus reimbursed hospital care, a structural arrangement that was inherently inflationary, with financial incentives to yield significant inappropriate care, increasing huge administrative overhead, in addition to fraud and abuse. There has been demonstrated ineffectiveness, with employers starting to see this arrangement as *costly expenses*—rather than *investment in workers' health*, or a worthwhile investment for the general population!

This payment structure, however, was so acceptable to providers and insurers that later in the 1960s, both Medicare and Medicaid were crafted with the same reimbursement, even though the several prepaid group practices that did evolve seemed superior in performance for cost, effectiveness, and consumer acceptability (Brindle, 1969; MacColl, 1966; Saward, 1969a, 1969b; Prussian, 1972). Provider political strength at the time of legislative passage foreclosed the debate that later surfaced with justification for the Nixon's health maintenance organization strategy in the late 1960s.

The crucial policy issues remain about the longer-term solvency of the Medicare trust fund and the strain on federal general revenues that fund the care for both seniors and the disabled (Munnell, 1985). Ongoing debates across decades for tighter cost controls recognize the demographic shift of more elderly people needing greater cash to cover costs, with less labor force participants paying taxes. The search for new or restricted payments remains contentious in order to get costs under better control; prepayment is considered in various ways. Health maintenance organizations helped some, along with diagnostic-related groupings reimbursement, and now value-based care. Nevertheless, considerable controversy persists over the terms for altering the health cost trend with a spectrum of philosophical differences and vested interests behind each step. There remain feasible ways to save funds to pay for care, but most will involve cutting provider incomes and pushing more burden on patients. Solving the long-term Medicare financing will need to be addressed given aging cohorts and now with calls for "Medicare for All." The method and level of payments to providers will affect both beneficiaries and the health system as a whole far beyond the immediate transactions at the cash nexus (Vladek, 1985). Republican market-based policies for cost controls seek cuts to providers and more cost-sharing by patients, whose origins and continuation began in the Nixon/Reagan/Bush administrations and now Trump.

The Health Maintenance Organization Strategy

The passage of Medicare and Medicaid for the aged and indigent drove overall health expenditures upward from 1965, along with other Great Society programs (Brown, 1983). The subsequent Nixon Administration sought to eliminate programs through cutbacks and rescissions to curtail outlays, as all subsequent Republican administrations seek to undo previous Democrat established programs. Total health expenditures had grown to reach $69.2 billion and 7.2% of GDP (Salmon, 1978, p. 136). Yet, the opening of access for the two large uninsured populations of aged and indigent greatly pleased providers, besides all in the medical-industrial complex, which had grown to attract new powerful players. After Medicare, Blue Cross Blue Shield plans began to lose market dominance to giant commercial insurance companies (Aetna, Metropolitan, Prudential, Travelers, Cigna, etc.); the latter competitors packaged health benefits into their other insurance product lines sold to large corporations, to undercut rates by the non-profits who lost rapidly in many locales. Blue Cross of Philadelphia was said to see its 90% market share fall precipitously to the commercial firms. Blue Cross negotiated friendly cost-plus contracts, while the commercial plans paid hospital charges for each item of service. Thus, while generally less ill, commercial patients brought more profits to hospitals.

At the same time, the sector's largess and potential returns began to entice investment capital into proprietary hospital and nursing home firms to explore profit-making opportunities in the delivery of services (Salmon, 1990). The Nixon Administration planners sought out their business friends, who also witnessed huge increases in employee health outlays, so employers came to believe in the health maintenance organization (HMO) as a favored model (Morgan Guaranty Survey, 1972; Conference Board, 1972). Nixon's proclaimed in his "healthcare crisis" speech in 1971 that it was chiefly the concern with costs: costs in the economy, costs to the corporate class as employers, and costs to the government for

Medicare/Medicaid recipients. He ambitiously declared HMOs to be the corner-stone of his restructuring of the *entire* healthcare system.

A totally new configuration was being shaped through his HMO strategy, along with added proposals for Health Systems Agencies (HSAs), Area Health Education Centers (AHECs), Professional Standards Review Organizations (PSROs), and Nixon's own national health insurance plan. These newly designed federal interventions were intended to revamp the entire sector (i.e., health planning, professional education, quality assessment, and financing) (Salmon, 1978). Dr. Paul Ellwood, known as the "father of the HMO," essentially took the CCMC recommendations for prepaid group practices and reformulated them into the HMO concept, only updated for corporate bottom-line pursuits. In essence, the HMO was intended to embody a *group practice of physicians* as part of a *coordinated delivery system* to offer a *benefit package* to an *enrollee group* that *prepays the fixed premiums* for care (Ellwood, 1971, 1973).

Nixon was faced with escalating expenditures under federal and state health programs, while his Vietnam War effort remained unabated and very expensive. He also heard from his friends among the corporate class who were alarmed by their rising outlays for workers' health insurance during a tough economy. Several corporate planning bodies issued widely publicized major reports (e.g., Washington Business Group on Health, Business Roundtable, Conference Board, US Chamber of Commerce, among others). At the same time, dozens of conservative ideological entrepreneurs urged health policy restructuring to favor their class interests; essentially a chorus broke out all singing the same song for HMO restructuring to contain costs (Salmon, 1977). A burgeoning business literature also carried forth, along with a popular press, to foment widespread HMO support (Rothfeld, 1973; Salmon, 1984).

Being from California, Nixon was enamored with the Kaiser Permanente system—corporate-initiated private large-scale group practice of medicine (Saward, 1970; Saward, Blank, & Greenlick, 1968; Fleming, 1971; Williams, 1971, 1972). So Ellwood envisioned a thousand Kaiser-like giant HMOs across the United States to reduce costs and improve care to the working population while tightening up services to the aged and poor—which were considered by businesses to be a "social drag" on the economy. This was part of the agenda to bring government beneficiaries into organized systems of care to get a grip on their overutilization (Schneider & Stern, 1975).

The very structure of the HMO was designed for profit-taking: costs for providing services under the benefit package contract would be deducted from prepaid revenues, yielding the profit margin, which would become *the measure of success.* Taking care of patients would later be termed "medical loss ratio" as greed became evidenced in many fast-buck HMOs or the poorly managed plans:

According to Ellwood, the HMO strategy will strengthen the role of "competition" by introducing "economic incentives" and minimize the need for "regulation" by relying upon "market mechanisms." The promise of a rational, well-organized delivery system of HMOs sounds convincing to cost conscious employers who purchase the bulk of health insurance for their employees, and to individual consumers who face problems of cost, quality, accessibility, and availability of services. As Alford [1972] points out, those proposing "solutions" of corporate rationalization gained support from consumers who are hard pressed for improved health care services. (Salmon, 1990, p. 86)

Profitability was introduced to the picture as the key to HMO growth and survival; this legitimation of profits in health care would propel the corporate takeover of American medicine our nation faces in the twenty-first century. Ellwood invited private corporations to lend their "industrial know-how" because they are experienced in "the application of modern management" and had the ability to generate effectively used capital resources. The Nixon Administration was intent on attracting private capital to invest; corporate takeover mechanisms were designed to entice commercial insurance companies, industrial employers, and workplace integration of industrial medicine with family medical care (MacLeod & Prussin, 1973; Salmon, 1975). By 1974, a flurry of activity in the marketplace saw 177 operational HMOs, 204 in the "formational" stage and 88 in the "planning" stage. About seven million people were actually covered in HMOs by this time, which was *not* considered an impressive number. Quite a number had been in the earlier prepaid group practices. Almost all newly initiated HMOs were for profit, while by the 1990s, several of the earlier managed care plans would come to a "biblical conversion" like Paul on the road to Damascus. Blue Cross plans (e.g., Anthem, WellPoint, among others) reorganized as for-profit corporations, a kind of "why doth thou not pursue huge profits when one can?" By this time, marketplace ideology had become so ingrained in the healthcare consciousness. Surely executives would reap greater bounty for themselves, which they in fact did!

Contextual developments in the larger society had much to do with this policy failure. The economic recession occasioned from the OPEC (Organization of the Petroleum Exporting Countries) crisis resulted in an abrupt rise in the price of oil with the long waits in gas station lines. This, in turn, spun the world economy into recession amidst troublesome inflation. Additionally, on the political front, the Watergate scandal led to Nixon's downfall, massively disrupting the District of Columbia bureaucracy and subsequently eroded Republican health reform effort after his resignation. Federal funds for HMO development had been limited, often taken from other agencies' budgets (Bauman, 1976). Private capital found other investment alternatives during the recession; so, this was a disappointing response to the cheerleading of the Nixon and later Ford administrations.

Federal health policy under the Ford Administration carried forth enactment of Professional Standards Review Organizations (PSROs) for quality monitoring and Health Systems Agencies (HSAs) for local health planning. HSAs incidentally grew more corporate over the Great Society's Comprehensive Health Planning Agencies, which had been filled with inner city activists (Health Information and Action Group, 1975). The dozen or more proposals for extending national health insurance all died in Congress. Of note, most major players in the health sector had a submitted proposal to suit their vested interests, including Nixon's own in anticipation of its enactment, opposing that of Senator Ted Kennedy's liberal standard.

By 1974 the idea of making explicit profits in health care did, however, firmly take hold. Several large Fortune 500 firms began to explore developing their own in-house clinics for their employees. The concept of integrating industrial medicine with family medical care was being tested out by certain firms because they recognized assuring employee health might lead to enhancing their labor productivity, along with getting control over climbing expenses. Moreover, replacement costs of managerial, technical, and highly skilled personnel (particularly in tight labor markets) run high; to this day, recruitment remains a difficult task for HR departments in many industries due to the unavailability of specialized employee pools.

This industrial medicine model has occasionally surfaced in business circles up until today. Corporate planning bodies, which had "discovered" the need for "efficiencies" in healthcare delivery, widely publicized their major policy reports and began to lobby in new ways for policy changes (Rothfeld, 1973: Salmon, 1976). This phase of corporate involvement in health care, however, witnessed many twists and turns, which represents the interconnected complexity of "health reform," the huge learning curve to grasp our dynamic health sector, as well as divisions among vested interests that persist until today. Revenue seeking by all parties comes up against imposed cost constraints, which have been stiffly resisted. Oppositions can usually forestall forward movement.

Still, the vision and direction of the Nixon Administration HMO planners was never quite embraced. Private investors in HMOs had been explicitly encouraged for healthcare profit-taking by Nixon officials (Salmon, 1984), so it became a natural outcome that other health endeavors would be seen similarly for lucrative returns. Dr. Charles Edwards, Under Secretary of Health, Education and Welfare, had been recruited from Booz Allen and Hamilton, a corporate consulting group, so past Democratic Public Health Service Commissioned Corps officers were replaced by business-oriented staffers with a larger corporate orientation and connections.

The HMO movement engendered by the bipartisan HMO Act of 1973 mandated the dual option where employees were to be offered a prepaid plan versus a fee-for-service plan, which the employer both decided, while simultaneously the feds spurred on Medicare and Medicaid managed care (Bauman, 1976). An influx of commercial insurance companies, employers, and hospital systems, among other providers, slowly adopted this new prepaid delivery arrangement, which significantly began to impact the culture of medicine (Young, 2013).

While staff model HMOs employed doctors, private practitioners defensively banded together in prepaid independent practice associations (IPAs) to keep their patient base from being syphoned off by local HMOs. Physicians around this time started to see the lessening of their autonomy and feel the erosion of their independence. Also, there were some observable differences between for-profit and the more traditional HMOs (Schlesinger, Blumenthal, & Schlesinger, 1986), but such began to ease over the decade as competitive behaviors converged.

Rise of For-Profit Hospital Chains

Profit was becoming the accepted underlying motor force for the sector development, with investment capital coming in, spurring more job creation, and boosting the entire economy (Fuchs, 2013; Healthcare is going gangbusters for the economy, 2018). Concentration and centralization in the delivery of health services proceeded with pursuit of ever-larger revenues with higher margins becoming central. After a while, the outmoded "not-for-profit" designation became camouflaged and blurred. The delivery system was now officially businesses competing for their economic growth under a changing reimbursement environment. The marketplace became a struggle for gain, or, in some cases, survival. As a Catholic nun administrator aptly stated to the author while researching hospital closures in Chicago: "No margin, no mission" (Whiteis & Salmon, 1990a). Convergence of organizational behaviors had come to no longer distinguish the two camps.

While HMOs nationally failed to attain the market penetration previously predicted, almost a dozen investor-owned for-profit hospital chains arose and rapidly advanced during this time in the 1970s (e.g., the earliest entrants, Humana, Hospital Corporation of America, National Medical Enterprises, American Medical International, Universal, among several others). Across the next two decades, more firms joined the proprietaries as new business line combinations, takeovers, and mergers ensued and continued lasting until today's ridiculously consolidated and integrating stage.

From out of this, Wall Street became enthralled. Backed by investment capital acquired from hedge funds and the stock and bond markets, such proprietary chains initially built smaller modern facilities in growing well-insured middle-class communities. Later the chains strategically absorbed certain hospitals and then started bringing endangered institutions under their management contracts, but the latter without any capital outlay for ownership. This added revenue to the lucrative supply chains from bulk purchasing pharmaceuticals to using sophisticated information technology. The chains attracted physicians by financially incentivizing them to hospitalize their patients there. The concept of an organization conducting a patient "wallet biopsy" was put into effect so that top-flight insurance and cash-rich patients filled their beds to boost bottom lines; profits were reinvested for greater growth and more takeovers. The uninsured and Medicaid patients were screened out and "dumped" to the public sector or to nearby "not-for-profit" hospitals that still were able to maintain a little charitable impulse to serve their surrounding communities, or could not easily turn them away.

Objective measurement of the extent of this tragedy across the nation was difficult to assess by the US Inspector General in 1988 since no record keeping was required. The US Commission on Civil Rights told President Barack Obama many years later in 2014 that lack of enforcement of the Emergency Medical Treatment and Active Labor Act (EMTALA), which had been signed by Reagan to prevent patient dumping, had not stopped this practice of refusing needy patients (Commission on Civil Rights, 2014). The law failed to provide financing its mandate, so violations were common by providers (Meyer, 2016). Estimates of hospitals believed to experience acts of dumping at least once a month was 45%—after President Bill Clinton again signed COBRA in 1993. The political stand for prohibiting the practice was by Dr. Ron Anderson at Parkland Hospital in Dallas, Texas (Hudson, 1986; Kutscher; 2014). Enforcement across Texas was exemplary for eventually provoking the COBRA action by President Clinton for a national prohibition. But policies that are not strictly enforced usually do not mean much.

Working out a methodology to monitor dumping patients, studies at Cook County Hospital in Chicago (Schiff et al., 1986) were absolutely key to such "wallet biopsies" that risked death and/or deterioration of clinical status in such unwarranted transfers. Patient dumping is thought to continue today as bottom-line dictates have continued to prevail (Can a hospital emergency room delay or refuse care, 2017).

Dr. Quentin Young, founder of the Physicians for a National Health Program, made the observation of the "vampire effect" (Young, 1995): once bitten, the so-called "not-for-profit" providers *became just like the for-profits—the only difference they don't pay taxes*! In a short while, it became difficult to distinguish the two camps within the uneven playing field; a series of convergent behaviors were becoming apparent as reimbursements tightened. Multihospital systems were grabbing up doctors' practices as smaller well-situated institutions in most urban areas became engulfed into larger entities (Salmon in Ginzberg et al., 1993); other hospitals added to the hospital closure trend, 15 in Chicago alone in the 1980s (Whiteis, 1992).

The far distant corporate chain management presiding over dozens of scattered hospitals lent itself to the preference for contracting out services over actual building or buying hospitals; this proved much less risky and more profitable since any acquisition under the management contract enriched returns from the corporate bulk purchase supply chain. Multihospital systems also became prominent in the so-called "not-for-profit" sphere as well; all sector parties saw an amazing surge in M&A fervor to better compete, as numerous hospital closures became more evident (Whiteis, 1992):

> Between 1974–77, eighty-five public hospitals closed. Twenty-one county hospitals in California were closed or sold during the last six years of the [1980s]. In New York City alone, twenty-nine hospitals were closed between 1976 and 1980, seventeen were considered "financially distressed" in 1982 along with a total of 160 hospitals nationwide according to the U.S. Department of Health and Human Services. (Salmon, 1990, p.61)

In the better-off proprietaries, centralization took form in aspects, such as combined dietary, laundry, and housekeeping services; bulk purchasing of pharmaceuticals, medical equipment, and supplies; and health information technology. This centralization achieved real profit enhancements as more hospitals were engulfed into the chain orbit without substantial investment. Not uncommon with takeovers were lower-level workers losing jobs to enhance the chain's profit levels. Hospital cutbacks also restricted emergency services and former outpatient departments affecting the greater size communities they had supported (Salmon, 1993). Independent doctor offices were acquired by hospitals, and new clinical buildings attracted specialists, who could be fed by the primary care physicians. Understand Andre Gunder Frank's development in the face of underdevelopment contradiction (Whiteis & Salmon, 1990a). Using systems theory, Frank analyzed within interregional global capitalism that certain sectors advance, but often at the expense of other sectors that lag behind. In brief, they tend to go hand in hand but structured for the advantage of the dominant.

The proprietary chains slowed their acquisition of failing hospitals to morph more toward hospital management contracting strategically to enrich their size without high capital outlays. Smaller public hospitals in rural areas and failing urban institutions were gobbled up in large numbers without much effort; these could be abandoned if corporate metrics were not achieved in a few years. These changing partners in the hospital industry dance led to many geographic relocations across the nation as large chains sought to maintain their profit levels from their glory days, at the expense of the communities they served (Whiteis, 2000). Significant care access issues ensued with abandonments and economic misery with loss of jobs in rural and inner-city areas.

Saint Anne's Hospital in the Austin community of Chicago, a 400+ bed facility—the largest hospital closing to date then—majorly impacted its residential area beyond the denial of health services. Doctors, nurses, pharmacists, and other professionals could obtain jobs elsewhere; however, lower-paid staff, who lived in the surrounding community, would eventually face neighborhood business failures, deteriorating housing stock, and policing reductions for a crime surge. Local stores that once thrived abruptly closed with no more hospital visitors and staff customers; property values plummeted, insurance costs increased, and more, *until* noticeable change in social support came when community activists mobilized replacement of health and human services to preserve a safety net. Several agencies restored the ambulatory building and attracted a CVS drug store—no more pharmacy wasteland! Black community leadership then was strong, with some charitable and academic help, to create a success story. Nonetheless, across the country many closed facilities remain abandoned as dead capital.

Around this time, outsourcing by many hospitals became a standard practice of the privatization trend (Ginzberg et al., 1993). Many hospital administrations found hazards in contracting out due to a lack of due diligence. DeGroote, Paepe, and Unger (2005) note conditions to be met to avoid potential calamities: (1) real competition must exist between competent and substantial private providers and suppliers; (2) adequate capacity must be present to assess needs and negotiate and monitor contract terms; (3) a legal and political environment must exist to enforce regulations and resist patronization and corruption (Mills, 1998). Such conditions are most critical for public systems in developing nations where privatization ran rampantly. Careful watch was not always adhered to, as some US hospitals became shells with a variety of private entities from consultants to clinical services taking operational and clinical responsibilities off premises. Nursing homes are notorious for such outsourcing practices (see Chap. 2).

The Broader Transformation

Over time, the American healthcare system—which had previously been based upon thousands of practitioner entrepreneurs and smaller-scale provider organizations except large firms in the peripheral supply role—began to be transformed in structure, control, purpose, and ethics, partly due to the tightening umbilical cord from the US Treasury (Young, 1999). Overall, *professional altruism* and *the charitable impulse of community hospitals* waned. All sector parties saw an amazing amount of M&As to expand their size to better compete. Outpatient departments and Emergency Rooms were scaled back, while private physician practices were acquired by hospitals in the quest to fill beds with paying patients and for better control over the means of medical production. Community cutbacks were deemed necessary to restrict unprofitable patients and clinical services. Such combinations and cutbacks were forged for "economies of scale" and "cost-efficiency" but were always sold under the banner of "serving the public better."

Other business ideas and behaviors crept into a broad swath of provider management as highly paid MBAs took the reins. By the late 1960s through the 1980s, at the operational level, a new breed of financial and marketing managers found employment supposedly to handle new complex issues, create "efficiencies," and enlarge the now defined "customer base." These managers over time tended to displace medical professionals in key decision-making roles.

In particular, proprietary firms set off heavy marketing campaigns to advertise their "superiority" as modern. They had newer facilities built in areas near the well-insured populations instead of being hospitalized in well-worn urban institutions placed near poorly insured areas. This was the age of roadside billboards and TV spots to advertise firms with what was to hopefully entice patients into changing providers. It was also the time of increasing managerial buildups in hospital ranks for the added sophistication needed to compete in a rapidly changing and challenging marketplace and to handle the complex financial conditions. Larger amalgamations, however, led to much higher administrative overheads, which in the calculation meant less money given to caregivers. Higher overheads included expanding their profit margins markedly; subsequently, this allowed certain firms to branch out internationally (Salmon, 1984, 1990).

Thus, *the new medical-industrial complex* (MIC) arose as a vigorous and varied group of investor-owned entities to serve those able to pay. Patients became "customers" who could sustain their growth for continued profit levels; Wall Street loved these rising stars as the new American wave of health care. This is the very expanse that Relman designated as "the most important recent development in American health care." (Relman, 1980, p. 963). The rapid growth of for-profit providers included investor-owned hospital and nursing home corporations, diagnostic labs, mental health and home care agencies, hemodialysis centers, freestanding ambulatory, surgicenters, MRI units, and emergency centers and a variety of other services. This grouping soon produced between $35 and $40 billon dollars (25% of personal health expenses) in 1979, a percentage much greater today. In 2018, the American Hospital Association listed 1035 investor-owned entities or 21% of hospitals accounting for the $902,891,035 expenditure (AHA, 2017).

Outside contractors in the supply side ballooned (especially administrative, consulting, and information technology) during the restructuring, alongside physicians and hospital executives witnessing administration becoming vastly dense. *Modern Healthcare* (2017a, 2017b) lists the largest management consultant firms making billions in health care (#1 Deloitte taking in $2.6 billion annually from 12,000 contracts) and the largest public relations and marketing agencies again with contract revenues in billions (#1 Omnicom Health Group billing $808 million in 2016).

Medicare and Medicaid initially had made little change in the actual delivery system beyond bestowing a massive provider subsidization under the fee-for-service and cost reimbursed financing mechanism. These market improvements did grant better access as millions of Americans received needed care; however, inflationary pressures with little price accountability created problems for both government, employers, and consumers. Importantly, the government largess invited a plethora of firms to jump on the healthcare bandwagon, which they did in droves with sales to providers. This collectivity joined all the other MIC firms to feed off the constant federal funding.

In effect, Medicare and Medicaid accelerated and aggravated both federal and state policy problems, to reveal major structural defects in the system. Neither federal financing program challenged the historic provider-preferred premise of underwriting virtually any expenditure physicians chose for patient care. It was the public and private funding largess, amidst a lack of regulatory oversight, that attracted the host of investors, including fast-buck operators.

The *more is better* philosophy had taken firm root in the system with *more* service utilization, *more* technology, *more* growth, *more* layers of management, and assuredly *more* profits. This perversion was accompanied also by *more* admissions, *more* unnecessary surgery, *more* inappropriate prescribing, *more* diagnostic testing, *more* fraud and abuse, *more* days in the hospital, *more* readmissions, and *more* of whatever made *more* money. Such were the results of the now fading structural arrangement for financing.

While the private market during this period provided many innovative changes that advanced care for some Americans, the direction did not seem to contribute to the public's overall health (McKinlay, McKinlay, & Beaglehole, 1989). Many Americans continued to face significant access barriers as the price of care continued to spiral out of control. Moreover, the overall medical measures of mortality and morbidity were found *not* to be declining (McKinlay, McKinlay, & Beaglehole, 1989). Yet, the medical marketplace remained heralded for all its attributed splendor by those who were richly benefiting.

The Reagan Era of the 1980s

The one-term Ford and Carter administrations launched few health policies of much significance. President Gerald Ford implemented Nixon's PSROs and signed the health planning legislation to establish Health Systems Agencies (HSAs), replacing the former Democrat-passed community-based Comprehensive Health Planning Agencies, which ceded influence over local health planning to more corporate entities (Health Information & Action Group, 1975). Some block granting for Medicaid to the states was also established (Ford, 2017). President Jimmy Carter's Voluntary Effort (VE) failed to impact hospital cost inflation, since the private sector went back to business as usual right when constraints were lifted after 1 year (Carter, 1977). The explosion of federal and employer budget costs later provoked the

Reagan fetish for cost controls and cutbacks. Economists saw their star rise, while concerns for access and quality took a back seat in policy discussions; again, huge policy reversals were set in place for market-driven ideology after Democrat Carter left office.

Health care as a percentage of GDP nearly doubled from 1965 to 10.5% by 1980. So it became clear to federal policymakers—and their corporate class sponsors— that not just the inflationary spiral but *the allocation of those dollars* and their outcomes deserved stronger policy attention. During the Reagan Administration, the Health Care Financing Administration (HCFA) began to wield enormous power, as did the Office of Management and Budget (OMB) (Etheredge, 1983). The former conducted utilization review, but in subsequent years, the agency morphed into *utilization management*; the latter review challenged provider behaviors. As the clinical decision-makers on patient care, doctors tended to be targeted as cost drivers (Schlesinger, Blumenthal, & Schlesinger, 1986). Victim-blaming patients for lifestyle behaviors and noncompliance for therapies and their subsequent utilization became prevalent (Ryan, 1976: Knowles, 1977; Crawford, 1977, 1978, 1979, 1980).

It might be recognized that HMOs were not easy to establish due to needed upfront funding and technical expertise which came at a high cost. Many existing providers shied away from the challenges presented with a break from the fee-for-service market. Thus, the superiority of organized systems did not hold up as an argument necessarily against the lucrative and entrenched vested interests at that time. Additionally, the conservative antipathy to extending any more access to the poor, disabled, elderly, women, and children kept alive the fetish for cost control in federal outlays. Profound economic shifts over time became evident.

As HMOs engulfed greater portions of fee-for-service markets across the country (Mechanic, 1991), preferred provider organizations (PPOs) by commercial insurance firms emerged, taking aim at the doctor-sponsored independent practice associations (IPAs), which had been physicians' preferred model to mitigate patient migration toward HMOs. Employees usually had a choice between a few options, but it was the employers deciding on what local insurance plans would be chosen, their benefits, and amounts of patient cost-sharing. IPAs faced a competitive disadvantage against PPOs, which had larger networks of hospitals and providers. As a result, PPOs became the instruments of hospital chains and insurance companies.

As premiums rose, benefit packages with greater consumer cost-sharing shifted the burden from government and corporations at a time of declining living standards. An insufficient number of health professionals spoke out about consumer health cost controls under the Reagan Administration and its class nature (Navarro, 2017). Policies emphasizing cheaper front-end ambulatory services were not regarded as a health improvement if the price was the sacrifice of necessary hospital, rehabilitation, and end-stage care for certain patient segments. The bulk of private investment was situated in the higher-cost multihospital systems and academic medical centers. Case in point, the HIV/AIDs crisis arose in the early 1980s, and Reagan simply denied its existence (Cohen, 1985).

As Reagan led a huge buildup in military expenditures, the Economic Recovery Tax Act of 1981 coincided with a sharp increase in revenues by the four major hospital management companies. Investor capital flooded into these companies and other proprietary ventures while their stocks climbed.

Nascent health information technology (HIT) enabled hospital financial executives to examine specific departmental costs to carry out greater rationalization of the labor process and to reduce expenditures within hospital operations. Across the globe, computerized systems continue to be developed in the rush to build "Big Data" to gain control over healthcare activities and to further scrutinize the appropriateness of services and practitioners' output (The 2019–2014 World Outlook for Internet, 2018). This burgeoning segment of American health information technology, today concentrated into four- or five nation-wide firms, began to play a critical role in tracking physician performance. The Obama Administration's Medicare Access and Children's Health Insurance Program Reauthorization Act (MACRA) of 2010 later further extended such monitoring (Feinglass & Salmon, 1994; Glassman et al., 1996; Hyans et al., 1996). Malpractice investigations took on greater meaning with HIT advances (Perna, 2018), with physician resistance to such electronic health records being a factor (Wigger, 1996).

HIT systems have come a long way over this past decade, and with greater big IT firms bringing greater sophistication into health care, it remains to be seen how such HIT systems may evolve: who designs and controls the metrics for what chosen analytics, for what purposes, and what directions. Whether the Trump Administration moves more aggressively on the MACRA implementation may be in doubt; CMS seems at times to rely upon private sector initiatives setting directions. Certainly, today's Accountable Care Organizations (ACOs) are using their own performance monitoring of costs and quality in varying ways, as will later be explored.

By the time Reagan introduced diagnostic-related group (DRG) reimbursement for Medicare, expenditures had climbed substantially. DRG categories established set amounts for diagnosis upon admission, and hospitals sought their profit by minimizing services, or as many consulting firms helped them to benefit through various managerial techniques. Hospitals sought contracts with a burgeoning array of consultants that sprung up to populate health trade shows and professional meetings. This demand for expertise led to a burgeoning healthcare management consulting industry, sporting firms like Deloitte, Optum, and Navigant, among a couple dozen others, raking in as high as $3 billion per year (Largest healthcare management, 2018, p. 34). DRGs supported widespread profit-seeking within the hospital industry.

Even with cost reductions in certain spheres, the fundamental belief in the private market for the bottom line remained the primary sign of "success." Each diagnostic group received a fixed payment for an admission with generally multihospital systems and larger hospitals able to maximize payment excesses. As a result, larger firms with specialized internal staff or outside private consultants won out by *gaming the system*. State Medicaid plans and private insurers followed suit with prospective payment soon thereafter, greatly complicating hospital reimbursement across the 1980s. Rearranging incentives, however, does not necessarily reduce overall cost outlays.

Certain clinical services were driven out of the hospital setting—a loss to physicians *not* jumping on the ambulatory bandwagon. Physician and corporate-sponsored surgicenters and diagnostic centers sprung up all over, completely unregulated and causing much local disruption. Any Medicare Part A DRG hospital budget "savings" were soon gobbled up under Medicare Part B physician payments. This is where the "vampire effect" became much more noticeable in many urban centers where so-called not-for-profits came up against the proprietary chains (Ginzberg et al., 1993).

Across the 1980s, for-profit hospital systems owned about 20% of nongovernment acute general hospital beds and more than 50% of nongovernment psychiatric beds. Yet this "development" went together with an "underdevelopment" of the less fortunate hospitals in poorer communities, as economist Andre Gunder Frank has said characterizes the capitalist system (1967). The 1970s growth in facilities and bed numbers in the proprietary sector contrasts dramatically to the contraction in the "not-for-profit" voluntaries and government segments of the industry who were left to serve the poor, minorities, and uninsured. Two major and interconnected issues became public and voluntary hospital failure in the face of the rapid encroachment by the for-profit sector (Whiteis & Salmon, 1990b).

A *Modern Healthcare* survey revealed a 15% increase in the total beds owned, leased, or managed by investor-owned multihospital chains between 1982 and 1983 and a similar 15.1% increase between 1983 and 1984, where the profits of investor-owned chains rose 28.5%. This continued trend had shown a 37.7% profit increase between 1982 and 1983 (*Modern Healthcare*, 1990, p. 66).

This examination of hospitals reveals the financial crisis among *those unable to tap into capital reserves*, as well as compete for better-paying privately insured patients. Financing their futures, many larger non-profit systems pursued tax-exempt bonds to expand to compete. However, 156 community hospitals closed between 1980 and 1984, with the single greatest concentration of closings (almost 30%) being in large metropolitan areas with populations over 1.5 million, the areas with the greatest health needs. These hospitals that closed tended *not* to be part of multihospital systems (Whiteis & Salmon, 1994). Underdevelopment was seen in the huge losses by public hospital systems, which recorded a $360 million deficit for 1984, 57.2% greater than the $229 million deficit in the year before.

In this era of cost cutting and retrenchment under Reagan policies (McKenzie, 1994), many hospitals and their served communities remained in jeopardy. Federal policy exacerbated the financial damages on hospitals that were most at risk. Restrictions on access for the uninsured and Medicaid patients, and the later impact of "dumping" patients on already overcrowded financially burdened public institutions, were noted in studies (Schiff et al., 1986).

Corporate concentration—under the guise of competition—led to a rapid and insidious trend, with insufficient policy concern for the massive disruption across the entire health system, including its profound impact on the culture of medicine (Stoeckle, 1994). As Whiteis and Salmon (1990a, p. 119) summed up:

In the wake of this push toward corporate consolidation, those left behind -- the working poor, the unemployed, racial minorities, many elderly women, and children [were] gradually being denied access to the vital resources needed to participate actively in their own health and the health of their communities. ... the structure of the health care industry, its long history of technological-intensive intervention, and the current trends toward for-profit care with the removal of services to those left behind in the wake of the corporate siphoning of public resources are all of a piece. They are signs and symptoms of the larger illness, the underdevelopment of public resources under corporate development.

This corporate takeover of health care coincided with the huge growth in the ranks of the uninsured, which rose dramatically during the Reagan years of neglect, continuing to balloon to 47 million Americans under the second George W. Bush Administration. Simultaneously, the number of *underinsured* (those with chronic diseases with poor coverage) has been estimated to be about equal in number. In addition, from the Reagan through George H.W. Bush years, economic crisis and hospital closure among institutions serving the poor and minority populations in major US cities created an access dilemma unaddressed by any public policy until the Affordable Care Act gave insurance coverage to some 20+ million.

The national health insurance failure by the Clintons in 1993 (Starr, 2011) stood beside the initiation of the Children's Health Insurance Program, which has aided some families with sick kids, but again became a subsidization to private insurance firms that had long neglected this cohort as unprofitable without federal largess. Clinton's approved health plans, while settled in the private sector, came with federal oversight that the insurance and pharmaceutical firms decided were not palatable. They chose to go on their own ways with the market.

Community hospital failures during the 1980s had multiple impacts to declining communities; closures displaced many unskilled and semiskilled workers who lived in adjacent neighborhoods delivering a double whammy to many urban and rural communities (Whiteis, 2000). Doctors, nurses, pharmacists, and other professionals could find jobs elsewhere, but unskilled workers did not easily regain employment. An accompanying disruption was the small businesses formerly sustained by the hospital traffic that closed, as the surrounding housing stock faced disintegration as well (Whiteis, 1992).

Globally, the move toward privatization in health care as well as for public services led to the removal of many state-guaranteed public services and instead provided private services across many nations (Navarro, 1984). Often inspired by the US and international financial institutions (Alvarez, Salmon, & Swartzman, 2011; DeGroote, 2005), the ideology of marketplace medicine was majorly exported and fostered multitiered healthcare systems in several nations, being shaped where larger social policies and processes were promulgated by increasing multinational corporate power and economic consolidation (Homedes, Ugalde, & Rovira 2005). The ideological significance lies in the accompanying decrease in the provision of human services and economic support to those considered "unproductive" segments of the population and their respective communities.

With the growth of corporate hospital profits, these firms moved into related areas of care. The sector saw a continuum of investor activity popping up in diversified areas of freestanding health centers, surgical, MRI and other diagnostic centers, and home healthcare agencies. Despite the contraction of services at the bottom layer of health institutions serving the less fortunate, services sold to well-off insured patients became money making enterprises. Retail store eye and dental centers, ambulance services and other profit-seeking entities filled the vacuum once provided by hospitals.

More recently, chain drug stores diversified into primary care clinics—an entry which blindsided community physicians (see Chap. 2). Today these clinics pose significant threats to primary care physicians and represent another intrusion of "marketplace competition" which has long been heralded by conservatives and investors as an example of innovation and improvement that can only be possible in a *free market health system* (Woodson, 2017) (sic).

Physicians then began to realize that their own remuneration was to be similarly subjected to conserving by both government and private insurance monies: "incentivizing" by the resource-based relative value scale (RBRVS) reimbursement began to set physician fees. RBRVS is based upon predetermined resource costs to provide various services, with the policy intention to stabilize the payment system while continuously trying to constrain outlays. This doctor reimbursement was Reagan's Centers for Medicare & Medicaid Services (CMS) new way to reduce doctor income. Physicians over time adapted to this regulatory constraint, but further restricted payments would lie ahead in the Medicare Part B reimbursement changes and then Obama's MACRA further tightening.

In their heyday, "free market" health economists (Fox, 1997) carried out studies to appeal to the corporate and governmental focus for cost containment. Advocacy and critique took a backstage to policy journals' focus on articles about provider reductions and higher consumer out-of-pocket payments as attempts to curtail expenditure growth. The President of the Federation of American Hospitals, the lobbying arm for the proprietary hospital chains, explained:

> …an administration opposed to government regulation of our industry, opposed to comprehensive national health insurance, opposed to cost controls, opposed to planning, and receptive to new ideas… we have never been in a better position in our history. (Federation of American Hospitals, 1981, p. 2)

The vampire effect was clearly in full swing with most "not-for-profits" obviously choosing bottom-line oriented strategies. Operating surpluses instead of profits are produced by so-called "not-for-profit" voluntary hospitals, which are manifested in higher executive salaries and expense accounts for administrative personnel, trustees, and their business associates who may furnish services or products to the hospital and, indirectly, the medical staff. *Modern Healthcare*'s executive compensation survey in 2019 (Kacik, 2019a, 2019b) revealed average pay for hospital administrators above a half million dollars, with larger systems' CEOs making well into tens of millions in payments per year, all increasing by 6.8% annually—far surpassing the average hospital worker's increases. As mentioned previously, the medical-industrial complex suppliers, who benefit by the pass-through federal/state and private funds, hyped up the purchase of new fancy equipment and supplies supposedly for competition's sake (McKinlay, 1984).

Thus, provider competition, and tougher reimbursement for patient care, created a climate that tended to lessen the enhancement of the population's health in their surrounding communities. What was more apparent was selective marketing to more desirable patients, and "demarketing" to others, along with efforts to build larger systems through diversification schemes. The rhetoric was for a "cost-effective, business-like basis" often with physicians being blamed for high utilization decisions for their patients. The object was to provide greater billable service to those patients who may likely not need more care, but who possessed good coverage for reimbursement and then provide less to those who may very well need more care, but possessed little or no reimbursements.

Further Implications

The magnitude of this proprietary presence and its rapid growth in a new realm of ambulatory entities remains completely unique to the US healthcare system. No other national health system across the globe has such a large and powerful medical-industrial complex with such a heavy corporate provider presence. Nowhere else is profit the main driving force in health care, though this may be changing in several nations. Other nations have traditionally constructed public healthcare and/or not-for-profit systems, though many nations are now privatizing often with the same collection of American health corporations currently making inroads into international markets (Berliner and Burlage, 1994).

With a change in values and purpose of the overall healthcare enterprise, corporate forces abandoned a public health orientation while directing the entire system to their commodity production purposes. Similar ideologies brought along employers who bought the arguments for HMOs, deregulation, and no national health insurance. Across this time, the industrialization of the sector seems directed more toward delimiting the allocation of resources to certain population segments. Individualistic solutions took precedence over communal approaches toward public health; the admonitions favoring social medicine fell on deaf ears among the professions. Corporatization has altered the nature of doctoring and will continue in the future in more dramatic ways (Stoeckle, 1994).

In our healthcare system today, profits subsidized from public funds (which amounts to almost 50% of total US expenditures) give ample reason for these powerful entities to exert influence over policymaking; their proposals are often at odds with the overall public's health. Regulatory constraints imposed by the government to redirect efforts to address public health is stiffly resisted in this medical marketplace, estimated to be around 2–3% of total health expenditures. Thus, the mission of underfunded healthcare entities to further the public's health will continue to erode substantially.

One might pose the question: How did this corporate transformation of US health care occur so fast? Not long ago, the medical profession was considered to be the dominant power in US health care; almost all hospitals were "not-for-profit," as was the largest insurer, Blue Cross Blue Shield, and the largest health maintenance organization, Kaiser Permanente.

Fading of late, the ethics of professionalism spoke to a calling to *public service* for physicians, nurses, and other practitioners while maintaining a *caring purpose* to *alleviate suffering* from disease in their patients *and their communities*. In the halcyon days of the 1950s, physicians were once "the captain of the ship" and used to be their own agents, with personal relationships with their patients, who used to come from communities of which they were both apart. Patients were patients—not considered "customers." Such an agency relationship has been fundamentally altered today (White, Salmon, & Feinglass, 1994).

Back then, insurance under Blue Cross Blue Shield did not interfere in those doctor-patient relationships, nor much in hospital dealings. In fact, payments worked to the clear benefit of providers who were generally happy with the relationship and their funding. Hospitals were paid cost-plus by Blue Cross, and when Medicare and Medicaid came into being in the mid-1960s, reimbursement was similarly designed. Doctors got fee-for-service crafted with hospital payments under the creed that "more is better"—"whatever it takes for patient care." Clearly more in this case meant free reign for getting higher provider revenues. The overriding paradigm was that services were always indicated if a physician ordered them, and they surely did so; use of facilities and newer technologies in greater quantities naturally exploded costs.

Nonetheless, this structural payment arrangement proved to be highly inflationary and packed full of unnecessary and inappropriate utilization, as well as documented iatrogenesis (doctor- or health system-caused disease) both clinical and social (Illich, 1976). *Social iatrogenesis* addresses the widespread medicalization of social problems and the created dependency on pharmaceuticals and medical care; over 90% of physician visits result in prescriptions. Federal and state governments felt the burden of exploding costs, and employers became upset over their uncontrollable outlays for workers' benefits with little gains in improved productivity, nor in overall population health (Salmon, 1973). Consumers constantly face higher and higher premiums, co-pays, and deductibles, still wildly escalating under both the Obama and Trump administrations.

While stronger cost controls appeared highly needed, the system's excesses and inefficiencies mounted, while excess greed prevailed and was increasingly identified but rarely addressed. The United States has *not* sought strong pathways for social prevention for broader occupational and environmental actions; these were opposite to the Republican policy agenda. Therefore, the ongoing corporate transformation spread rapidly as marketplace ideology heralded private interests; health sector corporations became powerfully involved in policymaking across all segments of the sector and then shaped it to their own self interests.

Physicians seem to have been slow to grasp implications from their loss of authority, but recent conditions and the surging burnout make it more evident, maybe to spur a new consciousness (see Chap. 6). The anti-government sentiments, historically expressed by organized medicine, may have tended to obscure threats from the encroaching corporate players. The profession can be characterized as highly fragmented. It now finds itself divided into dwindling private practitioners, paid employees (over 50% of the total practicing), as well as specific segmented divisions: primary care, specialty care, subspecialties, contract physicians, and an administrative class. Its professional elite in leadership roles has often wavered more in narrow self-interest than advocacy stands for the entire population's health and well-being.

Many physicians feel bewildered as they watch mega-corporate health groups and the insurance industry gather performance data to evaluate their clinical decision-making about their now *insurer-owned customers*—no longer *doctors' patients* (Feinglass & Salmon, 1994). Physician professional groups like the American Medical Association remain acutely disturbed by governmental actions into their professional affairs; nevertheless, they appeared to have been blindsided by the encroachment of private administrative entities over the practice of medicine. Relman foresaw the emergence of explicitly for-profit entities, but his voice and a few others failed to echo across the wider profession. Bitten by the vampire for-profit providers in the competitive struggle, the "not-for-profits" began to emulate them with convergent marketplace behaviors: creating patient barriers to entry, scaling back on not-so-profitable community-based services, building service lines that yielded attractive returns on investment, eliminating unprofitable service lines, and dumping patients who were unfunded or underfunded.

These overall conditions were promulgated by government policies, and part of the unplanned marketplace medicine left to the desires of numerous vested interests. The uneven playing field gave way to common bottom-line practices that mimicked across all provider systems. Moreover, administrative functions have now greatly expanded, so physicians find their autonomy more at risk (White, Salmon, & Feinglass, 1994).

From Obamacare to Trump's No Care

The above highlights prevailing conditions and issues before the election of Barack Obama: marketplace medicine was advancing, while 47 million Americans went uninsured, with many denied services; perhaps an equal number were underinsured due to high out-of-pocket outlays; insurance company practices were blatantly discriminatory; and many more health providers became financially at risk. Despite their substantial subsidization by George W. Bush's Medicare Part D, drug company price increases were seen as even more outrageous.

Forces of corporatization had grown steadily since the defeat of the Clinton reforms back in 1993, but the Democrats under Obama now seemed willing to deal and to use massive subsidization for a segment of the uninsured. Obama spoke to the national need to extend coverage while campaigning against insurance company practices. Waitzkin and Hellander (2016), however, note that:

> With funding from the insurance industry and financial corporations linked to Wall Street, Obama became the first presidential candidate in history able to turn down government funds for his campaign.

One wonders where his campaign funding came from other than the many small donors who flocked to his campaign of hope. Subsequently, the Obama Administration would obtain both insurance and pharmaceutical industry support for the Affordable Care Act by providing over $600 billion in funds to the insurance industry, with a continuation of Bush's promise not to regulate drug prices. The marketplace would benefit with new federal funds and minimal regulation. While Obama inherited an economy in shambles, his Administration dumped an additional $700 billion bailout of Wall Street and the banking industry, as Bush had previously performed such a stimulus of a similar amount.

There remains little ideological difference on each party's support for corporate health care even given Republican hostilities toward Obama. On health matters, both parties have generally been centrist since the liberal days of President Lyndon Johnson with his passage of Medicare and Medicaid in 1965. Neither party has supported universal health coverage, preferring incremental and minor adjustments to extending access, which tended to serve certain vested interests (see Chap. 2). Corporate health parties backed many financing modifications so that more government dollars flowed into the medical-industrial complex while consistently preventing regulatory oversight and resisting the push for insurance for everyone.

Coming after the Johnson Administration, Republican policies changed from administrative reform giving way to budget cuts, deregulation, and tax credits: from practical insights on how to improve operations to cutbacks (which Nixon called "rescissions"). Administrative science parlayed in business schools at this time was not prevalent in health care. Agency history, mission, constituency, and ideology were changing with a different party in control. Republicans followed a tendency that rejected the character and competency of the past Democratic direction to extend access to new groups in need; they fell into managerialism as seen in Nixon's new restructuring. The role of policy in the larger political economy was constrained by the Executive Branch, Congress, and the courts, so proposing that health services merely required better management was rather simplistic. Nevertheless, Republican's cynical ideological support for all things in the medical marketplace does not restrain costs as it is increasingly witnessing that price increases across the sector are the major culprit. Neither party will likely choose to tackle price controls in hospitals, pharmaceuticals, and every other health expenditure partially as the result of relying on campaign funding from these very industries. Thus, leaving the status quo in place means growing expenditures and a shift of costs to employees and consumers.

Republicans have heralded the status quo for private interests in health care; there was a continuum of shifts back and forth without much harmonious agreements between the parties on policies. Much of the dispute centered on entitlement programs in the Great Society health and social programs; diametrically opposed policy goals existed over any extension of access. Since their enactment Medicare and Medicaid both boomed to consume greater federal dollars, considered *expenses* for "unproductive groups" versus investment for workers' health. Some in Democratic circles held a value orientation for providing greater coverage, but they also responded to traditional health providers lobbying for more subsidization, plus being aware of ways to solidify their voter base through advocacy, if not legislative passage.

The Nixon Administration's emphasis on restructuring and managerialism gave way to Reagan's stricter cost controls. Both facilitated economists to gain prominence in health circles to formulate technocratic "solutions" in service to Republican Party market-oriented policies. With provider largess under fee-for-service discredited, prepayment incentives were championed. HMOs and DRGs demanded boosting analytical capabilities developed by business types whom Nixon brought into the bureaucracy, along with academic economists and consultants who festered over climbing costs in their reports and studies.

The aging of the population and the pent-up demand from historic lack of access amidst poor social conditions led to the realization that the scope of chronic disease and their future costs in current health care delivery was never taken into account by the government planners. There were a series of failures to hold the line on utilization until Reagan's bargaining with providers to curtail reimbursements. Unfortunately, once the providers found what would be paid for expenditures just shifted from Medicare Part A to the medical side Part B as for-profit ambulatory services increased substantially. Given this cost obsession, imperfect analytic capabilities along with a bottom-line mentality forsook greater focus on quality and hindered care coordination which is so key in chronic disease treatment and control. Overall, Reagan's cost control fetish became the rationale for prohibiting extension of health care access to all Americans, but allowed for vested health care interests to benefit handsomely. Republican health policies have historically been slanted toward market-based solutions with heavy investment into private corporations; it is worthwhile to point toward the brief review in Chap. 2 to see how special vested interests have advanced during past administrations.

In brief, Republicans have been recycling failed ideas for a long time. Now an untested promise of Big Data on steroids is being promulgated within the medical marketplace (see Chap. 5). This comes amidst compassion fatigue across the society for those left behind—over 23 million and growing under Trump. Buried deep in the House of Medicine's reductionism and fetish for the cellular bits and body parts, the medical profession can no longer identify the social and environmental causations of disease in population groups. Confusion persists among health professionals who need to awaken to their changing social context and return to being a noble profession in the Oslerian tradition of early last century—seeing and talking to patients to know them beyond their disease (Osler, 2008). This lineage of the Johns Hopkins University Professor of Medicine, William Osler, who urged physicians to be utmost devoted to their patient as a person and the populace was lost (Bliss, 1999; Silverman et al., 2008).

Notwithstanding Republican opposition, the Democrats and the Obama Administration failed to enact more progressive health policies (Medicare for All, public option, infrastructure development, etc.) when they held the majority of Congress and ultimately fed the corporate monster. Even with the Affordable Care Act decreasing the number of uninsured by 41% in 2017, some 20+ million remained uninsured, many without access to health insurance at any cost.

To reiterate, the ACA giving someone an insurance card is *not* in reality granting access. Access to care means assuring availability of affordable, comprehensive, quality care that is continuous by lowering social and cultural barriers to that care. This means guaranteeing substantial infrastructural improvements in communities so that physicians are there for relationships with patients and families, which the ACA did not do! Even while some funds for community health centers were made available with the disproportionate share hospital (DSH) monies, only small segments of the populace received improved health services.

Reflecting on the Affordable Care Act a decade later, it is important to understand the ambitious effort that was carved out during venomous Republican opposition aiming at its voluminous details. Many aspects of the Affordable Care Act needed to be launched at the same time upon an already complex and dynamic healthcare system; this made it difficult to coordinate the changes being implemented and gave the law's opponents fodder to attack government incompetency (Blumenthal & Abrams, 2020).

The ACA did solidify a commitment for what employers wanted: introducing value-based payment to change incentives from fee-for-service medical practice; the idea linking physician compensation to monitored performance by using information technology received broad acceptance. As an attempt to reduce costs by targeting quality of care, hospitals—the largest expenditure of any medical care component—got particular attention. Under the historic Medicare and Medicaid programs, cost reimbursement (or rather cost-plus reimbursement) had been the basis of payment, obviously being highly inflationary over decades. The ACA reduced payments to hospitals in various ways.

Medicare Advantage Plans run by private insurers saw reduced payments. The idea that got the hospital buy-in to ACA was that some 20 million of the uninsured would be brought into the system, thus reducing uncompensated care. The downside was that the federal government would begin to look at quality of care through the Hospital Readmissions Reduction Program which intended to have hospitals take responsibility for patients unduly readmitted for their clinical conditions soon after discharge. Wide variations in Medicare readmissions had been found (as high as 24.7% among patients with certain conditions). Identified hospitals with above-average risk-adjusted rates of readmission within 30 days were found unable to quickly alter their practices, so they received federal penalties, estimated to be 50% of the nation's hospitals the following year—an indicator of how difficult redirecting engrained practices are for quality improvement!

Another area of concern was hospital-acquired conditions; its program sought to identify how to measure and limit those conditions in groups of people occurring disproportionately. Hospital safety has been improving under the ACA, but it is unclear if the law actually produced such improvement or other factors contributed (Blumenthal & Abrams, 2020). Much more over the future needs to be done in hospital safety, with better studies to guide directions too (See Chap. 4).

Accountable Care Organizations

The major significant introduction of the ACA was Accountable Care Organizations (ACOs) which were designed to measure and reward physician practices based upon much greater scrutiny over physician decision-making with particular attention to costs and quality. Fifteen hundred ACOs were begun by hospitals and physician groups resulting in enrolling 44 million Medicare patients. While getting these public and private organizations off the ground from a policy perspective, as well as operationally, seemed formidable, the Trump Administration has not followed through with CMS emphasis as was the intent of Obama. Yet, as ACOs yield different performance with their control over quality and finances, questions remain whether many of their innovations will be proven worthwhile after assessment by good health services research and what it will take to replicate the worthwhile ones in other settings. In this era of Big Data with improved analytics, will the colossal IT firms sweep in with capabilities that will be used to serve consumers to lower costs and advance their health literacy? Or will marketplace disruptions locally, regionally, and nationally mount with lesser providers losing out? Will national health policy attempt to make health services available to all citizens? Will the nation be able to advance health promotion and protection for the whole population? Social, occupational, and environmental conditions for healthier communities need to be fully recognized, researched, and addressed beyond just cost-efficiencies in medical care, which is only part of improved population health.

For the most part, ACOs have modest net savings in the different types of ACOs, likely due to nuances of their design features and the sponsoring operational management. Physicians and hospitals also found the high-cost questionable quality procedures addressed through the Bundled Payments for Care Improvement Program, the idea being that providers would receive a single prospective payment for treatment of a medical or surgical condition and could retain savings or absorb excess costs in order to meet imposed quality criteria. Over a thousand hospitals and physician groups participated in this, again having mixed results, but some surgical procedure expenditures (such as hip and knee replacements) saw some cost restraint; while most of the program "was less promising with more chronic conditions" (Joynt Maddox, Oray, Zheng, & Epstein, 2019).

The ACA also looked to improve performance by strengthening the nation's primary care infrastructure. Increased monies were channeled into community health centers, and further support for hospitals came with the DSH initiative; designated safety net hospitals received enhanced reimbursement for taking care of more uninsured people. The Comprehensive Primary Care initiative sought increased payments from both public and private sources in order to reduce emergency department visits. Approximately 15,000 primary care practitioners were given enhanced payments, but the results of this remain to be determined (Peikes, Dale, & Ghosh, 2018).

Obama's goal of remaking the healthcare system (Pear, 2009) was beset by an ailing economy that exacerbated concerns over its eventual costs and stern opposition from the Republicans. His predecessor George W. Bush had poured $700 billion into Wall Street, and Obama repeated the transaction for another $700 billion to save the banking industry. For the ACA, health providers remained skeptical of new "efficiencies" that supposedly would help to control costs, though the ACA really did not have much in cost and quality controls, nor stiff regulation. The "46 million uninsured" was not a rallying cry that could dampen the ominous Republican opposition, who formed themselves into the Tea Party Caucus to express its bitter dismay over government intrusion into the healthcare market. Republicans in Congress stood as "deficit hawks" seeking to cut the federal debt and limit Executive power. The now evolved albeit diluted Freedom Caucus clowns now have had their wings clipped under Trump's military buildup and huge tax cuts, leading to the biggest federal deficits in history. The bailout bills to get the "economy back" ballooned the deficit even more with the CARES Act following the COVID-19 pandemic lasting through 2020.

The ACA implementation did not balloon costs in a huge way, yet the Republican budget hawks always objected to Obama spending. Increased spending and deficits under President Trump apparently don't stir the same dire warnings as we heard back during the Obama Administration. In fact, there was a modest increase in total health expenditures between 2010 and now before COVID-19 took hold. Employer-sponsored benefit spending also did not jump in a great way, partly because benefit packages were changed, less uncompensated care costs shifted to the private sector, and the health insurance exchanges took over some employees.

Besides the overall complexity of the ACA law, sad mistakes in its startup (especially with the website used to apply for coverage), and its slow implementation, the ACA proposed a federal "marketplace" to be run by the government for roughly 2/3 of the states, offering a set of benefit plans by private insurers (bronze, silver, and gold levels) with three added silver options for people qualified for cost-sharing reductions based on their income. The federal outlay was estimated to be over $650 billion. States were to receive extra funds to sign up their uninsured citizens plus a few years of federal subsidization in their Medicaid programs; several Republican-held states refused this Medicaid expansion. Private insurers were not required to offer standardized plans on the federal and the individual state marketplaces, an obscureness which tended to baffle consumers. Republicans seized upon talking points that revolved around taking your private health insurance away and not being able to keep your doctor. Alaskan Governor and then Vice-Presidential candidate Sarah Palin's fictitious "death panels" took hold with notions of killing grandma all in the service of the Affordable Care Act mandates. The Administration's promises of no changes in Americans' usual health care proved to be a stretch, so the opposition seized on that false claim.

Regardless of these missteps, 20 million of the 47 million received some access to coverage, even if the ACA popularity was tarnished by its inability to cover more and the determined opponents who continue to seek the law's "repeal and replace." Through the spectrum of these previous events, one can witness that *the popular mandate for health reforms* from the late 1980s through the early 1990s had called for an overall restructuring of the entire system (Sommers, Maylone, Blendon, Oray, & Epstein, 2017). Nevertheless, criticisms of the ACA were able to turn the tide during its complex implementation. This was aided by its slowness to deliver what was promised and its widely felt startup problems and confusion. The original federal website for signups failed at first. The exchanges proved to be too difficult to comprehend, were often misunderstood and that was if you were able to get through to the actual website. One major outcome was that low-income adults benefited well after a few years (Sommers, Maylone, Blendon, Oray, & Epstein, 2017).

Awareness of price increases by providers, insurers, and drug companies did emerge during this period of cost containment. Now it appears widely acknowledged as a key cost push in the overall expenditure. Constraints to ease into value-based reimbursement are a trend. Experimentation with these different programs and the ACOs has created an altered condition for payment practices. Quality appears to no longer just be rhetoric, with designs being put in place to bring about serious discussions with some concerted interventions. To its partial credit, the ACA brought necessary attention to evidence-based medical practice with its series of attempted cleanups. Comparative effectiveness for drug evaluations are now seen as so necessary built upon real-world data. Whether routing out the non-useful and harmful results in drug therapies, and how fast, remains to be seen in the current insurer/PBM industry. Tools are on the way to aid physicians and pharmacists in this clinical decision-making, so that practitioners can make better informed choices without being bludgeoned by administrators!

Existing patterns of testing and treatment can be scrutinized through electronic health records (EHRs) with new information technology capabilities and analytics—depending upon who controls these new tools. It is not clear if medical experts will prevail, or merely cost-cutting corporate administrators stay in charge of this direction; nevertheless, it is absolutely necessary that protocols receive sufficient physician participation in their development and give feedback on their utility for quality improvements. Practitioners should not be dictated to! Maintaining such dialogues will be critical if we are to see a system-wide reduction in the dramatic variations in medical practice and find better strategies for chronic disease control.

The authors, as academicians ourselves, would prefer studies by health services researchers that get peer reviewed, rather than leave observations and "studies" at the whim of the marketplace. Clinical practice must be balanced with practitioners, obtaining better understandings of evidence generated on solid scientific foundation—not by some newly designed corporate AI system. Surely, comparative effectiveness for pharmaceuticals cannot be left to the pharmaceutical firms.

A new policy perspective should reach awareness that powerful economic actors must be held in check so that society heads toward more progressive directions toward social justice and health equity. Demanding new accountability by the vested interests is a step toward breaking up the monopolies that have so controlled medical practice and medical science itself. Drug therapies should be scrutinized in ways that the pharmacy benefit managers have never chosen because of their profit-taking. Millions of Americans are on a multitude of drugs that may not really be helping them as much as they have been told, and in fact in many cases could be harming them. The ACA urged outcome studies which must be developed and funded with new trends for designing overall system performance.

Had the ACA not received such staunch Republican resistance and undermining, the Obama Administration may have been able to move forward on some of these activities in a better and clearer way. For sure, the issue of accountability is more pronounced policymaking debates. The recent explosion of many urban health conditions due to the coronavirus may provoke new demands for improvement in new accountable forms also.

To its partial credit, the ACA brought attention to evidence-based medical practice with its series of attempted cleanups. Comparative effectiveness for drug evaluations are now seen as so necessary to rout out the non-useful and harmful. Tools are on the way to aid physicians and pharmacists in this clinical decision-making, so that practitioners can make better informed choices. The outside power of the pharmaceutical industry may be required to be curtailed for real progressive reforms.

Existing patterns of testing and treatment can be scrutinized through EHRs and new information technology capabilities and analytics—depending upon who controls these new directions. It is not clear if medical experts and professionals are in charge of medical care usage instead of cost-cutting corporate administrators. It will be necessary that protocols receive sufficient physician participation and feedback so that there is buy-in and practitioners who will use the tool will not feel dictated to. Maintaining dialogues between providers and payers are critical if we are to see a systemic end to, or reductions, in significant variations in medical practice.

Demanding new accountability by the vested interests may be a step toward breaking up the monopolies that have so controlled medical practice and medical science itself. Drug therapies should be scrutinized in ways that the pharmacy benefit managers have never chosen because of their profit-taking. Millions of Americans are on polypharmacy that may not really be helping them, and in fact in many cases is harming them (Manasse, 1989). The ACA urged outcome studies to be developed and funded with new trends for designing overall system performance.

Trump's Divide

The 45th President caused many Americans to disbelieve and distrust the institution of the Presidency. For some Americans, it began with the actual election and followed by inauguration and later for many who may have voted for him but gradually came after continuous shenanigans. Indicators point to his incompetence in addressing the COVID-19 pandemic and an economy in free fall only to be compounded by protests after the George Floyd killing by Minneapolis Police in late May 2020. Trump's election to the Presidency dismayed a huge portion of the American population.

As president, Trump continues to secure and support his base versus an ever-enlarging defined enemy of Democrats, "establishment elites," including the media, intelligence community, and everything done within the past Obama Administration.

It has been reported he does fail to read many reports coming across his desk, nor does he seek advice from his advisors and cabinet. In the absence of a coherent governing strategy, Trump has consistently continued to campaign and has *never* pivoted from that to running the government as the chief executive. After FBI Director James Comey told him of Russian influence over the American elections (and all top intelligence agencies confirmed the interference), Trump reacted against the intelligence community and the media by promoting the idea of a "deep state" and haranguing about "fake news" and "very dishonest people." His performance led to much skepticism and criticism by the public that has in some ways allowed him to get away with it by maintaining what was called "America's Great Divide" (Frontline: America's Great Divide, 2020).

In his inaugural address, Trump appealed to his base, the forgotten men and women, aka the "deplorables" to begin to continue to accentuate the divide between them and everyone else. The largest protests in American history came shortly after his inauguration with women in the hundreds of thousands protesting in early 2017. Here was when the idea of "alternative facts" emerged, which presents us with an Orwellian sense of a dangerous and unstable environment that may allow a person to believe whatever one wants to believe in the Great Divide. Nothing gets accepted at face value; thus the Trump Administration rescinded nearly 200 Obama executive orders on the ACA, the environment, immigration, and whatever else President Obama had done. In his ongoing efforts to roll back all aspects of the ACA with an eye upon his base, his Administration took away transgender protections allowing doctors and hospitals to discriminate citing religious reasons (Armour, 2020). The first acts against the Affordable Care Act were designed to strip it of its powers.

His prime directive was to keep immigrants out of the United States by building the border wall and fighting Hispanics on the immigration issue; restricting DACA students; and going after Muslim "terrorists" by blocking seven Muslim nations with a travel ban. In response to the Charlottesville "Unite the Right" rally in 2017 which wound up with a right-wing supporter killing a protester with his car, the President merely dismissed the violence as there were many "good people on both sides." And his crude and mostly unsuccessful trade dealings with China, Europe, Mexico, and Canada have perpetually gyrated the financial markets. And yet for some reason his base remains loyal, supportive, and are very vocal, and the corporate sector enjoyed the tax cuts and easing regulations.

The Trump Administration has not followed through with Obamacare's emphasis on ACOs; instead he has singularly sought to totally dismantle the ACA. Sixty-five attempts by the Republican Congress to end Obamacare and two Supreme Court decisions, plus Trump's own executive orders, greatly interfered with its implementation over time, but to date the Affordable Care Act remains albeit with growing appreciation.

Nevertheless, when it became time for Republican legislation to "remove and replace," there were no ideas for the "replace" part. The GOP game plan was merely to repeal a somewhat popular entitlement that a Democratic Congress and President had enacted with zero plans by the opposition to replace. Their idea was simply to revert to the system that existed in 2010 that would throw millions of people off the health insurance rolls.

So after Trump had continually boasted he would deliver the "a wonderful plan," "the best care," and "for every American," Trump and the Republicans (proved this time to be the Party of no ideas) pressed on to strip the Medicaid expansion away from the several states who have signed on (Eilperin & Goldstein, 2017). Most Americans will remember the infamous John McCain's fateful Senate "thumbs down" vote that defeated Senate Majority Leader Mitch McConnell's attempt to repeal the ACA. In his second year of office, Trump slashed outreach efforts for navigators to enroll more eligible persons to help the ACA to "implode" (Sullivan, 2017). Hard-pressed folks would still sign up, though in small numbers.

COVID-19 Pandemic

The veniality of Trump has been exacerbated by his poor response and incompetence to the COVID-19 pandemic. Was it clear to the White House the virus would cull the ranks of minorities, the aged and disabled, the homeless, Native Americans, and prisoners? Or were they holding back widespread testing and their supply chain mismanagement after it was seen who was dying? Or did they just not care believing ultimately that they were dealing with "just the flu" and that this outbreak would run its course like the seasonal flu? Historians will hopefully delve into this clash of politics and public health.

During the Trump Administration, under both Secretary Price and Alex Azar, CMS made a wide range of temporary adjustments to Medicare and Medicaid, with exceptions for value-based services and delaying the MIPS incentive payments (Brady, 2020). ACOs will benefit from these CMS actions. The first CARES Act bailout law gave a $175 billion package for hospitals. The Trump Administration proceeded to distribute the funds—not to the neediest facilities facing the luge of coronavirus patients—but to wealthier hospital chains (Drucker, Silver-Greenberg, & Kliff, 2020). Regrettably, hospitals serving low-income patients did not fare well against the wealthiest who benefited; most of the former hospitals have insufficient cash on hand to finance operations during the epidemic (Cohrs, 2020). A high number are at risk for closure. Laid off workers who lost their coverage face a 60-day sign-up for Obamacare or Medicaid if eligible (Alonso-Zaldivardo, 2020). More folks quickly obtaining coverage may keep certain hospitals afloat.

Up until the Minneapolis Police murder of George Floyd in May of 2020, and the death of 100,000 Americans from the COVID-19 virus, Trump's approval rating stayed in the 30 to 40 percent range. Now Democratic Presidential nominee Joe Biden is leading in the polls based on anti-Trump sentiment as seen by the nationwide protests in almost every city, with some rioting and new calls for defunding police over a series of racist actions that resulted in multiple deaths, which have lessened Trump's approval rating, putting his reelection in jeopardy.

The recent implosion of several urban health conditions and ravaging state budgets (Mervosh & Harmon, 2020; Kelton, 2020) due to the coronavirus points out the paucity of analysis as Trump's basis of what to do. Delays, improper supply chain actions, and untimely travel bans may have actually compounded his Administration's response to COVID-19. His *playbook that wasn't* revealed a systematically dismantled pandemic preparation commission and then subsequent cuts to the National Institutes of Health and Centers for Disease Control and Prevention budgets, along with his antagonisms to the World Health Organization. He also failed to act more quickly on travel bans, with little decent national management over testing, and the supply chain for masks, gloves, swabs, and other medical personal protective gear. It is clear that the increased potential death and case rates can be laid squarely at the feet of President Trump and his Administration and his response, or more accurately lack of response, were criticized widely (Media Outlets Examine Trump Response to COVID-19 Pandemic, 2020). His continued push to restart and reopen the economy driven by his reelection campaign is likely to backfire with states in the south and west that saw little in the way of COVID-19 cases and deaths, but now are starting to show large increases in both. Reopening the economy before the pandemic was under better control in a number of states likely accounts for a second wave of infections and maybe reach the 200,000 death mark before the election (Stacey & Crow, 2020; Kuchler, 2020). It's ironic that many of the states that had lax "stay-at-home" and no required mask orders, plus an earlier opening, have faced the fastest spread of the coronavirus. And these are Trump states of Florida, Arizona, and Texas, among others (Masson, 2020). Ironically it seems this desperate push to reopen the economy, decrease unemployment, buoy the stock market, and bounce consumer confidence may actually wind up costing the President the very voters he was counting on to get reelected.

What is clear is that we will never see a progressive national health policy agenda ever arise under these sordid conditions of crisis. The calamity of a pandemic, Depression-era unemployment, widespread national protests, and a clueless Administration can only mean more hardship for the already hard-hit population. How will all of this be debated over the election campaign remains to be seen with facts, reasonable analyses, understanding, and reconciling of divergent perspectives. This is an expectation of a decent civil campaign.

Locally, Governors and Mayors are greatly perplexed over strategies, not just to address the popular health conditions but also for funding dilemmas that obviously delimits their ability to resolve their impending respective health crises in 2021. The resulting double whammy of the economic effect of the pandemic coupled with systemic community disinvestment (Harrison, 2020), give these communities cause to remain very angry. Coupled with spending on the pandemic, states have little room to address any other issues in their already strained economic situation. The opening of schools is an especially disheartening management decision for local areas.

Marketplace players, however, are planning to sweep in to explore the multitude of new opportunities, from state database constructions to software for contact tracing. Yamey and Jamison (2020) calculate the US death rate is a hundred times greater than it is in China. Other nations that acted early and effectively on available information avoided their worst-case scenarios; however, the Trump Administration still lingers well behind for improved public health programming to address the epidemic and financial assistance to providers. Americans justifiably have psychological uncertainty over the society in which we live.

Despite campaign promises to replace with the "best," "everyone covered," and "pre-existing conditions protected," no alternative plan was ever suggested. His vilifying China for his economic problems and other Twitter rants mean Trump needs issues for a comeback, even perhaps to maintain his loyal Republican ranks. This is key given how central health has become in the American consciousness. While the GOP and the Trump Administration have never actually had an idea for replacing the ACA, or reforming it in any ways other than vindictive rhetoric, the recent events of both the COVID-19 pandemic, the huge unemployment and loss of insurance coverage, and the protests surrounding the George Floyd killing may eventually renew interest in concerted healthcare reform. Let us see what the Presidential campaign reveals in the near term.

Conclusion

Today's mega-mergers of insurers, PBMs, and the sight of other large-scale cross-corporate amalgamations cannot help but provoke new deeper ponderings on the future of medical practice over the twenty-first century (McKinlay & Stoeckle, 1994). Beyond the entry of for-profit corporations into the delivery of care, other forces were endemic to the overall health system leading into the transformation of the sector. Corporate entities from pharmaceuticals and hospital equipment and supplies through accounting and legal firms had secured a strong foothold. All sought to enrich themselves to maintain the supply function to the delivery of health care. It remains all of the same piece.

In the 1860s Karl Marx made the point (O'Connor, 1981) which remains critical today for health care: production thus produces consumption. When we examine modern medicine, it is important to note that true objective health needs are hidden by mere medical care utilization, which is how the system defines as *health*. Here is where Illich's conception of *social iatrogenesis* becomes crucial. What has evolved over time is what has been offered in its commodified form of services; does utilization truly reflect either a patient's or the population's health and well-being? An ongoing critique of modern medicine in its current form has displayed many aspects, and it is worthwhile to ponder its questioning (Cousins, 1976; Carlson, 1976; Bishop, 1977, 1980, 1981; Waitzkin, 1978).

The definition of health has been argued and debated over time as the ideology and content of modern medicine has been critiqued (McNeely, 2002; Roemer, 1956, 1978; Waitzkin, 1978; Szasz, 1977; Kelman, 1984; Illich et al., 1977; Zola, 1972; Geiger, 1976; Thomas, 1976; Anderson, Smith, & Sidel, 2005; Dossey, 1982; Salmon, 1984).

The authors believe in a broader conception of *public health*, and we hope to contribute insights into overall healthcare system dynamics so people might begin to question its purpose and organization; we believe such an approach can assist making better choices for policy changes toward the *sustenance of well-being of the entire population*—apart from merely the clinical condition of an individual patient's doctor-designated services. This includes the broader social, political economic, and ecological context in a given society for varying cohorts, as well as the societal commitment to health care as a basic human right.

Since the 1970s corporate health care has been reorganizing the production of health services, yielding new production techniques, producing many new products and services, and reaping bountiful profits, some extracted by executives and investors, others reinvested. All of this is changing relationships between patients and health professionals. Through these processes, different expectations and new *needs* have arisen. These processes also create additional needs that production in a variety of ways attempts to satisfy, if profits can be made; nevertheless, these new discovered *needs* may be manufactured and not be helpful for advancing true public health for the entire population. They instead are designed to be suitable as more high-tech costly procedures to feed the medical-industrial complex.

The profit-based means to satisfy designed health needs are always changing, but a few constants remain. Medicine continues to seek out advancements to prolong life and supposedly improve quality of life. In a perverse way, it seems that American Health Care in particular is engaged in a desperate search for a cure for death and is willing to spend any amount of money to achieve it. So, is the nation ready to spend whatever is necessary to keep death at bay? Without a doubt, the medical-industrial complex stands ready to do those things for people provided the funds are given to pay for them. Availability of new technologies multiplies production possibilities and further offers commoditized versions of what is to be consumed, usually with explosive costs. For example, a new drug introduction onto the market can become a blockbuster, leading to often billions of new expenditures in a few years. Rarely are pharmacoeconomic studies performed to demonstrate any other downstream system savings: Should this be an FDA requirement even after the introduction, let alone, before it becomes embedded as standard care? Technology assessments need to become standard fare especially given the history and makeup of the MIC.

The pharmaceutical industry has come up with a plethora of drugs to address unwanted adverse drug reactions (or combo drugs that fuse two older drugs of shown ineffectiveness and more recently add-on drugs when the earlier ones don't work that well as the DTC ads reveal), which are created by use of other prescribed drugs. Firms advertise entities directly to consumers to stimulate demand often around restrictive PBM formularies. Such production and promotion require many people to buy into the constructed system rather unquestioningly (O'Connor, 1974). In a convoluted manner, the market and financing determine what gets produced, while at the same time, what gets produced has usually received payment to benefit providers and suppliers.

The impact on costs for bringing in large numbers of uninsured has been notable. Healthcare costs rose phenomenally from 2007 to 2015 with certain components doing better. Drug costs rose 15.8% in 2015 alone with existing brand drugs seeing new price increases to bring healthcare expenditures up to 19.2% of GDP. Back in 2015, a family of four was estimated to be spending $25,826 dollars per year for health care. For 2020, overall expenditures for health care in the United States reached $4 trillion annually, which may jump considerably with COVID-19, going beyond a fifth of the gross domestic product.

This sum remains a significant "expense" to the larger economy, which conservatives feel is burdensome on employers for competitiveness abroad, all government budgets, and their wealthy donors. Beyond the weight upon consumers themselves, corporate employers have dealt with increasing health expenses. Republicans seeking entitlement reductions propose cuts in Medicaid, Medicare, and other health programs. They are crafting coverage schemes (e.g., health savings accounts, narrow networks, short-term and skinny benefit plans, etc., along with changing disproportionate share hospital payments) to limit benefits and impose large caps, as was their agenda in the rollback of the ACA. Most of such ideas are unlikely to be well-received by the working and middle class and completely unmindful for the less fortunate among us.

The object of these policy directions is rooted in the belief that people should be responsible for their own health and if one wants something, then just go out and earn the necessary funds to pay for it; otherwise, the person is likely to be deemed *undeserving* of help from the rest of us. This victim-blaming perspective is anathema to the premise of health as a fundamental human right with universal coverage!

Capital flooding into any sector of the economy tends to create bubbles, which typically suddenly deflate when better opportunities for investment arise elsewhere. Renewed attempts to keep the present system intact appear to many as both untenable and unsustainable. Policymakers beyond the "slash and burn" ultraconservatives may come up with a twisted option, instead of that of progressive Democratic Presidential candidates "Medicare4All," but perhaps a vastly limited legislated *Medicaid for All* form may evolve—such may have the CMS contract with insurers to handle back end functions of insurance and payment much like many private insurance firms do now under Medicare contracting.

The current Democratic presidential nominee Joe Biden does not seem to be on board the single-payer bandwagon, so the articulation of the design and its implementation of something new beyond "build upon the ACA" has a very long way to go. Do the Congressional Democrats have the wherewithal to come up with a winnable legislative set of real solutions and to resist compromise in such a manner as mentioned above?

A fear should arise that such a compromise arrangement to gain feasible passage would likely be designed to remove risk from insurance companies, whereas finance capital might end up dictating more restricted conditions for health providers. Rate setting, along with other mechanisms, could be established at state levels, supposedly favored by Republicans (i.e., work requirements for Medicaid recipients). Other ideas should be explored to oppose the more draconian reforms led by the Trump Administration, like "skimpier health plans" pushed by US Secretary of Health and Human Services Azar (Armour, 2018).

In the final analysis, the authors here believe that our nation should guard against what may lie ahead as conservative health policies that favor those who wish to privatize the gain and give the public the losses—while Medicaid recipients and uninsured cohorts may go with limited options for the interim, particularly in states that didn't expand Medicaid.

However, popularity for the ACA has never been higher as witnessed in voters choosing Medicaid additions last election in 2016. In short, well-connected private entities that are better-managed and connected stand to do well financially, while many other providers may face closure (Goldsmith, 1985). In the meanwhile, patient cohorts can expect increased outlays, restricted access, and worsening health outcomes.

Health care in America has become solidly more corporate as the next chapter will demonstrate, with many Americans agreeing that profit seems to drive most aspects of the healthcare delivery system, including providers, PBMs and insurance companies, retail clinics, and peripheral supply firms, such as the pharmaceutical industry. Their purpose appears *not* to be enhancing the entire population's health and assuring access to needed services, nor especially raising the larger public health. This is not so easy to state since most physician and practitioners have devoted their careers to serving their patients, and many provider institutions do seek to perform to their utmost under challenging circumstances to serve their communities. When we examine modern medicine, it is important to note that true health needs in the population are grossly obscured by mere medical care utilization. What has evolved institutionally with the offered commodified form of medical services does *not* truly reflect a patient's, nor a population's, health and well-being.

We wish readers to ponder a new broader concept of public health as they examine our writing: the sustenance of well-being among the *entire population*—apart from the clinical condition of a single "individual patient's" designated services. This assumes the social, economic, political economic, and ecological contexts of life for varying cohorts in our society and the world; thus, a strong commitment to health and health care as a basic human right is fundamental.

References

Alinsky, S. (1950). John L. Lewis: An unauthorized biography. *JSTOR, 44*(4), 1019–1021.
Alvarez, L. S., Salmon, J. W., & Swartzman, D. (2011). *Int J Health Serv*, 41(2):355–370.
Anderson, M. R., Smith, L., & Sidel, V. W. (2005). What is social medicine? Monthly review magazine. Available via DIALOG. https://monthlyreview.org/2005/01/01/what-is-social-medicine/. Accessed 1 Mar 2018.
Armour, S. (2018). Skimpier health plans get boost. *The Wall Street Journal*, 21 Feb 2018.
Arnsdorf, I., & Greenberg, J. (2018). The VA's private care program gave companies billions and vets longer wait. *ProPublica*. Available via DIALOG. https://www.propublica.org/article/va-private-care-program-gave-companies-billions-and-vets-longer-waits. Accessed 14 Sept 2019.

Aronowitz, S., & Giroux, H. (1985). *Education under siege: The conservative, liberal, and radical debate over schooling*. London, UK: Routledge.

Baran, P., & Sweezy, P. (1966). *Monopoly capital: An essay on the American economic and social order* (pp. 1–389). New York: Penguin Books.

Barnet, R. J., & Muller, R. E. (1974). *Global reach: The power of the multinational corporations*. New York: Simon and Schuster.

Bauman, P. (1976). The formulation and evolution of the health maintenance organization policy 1970-1973. *Social Science and Medicine, 10*, 129–142.

Bell, C. W. (1996). U.S healthcare piques interest abroad. *Modern Healthcare, 26*(13), 78.

Berliner, H. S. (1977). *Philanthropic foundations and scientific medicine*. Unpublished thesis at Johns Hopkins University, Baltimore, MD.

Berliner, H. S., & Regan, C. (1987). Multinational operations of US for-profit hospital chains: Trends and implications. *American Journal of Public Health, 10*(77), 1280–1284.

Bhagwati, A. (2019). Private care for vets. *The New York Times*.

Bosch, S. J. (2000). Is Argentina ready for managed care? *Community Health, 25*(2), 89–94.

Brasfield, M. H. (1993). Health politics and policy, by Theodore Litman and Leonard Robins. *Journal of Health Politics, Policy and Law, 18*(4), 1001–1003.

Bresnick, J. (2018). DOJ recovers $2.5B in healthcare fraud, false claims in 2018. Health payer intelligence. Available via DIALOG. https://healthpayerintelligence.com/news/doj-recovers-2.5b-in-healthcare-fraud-false-claims-in-2018. Accessed 25 Jan 2019.

Brindle, J. (1969). Prospects for prepaid group practice. *American Journal of Public Health, 59*, 37–45.

Brinkerhoff, M. B., & Kunz, P. R. (1972). *Complex organizations and their environments*. Dubuque, IA: WC Brown Co.

Brown, E. R. (1976). Public health in imperialism: Early Rockefeller programs at home and abroad. *American Journal of Public Health, 66*, 897–903.

Brown, E. R. (1983). Medicare and Medicaid: The process, value, and limits of health care reforms. *Journal of Health Policy, 4*(3), 335–366.

Brown, E. R. (1990). DRGs and the rationing of hospital care. In V. G. Anderson & G. R. Anderson (Eds.), *Hospital ethics: Guide for ethical thinking and decision making* (pp. 69–90). Germantown, WI: Aspen.

Brown, L. D. (1985). Technocratic corporatism and administrative reform in Medicare. *Journal of Health Politics, Policy, and Law, 3*(10), 579–600.

Brown, M., & McCool, B. P. (1986). Vertical integration: Exploration of a popular strategic concept. *Health Care Management Review, 11*(4), 7–19.

Capitman, J. (1996). HMOs and the elderly. *Journal of Health Politics, Policy and Law, 21*(2), 380–384.

Cassel, C. K. (1985). Doctors and allocation decisions: A new role in the new Medicare. *Journal of Health Politics, Policy, and Law, 3*(10), 549–564.

Church, J., Gerlock, A., & Smith, D. L. (2018). Neoliberalism and accountability failure in the delivery of services affecting the health of the public. *International Journal of Health, 48*(4), 641–662.

Cohen, J. K. (2019). VA, Defense to establish new office for HER projects. *Modern Healthcare*.

Cohen, R. L. (1985). Aids: The impending quarantine. *Health Policy Advisory Center, 4*(16), 9–14.

Di Leo, J. R., Giroux, H. A., McClennen, S., & Saltman, K. (2013). *Neoliberalism, education, and terrorism*. New York: Routledge.

Disch, L. (1996). Publicity-stunt participation and sound bite polemics: The health care debate 1993-94. *Journal of Health Politics, Policy and Law, J21*(1), 3–34.

Donay, C. (2018). *Innovation drives deep changes in the structure of economies*. Pictet's View.

Dossey, L. (1982). *Space, time, and medicine*. Boulder, CO: Shambhala.

Doyal, L., & Rennell, I. (1979a). Health, illness and the development of Capitalism in Britian. In *The political economy of health* (pp. 96–138). Boston, MA: Little, Brown.

Doyal, L., & Rennell, I. (1979b). Understanding medicine and health. In *The political economy of health* (pp. 11–46). Boston, MA: Little, Brown.

Dranove, D. (2017). The Anthem-Cigna merger: A post-mortem. *Health Affairs*. Available via DIALOG. https://www.healthaffairs.org/do/10.1377/hblog20170905.061802/full/. Accessed 7 Feb 2019.

Dranove, D., & White, W, D. (1997). *Medicaid-dependent hospitals and their patients: How have they fared?* Dissertation, Northwestern University, University of Illinois at Chicago.

Drucker, J., Silver-Greenberg, J., & Kliff, S. (2020). Wealthiest Hospitals Got Billions in Bailout for Struggling Health Providers. Available at: https://www.nytimes.com/2020/05/25/business/coronavirus-hospitals-bailout.html. Accessed October 11, 2020.

Edwards, R., Reich, M., & Weisskope, T. (Eds.). (1972). *The capitalist system*. Cambridge, MA: Harvard University Press.

Engel, G. (1977). The need for a new medical model: A challenge for biomedicine. *Science, 196*, 129–136.

Ellwood PM, Anderson NN, Billings JE, Carlson RJ, Hoagberg EJ and McClureW (1971) Health Maintenance Strategy (Papers from the Workshop on International Studies of Medical Care), Medical Care 9(3), 291–298.

Ellwood, P. M., Jr., Herbert, M. E. (1973). Health care: Should industry buy it or sell it? Harvard Business Review. (51):99–107.

Etheredge, L. (1983). Reagan, congress, and health spending. *Health Affairs Journal*. Available via DIALOG. https://www.healthaffairs.org/doi/abs/10.1377/hlthaff.2.1.14. Accessed 12 Jan 2018.

Etzioni, A. (1961). *A comparative analysis of complex organizations on power, involvement, and their correlates*. New York: Free Press/Collier-Macmillan.

Eyer, J. (1984). Capital, health, and illness. In J. McKinlay (Ed.), *Issues in the political economy of health*. New York: Tavistock.

Fanu, J. L. (1999). *The rise and fall of modern medicine*. New York: Carroll & Graf Publisher.

Federation of American Hospitals. (1981). *Federation of American Hospitals 1981 in review: Annual report*. Little Rock, AR: Federation of American Hospitals.

Ferguson, M. (1978). A new perspective on reality. *Mind/Brain Bulletin, 3*, 1–4.

Fisher, I., Committee of One Hundred on National Health., United States. National Conservation Commission. (1909). *Bulletin 30 of the Committee of One Hundred on National Health: being a report on national vitality, its wastes and conservation*. Washington: Govt. Print. Off.

Fleming, S. (1971). Health maintenance organizations. A prototype: California - Kaiser Foundation-Permanente Program. *Hospitals, 45*, 56–57.

Ford, J., & Plimmer, G. (2018). Britain was once the pioneer in privatization but now many people believe that investors have run rings around the regulators. That has prompted a rethink about how public utilities should be managed. *Financial Times*.

Fox, D. M. (1979). From reform to relativism: A history of economists and health care. *Milbank Memorial Fund Quarterly/Health and Society, 3*(57), 297–336.

Frank, A. G. (1967). *Capitalism and underdevelopment in Latin America: Historical studies of Chile and Brazil*. New York: Monthly Review Press.

Frank, J. (1963). *Persuasion and healing: A comparative study of psychotherapy*. Schocken, NY: JHU Press.

Freidson, E. (1970a). *Professional dominance*. New York: Atherton Press.

Freidson, E. (1970b). *Profession of medicine*. New York: Harper and Row.

Freidson, E. (1973). *The hospital in modern society*. New York: Free Press.

Freidson, E. (1980). *Doctoring together*. Chicago, IL: University of Chicago Press.

Friedman, E. (1978). The end of the line: When a hospital closes. *Hospitals, 52*, 69–75.

Gilbert, J. (2019). GOA: Veterans health administration: Greater focus on credentialing needed to prevent disqualified providers from delivering patient care. Available via DIALOG. https://www.fedhealthit.com/2019/03/gao-vha-greater-focus-on-credentialing-needed-to-prevent-disqualified-providers-from-delivering-patient-care/. Accessed 17 Sept 2019.

Ginzberg, E. (Ed.). (1991). *Health service research - Key to health policy*. Cambridge, MA: Harvard University Press.

Goffman, E. (1961). *Asylums: Essays on the social situation of mental patients and other inmates* (pp. 1–386). Garden City, NY: Aldine Transaction.

Gold, J. (2019). Will ties to a Catholic hospital system tie doctors' hands? Kaiser health news. Available via DIALOG. https://californiahealthline.org/news/will-ties-to-a-catholic-hospital-system-tie-doctors-hands/. Accessed 14 Sept 2019.

Gooch, K. (2018). Dignity health workers protest amid pending CHI merger. *Becker's Hospital Review*. Available via DIALOG. https://www.beckershospitalreview.com/human-capital-and-risk/dignity-health-workers-protest-amid-pending-chi-merger.html. Accessed 18 Jan 2018.

Gray, B. (1983). *The new health care for profit: Doctors and hospitals in a competitive environment*. Washington, DC: National Academies Press.

Groote, T. D., Paepe, P. D., & Unger, J. P. (2005). Colombia: In vivo test of health sector privatization in the developing world. *International Journal of Health Services, 1*(35), 125–141.

Hagland, M. (1998). Americans abroad. Why United Healthcare went to Germany and what it learned there. *Healthplan, 39*(5), 67–72.

Ham, C. (1995). International models of managed care. *Health Care Management, 2*(1), 143–150.

Hastings, A. C., Fadiman, J., & Gordon, J. S. (1980). *Health for the whole person*. Boulder, CO: Westview Press.

Hensley, S. (1999). Brazilian healthcare at a crossroads. *Modern Healthcare, 29*(20), 34–38.

Hermann, E. S. (1981). *Corporate control, corporate power*. Binghamton, NY: Cambridge Books.

Homedes, N., Ugalde, A., & Rovira, F. (2005). The world bank, pharmaceutical policies, and health reforms in Latin America. *International Journal of Health Services, 45*(4), 691–717.

Hotchkiss, D. R., & Jacobalis, S. (1999). Indonesian health care and the economic crisis: Is better managed care the needed reform? *Health Policy, 46*(3), 195–216.

Hurley, E. R. (1995). Promise and performance in managed care: The prepaid group practice model. *Journal of Health Politics, Policy and Law, 20*(4), 1051–1062.

Hyans, L. A., Shapiro, W. D., & Brennan, A. T. (1996). Medical practice guidelines in malpractice litigation: An early retrospective. *Journal of Health Politics, Policy and Law, 21*(2), 289–314.

Illich, I. (1976). *Medical Nemesis. The expropriation of health*. London, UK: McClelland and Stewart Limited.

Institute of Medicine. (1986). *For-profit enterprise in health care* (pp. 1–556). Washington, DC: Institute of Medicine.

Institute of Medicine. (2011). The Future of Nursing: Leading Change, Advancing Health, Available at: https://www.ncbi.nlm.nih.gov/books/NBK209881/. Accessed on December 2, 2020.

Institute of Medicine Study, Gray, B. H., & WJ, M. N. (1986). For-profit enterprise in health care. *New England Journal of Medicine, 314*, 1523–1528.

Japsen, B. (2018). California clears CVS-Aetna deal after concession to 'not increase premiums.' Available via DIALOG. https://www.forbes.com/sites/brucejapsen/2018/11/15/california-clears-cvs-aetna-deal-after-concession-to-not-increase-premiums/#68334ee19814. Accessed 24 Jan 2019.

Johnson, D. E. (1984). Multi-unit providers: Survey plots 457 chains' growth. *Modern Healthcare, 14*(5), 65–84.

Jopson, B., & Sevastropulo, D. (2017). Trump takes big steps to unwind Obamacare. *Financial Times*. Available via DIALOG. https://www.ft.com/content/f2ab3844-afc9-11e7-aab9-abaa44b1e130. Accessed 18 Jan 2018.

Joynt Maddox, K. E., Oray, E. J., Zheng, J., & Epstein, A. M. (2019). Post-acute care after joint replacement in Medicare's bundled payments for care improvement initiative. *Journal of the American Geriatrics Society, 67*, 1027–1035. https://doi.org/10.1111/jgs.15803

Jung, Y., & Kwon, S. (2018). How does stronger protection of intellectual property rights affect national pharmaceutical expenditure? An analysis of OECD countries. *International Journal of Health, 48*(4), 685–701.

Kacik, A. (2019a). Catholic health initiatives and dignity health complete merger. *Modern Healthcare*. Available via DIALOG. https://www.modernhealthcare.com/article/20190201/NEWS/190209994/catholic-health-initiatives-dignity-health-combine-to-form-commonspirit-health. Accessed 14 Sept 2019.

Kacik, A. (2019b). One of the constants of healthcare: Rising executive pay. *Modern Healthcare*, pp. 26–30.

Kacik, A., & Bannow, T. (2017). CHI- dignity mega-merger to test co-CEO model. *Modern Healthcare*. Available via DIALOG. https://www.modernhealthcare.com/article/20171209/NEWS/171209851. Accessed 12 Feb 2019.

Kelman, S. (1971). Toward political economy of medical care. *Inquiry, 8*(3), 30–38.

Kennedy, L. (1985). The losses in profits: How proprietaries affect public and voluntary hospitals. *Commentary, J23*, 3–10.

Keohane, D. (2018). France prepares for privatizations take-off. *Financial Times*.

Kheel, R. (2019). VA unveils proposal to expand private health care for veteran. *The Hill*. Available via DIALOG. https://thehill.com/policy/defense/427704-va-unveils-proposal-for-expanded-private-healthcare-for-veterans. Accessed 7 Feb 2018.

Kinney, D. E. (1995). Malpractice reform in the 1990s: Past disappointments, future success? *Journal of Health Politics, Policy and Law, 20*(1), 99–136.

Knowles, M. (2019). Why hospital mergers may harm care quality. *Becker's Hospital Review*. Available via DIALOG. https://www.beckershospitalreview.com/quality/why-hospital-mergers-may-harm-care-quality.html. Accessed 17 Sept 2019.

Kolko, G. (1963). *The triumph of conservatism. A reinterpretation of American History, 1900-1916*. New York: The Free Press.

Krippner, S., & Villoldo, A. (1976). *The realms of healing*. Millbrae, CA: Celestial Arts.

Lawlor, E. F. (1989). *The rest of the story: Insights from a cluster of Chicago hospital closures*. Dissertation, The University of Chicago.

Lawthers, G. A., Localio, R. A., Laird, M. N., Lipsitz, S., Hebert, L., & Brennan, A. T. (1992). Physicians' perceptions of the risk of being sued. *Journal of Health Politics, Policy and Law, 17*(3), 463–482.

Leichter, M. H. (1993). Paying for health care: Public policy choices for Illinois. *Journal of Health Politics, Policy and Law, 18*(4), 1008–1010.

Light, D. W. (1986). Corporate medicine for profit. *Scientific American, 255*(6), 38–45.

Light, D. W. (1991). Commentary: Professionalism as a countervailing power. *Journal of Health Politics, Policy and Law, 16*(3), 499–506.

Liu, F., & Salmon, J. W. (2010). Comparison of herbal medicines regulation between China, Germany, and the United States. *Integrative Medicine: A Clinician's Journal, 9*(6), 42–49.

Ludmerer, K. M. (1985). *Learning to heal: The development of American medical education*. Rochester, NY: Johns Hopkins University Press.

Luthi, S. (2019). GAO: VA kept medical staff despite misconduct allegations. *Modern Healthcare*. Available via DIALOG. https://www.modernhealthcare.com/politics-policy/gao-va-kept-medical-staff-despite-misconduct-allegations. Accessed 14 Sept 2019.

MacColl, W. (1966). *Group practice and prepayment of medical care*. Washington, DC: Public Affairs Press.

MacLeod, G. K., & Prussin, J. A. (1973). Special article: The continuing evolution of health maintenance organizations. *New England Journal of Medicine, 288*, 439–443.

Maio, F. D., & Ansell, D. (2018). "As natural as the air around us": On the origin and development of the concept of structural violence in health research. *International Journal of Health, 48*(4), 749–759.

Market Research. (2018). The 2019–2024 world outlook for internet of things (IoT) healthcare. Available via DIALOG. https://www.marketresearch.com. Accessed 5 Jan 2018.

McKenzie, N. F. (1994). *Beyond crisis confronting health care in the United States*. New York: Meridian.

McKinlay, J. B., & McKinlay, S. (1979). *Examining trends in the nation's health*. Paper presented at the American Public Health Association Annual Meeting, New York, November, 1979.

McKinlay, J. B., McKinlay, S. M., & Beaglehole, R. (1989). A review of the evidence concerning the impact of medical measures on recent mortality and morbidity in the United States.

International Journal of Health Services. Available via DIALOG. http://journals.sagepub.com/doi/abs/10.2190/L73V-NLDL-G7H3-63JC. Accessed 20 Feb 2018.

McLafferty, S. (1982). Neighborhood characteristics and hospital closure: A comparison of the public, private, and voluntary hospital systems. *Social Science & Medicine, 16*, 1667–1674.

McLafferty, S. (1986). The geographical restructuring of urban hospitals: Spatial dimensions of corporate strategy. *Social Science & Medicine, 23*(10), 1079–1086.

Mechanic, D. (1991). Sources of countervailing power in medicine. *Journal of Health Politics, Policy and Law, 16*(3), 485–498.

Meyer, H. (1997). Exporting expertise. *Healthplan, 38*(1), 44–50.

Meyer, H. (2016). Why patients still need EMTALA. *Modern Healthcare*. Available via DIALOG. https://www.modernhealthcare.com/article/20160326/MAGAZINE/303289881. Accessed 7 Feb 2019.

Meyer, H. (2019). VA launches expanded private care as stakeholders worry about glitches. *Modern Healthcare*, p. 10.

Meyer, H., & Bannow, T. (2018). CHI- dignity merger cleared by Vatican. *Modern Healthcare*. Available via DIALOG. https://www.modernhealthcare.com/article/20181016/NEWS/181019911. Accessed 12 Feb 2019.

Meyers, H. (1970). The medical-industrial complex. *Fortune, 81*(1), 90–126.

Miliband, R. (1970). *The state in capitalist society: An analysis of the system of power*. London, UK: Weidenfeld and Nicholson.

Miller, I. (1992). *The blue cross association's voluntary institution building approach to HMO policy: Social learning, leading and language*. Unpublished thesis. Union Institute, Cincinnati, OH.

Mills, A. (1998). To contract or not to contract? Issues for low and middle-class income countries. *Health Policy and Planning, 13*(1), 32–40.

Milmo, S. (1987). Private healthcare expected to grow in Europe. *Modern Healthcare*, pp. 94–95.

Moccia, P. (1994). Percent distribution of selected health care practitioners by gender (chart). In *Beyond crisis confronting health care in the United States* (p. 384). New York: Meridian.

Modern Healthcare. (2017a). Largest healthcare management consulting firms. Ranked by 2016 Total healthcare revenue, in millions. *Modern Healthcare*.

Modern Healthcare. (2017b). Largest U.S healthcare public relations and marketing agencies. Ranked by 2016 U.S. revenue, in millions. *Modern Healthcare*.

Modern Healthcare. (2018a). By the numbers: Resource guide 2018–2019. *Modern Healthcare*.

Modern Healthcare. (2018b). CHI- dignity merger cleared by Vatican. *Modern Healthcare*.

Modern Healthcare. (2018c). Largest healthcare management consulting firms. *Modern Healthcare*, p. 34.

Modern Hospital. (1971). Kaiser plan: Planned surplus gives doctors incentives, keeps facilities up to date. *Modern Hospital, 116*, 91–93.

Monica, K. (2008). McKesson wins $400M DoD imaging health IT system contract. *EHRIntelligence*. Available via DIALOG. https://ehrintelligence.com/news/mckesson-wins-400m-dod-imaging-health-it-system-contract. Accessed 7 Feb 2018.

Morrisey, M. A., Gibson, G., & Asby, C. S. (1983). Hospitals and health maintenance organizations: An analysis of the Minneapolis-St. Paul experience. *Health Care Financing Review, 4*(3), 59–69.

Mowery, C. D., & Mitchell, V. (1995). Improving the reliability of the U.S. vaccine supply: An evaluation of alternatives. *Journal of Health Politics, Policy and Law, 20*(4), 973–1000.

Muller, J. Z. (2008). *Thinking about capitalism*. Lecture courses. Washington, DC: Catholic University of America.

Mullner, R. (1988). Modeling hospital closure relative to organizational theory: The application of ecology theory's environmental determinism and adaptation perspectives. *Social Science and Medicine, 27*(11), 1287–1294.

Mullner, R., & Gifford, B. D. (1986). Rural and urban closures: A comparison. *Health Affairs*, pp. 131–141.

Munnell, A. H. (1985). Paying for the Medicare program. *Journal of Health Politics, Policy, and Law, 3*(10), 489–512.

Navarro, R. P. (1995a). Exportation of U.S. pharmacy benefit management companies to Canada. *Medical Interface, 8*(7), 72–74.

Navarro, R. P. (1995b). Exporting managed care: Importing quality lessons. *Manage Care Interface, 11*(4), 61–62.

Navarro, V. (1976). *Medicine under capitalism*. New York: Prodist.

Nelson, E. (2018). The dismal cost of economics' lack of racial diversity. *Quartz*. Available via DIALOG. https://qz.com/1492283/economics-has-a-crisis-of-diversity/. Accessed 8 Jan 2018.

Newton, S. H. (1973). *The integration of occupational and family health services in a health maintenance organization*. Presented at 58th annual meeting of the industrial medical association, Currigan convention Hall, Denver, Colorado, 19 April 1973.

O'Connor, J. (1973). *The fiscal crisis of the state* (p. 196). New York: St. Martin's Press.

O'Connor, J. (1974). *The corporations and the state: Essays in the theory of capitalism and imperialism*. New York: Harper.

O'Connor, J. (1981). The fiscal crisis of the state revisited: Economic crisis and Reagan's budget policy. In *Kapitalistate working papers on the capitalist state* (pp. 41–62). New Brunswick, NJ: Kapitalistate.

O'Toole, P. (2019). Theodore Roosevelt cared deeply about the sick. Who knew? *The New York Times*. Available via DIALOG. https://www.nytimes.com/2019/01/06/opinion/theodore-roosevelt-health-care-progressive.html. Accessed 18 Jan 2019.

Oloroso, A. Jr. (1988). What's next? More inner-city hospitals imperiled. *Chicago Reporter*. Chicago, 2 October 1988.

Oloroso, A., Jr. (1989). Strapped inner-city hospitals sump patients to avoid red ink. *The Chicago Reporter, 19*(1), 6–9.

Owens, T. (2019). 1 big thing: A reality check on hospital mergers. *Axios*. Available via DIALOG. https://www.axios.com/reality-check-on-hospital-mergers-aha-economists-91007ae4-6776-4f33-9c61-db41c945482a.html. Accessed 17 Sept 2019.

Peikes, D., Dale, S., Ghosh, A., Taylor, EF., Swankoski, K., O'Malley, A. S., Day, D. J., Duda, N., Singh, P., Anglin, G., Sessums, L. L., & Brown, R. S. (2018). The Comprehensive Primary Care Initiative: Effects On Spending, Quality, Patients, And Physicians. *Health Affairs, 37*(6):890–899.

Pelletier, K. R. (1976). *Mind as healer, mind as slayer*. New York: Delta/Delacorte.

Perez-Stable, E. J. (1999). Managed care arrives in Latin America. *The New England Journal of Medicine, 340*(14), 1110–1112.

Perna, G. (2018). Avoid an HER-related malpractice lawsuit. *Medical Economics*, pp. 28–31.

Price, S. L., & McGillis Hall, L. (2013). The history of nurse imagery and the implications for recruitment: A discussion paper. *Journal of Advanced Nursing, 7*(70), 1502–1109.

Quinton, S. (2017). Team approach to health care means new role for doctors. *Health & Spirit*. Available via DIALOG. https://www.arcamax.com/healthandspirit/health/healthtips/. Accessed 6 Feb 2018.

Rau, J. (2017). Nursing home industry wins as penalties are relaxed. *The New York Times*. Available via DIALOG. https://www.nytimes.com/2017/12/24/business/trump-administration-nursing-home-penalties.html. Accessed 24 Jan 2019.

Rau, J. (2018). Care suffers at nursing homes as profits rise. *The New York Times*. Available via DIALOG. https://www.nytimes.com/2018/01/02/business/nursing-homes-care-corporate.html. Accessed 24 Jan 2019.

Reich, R. (2018). The privatization myth: Here are 5 ways conservatives' free market ideology can destroy public goods. *Alter Net*. Available via DIALOG. https://www.alternet.org/2018/12/privatization-myth-here-are-5-ways-conservatives-free-market-ideology-can-destroy-public/. Accessed 8 Jan 2018.

Relman, A. S. (1980). The new medical-industrial complex. *New England Journal of Medicine, 303*, 963–970.

Reverby, S. (1994). Nursing and caring: Lessons from history interview. In *Beyond crisis confronting health care in the United States* (p. 386). New York: Meridian.

Rich, R. (1982). The political economy of public services. In N. Fainstein & S. Fainstein (Eds.), *Urban policy under capitalism*. Beverly Hills: Sage.

Roemer, M. I. (1956). *Medical care in relation to public health*. Geneva, Switzerland: World Health Organization.

Roemer, M. I. (1978). Social medicine: The advance of organized health services in America. *Springer Series on Health Care and Society, 3*, 1–560.

Roemer, M. I., & Shain, M. (1959). *Hospital utilization under insurance* (p. 39). Chicago, IL: American hospital association.

Rorem, R. (1931). *Private groups clinics*. Chicago, IL: Milbank Memorial Fund.

Rosen, G. (1958). The bacteriological era and its aftermath. In *A history of public health* (pp. 294–343). New York: MD Publications.

Rosen, G. (1963). The hospital in modern society. In *The hospital: Historical sociology of a community institution* (pp. 1–36). New York: The Free Press.

Rosen, G. (1975). *Preventive medicine in the United States, 1900–1975: Trends and interpretations*. New York: Science History.

Rothfeld, M. B. (1973). Sensible surgery for welling medical costs. *Fortune, 4*, 110–152.

Sager, A. (1983). The reconfiguration of urban hospital care: 1937–1980. In A. Greer & S. Greer (Eds.), *Cities and sickness* (pp. 55–98). Beverly Hills, CA: Sage.

Salmon, J. W. (1978). *Corporate attempts to reorganize the American health care system*. Unpublished thesis at Cornell University, Ithaca, NY.

Salmon, J. W. (1990). *The corporate transformation of health care* (Vol. 1). Amityville, NY: Baywood Publishing.

Salmon, J. W., & Goepel, E. (1990). *Symposium papers of the international symposium on community participation and empowerment strategies in health promotion*. ZIF Center for interdisciplinary studies, Bielefeld, Federal Republic of Germany.

Saward, E. W. (1969a). *The relevance of prepaid group practice to the effective delivery of health services*. Presented at 18th annual group health institute, Ontario, Canada, 18 June 1969.

Saward, E. W. (1969b). The relevance of the Kaiser-permanent experience to the health services of the eastern United States. *Bulletin New York Academy of Medicine, 46*, 707–717.

Saward, E. W. (1980). Health maintenance organizations. *Scientific American, 4*(243), 47–53.

Saward, E. W., Blank, J. D., & Greenlick, M. R. (1968). Documentation of twenty years of operation and growth of a prepaid group practice plan: Kaiser foundation medical care plan, may/June 1968. *Medical Care, 6*, 231–244.

Schiff, R. L., Ansell, D. A., Schlosser, J. E., Idris, A. H., Morrison, A., & Whiteman, S. (1986). Transfers to a public hospital. *New England Journal of Medicine, 314*(9), 552–557.

Schlesinger, M., Blumenthal, D., & Schlesinger, E. (1986). The economic performance of investor-owned and non-profit health maintenance organizations. *Medical Care, 24*, 615–627.

Schlesinger, M., Gray, B., & Bradley, E. (1996). Charity and community: The role of nonprofit ownership in a managed health care system. *Journal of Health Politics, Policy and Law, 21*(4), 697–752.

Schneider, A. G., & Stern, J. B. (1975). Health maintenance organizations and the poor: Problems and prospects. *Northwestern University of Law Review, 1*(70), 90–138.

Shryock, R. H. (1936). Practice in a changing society. In *The development of modern medicine* (pp. 369–423). Philadelphia, PA: University of Pennsylvania Press.

Shryock, R. H. (1959). *The history of nursing: An interpretation of the social and medical factors involved*. Philadelphia, PA: Saunders.

Sigerist, H. E. (1960). The social history of medicine. In *On the history of medicine*. New York: Routledge.

Smith, R. S., & Lipsky, M. (1996). Privatization in health and human services: A critique. *Journal of Health Politics, Policy and Law, 17*(2), 233–254.

Snow, C. (1996). U.S. HMOs aim to go global via overseas deals. *Modern Healthcare, 26*(26), 130, 132, 155.

Sommers, B. D., Maylone, B., Blendon, R. J., Oray, E. J., & Epstein, A. M. (2017). Three-Year Impacts Of The Affordable Care Act: Improved Medical Care And Health Among Low-Income Adults. *Health Affairs, 36*(6):1119–1128.

Spurr, J. S., & Simmons, O. W. (1996). Medical malpractice in Michigan: An economic analysis. *Journal of Health Politics, Policy and Law, 21*(2), 315–346.

Starr, P. (2011). *Remedy and reaction. The peculiar American struggle over health care reform.* New Haven, CT: Yale University Press.

Steinhauer, J., & Philipps, D. (2019). V.a. to propose shifting billions into private care. *The New York Times.* Available via DIALOG. https://www.nytimes.com/2019/01/12/us/politics/veterans-administration-health-care-privatization.html. Accessed 7 Feb 2019.

Stevens, R. (1971). *American medicine and the public interest.* New Haven, CT: Yale University Press.

Stocker, K., Iriart, C., & Waitzkin, H. (1999). The exportation of managed care to Latin America. *New England Journal of Medicine, 340*(14), 1131–1136.

Sweeney, J. J. (1986). *International healthcare union conference on privatization.* Washington, DC.

Swider, S. M., & Kulbok, P. A. (2015). Creating the future of public health nursing: A call to action. *Public Health Nursing, 2*(32), 91–93.

Szasz, T. (1977). *The theology of medicine: The political-philosophical foundations of medical ethics.* New York: Baton Rouge Louisiana State University Press.

Tanenbaum, J. S. (1995). Medicaid eligibility policy in the 1980s: Medical utilitarianism and the "deserving" poor. *Journal of Health Politics, Policy and Law, 20*(4), 909–932.

Terhune, C. (2018). As billions in tax dollars flow to private Medicaid plans, who's minding the store?. *Kaiser Health News.* Available via DIALOG. https://khn.org/news/as-billions-in-tax-dollars-flow-to-private-medicaid-plans-whos-minding-the-store/. Accessed 18 Jan 2019.

The Committee on the Costs of Medical Care. (1932). *Medical care for the American people.* Chicago, IL: University of Chicago Press.

The Economist. (2014). *The $272 billion swindle: Why thieves love America's health-care system.* Miami, NY: The Economist.

The Economist. (2019a). How wising rail fares and falling punctuality undermine confidence. *The Economist.* Available via DIALOG. https://www.economist.com/britain/2019/08/15/how-rising-rail-fares-and-falling-punctuality-undermine-confidence. Accessed 14 Sept 2019.

The Economist. (2019b). *The treasury plans to privatise Fannie Mae and Fannie Mac.* New York: The Economist.

The Morgan Guaranty Survey. (1972). Changing the system of health care. *The Morgan Guaranty Survey.*

Traige Health Law Blog. (2019). Health care fraud leads $2.8 billion collection for false claims. *Lexology.* Available via DIALOG. https://www.lexology.com/library/detail.aspx?g=3ceb03cf-88d8-4fb4-bb4b-31b26db1edec. Accessed 25 Jan 2019.

Uzych, L., & Kinney, D. E. (1996). Medical malpractice and no-fault systems. *Journal of Health Politics, Policy and Law, 21*(1), 153–158.

Vladeck, B. C. (1985). Reforming Medicare provider payment. *Journal of Health Politics, Policy, and Law, 3*(10), 512–532.

Waitzkin, H. (1978). A Marxist view of medical care. *Annals of Internal Medicine, 89,* 263–278.

Waitzkin, H. (1983). *The second sickness: Contradictions of capitalist health care.* New York: Free Press.

Waitzkin, H., & Hellander, I. (2016). The history and future of neoliberal Reform: Obamacare and its predecessors. *International Journal of Health Services, 46,* 747–766.

Whitcomb, E. M. (1996). Commentary-physicians supply policy: A victim of politics in the era of pork. *Journal of Health Politics, Policy and Law, 21*(4), 855–862.

White, W. D., Salmon, J. W., & Feinglass, J. (1994). The Changing Doctor-Patient Relationship and Performance Monitoring: An Agency Perspective in: Salmon JW: The Corporate Transformation of Health Care – Part 2: Perspectives And Implications, Amityville, NY: Baywood.

Whiteis, D. G. (1992). Hospital and community characteristics associated with urban hospital closure. *Public Health Reports, 107*(4), 409–416.

Whiteis, D. G. (1997). Unhealthy cities: Corporate medicine, community underdevelopment, and the public health in the U.S. *International Journal of Health Services, 27*(2), 227–242.

Whiteis, D. G. (1998). Third-world medicine in first first-world cities: Underdevelopment and public health in the U.S. *Social Science & Medicine, 47*(6), 795–808.

Whiteis, D. G. (2000). Poverty, policy, and pathogenesis: Economic justice and public health in the US. *Critical Public Health, 10*(2), 257–271.

Whiteis, D. G., & Salmon, J. W. (Eds.). (1990a). The proprietarization of health care and the underdevelopment of the public sector. In *The corporate transformation of health care: Issues & directions*, pp. 117–131. Amityville, NY: Baywood.

Whiteis, D. G., & Salmon, J. W. (1990b). Public health care delivery systems in selected U.S. *cities: Findings of the urban public health care system study tours project*. Health and medicine policy research group, University of Illinois at Chicago College of Pharmacy, Chicago.

Wigger, U. (1996). *Medical students and primary care physicians' opinions and concerns on the use of information technology*. Unpublished dissertation, University of Illinois at Chicago.

Williams, G. (1971). Kaiser delivery system: Less utilization, more productivity. *Modern Hospital, 116*, 81–85.

Woodson, J. (2017). Future of the global retail clinics market- growth, latest trend, and forecast 2022. *Newsient*.

Young, Q. (1995). Personal communication. April 28. Chicago, IL.

Young, Q. (2013). *Everybody in, nobody out: Memoirs of a rebel without a pause*. Harbor, WA: Copernicus Healthcare.

Zola, I. K. (1972). Medicine as an institution of social control. *The Sociological Review, 20*, 487–504.

Chapter 2
Pharmaceuticals, Hospitals, Nursing Homes, Drug Store Chains, and Pharmacy Benefit Manager/Insurer Integration

Introduction

"Healthcare mega-mergers dominate in 2017" claimed a *Modern Healthcare* article in December 2017—a clear reality for firms across the entire health sector, all trying to achieve greater scale for financial advantage for their executives and stockholders; further marketplace consolidation would lie ahead (Nash, 2018). The extent of mergers and acquisitions (M&As) marked 2017 as a "year of mergers": horizontal, vertical, regional, national, and large and small scale (Kacik, 2017a). The opening of 2018 began a tumultuous consolidation of the market with the entry of Silicon Valley players.

This chapter will examine the continuing corporatization in the American healthcare system. First, the upsurge in consolidation is examined through the merger and acquisition activity of each segment of the industry: pharmaceutical firms, insurers, hospitals, and health systems, and the more recent intensely pharmacy benefit managers. Ongoing federal subsidizations now over 46% of total expenditures are revealed to provide the attractiveness for investment in health care for mighty lucrative returns. This incentive structure remains even while Republican efforts to restrain spending are chiefly targeting the indigent, seniors, and seriously ill (Pear, 2018). Employer reactions to persistent cost escalation are also examined with implications to workers' benefits and further rationalization. In closing, the huge recent incursions by information technology firms suggest that the American healthcare system may be on the verge of a further corporate takeover, instead of resolving issues of access, quality, cost, and accountability through a progressive public health approach.

© Springer Nature Switzerland AG 2021
J. W. Salmon, S. L. Thompson, *The Corporatization of American Health Care*,
https://doi.org/10.1007/978-3-030-60667-1_2

Merger Mania Amidst Policy Uncertainties

The New York Times Sunday Business post piece (Abelson & Creswell, 2018, p. 1) "Merger Medicine and the Disappearing Doctor" noted that 12,000 retail clinics formed by insurance companies and giant retailers were teaming up to dominate health care. Office visits to primary care doctors declined 18 percent from 2012 to 2016.

Meanwhile, Donald Trump and his Republican cohorts sought budget cutbacks amidst elimination of the Affordable Care Act, as well as the Medicaid program. By 2026, national health spending is predicted to reach 19.7% of the economy (Inserro, 2018a). "Americans used less care in 2016, but health costs still soared" headlined the Health Care Cost Institute (IHCCI) (Inserro, 2018b), which identified rising prices, "especially for prescription drugs, surgery, and ED visits." Overall spending grew further than at any time in the last 5 years!

Prices rose, but who paid for such prices increasing so much? What does this mean about the introduction of value-based care (VBC)? It seems *not* to be going away—at least for the quality reporting requirements for doctors! (Sweeney, 2018). This IHCCI report noted that direct out-of-pocket patient spending increased every year. In the meanwhile, prices for professional services—fees to physicians—saw their lowest growth and lowest prices overall. Patients and physicians may have a mutual set of concerns over the evolving structure of the delivery system.

The Kiplinger Letter cautioned about the sizzling pace of M&A activity in the economy, up to 60% in the first quarter over 2016—a total of $1.2 trillion in tie-ups, still marching on for the remaining months of the year. Low interest rates—about to rise more—aid the debt-financed deals, along with the burgeoning corporate coffers, thanks to the Trump tax cuts. Several health firms—along with most IT firms—have been cash-rich, floating bond offerings so they can horde cash to buy up any firms that may get beaten up by market swings over the near future. Stock buybacks are common to boost values in preparation for takeovers. It should be noted that R&D investments do not hold as much guarantee for short-term gain as such corporate behaviors. Together these conditions foster a health system bent on placing profits over public health. Yet Kiplinger (2018, p. 1) comments that these activities may signal that companies aren't able to grow their business from within and are instead relying on taking over competitors that may increase profits but at significant cost to the acquiring company.

These advisors maintain that these actions do not seem to be the case right now since "the US economy looks sound." Corporate debt levels are high, but manageable, so far. Many companies pursuing deals are reportedly positioning themselves for longer-term growth, not a quick, one-time earning hike. Health care and consumer goods are predicted to remain among the most popular arenas for deal making. Kiplinger notes that Amazon, Walmart, and other retailers are being pressured to get a lot bigger so that they can compete more aggressively.

But getting bigger in a difficult environment caused by increasing interest rates may make it harder to finance deals, a bear stock market may sour investors, worsening trade disputes will be provoked by Trump, and most of all antitrust rumblings from his Administration remain unclear. Can his Department of Justice reorient from its current fumbling over immigration to block future takeovers? The courts gave the go ahead in June 2019 for the Time Warner/AT&T merger; so it is rumored that this approval will open up a huge new surge in M&As overall and especially in communications. Most of all in terms of uncertainty is the $316 billion annual cost by the US Treasury on interest payments that are financing the Republican tax cut. This future cloud of $15.3 trillion looms over the overall economy, as particularly health care with federal resources drained to pick up this debt tab. One must bring to mind the Trump budget deficit spending to build the military amidst his colossal tax cuts for the rich, and that preceded the business bailout of 2020 after COVID-19.

Beyond the merger mania, escalating drug prices reached a "boiling point." From 2012 to 2016, drug costs rose 27%. Amidst a plethora of cybersecurity concerns from providers, there appeared a wide range of health-related smartphone apps, care moving more to community settings, and consumers becoming "money managers" to handle much higher deductibles and patient outlays (Gooch, 2015). Despite similar utilization rates for the United States compared to other nations, labor and goods (including pharmaceuticals) and administrative costs (including profits) are the major differences with health costs in America (Masterson, 2018). Beyond the growing and aging population, increased prices and the intensity and utilization of the costliest services are actually driving spending.

For seniors, Medicare healthcare costs remain a rising burden—they are expected to consume a larger share of their total income by 2030 (Cubanski, 2019). Medicare beneficiaries averaged out-of-pocket payment spending at 41% of the average Social Security income in 2013. As Republicans reduce funding for Medicare and Medicaid, this senior and indigent cost-sharing becomes highly problematic for them, especially for folks with debilitating chronic degenerative diseases. Over recent years, more attention seems being paid to these "high spenders" on costs rather than their access to improved quality care (Johnson, Brennan, Rodriquez, & Hargraves, 2018).

Substance abuse, chronic illnesses, and protections against infectious and food-borne illnesses, along with the socioeconomic determinants of health such as poverty, unemployment, and violence, are mere afterthoughts for those in charge of our healthcare policy:

> The new administration has also changed the health care landscape through the Food and Drug Administration, and its new commissioner, Scott Gottlieb, M.D.: Actions on high drug pricing, clearing orphan drug request backlogs, increasing drug review efficiency, and driving digital health technology and medical device innovation. (Vogenberg and Smart, 2018, p. 34)

In its first year, the corporate-pleasing Trump Administration became notorious for pulling all verbiage referring to climate change from federal websites, eliminating the Clean Power Plan, and withdrawing from the Paris Climate Accord, along with Scott Pruitt's litany of EPA travesties, which are also likely to have significant health consequences for people (Davenport, 2018; Talbot, 2018; Eilperin, Dennis, & Dawsey, 2018. The Children's Health Insurance Program finally was passed in December 2017 but only given a temporary 3-month reprieve by Congress, along with a modicum of added funding for community health centers (CHCs) to support vital infrastructure. CHCs in the past have garnered bipartisan support since one CHC has been carefully situated in almost every Congressional district.

Nevertheless, major funding uncertainties defined public health in 2017 (Johnson, 2017), thanks to Trump and his Republican cohorts. Of concern to public health professionals has been the significant relaxation and elimination of regulations to allow the marketplace to thrive unfettered. Nevertheless, public health funding by federal, state, and municipal governments has historically stayed at 2% to 3% of total US health expenditures (Himmelstein, & Woolhandler 2016).

As for corporate employers who are caught up on urging "cost management" on providers (Kalish, 2017), their influence ever grows as their climbing outlays propel forward high-deductible health savings plans (HSAs) for employees and greater risk-based contracting with providers. Larger corporations self-insure for their health benefit outlays. From time to time, certain employers have attempted stricter controls over what gets labeled as high costs, including their historically shifting a greater burden to employees (Young, 2005): fixed-sum health benefits to encourage workers to "shop efficiently"—a so-called "consumerism" approach in vogue of late. It is *not* well known what higher cost-sharing and reduced benefit coverage do for improved health and well-being of either their employee families or the overall population.

Corporate America lies behind the steady raising of co-pays and deductibles in the private insurance market—especially for drugs—to force employees to judiciously use services, like avoiding ERs, limiting doctor visits, and purchasing generics over brand drugs. Many firms have fallen into avoiding insurers through self-funding their health plans, with group stop-loss insurance in abeyance. The trend toward "direct contracting" with provider systems indicates employers supporting efforts for stricter "cost management" (Kalish, 2017). Direct contracting has been saving costs for some employers, but there are issues such as growing the network of providers and obtaining performance, constructing databases and developing analytics, and also conducting studies for good decision-making. Walmart is another firm that engages in direct contracting (Diamond, 2018), but one of the more prominent American corporations to go down this path was General Motors. Twenty-four thousand of its 180,000 workforce were placed in a 5-year direct contracting program with the Henry Ford Health System, circumventing insurance companies. Boeing also contracts in California for its employees. Plans provide discounts to employees who participate, but educating them to choose wisely for the "best doctors" and hospitals can be problematic. Integrating care among the set of providers takes effort, especially if they are not already formed into systems.

Saving on next year's employee benefit outlays has been the HR executives' goal for decades, seizing upon what can be cut out. Evermore such decisions are sought, backed up courtesy of Big Data extracted from provider performance. While analytics work has been reaching some precision, it does not always lead to the "best" benefit decision-making, nor what workers particularly need or want. Across the 2018 midterm election cycle, it became clear that health care dominates as a major issue to the overall public.

Overall benefit costs for employers have risen more than 24% in the last 2–4 years (Kalish, 2017), the same 24% rise as was for 2000 to 2004. Per capita growth in employee cost is driven by specialty drugs (Toich, 2017a, 2017b). Trump's recent repeal of the individual mandate under the ACA has caused anxiety among employers who fear potential adverse selection among their employee plans. In this context, policies and practices promoting these marketplace dynamics have been sustained by Republican Party-based ideology.

Chapter Purpose

This chapter will expand upon the previous chapter with the advances in corporatization across all segments of the American healthcare system. It will be seen that rather than merely a trend, there is a huge upswing in the amalgamation of providers and suppliers as profit-taking surges in the marketplace. Federal subsidization of specific areas is highlighted as about 50% of funding comes from government sources. Policy actions by not just Republicans when in power but also the Obama Administration's ACA favoring the private sector growth without much acknowledgment for its natural tendencies for greed with concerns for equity in health services get downplayed. Each private segment of the overall system discussed below from pharmaceuticals and pharmacy benefit managers to hospital and healthcare systems has done well and increasingly so. Privatization in the capitalist system seems to favor private entities so we see that nursing homes, prisons, higher education, and more succumb to similar moves for profit opportunities to transform them, resulting in what might be said numerous questionable outcomes. Chain drug stores rose to challenge ambulatory physician practices in the 1980s, again being the march of private corporate takeover. This chapter concludes with a lament that the population's health care remains solidly under corporate auspice, which presents many barriers to raising the public's overall health status.

Ongoing Corporate Federal Subsidizations

In almost all circles of payers and providers, a deep pervasive frustration bubbles over the current payment system—repeatedly said to be broken—with continuous attempts to contain cost inflation, many futile. Physicians are said to be moving toward single-payer Medicare for all (opinion favored by over 50% of doctors). Pressures toward "value-based payments" are not really seen as the best prospect in some quarters (Gittlen, 2017). Ascertaining value is very complex and politically holds a series of landmines for many parties, so we see fits and starts on this strongly intended direction.

It is undeniably true that Medicare and Medicaid bailed out health providers for the two groups, previously uncovered seniors and indigent, who paid out of pocket when they could to get care. This can be viewed as a social development with many people receiving needed services, and surely these funds boosted employment in the economy. These federal programs begat significant gains in financial access for millions of Americans; seniors and the poor were brought into health care in a wonderful way, but it came from an initial federal Medicare cost of over $3 billion in 1966 now growing to 2016 expenditures over $685.3 billion for Medicare and even higher for Medicaid of federal $344.4 billion; the states' share is about an equal additional amount (HHS.gov, 2016). Private parties benefited greatly under the huge federal funding from the mid-1960s fashioned after the Blue Cross Blue Shield deal of fee-for-service and cost-reimbursed hospital care. Medicare Part A was fashioned after Blue Cross, with its required stepdown accounting sheets prepared by the hospital administration to essentially receive cost-plus payments that of course ballooned over the years. Blue Shield was the model for Medicare Part B, paying doctors piecemeal for services previously either discounted for certain patients or provided free for the elderly. Thus, federal largess bailed out the healthcare system for seniors and the indigent and began an economic boom for all the vested parties that came to feed on the trough, i.e., the medical-industrial complex (MIC).

Historical review of the heavy cost inflation under fee-for-service medicine, the excessive inappropriate care, high administrative costs, and issues of questionable quality have been documented in health services research over time. This federal largess essentially invited in the host of proprietary firms documented in Chap. 1. All of this uncontrolled expenditure has provided ammunition to cost-cutting conservatives, who are currently intent upon dramatically scaling back its 14% of total federal spending, mainly because *the aged and indigent are simply not worth it*—to the Republican Right, which seeks budget program cuts, nor to Corporate America, which considers their expense to productivity for the overall economy.

An obvious government creation of corporate medicine was the End-Stage Renal Disease Program (ESRD) adopted under Medicare Part C by Nixon in 1973. Nowadays persons with chronic kidney disease do not face the horrendous access and cost barriers to get their blood dialyzed three times a week to forestall their death and perhaps wait for a transplanted kidney. In an article entitled, "God help you. You're on dialysis," *The Atlantic Monthly* (2010) reported that the US fatality rate was one of the worst in the industrialized world and costs more than anywhere else. Yet, this federal program, which covers any citizen diagnosed with kidney failure under Part C, regardless of age or income, piles huge sums of money into a mere handful of highly profitable corporate dialysis chains; in 2016, the ESRD program cost taxpayers $32.9 billion—considerably more than its initial projected price tag of $135 million.

In essence, this End-Stage Renal Dialysis Program yielded an entire corporate industry of nationwide and regional dialysis firms, which have grown wildly (e.g., Fresenius, DaVita, US Rural Care, American Renal Associates, and Satellite

Healthcare, among a few others). Academic medical centers still do some dialysis, but not for chronic care. The top two listed for-profit firms served 383,464 patients of the 477,476 in the program in 2014, that is, 80% of persons receiving dialysis; both firms have spread overseas too. Incidents of noted substandard care have been newsworthy (Atlantic, 2010; Oliver, 2017). A midterm election proposition in California sought to curtail ESRD firms' excess profits and address quality issues, but it was strongly opposed and defeated by the industry. Critics of the ESRD industry state that these for-profit clinics are seen as low-quality care and that performance is often hidden by the government from the patients and families who use that service (Atlantic, 2010). Medicare does not set staffing ratios, and "hundreds of clinics were cited for infection-control breaches." Even with such lax oversight, for-profit share of revenues in 2016 was 93% among dialysis providers. In contrast, Italy's public hospitals provide more than three quarters of the care (Atlantic, 2010). Marketplace medicine absent adequate federal oversight can be expected to hinder cost and quality issues for consumers.

During the 1990s, George H. W. Bush substantially buoyed the nascent pharmacy benefit managers (PBMs) with his Medicare Modernization Act simultaneously taking care of his friends in the pharmaceutical industry with the promise of *no cost controls over drugs*. Coverage of drug therapies was long overdue from 1965 Act and surely remains completely necessary to senior health care. This Act for the first time subsidized much of seniors' pharmaceutical costs with Medicare Part D. One hundred and eight billion again was given over right away to the pharmaceutical industry. Bush overnight spurred forth phenomenal growth and power in the private PBM industry, now enrolling 43 million plus Americans. This direct subsidization created the price escalation of drug prices, becoming a critical political economic dilemma now across this decade.

Again, marketplace medicine prevailed. The deal forestalled in legislation forever no drug price regulation on pharmaceuticals, leaving an escalation of prices to become a critical unabated political economic dilemma reaching to this day. It also remains remarkable that a fledgling industry from the early 1990s with a handful of firms today now has the largest pharmacy benefit managers dwarfing a number of long-established pharmaceutical firms, and these PBMs remain more profitable, setting them up as targets for the ongoing M&A fervor by insurers, now attracting Silicon Valley firms in 2018.

Not to be outdone with outright federal subsidization of corporate health, Barack Obama and the Democratic Congress dropped over $600 billion into the coffers of the private insurance industry with the Affordable Care Act, even after a strident critique of their crass practices of discriminating against sick and disabled patients and their families. Like the above provider groups, insurance firms have recently become dissatisfied without greatly increasing annually the federal largess.

As with most federal programs, it need not be said that some people indeed did benefit with new access to services. Beyond being intended to sway voting constituencies with the ACA, it can be pointed out that perhaps a different design for a public option might have curtailed the driving force away from its major corporate beneficence; states might have been able to conduct their own public plans, as was suggested, but dismissed by the Democrats. In contrast to what was passed, health infrastructural development could have been more substantial, going beyond the limited funds for designated safety net hospitals, risk corridors, and community health centers. Cost controls and quality improvements were downplayed as "regulatory" to quell the insurance and pharmaceutical industries, and provider antagonisms, though grievances from these vested interests emerged when the Republicans ranted "repeal and replace." Unlike the Bill Clinton days, corporate opposition had given way to Obama's accommodation strategy to reap marketplace advancement with heavy government support sans much strict oversight and regulation.

In the ACA, pharma was continued to guarantee *no federal price controls*; insurers expanded their market share with bountiful subsidized customers; so both vested industries decided *not* to oppose the ACA (as historically had been the case with almost all previous federal insurance extensions). Wonderfully, 20 million Americans received *access to insurance coverage* (but absent greater support for infrastructural improvements), *not necessarily access to proper continuous physician care!* Now with Trump reversing any and all of Obama's legacy, most of these folks appear vulnerable to losing it. Witness Congressional attempts to rid the Medicaid program in its entirety, not just its ACA expansion by Mitch McConnell's Senate attempt!

In 2016, 28.1 million Americans were still uninsured (8.8% of the population). This represented a slight decrease despite ongoing Trump attempts to repeal all of the ACA. Those maintaining coverage—many who still cannot afford care due to the high cost-sharing requirements—seem better off since a strongly disproportionate burden of uninsurance fell upon minorities. Lower-income Americans still have significant problems in obtaining adequate medical care, since income is so crucial to decent access and social determinants lead to ill health. Inequality continues to be a marked feature of American society; in recent decades, poorer Americans have borne more of a tax burden, while richer Americans pay less, especially after the Republican tax cut in 2017 (Himmelstein, Woolhandler, Almberg, & Fauke, 2018).

Such repeated historical federal largess with its mindful flow of funds to the medical-industrial complex, however, has tended over time to undermine what should be the social purpose of the American healthcare enterprise: to advance the overall health status of all Americans. Of note, during the George H. W. Bush and Clinton administrations, the health sector became a motor force for rise in employment, thus GDP growth. Nevertheless, the maldistribution of both health status and afterward healthcare resources has never been given top funding priority over feeding the beasts in the MIC. In the final analysis, the lobbying parties, who influence these federal programs and then support their funding, are the very ones who reap the spoils within the corporate health sector.

True, many citizens did clinically benefit from every of the above policy actions; such remains the key ideological selling point to the general public for each program's continued tax fund flow. The corporate welfare aspects usually remain unspoken, and often hidden, as does suggestions for closer monitoring of potential and real abuses.

Accountability has never been a hallmark of American health policy. Witness the estimated cost of fraud and abuse at about 3% of the near $4 trillion spent on health care. At the same time, all of these policy actions propelled a burgeoning health cost conundrum for the entire nation. An ever-expanding expenditure—coupled with declining standards of healthcare delivery—still poses uncertain outcomes for the population across this century without progressive policy remediation.

It should be pointed out that never has there been a national policy debate over whether such a corporate health system was the *best way to organize* Americans' health care, nor was there a debate over whether the American people *knew much about the corporate takeover*, nor more importantly whether they *actually wanted such profit-driven arrangements over their health.*

Notwithstanding, our nation surely needs to engage in popular debate to investigate the overall corporate consequences to health and health care. This should happen now as a national debate over "Whose healthcare system is it?" along with the rallying for "Medicare for All." The key question is: "Whom does it serve? People or profits?" More and more people today in all walks of life are coming to the conclusion that marketplace forces or the billionaire class cannot fix a broken healthcare system (Master, 2017).

The Pharmaceutical Industry

When one thinks of corporate health care in America, it is likely that the pharmaceutical industry first comes to mind. The industry has dramatically expanded and prospered long from early entrepreneurship origins at the turn of the last century with the likes of Merck Sharp & Dohme, Eli Lilly, Abbott, and Upjohn Brothers selling nostrums from covered wagons that traveled from town to town. Its presence is now negatively known from newsworthy portrayals of price gouging and its ubiquitous direct-to-consumer (DTC) TV advertising reaching $6 billion annually. Moreover, an ever-increasing percentage of Americans are consuming multiple drug products and experiencing growing out-of-pocket outlays (Dusetzina, Keating, & Huskamp, 2019; Terhune, 2016).

Recently, in addition to a heightened awareness of the costs of various drugs, there have been mounting doubts about drug safety and efficacy (Carcinoma-causing ingredients found in Zantac, 2019; Silverman, 2019a, 2019b; Dangerous contamination, 2019). At the same time, some firms have reported newsworthy zooming profits, political influence, and multiple miscreant behaviors (Opioid deaths taking a quarter Americans' lives; Data show a "tsunami" of overprescribed opioids across U.S. as death toll rose in 2019; Crow, 2018; Billionaire Sackler family owns second opioid drug maker, 2018; About the epidemic, 2018). Johnson & Johnson, a firm with a past prided reputation, became tarnished by association with the El Chapo-Sackler Family at Purdue Pharma in the opioid crisis (Economist: Big Pharma in Court, 2018).

The populace has also been introduced to the world's disease burden through news coverage of profit-taking from developing countries, particularly the Southern Hemisphere (RNCOS Global Vaccine Market Forecasts to 2017, 2013; Wechsler, 2020; IQVIA Global Medical Spending and Usage Trends, 2020).

Relief from double-digit inflationary drug costs, plus knowledge of fellow American citizens who cannot afford to buy needed medications, is now an emergent domestic political issue (Roland & Loftus, 2016). The Pharmaceutical Research and Manufacturers Association responded to these criticisms with a TV campaign blitz and more intense lobbying (Scott, 2017). House Speaker Nancy Pelosi's drug pricing bill following the impeachment inquiry does not hold any promise of passing, even if compromises ever come from Trump (Cunningham, 2019). Members from both parties remain at fault. Democrats and Republicans have taken plenty of cash campaign contributions from PhRMA (Facher, 2020).

New perspectives from payers and providers are additionally provoking demands for better pharmacovigilance due to drug mishaps and noted ineffectiveness (Pharmacovigilance & pharmacoepidemiology, 2019). A greater push may come from European drug policy standards, which according to STAT raise a huge question for US charities and NIH funding. Why don't our tax-exempt charities insist on reasonable pricing to protect access to the medicines they make? Why does the NIH refuse to enforce the contractual obligations in funding agreements (Love, 2019) related to the $1.2 million treatment of Zulema?

Perhaps, given all of this today, the pharmaceutical industry faces its most profound period of change since the turn of the last century when it was corporatized. It has been said that the collision of technology, business, politics, and culture has contributed to one of the most divisive times in US history. The pharmaceutical industry displays all such tensions. Nevertheless, it remains problematic in how the global pharmaceutical industry gets conceptualized. It is indeed much more than just brand drugs produced by multinational giants (now rebranding itself as the "life sciences industry"), along with generic houses in almost every nation of the world, the bulk coming from Israel, Brazil, Russia, India, and China. These BRIC nations each has a thriving industry making off-patent entities and shipping approved pharmaceutical ingredients (APIs), which are added to many US and European brand entities (PR Newswire, 2020). Sophistication in API development and manufacture has become serious; the bulk come from abroad and must be thoroughly tested for safety precautions after several highly publicized incidents and drug recalls.

Then there are thousands of firms contracted for equipment, glassware, parts and supplies, packaging, and added ingredients for production (Rowland, 2020). Additionally, firms assist in outsourced manufacturing, clinical trials, and an array of administrative services (Outsourcing Resources, 2019). Moreover, there is the plethora of firms which surround and feed off the industry, such as consultants, regulatory affairs and compliance, analytic, lawyers and lobbying, IT firms, and marketing firms. While much is described for consumption by industry sources (and generally unavailable due to huge prices for their insider publications), there has been little critique of ongoing drug marketing practices, clinical trial developments, and the rapid consolidation of the industry in the academic literature.

What may prohibit any new price controls or further regulatory attempts are the numerous vested allies of the pharmaceutical industry. Allies on Wall Street and Madison Avenue, Congress (Facher, 2020), Academia, and elsewhere have historically benefited from the largess of pharmaceutical companies. Moreover, "America's biggest charities are owned by pharmaceutical companies" (2019) so claimed by an *Economist* article. The industry is extant in its spread of influence, and it has truly mastered exerting political prowess over time.

It should be noted that the bulk of the world's almost eight billion inhabitants use alternatives to pharmaceuticals (herbals, Ayurveda and Chinese traditional medicines, other Latin and African nostrums, and a variety of over-the-counter substances). High costs, unavailability, and cultural preferences account for this preference (Salmon, 1985; Kleinman, 1984).

The corporate pharmaceutical industry has advanced mightily to address numerous health conditions in our nation and worldwide. Nevertheless, in pursuit of new profit opportunities, and to placate fears (for the new realities of global pandemics, with a burgeoning vaccine market, along with remedies promised for chronic disease cures and now, for the sales benefit, drugs for prevention); all this goes hand in hand in a continual public relation blitz full of hype and hopes (Wechsler, 2018).

Today, this industry is multinational, extremely profitable, and very ideologically political and powerful. But it is *still a relatively small capital* compared to giants like Walmart, General Motors, Microsoft, Apple, Amazon, and other titans of American capitalism (Fortune, 2020). The pharmaceutical industry has been noted as being one of the least transparent parts of the US healthcare system, yet its set of ongoing issues has brought it into the popular and political spotlight this decade. Due to public disapproval of the industry (Bulik, 2020), firms have been attempting a rebranding of sorts advertised as "life sciences businesses," with attempted diversifications. Seizing the opportunity to wear a big white hat after coming up with an effective vaccine against COVID-19, its declining drug industry image may be able to be redeemed.

Emerging technologies make up several small research-focused private biotech firms aimed at a specific tech platform, a mechanism of action, or a few early-stage compounds, not yet with revenue streams, but awaiting an IPO to enlarge richly, and/or for an eventual takeover by a big firm (Deloitte, 2018a). Few of the largest brand companies have produced blockbuster discoveries—like those in the 1980s— but they now buy entities through acquisitions, which have trended with a big surge in this century.

In this age of deregulation, one can easily identify a critical need for greater market oversight by governments. In an article entitled, "The Biotech-Industrial Complex gets ready to define what is human," Newman (2019, p. 2) writes that newly approved human-animal chimera procedures, although by scientifically and ethically questionable techniques, may be soft-pedaled by panels of experts influenced by financially motivated bio-entrepreneurs.

Mergers and acquisitions (M&As) have become a major characteristic of late-stage capitalism. All over the world, business entities are joining together with the sole purpose of increasing their market share and reaping higher revenues and profits. In numerous countries, much of the merger activity looks like swashbuckling. The allures of combinations are heralded as major economic steps forward. International combinations allow for cross-border transactions, and even within a single country, a merger could be a keyway to enter new markets, often seen in the pharmaceutical industry when a biotech firm is gobbled up to just obtain a single new product (Mergers and Acquisitions Take Center Stage, 2019).

Finance capital loves M&As because enormous bankers' fees are reaped, plus there is the ideological support for basically touting promised economic growth. Nevertheless, some mergers and acquisitions do not seem to work out; frequently, by 2 years down the line, when plants get close, worker layoffs result, and corporate culture clashes become difficult to resolve. Additionally, promises for the sale or takeover do not fully delight Wall Street. In the era of globalization, blurring lines between industries and the increasing technological disruption, M&As continued to flourish. If not actual takeovers and/or coming together, many firms seek subsidiaries in the form of joint ventures, which is like "friends with benefits." Such, along with licensing entities, may make sense for less risk and allow a better chance to get to know each other. However, the Federal Trade Commission is being pressured to examine the steady increase in Pharma M&A, noting the AbbVie/Allegan merger and the Pfizer combos (Lawmakers ask FTC, 2010). Reuters reported that the FTC later responded by asking for more information on the $63 billion deal (FTC requests AbbVie, Allergan, 2019). Consumer groups and unions are lining up to block this drug amalgamation now (Silverman, 2019c).

The largest drug company, Pfizer ($52 billion in revenues), is known less and less as an R&D research manufacturer. The *Chicago Tribune* noted that the firm went on a range of chronic acquiring (Johnson, 2016): $14 billion to buy Medivation, another $495 million for Bamboo Therapeutics, and $5.2 billion spent for Anacor Pharmaceuticals in 2016 alone (Pierson & Banerjee, 2016; Rockoff & Stevens, 2017). Pfizer's abortive deal with Allergan in 2016—a $160 billion failure—was essentially a tax avoidance scheme to relocate to Ireland (Growing Pains, 2016; Grant, 2017). Allergan ($16 billion), hurt some by the Pfizer mishap, later went with Allegiance in a strategic partnership to sell its products across Europe, Africa, and the Middle East. Abbott, now just drugs as AbbVie ($28 billion), tried to get out of a messy deal with Alere because the target had misrepresented its attractiveness (Schnecker, 2016). Back in the 1990s, eight of the blockbusters sold by Pfizer came from acquisitions as further evidence that drug firms are not intensely trying to discover new products from their own research.

The purchase of new products from other firms spurs much competition within the industry. Grocer (2019) points out that the hunt for finding new entities has been driving up the cost of takeovers. Over $146 billion was expended in the first few months of 2019 (Rockoff & Stevens, 2017). Pharma managements do not always make astute decisions, and with the industry under more intense watch, such decisions get amplified through the business and popular press. Within virology, as well as with chronic diseases, the repurposing of older drug entities has come into vogue.

Many firms are concerned for their public image. Recently, Novartis ($49 billion in revenues) was nailed for manipulating clinical trial data to get a faster FDA approval (Thomas, 2019). Witness Johnson & Johnson's sinking PR from its opioid involvement (Hoffman, 2019). Giving great publicity was one of the worst corporate decisions of late: Bayer of Germany ($49 billion) in its frenzied acquisition of Monsanto, the agribusiness company, in a $63 billion buyout. This is now seen as highly regrettable given the 13,000 court cases against the dangerous use of Monsanto fertilizers; the stock price of Bayer fell 40%, the kind of drop that leads to significant stockholder discontent (Bender, 2019).

The year 2017 was predicted to see a decline in M&A fervor (M&As driving chemicals, 2017). Yet, it should be remembered the strong M&A market is very pleasing to Wall Street bankers who arrange deals and profit for themselves handsomely. The coronavirus outbreak and resultant recession significantly derailed consolidations in 2020. Yet, large cash balances in some firms may restart takeovers, but not likely as much as past surges. Remember, some industries were bolstered by the huge Republican tax cut and with earlier increasing profits, but even with the low interest rate for borrowing, M&As will be selective. This economic environment will not spur deal making and other collaborative strategies across many business sectors.

Notwithstanding for the pharmaceutical industry, will the eyeing of Gilead by AstraZeneca stimulate new fervor among drug companies to consolidate (Lauerman, Ring, & Hammond, 2020)? A few companies are using the moment of the epidemic to "go lean" and may launch new efforts along the trends described above. Overall, the economy is facing unprecedented, near-term difficulties, which may give future-oriented firms time to assess core activities, competition, and a changing post-COVID-19 culture.

In a STAT article, "Pharmaceutical mergers and megamergers stifle innovation," Milani (2019, p. 1) stated that the industry puts profits over people with a huge percentage of all Americans believing that drugs cost too much and lowering them should be foremost on legislators' to-do lists. In the absence of Trump and the Republicans doing anything, several states are taking more than a glance at drugs with new policy initiatives (What other states can learn, 2014). Will state governments feel reinvigorated as they learn to cope with heavy post-virus fiscal burdens amidst damaged economies?

Such behaviors also yield the ups and downs of the biotech market, pressuring pharma more since their R&D expenditures have recently produced poor drug pipelines (Grant, 2017); thus, firms *must resort* to the acquisition of new products. In this climate, particularly in 2016—a high deal volume year—the biotech bubble came upon the industry (Grant, 2017). Another factor pushing this forward is patent losses that lead to seeking specific replacement entities. An example is Roche ($54 billion) outbidding for the biotech Spark for $4.8 billion (Massoudi et al., 2019). The synergy of acquiring products that work with the existing product line and/or what may be in the pipeline is key in many cases for success (Schencker, 2016).

Melding different corporate cultures, besides the technical nuances of bringing scientific endeavors in line, is always problematic; firms find results that do not work out to be how they were parlayed at first love.

Patent loss particularly hits the highly priced biologics (more difficult to make larger molecule drugs usually administered by injection or intravenous fusion in the doctor's office). These entities in oncology, rheumatology, and endocrinology are part of the specialty pharmacy category that is ballooning drug expenditures for employers and the Medicare Part D program. The global biosimilar market is estimated to grow by 6% by 2025, heralded by the top seven manufacturers ($7.7 billion in the United States in 2019) (Global Report Store, 2019). New generic biosimilars when eventually on the market may save up to $250 billion over the next decade. Over 125 biologics are under brand protection with entrenched company barriers in place, so few biosimilars are ready to be approved by the FDA (Public Citizen highlights efforts by biologics industry to maintain monopolies, 2015). While this issue remains a contentious policy direction, it is vital to resolve since specialty drugs now represent 45.4% of the total pharmacy spending ($218.6 billion), including orphan drugs for relatively few people with rare disease conditions. The federal government subsidizes companies for their orphan drug development. The increasingly stricter formulary management schemes by PBMs urged by employers don't lend themselves to the same tactics that seem to work on traditional medicines (Vela, 2019).

Financial Times in an article "Case of buyer's remorse over Pharma deals from 2015-16" pointed out that the frenzy for growth did not always work out the best for investors, nor obviously for the public's health. The perpetual hunt for new medicines to replenish dry pipelines to achieve higher revenues from drugs falling off the "patent cliff" was tempered in these few following years. Some multibillion-dollar deals do not appear to be well founded in hindsight. Again, the increased scrutiny by Wall Street over the drug industry makes managements subject to more critique than they have ever seen before.

There has been an internal industry discussion (as well as from Wall Street) about the wisdom of large conglomerate diversified firms versus the "pure play" drug firms that focus just on discovering innovative medicines. *Financial Times* raised the question that some firms may be too big to succeed, much akin to the behemoths in the information technology sector thought to be too big for expected growth. We have witnessed the shedding of [assets] by several drug companies, particularly in consumer medicines. GSK ($49 billion) broke off its over-the-counter brands into a joint venture with Pfizer (Roland, 2018; Reuters, 2019).

The *Economist* delved into the debate over whether diversified drug firms should break themselves up into more specialized units. Diversified firms are those that typically have consumer health divisions that offer low-margin products versus the "pure-play" with innovative medicines that usually command higher margins.

In the first camp are Johnson & Johnson, GSK, and Novartis each considering splitting off parts since investor believes they will be worth more. Pfizer dumped its consumer product division to J&J in 2006, and Merck divested its consumer unit in 2014 (Growing Pains, 2016).

Yet the *Economist* continues to point out that even a firm that publicly professes a desire to slim down is likely to buy others. Firms may be looking for new drugs to sell or to enter different geographical regions. The axiom from the industry is that drug pipelines matter enormously and Pharma bosses and investors may debate the merits of focus versus diversification, but doing deals will continue (Growing Pains, 2016, p. 62).

This direction has been ongoing through numerous years, along with reconsidering the maintenance of generic houses inside a firm. Under the weight of an acquisition, Teva ($22 billion), based in Israel, saw its shares tumble 24% in a day during the summer of 2017 (Scheer & Rabinovitch, 2017). Teva is the biggest seller of generic drugs (one in every seven generics worldwide).

Certain biotechnology firms have in the meanwhile advanced as major formidable players. Frost and Sullivan studied the biotechnology sector noting that Amgen, Chiron, Genentech, and Genzyme will lead the market, with licensing deals and risk management connections with most of Big Pharma. The Rise of Biotech Pressurises Pharma report in 2005 said high returns in biotech stocks will sustain investor interest in the industry to maintain R&D projects. The top ten US biotechnology companies have 186 products in the pipeline, nearly 20% in phase 3 to substantially impact market growth in the short term (Rise of Biotech Pressurises Pharma, 2005).

As with the entire concentrating health sector, there is also a set of medical technology firms seeking larger market shares from M&As; *Fierce CEO* reports on the top companies in this segment, who face the same terrain of changing partners to secure better positions amidst the uncertainty in the current dynamics (The Top Companies in Med Tech, 2017).

Housed in only seven advanced Western nations, multinational brand manufacturers discover new expensive novel therapies (or buy them by gobbling up smaller firms). An additional key industry segment is the decentralized global generics market that chiefly supplies pharmacy benefit managers (PBMs) in the United States. Many developing nations get much lower cost off-patent drugs, including APIs (approved pharmaceutical ingredients) that also get poured into branded entities made in the United States (Salmon, 2017a). The high potency API market is projected to reach $27 billion by 2023 (Active Pharmaceuticals Ingredients market size, 2018). Additionally, an abundance of over-the-counter (OTC) products (including analgesics, digestive agents, dietary substances, vitamins, minerals, and all kinds of herbal remedies) is readily consumed by people at out-of-pocket costs (Liu & Salmon, 2010). Worldwide counterfeit medicines that threaten the globe are a direct result of the unaffordable costs of needed drugs in most Southern Hemisphere nations.

Inflation in US drug expenditures for many years has far outpaced other medical expenditures (doctors, hospitals, nursing homes, etc.) despite efforts by managed care pharmacists to keep costs contained (CVS Health, 2017). Popularly used brand drugs for the elderly, as well most generic drugs, have seen continuous double-digit annual price climbs (Silverman 2016). Many long term generic drugs required by many diabetics to live, have seen unjustifiable price increases and shortages (Roland

& Loftus, 2016). A rash of drug price climbs became notable during the 2016 election campaign drawing both Presidential candidates' commentary, for example, EPI-pens rose in a huge hike (Skapinker, 2018). Other examples were noted in the press to provoke public ire. Thus, never have drug costs become a hot political topic in America and across the world.

Trump's campaign stumps spoke to drug price gouging to appeal to his working-class base and even found the mainstream media universally welcoming his promise to negotiate prices for the federal government. In *The New York Times* op-ed, Wu noted Trump's missed opportunity to back up his populist criticisms of pharmaceutical price gougers and be cheered on by everyone (Wu, 2017). Wu suggested beginning with the ten most outrageous incidences of excessive pricing, but Trump quelled his rhetoric from the White House as he met with Pharma leaders and later appointed a drug company executive as his Health and Human Services Secretary. Remember back that Trump ran as an economic populist to confront the pharmaceutical industry. Over 3.5 years, however, the price gouging business model remains in effect. The Trump Administration essentially has done little policy change here.

Spectacular investor returns make pharma stocks a favorite of Wall Street, hedge funds, pension plans, and individual investors, along with advertising firms loving the pharma money flowing richly to them (Deloitte, 2018b). Thus, the pharma industry's political allies are extensively implanted deep within the capitalist economy worldwide.

The remarkable rise of this unique industrial organization has often been cloaked as *the major contributor* to the world's health advances, though such is disputable. This assertion, however, has tended to grant pharma firms special privileges. In contrast, demographic research has indicated that declining death rates in populations overtime have much more to do with rising standards of income, as well as numerous public health measures (Powles, 1973; McKeown, 1971; McKinlay & McKinlay, 1977, 1979). Nevertheless, the industry repeatedly takes credit for their products, which indeed may aid many patients clinically, but not so much for overall populations.

The vaccine segment of the industry is foremost in its assurances for better world health, though policy researchers might ask for prior cost-benefit evidence before any developing nation spends countless billions on mere possibilities in prevention for its people, now including promises for eradication of several chronic ailments (BBC Research Global Cancer Vaccine Market, 2014; Adult Vaccines Market Analysis, 2014).

The manufacturing and sale of pharmaceuticals in America are highly regulated for purposes of assuring product and patient safety (Fincham & Wertheimer, 1991), as well as a result due to historic public outrage over past drug mishaps (Wolfe, Coley & Health Research Group, 1981). Regulatory policies became enacted after a historic series of calamities in drug use in our population for impure, unsafe, and non-efficacious ingredients, unsanitary production facilities and processes, fraudulent claims for effectiveness, and a huge host of marketing abuses. The US Food and Drug Administration (FDA) was founded and strengthened over time to address some issues, but not all such matters, and often insufficiently addressed according to some observers. While the industry complains that it is already overregulated and that the FDA is often cumbersome in reviews, others claim that regulatory science could be vastly improved and strengthened and that the FDA could do more in tightening up drug reviews and oversight of certain players and practices, particularly for safety purposes (Edlavitch & Salmon, 2006). Some critics ask for broader scrutiny over marketing practices too.

Additionally, the current ongoing concern for the federal government to address unbridled price climbs, amidst broader scrutiny over firms' marketing practices, has provoked a few states to step up for policymaking as Trump has substantially wavered and caved to industry largess (Salmon, 2017a, 2017b). In the absence of federal actions, numerous states have moved on drug pricing fixing and other confrontational issues with manufacturers (Ollove, 2019). Trump's major drug price pronouncement in May 2018 actually spiked drug stocks to indicate all will be well ahead for the industry.

The Bush subsidization of the 2006 Medicare Part D program today faces a huge surge due to the high costs, and more frequent use, of newer specialty drugs (Andrews, 2019). With the ACA "donut hole" going away, more elderly are entering the catastrophic coverage benefit period. Since this will greatly propel Medicare outlays, the Trump Administration has been considering spending caps for specialty drug use, which would increase beneficiaries' out-of-pocket costs. Biosimilar development by generic firms is unlikely to stem this drug expenditure climb by very much, given utilization trends (Biosimilar Drug Development, 2019).

Worldwide drug sales are projected to reach $1.5 trillion by 2021, up $370 billion from 2016 (Berkrot, 2016). US drug spending was $485 billion in 2017, expected to grow up to $655 by 2023 (Philippidis, 2019). Despite smaller capitalization in the US economy next to financial institutions and other manufacturers, as well as corporate giants from Silicon Valley, Pharma firms have achieved *disproportional political power* through huge bipartisan lobbying. Given a 3:1 ratio of its lobbyists to every Congressman, plus ample campaign donations to both parties' candidates, this industry has done very well to stem criticisms. There has been an industry/federal "revolving door" where politicians and bureaucrats float back and forth, maintaining the ideology of "wonderfulness of the industry." Academic medical centers have been richly funded, and health professionals have been lavished with bountiful generosity in their practices and professional organizations. Now that greater numbers of nurse practitioners and physician assistants prescribe drugs, pharma gift giving (meals, fees, grants, and other goodies) are being bestowed upon them also (Silverman, 2017). (See Retail Clinics section below).

All of this has been successfully strategic for decades. The public is daily swayed to consume drug products in the over $5 billion spent on direct-to-consumer (DTC) persuasive advertising. Few other nations of the world tolerate DTC ads. Scientific endeavors can be costly, though R&D outlays differ among firms, some of whom place marketing expenditures well ahead of drug discovery outlays.

Single entities can generate billions in revenues, most with double-digit sales gains year after year. The top 15 selling drugs range from $15 billion Lyrica (by Pfizer) to Humira's almost $20 billion (by AbbVie) (Philippidis, 2019). Trump and the Republicans may talk about restraining drug prices, but no direct policy actions have been taken through 2020. Generic drugs saw some entity prices triple with the General Accounting Office identifying more than 20% of generics increasing over 100% from 2010 to 2015 (Morgenson, 2017).

The pharmaceutical industry has mastered the same tactic that Trump has become famous for: John Oliver called the technique "Whataboutism?" (Oliver, 2017)— abruptly changing the subject to distract folks from a difficult or uncomfortable topic. When industry spokesmen are asked about price gouging, their commentary for distraction focuses on all the *great drugs in their pipelines* that cost a lot to produce (claimed to be a billion dollars or more each). This argument flies in the face of many firms which have promotion expenses far in excess over their R&D outlays. In other words, advertising to sway prescribers and constant direct-to-consumer TV ads take a greater portion of revenue than what their executives think about in terms of disease scourges and unmet clinical needs in populations—especially internationally. After botching the industry's response to fight the HIV/AIDS epidemic by restricting the availability of drugs, certain firms may now be attempting to approach international health differently. Of course, the white-hatted good guys are out there publicizing their efforts for COVID-19 vaccines and cures; commentators are asking if the epidemic will possibly assure the industry image improvement.

When critiqued about their marketing abuses, the "pay to play" blocking of generics onto the market, stock manipulations, and clinical trials gone awry, amidst other transgressions, industry defenders change the subject and retort a list of "whataboutisms": recent approvals in precision medicine, discovering genetic risks, genomic medicines and epigenetics, firms searching to understand the microbiome role in numerous conditions, molecular diagnostics in personalized medicine, and CRISPR, CAR-T, and RNA editing, amidst a continuing alphabet soup of new innovations, including vaccines.

This is not to suggest that significant findings may indeed come from such efforts, as already seems to be the case with cancer genetics knowledge (Cutting edge, 2018), but of late each firm's public affairs office seems to work overtime with press releases to inform us of how great they are to stem criticisms.

But what about industry's contributions in harnessing infectious microbes to prevent more social epidemics, like Ebola, Zika, SARS, drug-resistant malaria, and the rise of yet-known unforeseen diseases across the Southern Hemisphere that may spread fear to the United States and Europe? Granted, dozens of innovations in processes, production, and distribution arise from inside the industry (i.e., see industry newsletters and magazines: *R&D*, *MM&M Weekly*, *Pharmaceutical Executive*, *STAT Pharmalot*, *BioPharma Dive*, *Drug Discovery and Development*, among others).

Nevertheless, justifications of climbing prices and high profit margins at times disturb other domestic manufacturing executives (who may unequivocally struggle only to obtain lower margins), while all employers, large and small, confront constantly zooming employee benefit costs, with highest cost specialty drugs a formidable culprit (Terhune, 2016) and this drug component being unbridled. The industry caters to Wall Street analysts, who conduct in-depth regular financial reviews. Hedge funds give more attention to pharma firms, venture capitalists, and large healthcare investment banks that lend and invest heavily within the health sector (Modern Healthcare, 2018a, 2018b, 2018c, 2018d, 2018e, p. 34); they pay very close attention to what pharma firms research and their returns, as well as do pension funds and individual investors who have historically appreciated the constant climbs in drug stock price rises. 2017 saw health private equity investments totaling $83 billion, the only sector in the economy to receive more private equity over 2016 (Button, 2018). Money invested and made in pharma stocks is key to enhancing the industry's prowess.

Such financial tie-ins across the economy raise the stakes against any progressive political reform, but these very tie-ins also heighten the society-wide visibility for pharma and other parties. The latter scrutiny may eventually make for a new era for the industry longer term. Thus, the industry's embeddedness economically and politically makes change not very likely, especially given the Trump Administration's cozy dealings with pharma firms. Coupled with large donations to key representatives and senators, one can see that paying homage to the pharmaceutical industry will continue with corrective policy change difficult, if not impossible, to enact. Watch how individual firms seek to curry favor during the coronavirus epidemic while the desperate public yearns for the magic bullet of a vaccine.

While the above listing is a mere inkling of what pharmaceutical firms may have on their scientific agendas, many of their costliest products heralded from industry organs (which get catapulted by their public affairs staff early on into the popular press) contain measures of hope, and hype, that belies the fuller story of these promises for very costly entities: multinational drug firms historically have a poor track record across the globe in disease containment since profit *always* determines production pursuits. For example, *Financial Times* estimates the new gene therapies may cost $1 million per patient (Gene therapy, 2017)—a tough distribution even across insured middle-class Americans, let alone the less fortunate, especially internationally.

In all, pharmaceutical firms continue to reap extremely high profits compared to other industries; they remain a formidable force in public policymaking and have a very persuasive public presence, though lately their image has been doubtful in many consumers' eyes (Cubanski, 2019). Pharma rarely loses a political battle in Congress with only occasional setbacks from the FDA. The industry's constantly surging drug prices will not likely face price controls for a predictable time under Republican rule, but both party's stalwarts lately give voice to the issue because it sounds good in the news. Certain firms have lately restrained the huge hikes as seen in 2016–2017, but a 2020 surge was made evident. The United States has by far the largest dollar drug market in the world (nearly a half trillion dollars), understandably since almost every other nation negotiates lower drug prices for their populations and healthcare systems and many nations also restrain over prescribing much better.

For decades, pharma firms have been singing the same song, praising their requirement for high profits to maintain R&D to fight disease threats, but at whatever prices, firms choose to charge. From the 1980s, mass marketed *block-buster drugs* that most middle-aged and seniors get prescribed *for their lifetimes* (i.e., statins, antihypertensives, diabetes scripts, antidepressants, and more); this was *the major goal* of many manufacturers, not curing diseases! Nowadays, niche drugs and more federally subsidized orphan drugs with lesser patient numbers are being targeted, along with new specialty discoveries with the hope of forestalling any diminution in profit streams: the largest manufacturers don't appear to be bringing out many entities, but prefer purchasing firms and products. While blockbuster sales had often reach annually into multibillions, PBMs, payers, and employers have termed them *budget busters* and have begun to fight back some in an internecine blame game for drug costs.

The 2017 Republican corporate tax cut and the repatriation of profits from overseas predictably add to the ongoing Pharma M&A fervor; as in the past, it may lead to plant closings and worker layoffs—not an employment expansion. More so, in the pharmaceutical industry, those funds will be used for greater monopolization. We may also witness huge stock buybacks, which aid executives for their quarterly bonuses and investors with the buoying of their stocks.

In sum, while US firms in the past have generated some of the most innovative pharmaceutical products, other international firms in Japan, Switzerland, etc. have *lately led with outstanding new drug introductions*, even given foreign firms facing their homeland price controls, with mostly lower profit margins and less remuneration for their execs (Salmon & Gutkin, 2021).

Hospitals and Healthcare Systems

The US healthcare system was historically constructed as doctor-dominated, hospital-centric, disease-oriented, and curative in approach with much end-staged medicine. However, these "old ways" developed under fee-for-service medicine and cost-reimbursed hospital care are gradually being revised in the ongoing push for greater value and quality improvement. The escalating cost spiral, amidst growing ineffectiveness, has as much to do with the kind of medicine historically embedded, as it does *who has come to own and control the American healthcare enterprise*. Managed care will be more fully addressed later along with Accountable Care Organizations, but the discussion here pertains to large hospital chains and healthcare systems, sometimes called integrated health systems (IHSs), which all demonstrate the mixed and amalgamating collectivity of clinical entities operating within the American delivery system.

American hospitals were originally founded by religious groups and municipal governments to service surrounding communities. Their "not-for-profit" status indicated a bygone charitable impulse to serve all comers in need, particularly addressing infectious epidemic diseases. Over time with healthcare modernization and scientific advancement, quality was vastly improved. The early for-profit medical schools and hospitals prior to the Flexner Report in 1910 were all pretty much eliminated by the 1930s. Notwithstanding in the recent space of 50 so years, after the Nixon Administration legitimized money-making as the objective to both health maintenance organizations and later hospital services, ongoing disruptions now reveal an emergent new structural arrangement for American medicine: the push for the so-called value-based services is being heralded to intentionally alter provider incentives and behaviors, but importantly to establish monitoring and greater accountability, over practitioners. The implications for physicians and other professionals are becoming clearer with information technology and the changing agency relationship (Feinglass & Salmon, 1994; White, Salmon, & Feinglass, 1994).

It was shortly after the HMO strategy that for-profit hospital chains arrived on the scene with the "not-for-profits" facing stiff competition to their traditional inefficient ways. Hospitals consumed over 40% of healthcare expenditures, and doctors continued to use hospitals as their workshop, but not in the same way as previously. The culture of medicine was about to be changed, and the predominant kind of medicine that was practiced provided the foothold for the medical-industrial complex to benefit handsomely (McKinlay, 1984; Salmon, 1985).

The strengthened centralized administration over these scaled-up complex multi-hospitals became championed by the for-profits; they achieved much in local competitive battles given multiple advantages (access to capital reserves, newer facilities, locational superiority, economies of scale, consultancies, contract discounts, selective marketing, etc.). Over time, a transformation of most hospital services witnessed Quentin Young's vampire effect (for-profits biting the so-called not-for-profits who became just like them in character) for converging behaviors in most institutions (Young, 1997). Again, the marketplace often determines the overall orientation, plus the increase of administrative control over professionals was taking hold. Over time, a transformation of most hospital services witnessed Quentin Young's vampire effect, that is, for-profits biting the so-called not-for-profits who became just like them in character which resulted in a convergence of profit seeking behaviors in most institutions.

It still remains to be seen what impact the Accountable Care Organizations (ACOs) will have on the overall hospital industry; notwithstanding by the 1990s, HMOs had hit traditional hospital functioning hard (which will be covered later). Today the multi-hospital for-profit systems face notable management mess-ups at Community Health Systems and Tenet, among others (Ellison, 2019). The industry faces notable challenges with its current changing landscape, including the "not-for-profits" rapidly consolidating even more.

Tighter reimbursement issues and lost revenue during the epidemic will plague all firms as hospitalization costs remain hard to control, along with value-based care (VBC) being demanded by payers and elective money-making procedures postponed. It is uncertain how COVID-19 may affect the push for VBC (Livingston, 2020), but the pandemic looks like more hospitals may breach debt covenants due to the estimated well over $200 billion lost revenues (Bannow, 2002).

The large-chain hospitals expanded recklessly in their thirst for market share and ever-increasing profit margins. As Hoy and Gray pointed out in their 1986 book, most growth of the six largest for-profit hospital chains up to 1984 had occurred through acquisition of existing entities. Most of the hospitals acquired were previously for profit, but roughly 20 percent were non-profit. The acquisition of these hospitals created additional churning in ownership with some changing hands up to five additional times (Hoy & Gray, 1986).

By this current century, rising pressures make it difficult to grow as rapidly. Managing existing inventories of facilities, as recent news reports indicate, confronts Community Health Systems ($18.4 billion), which was the largest for-profit chain, since 2016 retrenching some (Evans, 2016a). It ran into significant management challenges, including disgruntled investors demanding spinning off a series of hospitals that did not meet required desired metrics. Shortly thereafter, Tenet Hospital System ($20.6 billion) arose in reports of spinning off a number of their facilities due to financial difficulties (Kacik, 2017b; Barkholz, 2017a, 2017b). These systems often provided the backbone of health care in many rural and smaller city areas but also represented significant portions of urban locales, such as Philadelphia and Chicago where Tenet hospitals have been recently sold (Schorsch, 2017; Cramer, 2020).

Management muck-ups are not confined just to the greedy for-profit chains (Chaffee, 2016). Despite high administrative overheads (which tend to soar in multi-hospitals), many systems face difficulties managing off-site facilities since their size indicates complex varying regional characteristics across a consolidated industry segment. Compensation patterns have been climbing dramatically for CEOs with multimillion-dollar pay packages not uncommon (Barkholz, 2016)—not a bad job that pays up to over $100 million! A reported 33% average bonus awaits a successful hospital executive. Remember that a hierarchy below the CEO also gets paid very well and there are hordes of subordinates in management. Yet these jobs are tough, so turnover is quite high. *Becker's Hospital Review* routinely reports multiple hospital CEOs departing their jobs weekly, perhaps for not making system-wide metrics given intense scrutiny over imposed standards of quality and patient satisfaction (the latter called "clinical transformation") (Gooch, 2020). Exiting a job may also be for better pay or burnout from brutal pressures. Indeed, it is tough to move such complex operations toward value-based care and still reap the desired profit levels. For proprietaries, outside investors seek greater returns on their stocks; they watch financials closely so that challenges to management are becoming commonplace. The *Modern Healthcare* survey of executive compensation (Kacik, 2017c) stated that as corporations acquire more hospitals and physician practices, they grow market share, but at the same time, they need to ensure that their services are best aligned to improve outcomes and more importantly generate returns on that investment (p. 19). As these organizations took on more risk, they responded with Accountable Care Organizations (ACOs), started their own health plans, and in general expanded services that required increasing administrative control which necessitated ever-increasing financial incentives to acquire sufficient executive talent to manage these new entities (p. 21).

Of note, seven out of ten of the most profitable hospitals are the so-called not-for-profits (Johnson, 2016), who since 2015–2016 are adjusting their strategies to draw in investors (Evans, 2016b). The top ten of these largest systems reached $10 to $60 billion in revenues with many obtaining outside private equity investments (Modern Healthcare's 2016; Hospital System's Survey, 2016; Modern Healthcare Systems Financial Database, 2020).

The hospital sector is taking a beating with COVID-19 with many failing institutions, which is extremely problematic in denying access to vulnerable urban communities and small rural towns. It will be prudent from a policy perspective to reinstate federal, regional, and state planning mechanisms to rebuild a proper distribution of medical resources rather than leave it to marketplace madness.

Corporatization Spreads: Nursing Homes, Prisons, and Education

Market ideology is so ingrained in American society that it is often automatically suggested that privatization is the preferred "solution" to numerous sectors, including public water system infrastructure (Ivory, Protess, & Palmer, 2016) and other municipal activities. Reaching out to Big Tech for help, post-epidemic should heed cautionary notes also (Klein, 2020). This "private sector can do it well" thinking is so pervasive that not much thought is given when turning over huge sectors of government and non-profits to corporate operators; too often contracts are not tight for performance measures and accountability, and enforcement tend to be weak. The result is often a changed *nature to the entire enterprise*: witness the nursing home industry, prisons, universities, and much more.

The phenomenon of corporatization ranges from hospitals to the nursing home industry (which has been predominantly for-profit ownership). The earliest hospital chains, Hospital Corporation of America and Humana, came out of nursing homes. Beyond the concentrating hospital industry nowadays, the increasing nursing home consolidation is solidly for-profit (about 11,000 out of 15,640 nursing homes are for-profit) (IQVIA, 2018a, 2018b). *MedPage Today* (Wynn, 2017) reports on the rate of complaints in nursing homes going up more than 37%, with increased severity too. More than half were characterized as "immediate jeopardy" or "high priority," the most serious types of cases. Findings by the HHS Office of Inspector General on state investigations into complaints at nursing homes usually do not bring change.

This discussion on the warehousing of our nation's elderly takes on special meaning as we observe the mass deaths in long-term facilities exceeding 50,000 from COVID-19 by June 2020, 40+ percent of the nation's almost 200,000 deaths (Kamp, 2020). Nevertheless, the common notion has held that both hospitals and nursing homes require "management," so private investment was naturally thought to be preferred. Proprietary hospital chains actually originated out of for-profit nursing homes (like private prisons both used "hotel services"). This occurs when some federal and state payments became available. The model of corporate ownership was from the likes of Hospital Corporation of America and Humana. Not as profitable as market, it was easy to jump into nursing homes, so several chains saw an aging population in middle and working class as a market with some government subsidy plus ability to pay from savings; thus more bodies in beds enlarged their supply chains, so expansions ensued.

As the coronavirus outbreak swept the nation, it was initially seen that the squalid conditions in any congregate living arrangements for the elderly were figuratively petri dishes for its spread. Historically, state agencies were reported *not to respond well* to patient and family complaints. Nursing homes have had high staff vacancy rates as well as high turnovers, due to low-paid salaries, with often scant professional supervision. Federal data has shown most nursing homes overstate their numbers of nurses and caretaking staff to the government. Therefore, fluctuations and gaps in care are common, affecting health code compliance, residents' meals, and medication regimens. Of those 14,000 nursing homes, 7 in 10 reported lower staffing levels based on the evaluation with an average drop of 12% (The Health 202: Medicare For All, 2019, p. 1). Such poor conditions of labor yield high profits for investors or even provide for staying financially viable for the so-called "not-for-profit" nursing homes, given persistent historically low State Medicaid reimbursements, which vary by region.

Beyond these conditions, lax scrutiny over abuses of residents means many cases go unreported, estimated to be over two million annually, according to Lawyers. com (Chant, 2019). Types of abuses in nursing homes include a range of physical abuses (cuts, bruises, torn or bloody clothing, pulled out hair, broken bones), plus emotional abuses, including intimidation, humiliation, isolating the patient from family and other residents, mocking, or terrorizing the patient, along with outright neglect; signs of neglect include malnourishment, dehydration, unwashed clothing or bed linens, and failure to administer medication properly (Chant, 2019). These cases of abuse go unnoticed, even by caring staff since as Rau has noted being like "ghost towns." He notes underreporting to the government on staff patterns, which bolsters family suspicions of inadequate staffing (Rau, 2018, p. 1).

The poor situation of how our elderly and disabled are treated in long-term care facilities has been developing for a long time; it is mighty complex, which will make it difficult to remedy unless there is determined public outrage in certain states over the virus revelations. Designing workable regulatory policy remains challenging, but all that may be needed is a few state reform models. Many targeting efforts in the past have not been corrected due to the ownership issue, their influence on state governments, and their outright seeking profits, amidst the low reimbursement climate by Medicaid. With ensuing lawsuits and the reality of folks not trusting these facilities to be safe, it just may come that investors pull out of this line of business, especially if regulatory oversight comes to pass.

The size of a nursing home facility can reach 1000 beds. The top 50 nursing home chains that own as many as 426 facilities in the largest chain, so nursing homes vary in size by individual facility and by the largeness of network-owned chains (Flessner, 2019).

The New York Times article "Nursing Home Industry Wins as Penalties are Relaxed" noted that the Trump Administration scaled back fines against nursing homes that harm residents or place them in grave danger of injury—part of a broader regulatory relaxation under Trump. Rau calculates that nearly 6500 nursing homes—4 of every 10—receive a citation at least once for a serious violation (Rau, 2018, p. 1). Another article in *The New York Times* entitled "Care Suffers as Profits Rise" reports that complaints are higher at nursing homes that feed money to their owners' other firms. Caring for the increasingly elderly population in America who need competent caring in nursing homes has been compromised by sinister capitalist arrangements, an increasingly common business arrangement where owners outsource a variety of goods and services to companies where they have a financial interest or control. More than 11,000, or nearly 75% of nursing homes in the United States, have business dealings known as related property transactions, according to an analysis of nursing homes' financial records by Kaiser Health News (Rau, 2017). Some homes even contract out basic functions like management or rent their own building from a sister corporation claiming this is an efficient way of running their business and can help minimize taxes (Rau, 2018, p. 5).

This financial gaming is commonplace to marketplace medicine across the industry, among multiple creative means to rake in greater profits. In another *The New York Times* piece, "Care Suffers as More Nursing Homes Feed Money into Corporate Webs" claims that contracts with related companies accounted for $11 billion of nursing home spending in 2015—a tenth of their costs—according to financial disclosures submitted to Medicare. Investigations, such as these superb *The New York Times* articles have been replicated by cub reporters from local newspapers across America for decades, recognizing and responding to patients' families' concerns. Mostly all conclude the nursing home industry is raft with corruption and financial craziness to benefit owners rather than the very patients they are supposed to serve. Nursing home presented conditions that allowed deaths to mount from the recent virus simply because residents' lives have been neglected. It has been noted that nursing homes with related companies received fines 22% more often for serious health violations than independent homes, with penalties averaging almost $25,000 (7%) higher.

Most of these were for-profit entities that solely existed for the enhancement of investors. In a section entitled "Piercing the corporate veil," the article maintained that utilizing separate limited liability corporations and partnerships gained popularity just as the industry consolidated by publicly traded companies, private investors, and private equity firms. This above article cites a 2003 piece in the *Journal of Health Law* (Casson & McMillen, 2003) that encouraged owners to separate their nursing home businesses into detached entities to protect themselves if governments ever tried to recuperate overpayments or if juries levied large, negligent judgments (Rau, 2018, p. 6).

Again, it should be clear that the care for our nation's elderly has long been placed in jeopardy by such financial shenanigans. Investigations and lawsuits following the mass negligence after COVID-19 infections will likely uncover much corruption. An article entitled "At Many Homes, More Profit and Less Nursing" claimed a typical nursing home acquired by a large investment company before 2006 was scored worse in national rates using indicators to track ailments of long-term residents (Duhigg, 2007). Those included bed sores, usually preventable infections, as well as the need to be restrained. Before they were acquired by private investors, many homes scored at or above national averages in similar measurements. Private investment companies have made succeeding in court difficult for plaintiffs, and for regulators, it is hard to levy chain-wide fines since such complex corporate structures obscure control of the nursing home. It should be noted large chains owned by investment companies earned $1700 a resident, according to reports filed by the facilities. Those homes, on average, were 41% more profitable than the average facility (Duhigg, 2007, p. 2). The way firms earned greater profits is that managers cut clinical registered nurses sometimes far below levels required by law. For-profit homes were seen to put profits first, so the epidemic brought these practices to greater light (Goldstein, Silver-Greenberg, & Gebeloff, 2020). In *The Washington Post* piece entitled "As nursing home residents died, new COVID-19 protections shielded companies from lawsuits," Cenziper, Whoriskey, Mulcahy, and Jacobs (2020) explain how Governors gave immunity to protect the nursing homes and their owners, plus appeals to Health and Human Services Secretary Alex Azar and Mitch McConnell went for naught. Families may have little recourse.

At the state level, rules and regulations over nursing home operations tend to be lax, and several states have more lenient surveillance and enforcement than others, typically drawing widespread criticisms. Our 50 states vary greatly in the quality of nursing home care under their supervision. In regulatory statues, definitions of "abuse and neglect" are usually insufficient. Staffing patterns and training issues of nursing assistants, who take care of patients' daily needs, are pervasively poor, so personal care standards are easily compromised. Beyond the training and supervision of these very low-paid staff is the turnover issue, which often split state agency regulation that does not adequately address. For example, in Illinois, the Department of Public Health provides for licensure, but the Illinois Department of Public Aid handles reimbursement. Coordination between state agencies can be problematic beyond interagency work with a Department of Mental Health also. This situation may be replicated across many states where licensure and certification and inspections are different from the financing issues, even while they are usually poorly reimbursed, or not adequately examined. Thus, legal problems notoriously arise over "informed consent" and families being notified of what happens to their relative.

The virus has devastated nursing homes across the country, before staff were regularly tested and given PPE, and visitors were prohibited (Healy, Richtel, & Baker, 2020). Chances for infection of their relatives became the main worry of families in the understaffed and underfunded homes (Reilly, 2020). This worry and the horror of deaths will likely lead into widespread lawsuits through 2021. Look for a withdrawal of investment dollars as facilities close and go bankrupt, particularly where severe occurrences in Nebraska, Wisconsin, Washington State, Illinois, and New York made headlines. In April 2020, *The Washington Post* claimed that one in ten nursing homes nationwide reported coronavirus cases (Cenziper, Jacobs, & Mulcahy, 2020). *The Wall Street Journal* said deaths topped 10,000 that same month in nursing homes (Kamp & Mathews, 2020).

It became apparent that the elderly, especially with underlying chronic disease, are highly vulnerable to death from the virus (Cavendish, 2020). Such should have been suspected with prompt preventive actions taken. Without professional quick response, which is generally lacking in this industry, along with limited testing by the federal government, it is reasonable that staff were likely bringing in the virus. Same goes for homes for the disabled and other social service agencies indicating just how badly the US healthcare system was prepared for the outbreak and how bad the national leadership was!

Obviously, states were not policing homes (Chicago Tribune Editorial Board, 2020b). Ornstein and Sanders (2020) maintain nursing homes allowed the virus to explode when they violated basic health standards like isolation, use of PPE, and failure to maintain social distancing. Thus, it was no surprise nursing homes turned into disaster zones. Will stricter regulation and enforcement now ensue (Yin, 2020; Kacik, 2020a, 2020b)? Perhaps a few states will step up as models, but reform of this industry segment will be formidable.

For sure, the impact on staff has been devastating, since nursing assistants and support staff are poorly paid with few decent benefits. An SEIU union in Chicago threatened a strike (Editorial: A Nursing Assistant Strike during COVID-19) seeking pay raises, sick pay, training, and prevention protections (Chicago Tribune Editorial Board, 2020a). Previously, CMS had intervened with nursing home penalties and cracking down on inspections (Castellucci, 2018; Brady, 2019). Change has come very slowly to nursing home reforms simply due to few state and federal priorities and the industry's power to resist. So most past attempts at change over time seem futile up to this present moment of crisis. In September 2019, CMS considered rewarding SNFs for outcome-based care in its Payment Driven Payment Model, which may in theory eliminate unnecessary therapy services designed to build profits (Kacik, 2019). This was intended for system change away from Medicare fee for service—a side effect is the imposed data sharing with hospitals. Nursing home professional staff will need to discover what is "clinically appropriate care" with this costly change. After hospital discharge, patients' needs today are more complicated, so facilities must gear up for complex cases by hiring additional nursing staff, which is costly, as payments get restricted. Such tinkering with reimbursements usually does not have adequate policy follow-up for neglectful practices in this segment of health care.

Financial watchdogs rarely pursue this industry except in one case in 2019: the US DOJ prosecuted Illinois and Florida nursing home operator Philip Esformes guilty of Medicaid fraud (Jackson & Ariza, 2019) for $1.3 billion. The judge in the case called the operator orchestrating a fraud unseen by anyone prior (Jackson & Ariza, 2019, p. 4).

If nursing homes had been thought of as "God's waiting room," they might after COVID-19 actually have morphed into Sarah Pain's vision of death panels!

Prisons and Immigrant Detention Camps

The phenomenon of corporatization is so prevalent across American society that it has spread from hospitals and the nursing home industries to the privatization of prisons, immigrant roundups, and for-profit universities.

Additionally, the coronavirus outbreak exposed the sad conditions in congregate living arrangements for prisoners and detainees before revealing the overall social injustice within minority communities, the police, courts, and criminal justice systems that are being protested and examined. Several prison systems were quickly highlighted as incubators for the virus as detainees found overcrowded and were not properly protected. Some jurisdictions released many merely recognizing the backlogs in the courts (those arrested who could not post bond, minor offenses, older at-risk prisoners, etc.). Cook County Jail in Chicago became a national top hot spot with 350 confirmed cases (Ivory & Williams, 2020) due to overcrowding of suspects.

Worldwide prisons (Coyne, 2020) quickly considered inmate release, sanitary cleanup, visitor bans, and other containment measures to quell prison powder kegs for rapid spread (Mancini, Cocco, & Shubber, 2020). Most prisons domestically historically have poor medical care, so coping with the outbreak proved impossible. As Ivory (2020) pointed out, these facilities are *not* hospitals able in any way to care for those infected, as attention focused nationally from the realm of local dilemmas, the plight of the Trump Administration's ongoing incarceration of immigrants by the Border Patrol. Most of these facilities for the "illegals" are contracted out to private entities at huge costs, which were never well-equipped to render sufficient medical attention before COVID-19.

Nationwide overall testing was so poorly conducted by the Trump Administration so it would not be expected to prioritize all at-risk groups in nursing homes, prisons, jails, and detention centers. Just on the basis of crowding in such facilities should have given reason to mobilize much greater efforts.

Social distancing in crowded prisons and immigrant detention centers, along with improper sanitation, lack of PPE, and medical capabilities placed these populations at very great risk. It was predictable that rates of infection would zoom disproportionally, and they did. The United States had 1.5 million citizens in state and federal prisons in 2016 (Gotsch & Basti, 2018). That makes 8.5% in private detention. States with the most private prisons are California, Florida, Louisiana, Mississippi, Oklahoma, Wisconsin, and of course Texas, with its high of 13,985 but down from 20,000 in 2008.

The Trump Administration placed 73% of immigrants in privately run facilities. Attorney General Sessions reversed the Obama Administration directive to phase out private prisons. From 2000 to the present, a boom in private prisons saw five times increase in people going to private prisons (Gotsch & Basti, 2018).

Factors for such an increase were the driving quest of profit and the tendency of federal and state officials to favor privatization schemes, along with how the war on drugs, mandatory sentencing, minimum sentences, and tougher policing expanded America's prison population beginning in the 1980s. One in 12 convicts receives a private placement, a 47% jump since 2000, while the total population increased by 9%. The two largest corporations are CoreCivic and GeoGroup that run private prisons with contracts exceeding $3.5 billion in 2015. Lesser offenders, not necessarily major felons, get housed in private places since security costs tend to be lower for them.

Over 26,000 immigrants are detained in privately run facilities. Contracts by U.S. Immigration and Customs Enforcement (ICE) are for beds even if not filled. There has been a 442% increase since 2000 into over 200 immigrant prisons and jails in the United States (Gotsch & Basti, 2018). Average length of detention can run as high as 100 days. Some facilities force work upon the detainees paying $1 per day. A heightened political issue with full press coverage has centered on separation of families and the poor conditions for women and children and lack of medical care (Gotsch & Basti, 2018).

Proponents for privatization of prisons argue cost-savings, but some research casts doubt on the validity of this line of thinking (Private prisons, 2020). The promise may not have materialized according to the US Bureau of Justice Statistics. So controversy continues as privatization remains an international phenomenon across many nations.

As to the effect from the epidemic, one would hope local, state, and federal enforcement would emerge with better quality performance measures and see that they are met transparently so that private contracting proves its so-called cost-savings. The ideology of privatization where for-profit entities take over formerly public functions must be fought on the basis of evidence, which Gotsch and Basti say is lacking. Known for lower staffing levels, correction officers in private prisons earn considerably less than public facility counterparts who receive superior training. Quality and performance concerns persist. Since for-profit prison growth trended with growing crime rates and tougher sentencing patterns, it may be hopeful to believe that the ongoing street protests for police and criminal justice reforms may eventually lead to an examination of this notion of letting the "free market" rule in private prisons.

Universities

The COVID-19 epidemic had an abrupt impact on higher education and may just provide a lasting transformation to the sector. University administrators were among the first to act as students were returning from spring break by shutting down classrooms and dormitory life to prevent the virus spread. Classes were cancelled, and students dismissed (Green, 2020a); colleges had their money for tuition, fees, and dorm rentals, so most colleges thought hastily assembled online courses a la Trump University might suffice for the end of the semester. Many faculties were insufficiently prepared for online learning, and students found growing frustration from not seeing friends and having a campus experience. Senior health science students needing rotations, science majors missing lab settings, and theatre arts and music students requiring interaction, among others, find online courses not decent substitutions, and surely not worth the costs (Minhaj, 2020).

Students and parents thought the replacement of classroom learning and the campus experience somehow was not worth the $30 to $60 thousand or more. In truth, universities faced a hard lesson (Jack & Smyth, 2020); they began to lose their constituencies. Parents at DePaul University in Chicago demanded their money back (Cherney, 2020). Other colleges will face lawsuits as folks are drawing up class action suits. Who knows how many international students, whom many institutions depend upon for their much higher payments, will return upset for being outright dismissed and/or for fear of the continued epidemic spread?

Then many students may just not return for the fall semester (Anderson, 2020; Hubler, 2020) believing downgraded University of Phoenix-type degrees will not be useful to a future job search. An estimate of 15% dropout has been made (Minhaj, 2020). College used to be aspirational as a mechanism for social mobility. The general public has now begun to assess what value a degree may have as costs are sure to rise. The virus requires continual testing (for the virus and not what students learn), eliminates lecture halls and sports events, and imposes social distancing, masks, single-room dorms, and other restrictions college students may not take to.

Recently, examinations of high administrative costs, use of endowments, expenses for sports activities, overall budget allocations, and other aspects of universities are now in play. For sure, fiscally strapped states will be unable to pony up extra funding for public universities; many may be in jeopardy for cuts if not closure. Since universities have been corporatizing over the last few decades, queries into administrative decision-making and priorities in operations will likely discover many points of critique. Over the years administrators have wrung profits from bookstores, sporting events, parking lots, dining facilities, etc. Yet, it is estimated that 1/5 of colleges are at risk financially, so along with the questionable fate of public universities which have become more dependent on tuition (Carey, 2020), a period of consolidation may be on the horizon for US universities. The shift will deepen from academic to corporate.

With college shutdowns this past spring, the online for-profit colleges saw an opportunity to snare students through renewed advertising campaigns (Kolodner & Burtrymowicz, 2020) though this segment of education still faces a tarnished image due to several firms leaving graduates with huge debt and questionable learning. As state budgets slowed and higher education saw cuts and stagnation in the early part of this decade, this for-profit segment grew. Like for-profit hospital chains, certain firms became darlings of Wall Street. Internet offerings were attractive especially to full-time workers. Large institutional investors swept into this industry, but concerns for quality saw enrollments drop from the heydays of 2010–2013 along with lower student loan repayment rates and lower graduation rates. For-profit higher education corporations received $32 billion in Title IV funding, approximately 70% of their funds. America's largest university, University of Phoenix, enrolled nearly a half million students in 2010 with revenues approaching $5 billion to demonstrate the advertising and political connects count.

As in primary and secondary education with US Education Secretary Betsy DeVos trending toward privatization, political revamping will have profound effects (Green, 2020b). For sure, the Big Tech firms have become entrenched in both hardware and software, strengthening their grip with the stay-at-home schooling orders. Google for Education, Apple, and Microsoft have long had major involvement in education, though critics feel much is not meeting the high expectations (MSNBC, 2020). Over the past few years, Google Educator has gained entry into many school districts to sell Chromebooks and to promote reliance on its search engine, Google DOCs, and drive. Teacher resources are also provided.   Its dominance not only defeats competitors but also extinguishes the possibility that competition may occur, besides engraining a certain system dependence over time, according to Duhigg (2018). Likely the school market for online instruction from IT firms exploded after the epidemic led to school shutdowns, and individual families who are home schooling can be customers too.

With the ongoing economic turndown, the job market for the 3.9 million spring college grads appears uninviting (Weaver, 2020). As with the 2008 global financial crisis, a generation of young people, debt-ridden from their education expenses, will face tough life prospects, and so it may be for a few years for the current enrolled group of students given the state of the economy.

This entire social situation demands astute minds to consider progressive man/woman power planning for this generation for a productive future, and not rely upon an erratic market scramble for chaotic guidance. If the Trump Administration should try to resolve issues in the education sector, Betsy DeVos' outright support of for-profit schools can give indication of the policy drift (Dayen, 2019).

Drug Store Retail Clinics

HMOs were sporadically resisted by the medical profession; certain doctors found the competition shrunk their practices by siphoning off paying patients after the 1973 dual-choice HMO mandate fell into the hands of employer HR offices. The HMO effort proved to be less encompassing of the profession as practices became bought up by hospitals to feed their specialists and admissions. Greater numbers of doctors began the trend toward employment contracts, now approaching 50%.

Not really anticipated by the profession was the fast diversification of chain drug stores that spread all across the nation in huge numbers. There are now an estimated 3000 in-store clinics, 14 times an increase over 10 years to 2018 (Retail Bus Tour, 2014, Statista, 2018). Additionally, there are 7.639 urgent care centers, now itself an $18 billion segment of health care, offering perhaps a higher acuity service with corporate physician staffing (Japsen, 2018). For cost concerns, this ambulatorization of medicine seemed to be heralded, along with surgicenters and MRI units, but they became mainly corporate in sponsorship over time, usually shifting doctors out of hospitals (Lovrien & Peterson 2016a, 2016b).

Pharmacies had begun to morph beyond just dispensing prescriptions into more clinical services to complement their general store functions in many neighborhoods. Walmart and other big-box firms, many chain food stores, and the Walgreens, CVS, Rite Aid, Target, Health Mart, Rexall, Kroger, and the like pharmacy industry identified the opportunity in being the "most accessible healthcare resource." Their general store function provided front-end consumer products to attract customers, so why not design retail clinic space?

With the purported demand for primary care and consumers seeking better access to convenient care, store managements set out to hire nurse practitioners and physician assistants from their ample supply to directly compete with family medicine and pediatrics, whose patients seem to prefer shopping while waiting for their appointment, as well as getting the prescription right from the pharmacy in the next aisle. Retail clinics began to handle minor medical needs, well childcare, vaccinations, and preventive care. Several have moved into chronic care management and lifestyle change strategies for reimbursements and out-of-pocket payments.

Moreover, it was the lower cost of care over physicians, free parking, and most of all easy and convenient care that consumers tend to like, supportive of the "consumer-centric" rhetoric that has become common in the healthcare system. Besides, one can pick up drugs, groceries, and other sundries afterward or while waiting—reportedly always less time than hanging at the doctor's office with sick people. Moreover, there is a huge rack of magazines in the store to choose from, since some patients have complained about old used reading materials in doctors' offices, besides other historic gripes. This last comment is intended to point out that consumerism is not always that great.

Retail clinic visits are to the dismay of local medical practitioners who get to hear favorable satisfied reports from their patients, who regularly prefer retail clinics and tell their doctor if not records having transferred. Some areas of the country saw a doctor backlash as editorials in medical journals questioned their quality management or sought to besmirch nurse practitioners. Research from RAND has shown that retail clinics do not necessarily reduce ER use and may actually be contributing to higher overall spending. Records are not readily shared unless a hospital system connection has been established. Many hospitals have recently begun to affiliate with a number of retail clinics to establish referral mechanisms and to actually participate in this rapidly developing change in medical care delivery.

Pharmacy Benefit Managers

Rising like a phoenix in the desert, pharmacy benefit managers (PBMs) have ballooned as gigantic newcomers to corporate health in a very short time. Several PBMs now have greater revenues and even higher profit margins than the largest pharmaceutical firms—remarkable since PBMs have only been around since the early 1990s. In the late 1980s, their predecessor third-party administrators (TPAs) organized to pay prescription bills to pharmacies. Since many pharmacies had already computerized to maintain their growing inventories and conduct online ordering from drug distributors, it became possible later on for online claims adjudication and eventually to direct pharmacists for clinical oversight, beyond just payment collection.

Thus, PBMs represent the quintessential opportunity for quickly amassing huge revenues and profits in the American healthcare market, which incidentally makes them valuable takeover targets of late. They piled up significant political power when President George W. Bush designated them as the handlers of the Medicare Part D drug program; they serve private insurance firms who carve out their drug benefit and self-insured corporate employers too—they perform a necessary overall administrative function for handling the over five billion prescriptions written every year. Again, the rapid industrialization of the healthcare sector brings such kinds of administrative oversight in all phases of health care.

The early and evolving PBMs were pharmacy card system (PCS) and diversified prescription system (DPS), both fast growing and later absorbed by pharmaceutical companies Eli Lilly and SmithKline Beecham, respectively. Pharmacists in stores liked this model that allowed them to maintain their customer base and get paid, stores being then mainly independently owned while the big store chains began to grow.

The potential for industrialization of drug distribution became evident as more drug entities came onto the market and prescribing zoomed. The upgraded industry expansion was found to lie in mail order pharmacies, where the RX was electronically transmitted from the prescriber and then shipped out from gigantic automated dispensing warehouses to patients' homes. Bulk purchasing of generics from overseas became commonplace; automation allowed a robot to fill up to 50,000 scripts per day, which enabled employer demands for cheaper generic substitutions to be met. Fewer professional pharmacists were left in the community.

Nevertheless, the industrial model for centralized dispensing (MEDCO, a PBM later acquired by Merck) had provoked the ire of practicing pharmacists in independent operations; their customers no longer came to the pharmacy for their prescriptions, nor to buy various dry goods and sundries. With mail order pharmacies now dominant today (between 80% and 90% of the total United States' 5.4 billion scripts are handled by all PBMs), PBMs get rich on volume dispensing so—like with Trump, the argument of *no collusion* —between PBMs with Pharma seems like thin gruel. PBMs sought special relationships with pharmaceutical firms who pay them for preferred brand status on their formularies; they jointly conduct disease state management programs to push preferred entities, and PBMs sell their valuable data to drug firms if not producing bountiful health services research from their data warehouses (Dedhiya & Salmon, 1998). Notwithstanding, in the "blame game" over drug pricing, greater antagonisms between the two are emerging with recent public attention to increasing drug prices.

More so, an aging cohort of BS-trained burgermeister pharmacists was retiring, so thousands of small stores closed per year in the 1990s. As a result, pharmacy wastelands arose in rural and inner-city neighborhoods (Qato et al., 2014), with no infrastructural relief other than big-box Walmart mushrooming across the land—an additional factor driving out small community pharmacies. Pharmacies were never under federal health planning (CHPs or HSAs) guidelines; business owner pharmacists were never involved partly due to the professional socialization for business owner pharmacists. Such massive closures over this decade were *not necessarily merely managed care-driven* per se, but complicated by the rapid expansion of chain drug stores, several of which had started their own PBMs. Again, demonstration of health marketplace disruption and destruction was clearly witnessed, with professionals at most risk ceding to more powerful corporate entities.

As corporate chain drug stores ballooned (Walgreens, CVS, Rite Aid, Kroger, Albertsons, Kmart, and more), the top ones garnered between 2000 and up to over 7000 locations, expanding beyond regional to nationwide operations. PBMs added to their lines of business when George W. Bush rewarded them with Medicare Part D; profits for both chains and PBMs grew quite handsomely.

PBMs make money processing each prescription Rx claim and using profitable mail service that allows generic substitutions. They also sell usage data to pharmaceutical companies, who also discount their brand cost for preferred formulary status. Commonplace today are tiers for co-pays to incentivize patients to buy cheaper generics, prior authorizations to push prescribing away from costlier entities, and directed clinical interventions at the pharmacy counter toward practitioners for patients and both now part of the more invasive modern PBM. Some PBMs have even broken down the silo of medical and pharmacy benefit data integration to promote some coordinated care, particularly at the request of larger employers for cost savings. Each administrative "innovation" may be beneficial in ways for patient care. Nevertheless, highly profitable PBMs remain essentially unregulated in the ongoing marketization of drug benefits, which are becoming highly complex and often undiscernible to even insiders.

Then at the end of 2017, the business press was ablaze about pointed developments related to pharmacy benefit management, but existing firms became more and more alarmed by the new competition while their stocks plummeted, when IT industry firms even mentioned, let alone actually stepped in (Schencker, 2018). Earlier in 2017, insurer Anthem initiated a shake-up by ditching the number one PBM, Express Scripts (a not-so-uncommon industry practice of changing partners), following legal suits and countersuits. Anthem reportedly sought "complete control over its formulary," meaning an attempt to lower outlays to keep more money for itself.

Given the historical trend of divorces within the PBM industry, consumers might still need to adjust to new benefits, different drugs, new pharmacy sites, higher co-payments, and deductibles—as drug prices will surely continually rise. *Modern Healthcare* (2017, p. 17) has highlighted this trend when they noted that PBMs are under a consolidation trend with insurers opening their own PBMs to more effectively control costs, as well as gain them access to more patients and physicians.

As consolidation continues, a *Becker's Hospital Review* article (Haefner, 2018) stated that OptumCare is employing a huge amount of all employed doctors and scaring both Kaiser and hospitals in general. Insurer United is said to direct its insured customers toward its acquired physicians. So, it can be seen that insuring populations corporately controlled leads to greater administrative control over physician behaviors, along with their prescribing, all adding more layers of cost.

PBMs control prescription drug benefits for employers, insurers, and the CMS. Since their early stages, firms have sought to negotiate discounts with pharmaceutical companies and establish pharmacy networks in order to implement their own created drug benefit plans. Lately with the societal concern over exorbitant drug price escalations, the "blame game" has drawn greater attention to PBMs for *not doing more* to restrain pharmaceutical manufacturer prices. Trump recognized the PBM political vulnerability and chose to leave his friends in the drug industry less culpable for high prices. Needless to say, PBMs' activities and their extra profits do create a greater patient burden from every consumed drug after the PBM pockets any discounted savings and then adds administrative overhead, which policymakers should find embarrassing for the United States compared to all other nations. Criticisms are now levied that PBMs have not done much over 20 years to restrain the consumer drug price climb, so as with many Trumpisms, it seems implausible to believe that "There is no collusion."

The healthcare industry is now awash with discontent between and among PBMs, manufacturers, hospital systems, insurers, specialty pharmacies, wholesale distributors, and chain drug stores all pointing fingers at each other over horribly high costs in the midst of their collective richly lucrative business model; this business model based upon increasing profits appears to ultimately *not benefit consumers*, nor many employers for that! Partly the long persisting "silo effect" has precluded coordination in the delivery system (fragmented doctors disconnected from pharmacies unconnected to other clinical facilities). This outmoded structure may now be giving way with industry vertical integrations. Many thinkers may see integration as the answer to the cost and quality problems, but we should ask in what ways and importantly under whose auspices and for what purposes. Integration does not by itself yield the key care coordination.

The year 2017 initiated a tidal wave of changes across the health sector. Express Scripts allegedly overcharged Anthem over several years, leading the insurer to end its outsourcing to an external PBM (Matthews, 2017). A number of new permeations in the consolidation process are rapidly proceeding—all under the banner of providing better service for less money and improved efficiency (Spitzer, 2018c). Noted from the above comment, should disbelief be warranted in more "whataboutisms"?

Anthem's deal with its IngenioRx, with CVS arranging for distribution, is said to save Anthem $4 billion annually (Haefner, 2017a, 2017b, 2017c). Firms' moves to consolidate for their own interests can be seen in the example of constructing "preferred pharmacy networks." For 2018, 99% of Medicare Part D pharmacy drug plans (PDPs) are distributed through "narrow networks" that incentivize filling of scripts at certain chosen pharmacies contracted within the network. Five giant insurers and two dominant PBMs control these networks, a corporate consolidation that again reflects taking advantage of federal Medicare funding (Fein, 2017). Restricted networks restrain pharmacist-owned stores that have historically complained that managed care arrangements are squeezing them out, while larger chain stores have gradually taken over the bulk of the ambulatory prescription market share. PBM middlemen select drugs and negotiate discounts with manufacturers and then set rates for what pharmacies are selected to be part of their networks.

The current crop of PBMs has been enlarging over time with a flurry of previous M&As and some integration. Trace back any larger company to see a history of industry amalgamations usually with support by employers, insurers, and the federal government under the Part D program. However, these earlier happenings were by no means the biggest developments to shake ups in the PBM industry; the PBM industry's current fluidity appears to be a consideration by Amazon to enter the field based upon the ongoing trajectory of this lucrative enterprise (Bond, 2018).

As the giant IT firms of US capitalism jump into health care, it is probable that their individual and collective impact will be momentous. Amazon is the "new kid on the block"—much bigger, much more powerful, and with greater ability to reshape the PBM industry due to its size, scale, and past behavior—Amazon has established pharmacy business Pill Pack as an adjunct to its e-retailing business. Existing players who realize hundreds of billions of dollars are at risk for a reinvention of the industry (Martino, 2017). Drug store stocks plummeted in June 2018 with Amazon's acquisition of PillPack after rivals had voiced fears of its entry (Kim, 2018). The adjunctive Buffett-Amazon-Dimon ("BAD") collaboration adds still the unknown unknowns since this business of health care and drugs is indeed very complicated. Remember Trump's point: "Nobody knew health care could be so complicated."

Nevertheless, the strong national brand image of Amazon, and its generational following among younger online buyers (92% of online shoppers have bought from Amazon) makes entry of competitors all but impossible. Vartorella (2018) maintains Amazon has forced established PBMs toward "bolder decisions" to rethink the value proposition in the PBM industry, according to Martino. Customer service a la Amazon will be quite a challenge for a more compelling assessment of value (Martino, 2017). Its first move into pharmaceutical distribution to hospitals was labeled "disruptive," even before the final decision was made by the company to buy PillPack to directly sell drugs to consumers. Both announcements dropped stock prices of chain drug stores and had most innovating trying to move toward improved customer service, since Amazon's entry will hit bottom lines hard and maybe remove some of their customer bases. Amazon took steps to obtain pharmacy licensing in multiple states to sell drugs online, as well as open 450 whole food pharmacies. PillPack already has those state licenses. The total market for prescription drug distribution currently is around $560 billion a year, which will give the mega Silicon Valley firm plenty of business to siphon off. The Amazon entry to become a major hospital supplier (Paavola, 2018) represents the growing hegemony of the corporate tech industry over multiple facets of American life, now analogous (but much more pervasive) to the auto industry's reshaping the society, along with American culture in the twentieth century.

Nevertheless, as a new entrant, Amazon will find that the prescription distribution market is highly complex with a huge varied number of entities in the insurance, hospital, nursing home segments, as well as 56,000 nationwide chain pharmacies (Sharif, 2017). For sure in the American retail marketplace, a cultural change has been taking place, where consumers are seemingly more demanding for quality and service, and they are armed by the Internet with much more information about products and prices. The Amazon transformation of the PBM industry would not eliminate brick and mortar stores by the chains since they can design customer experiences beyond mere mail order, so they will likely survive in some new form, particularly with their retail clinics. Yet, the might of Amazon is amazing; 354 million different products are under its warehousing, so adding 8 to 10 thousand drug entities may be easy. Moreover, Amazon is known as a highly competitive company going for scale to drive down prices (as seen in groceries), so what it does in drugs remains to be seen. Amazon is also working with Chase Bank and Berkshire Hathaway on their direct contracting scheme. Its potential entry into drug distribution may have also provoked CVS and its deal makings with Aetna, with more predictable overall changes to come.

After the failure of the Aetna-Humana combination in 2015, this large insurer waited as CVS took a long time to go for its $240 billion market combination. CVS is the number one drug store in the country with its Caremark PBM arm. The CVS/Aetna arrangement will have greater leverage over reducing Pharma prices. If the merger goes through, it will be the biggest deal of 2017: $66 billion in sales where CVS is offering a 25% premium on the stock price of Aetna. Higher drug costs have been said to be a contributing factor in this arrangement (Terlep, Matthews, & Cimilluca, 2017).

Successful PBM/insurer amalgamations can be seen in UnitedHealthcare/OptumRX with other insurers considering owning in-house PBMs rather than outsourcing (Sorkin, De la Merced, & Tsang, 2017; Grant, 2017). UnitedHealthcare, the largest insurer, has also been exploring partnering with a pharmaceutical firm. United made $50.3 billion in its third quarter, which was up to 9%, with its PBM profits reaching $1.7 billion, up to 15.7%. CVS gets more customers for its PBM out of the deal and can strengthen its retail clinics and other store activities. It represents, as several have stated, companies climbing up the "healthcare food chain" to integrate in order to grab a larger market share. Many big companies are rushing to integrate different business lines for cost efficiencies to achieve dominance in the market (Mattioli, Terlep, & Mathews, 2017).

Recently, drug stores have seen declining sales in their non-pharmacy retail operations, so the pharmacy and drug sales remain a higher percentage of their revenue (estimated up to 75% for some firms and growing lately). Of course, when customers walk in to pick up their prescriptions (rather than using mail order), they grab a shopping cart to buy sundries on the way to the back of the store. The Federal Trade Commission (FTC) intervention against horizontal mergers led Walgreens/Boots to buy only half of the Rite Aid stores across the country; this was the largest and most controversial M&A of late. Other integrated drug chain stores may now be explored and not necessarily be FTC opposed. The CVS/Aetna combination is thought to be better able to face off against not just pharmaceutical manufacturers but also the powerful giant hospital systems, both of which are on their own seeking to merge, integrate, and expand.

Humana, the $37 billion insurer heavy in the Medicare space, was unable to consummate its horizontal deal with Cigna (U.S. District Court, 2017). So Walmart ($500 billion revenues) is seeking to forge another profound shake-up in the benefit industry (Mayer, 2018). Never a paragon for its workers' health care, the giant retailer may seek to leverage its 4700 nationwide stores to provide primary care for both employees and the general public (Tracer & Hammond, 2018). By owning Humana and bypassing other insurers, Walmart can remove the middleman and deliver directly to consumers while at the same time use its massive bargaining power to lower prices (Bloomberg, 2018a, 2018b, p. 2). With the highest revenue corporation in the world, Walmart's profit fell 42.1% in the 4th quarter 2017 year over year. This mammoth is moving from merely big box to delivery of products during COVID-19, now requiring masks 6 weeks after the beginning of the outbreak.

The business press, along with the healthcare press, has lit up over all of these "disruptions" with *Modern Healthcare* declaring it "has reached its tipping point" (Disrupted, 2018). Much of the business coverage accepts the corporate line of great things to come for lower costs and improved services, though it might be advisable to remain skeptical at this point in time. Indeed, the flurry of corporate consolidation is unprecedented with the new configuration yet hard to imagine. All of these nascent marketplace developments rest essentially at the announcement stage and wait to be achieved; none at this stage appears to be easy going, given the detail of the study to mount each effort amidst complicated market dynamics, besides the regulatory oversight, though rather weak if may currently be.

Back to the PBM industry, it should be noted that these firms perform a socially necessary function in administratively handling over five billion scripts annually written by physicians and other prescribers; it surely beats the workflow inefficiency and minimizes the mistakes of pharmacist dispensing in the community setting. Given that more powerful and dangerous pharmaceuticals are regularly dispensed lately and greater numbers of patients are consuming numerous entities at the same time, PBMS have corrected or rather eased a few of the potential mishaps.

Nevertheless, the facts are that PBMs are profit-based, essentially unregulated and have tended to serve little or no outright public health functions—this undergirds a clear policy mistake under the Bush Administration for neglecting how the states might together had designed a decentralized R model in the 1990s following their history of Medicaid script processing to conduct a similar function—though publicly performed and accountable. Providers may snicker at this given the way the Medicaid program addresses drugs, but little cleanup of this Medicaid payer system has ever received adequate policy attention. All the Republican rhetoric of devolution to the states and strengthening their role in health care to be closer to people seemed not to be considered in the policy debates over Part D. But instead Bush promoted the corporate takeover of Medicare Part D drug distribution. Federal grants to upgrade the states likely would have socially cost much less than the profit streams of existing private PBMs! A large public database for pharmaco-epidemiology would have been a public health researcher's dream to improve drug usage in patients, thus potentially improving the health of the American population. Or we can wait for Amazon.

Private PBMs compete and rarely cooperate on much (except lobbying), particularly addressing the issues of rampant drug misadventuring in American society (Commonwealth Fund, 2019). The gigantic data warehouses they have amassed have *not* been fully utilized in research for the most part; academic researchers rarely get privy to their proprietary data to publish in peer-reviewed journals. Volume-driven by making money for every script processed, only their strong generic substitution has restrained drug expenditures in the past from escalating even more; deals with manufacturers to push certain pharmaceuticals on preferred lists bridged ethical lines at times. A few firms have, however, sought interventions to improve pharmaceutical care among their enrollees.

Notwithstanding, the difficulty in critically assessing this profit-driven segment in health care rests in the overall corruption of overmedicating Americans with many tie-ins to what PBMs *could be doing differently.* The huge uptick in the cultural medicalization of everyday life and social problems (Illich, 1976) contributes heavily to this phenomenon, but when profits lead, criticism, let alone insider awareness, tends to remain absent. Consider over drugging with many drug categories— amidst the current opioid epidemic—that have created a catastrophic public health crisis among school children, incarcerated minors, prisoners, and especially the elderly in nursing homes.

Summary Thoughts

When considering any assessment of a national healthcare system, it is important to distinguish between the micro and macro levels, given that most health professionals have little or no preparatory course work in health policy analysis in their education, nor much orientation through their professional associations. Nor has there been much in-depth coverage to the complexity of macro-level issues in their journals (until just recently in a select few). It is easy, therefore, to understand the lag in consciousness among professionals; many physicians have not seen clearly and thus misinterpreted much over the last couple of decades.

The corporate takeover differs from the meddling by government that always seems to create antagonisms, though the federal government often serves as an instrument for vested financial powers in health care as depicted above.

At the micro level, one can detect functioning of provider organizations, where the clinical work of practitioners takes place and involves them deeply. Questioning management actions is on this level, though not often viewed in a larger political economic context. Physicians' concern is understandably for patients and community needs—those who seek care. But they tend to see care at the level of the individual patient's presenting symptoms. Few tend to examine the larger picture of the public health realm from which patients collectively rise, though a new awareness has been provoked with COVID-19 for sure. Nor has the profession done well in assessing federal actions beyond a narrow self-interest, falling into the trap of little critique of the large medical marketplace (Sidel & Sidel, 1977).

Our nation has neglected for a long time, even given well-meaning attempts, to effectively address the greater unmet needs of the poor, minorities, LGBTQ, disabled, and other special populations despite numerous reports. In a market-based system, the indigent with often complex cases brings little of value to the transaction; thus, they are often ignored, except by the dedicated though underfunded and overwhelmed public hospitals and clinics, community health centers, and maybe select academic medical centers. By focusing on the micro level, one can however, become cognizant of the multitude of variations in our complex delivery system—from the maldistribution of resources to the diversity of population groups; such critical differences in the *nature of care delivery systems* are to be noted, though greater understanding derives from analytically viewing such developments from the larger macro level.

In contrast, this larger level is determined by the societal character; in turn, it affects all the nuances of the unique healthcare structure and the social policies that evolved historically. Service capacities can be assessed, along with the history of health policies at the national and state levels. The social epidemiology (the population's objective health needs) can be discerned to shed light to both the nature and effectiveness of health policies, the services delivered, and the overall societal character.

Here also at this level are advances in medicine, the forces of science and technology, and the roles of supply industries (in the United States, determined in the political economy of the medical-industrial complex), academic medical centers, the National Institutes of Health, Food and Drug Administration, Centers for Disease Control and Prevention, Centers for Medicare & Medicaid, philanthropic foundations, and policy research centers. Each should be examined in light of its ability to stand and serve the public's true health interests, rather than be influenced by the market structure, its corporate parties, or the political party in power. Unfortunately, individuals among this collectivity may harbor critical views of marketplace medicine, though they mostly accept the overall situation as given and immutable. Case in point is the Centers for Disease Control and Prevention under Trump!

But it is crucial to note that looking at the macro level provides us with a broader understanding of the major players and their power and influence, exerted not just in everyday life of the healthcare workforce and provider institutions but also in the setting of the tone, purpose, and direction of public policy.

Roemer's (1990) description points out that there are unique characteristics of each and every national health system across the globe. All of them struggle with resolving problems of access, cost, quality, and accountability to advance their population's health. Assessing overall system trends is important to grasping the micro and macro dynamics over time. The mode of financing health care and the share of public and private funds supporting resource allocations are important to recognize. The resolution of problems that crops up in the US healthcare system, whether concerning costs or the general effectiveness of the overall system, may depend upon popular demands for specific policy remediation. Redirections depend upon their orientation (market development vs. public health), as well as levels of sophistication, informed by critical health services research in the public interests.

To that end, we are witnessing in the national debate renewed efforts to uncover a more detailed comprehension of what has been happening. The level of health information technology has the potential to identify population disease patterns and design proper utilization of services to not only better treat but to prevent disease occurrences. Notwithstanding, it is crucial to note *who controls this technology and for whom*. In the United States and worldwide, the growing attention to analytics is crucial, both in terms of capabilities to examine sufficient Big Data for decision-making, including differentiating social determinants and demographics which remain lagging. Most importantly, *who controls the analytics work, the metrics chosen by whom*, and *how they will be used for whose purposes*? Vested corporate health interests are excited about Big Data, which should give pause to those concerned about the large public's health or, for that matter, your own health.

All across the world, information technology is entering healthcare systems to illuminate issues that were only vaguely understood. Today though, a major problem arises when American multinationals swoop down on new foreign markets with suggested national policy changes to entrench their own interests (Human Development Network, 1993). Thus, the paramount issue becomes who owns and controls the chosen analytics, for specifically questioning institutions that facilitate the influence of multinational health corporations present on new markets after privatization schemes gets encouraged to various governments.

The United States remains the largest and richest national health system; it has perhaps the highest level of science and technology across many fields. Yet, the United States will spend $4 trillion in 2020 (now approaching 20% of GNP). Its profit-based system continues to have the highest inflation rate year after year over any other nation of the world. The difference between Canada and Germany (the next highest spenders after the United States) and yet the former two provide universal coverage to their respective populations, which are healthier, but at a cost about 40% lower of what the United States spends per capita. Federal estimates of our projected growth are now being recalculated with the Trump Administration and Republican control over the Senate. Still over $10,000 dollars are spent per capita with more than 12% of Americans lacking coverage (even after Obama's ACA enrolled 20 million of the uninsured). This makes this expenditure highly problematic to government, businesses, and consumers alike. The ballooning costs affect the federal and state budgets who need to put in place austerity measures. Corporate employers have constrained their outlays for employee health and seem to have few clear options ahead.

Rather than examining the international community for ideas to develop a decent system that is more sensible, equitable, and cost-effective and move to achieve universal access, the authors believe that the Trump Administration and GOP Congress will double down on private market initiatives to "fix" what they think ails the US system, first aiming, however, to disenfranchise the indigent and then on to seniors—both considered unproductive segments of the economy. We can predict an explosion in an already bloated expenditure, as well as reduced access to more Americans. For those with current coverage, they may expect being subject to sometimes substandard, ever more expensive, and often unnecessary services while at the same time facing iatrogenic care induced by an unregulated market system tending to medicalize all that appears wrong with us. This is not a hopeful scenario.

Conclusion

Health care in America is solidly corporate; most Americans may agree that profit seems to drive the healthcare delivery system, including providers, insurance companies, PBMs, chain drug stores, and peripheral supply firms, such as the pharmaceutical industry. Their collective purpose appears *not* to be enhancing the entire populous' health by assuring access to needed services, nor especially concerned with raising the larger public health condition through other measures. This is not so easy to state since most physicians and practitioners have devoted their careers to serving their patients and many provider institutions do seek to perform to their utmost under challenging circumstances to serve their communities. Notwithstanding, corporate dominance in American health care and trends in public policy often act against the interests of health professionals (e.g., MACRA) with policies that greatly influence behaviors.

In the 1860s, Marx made the point that today remains critical: production thus produces consumption. When we examine modern medicine, it is important to note that true health needs in the population are grossly obscured by mere medical care utilization; here, Illich's conception of social iatrogenesis appears crucial. What has evolved institutionally with the offered commodified form of medical services does not truly address a patient's health and well-being, nor a population's health. The definition of health has been argued and debated over time as the content of modern medicine has been critiqued (Kelman, 1975; Illich, 1976; Zola, 1972; Salmon, 1985).

We wish readers to ponder a newer broader concept of public health as they examine our writing: the sustenance of well-being among the entire population—apart from the clinical condition of a single individual patient's designated services. This assumes the social, political, economic, and ecological contexts of life for varying cohorts in our society and across the world; thus, a strong commitment to health and health care as a basic human right is fundamental.

References

Abelson, R., & Creswell, J. (2018). The Disappearing doctor: How mega-mergers are changing the business of medical care. https://www.nytimes.com/2018/04/07/health/health-care-mergers-doctors.html. Accessed 19 June 2020.

Anderson, J. (2020). Coronavirus is giving online higher education a second chance to prove its worth. Quartz. Available via DIALOG. https://finance.yahoo.com/news/coronavirus-giving-online-higher-education-141850370.html. Accessed 16 June 2020.

Bannow, T. (2002). Pandemic could lead more hospitals to breach debt covenants. https://www.modernhealthcare.com/finance/pandemic-could-lead-more-hospitals-breach-debt-covenants. Accessed 19 June 2020.

Barkholz, D. (2016). Special deals, circumstances propel healthcare CEO pay. https://www.modernhealthcare.com/article/20160416/MAGAZINE/304169933/special-deals-circumstances-propel-healthcare-ceo-pay. Accessed 19 June 2020.

Barkholz, D. (2017a). Tenet CEO Fetter stepping down; company adopts poison pill. https://www.modernhealthcare.com/article/20170831/NEWS/170839967/tenet-ceo-fetter-stepping-down-company-adopts-poison-pill. Accessed 19 June 2020.

Barkholz, D. (2017b). There's no quick turnaround for next tenet CEO. https://www.modernhealthcare.com/article/20170901/NEWS/170909980/there-s-no-quick-turnaround-for-next-tenet-ceo. Accessed 19 June 2020.

Bender, R. (2019). *Bayer shares fall after jury finds exposure to roundup helped trigger cancer.* Available at: https://www.wsj.com/articles/bayer-shares-fall-after-legal-setback-on-roundup-weedkillers-11553077610. Accessed 11 Oct 2020.

Berkrot, B. (2016). *Global prescription drug spend seen at $1.5 trillion in 2021: Report.* Available at: https://www.reuters.com/article/us-health-pharmaceuticals-spending/global-prescription-drug-spend-seen-at-1-5-trillion-in-2021-report-idUSKBN13V0CB. Accessed 11 Oct 2020.

Bloomberg, M. R. (2018a). Walmart said to be in talks with Humana to provide health care. *Fortune.* Available via DIALOG. http://fortune.com/2018/03/30/walmart-humana-merger/. Accessed 9 July 2018.

Bloomberg, M. R. (2018b). Google turns its back on America's security. *Chicago Tribune.* Available via DIALOG. http://www.chicagotribune.com/news/opinion/commentary/ct-per-spec-google-artificial-intelligence-national-security-project-maven-america-0607-story.html. Accessed 24 Aug 2018.

Bond, S. (2018). *Amazon's ever-increasing power unnerves vendors.* Available via DIALOG. https://www.ft.com/content/c82ce968-bc8a-11e8-94b2-17176fbf93f5. Accessed 23 July 2020.

Brady, M. (2019). CMS will crack down on nursing home inspectors. *Modern Healthcare.* Available via DIALOG. https://www.modernhealthcare.com/safety-quality/cms-will-crack-down-nursing-home-inspectors. Accessed 16 June 2020.

Bulik, B. S. (2020). *Pharma sees more post-M&A rebrands than other industries—and it does them better, too.* https://www.fiercepharma.com/marketing/pharma-leads-industry-rebrands-new-research-assessing-pros-and-cons-name-changes-after-m. Accessed 11 Oct 2020.

Button, K. (2018). Healthcare private equity investments were up in 2017, despite Obamacare uncertainty. *Mergers & Acquisitions.* Available via DIALOG. https://www.themiddlemarket.com/news/private-equity-investing-in-healthcare-rises. Accessed 9 July 2018.

Carey, K. (2020). As states' revenue disappears, so might the 'public' in public colleges. *The New York Times.* Available via DIALOG. https://www.nytimes.com/2020/05/05/upshot/public-colleges-endangered-pandemic.html. Accessed 16 June 2020.

Casson, J. E., & McMillen, J. (2003). Protecting nursing home companies: Limiting liability through corporate restructuring. *Journal of Health Law, 36*(4), 577–613.

Castellucci, M. (2018). Most skilled-nursing facilities penalized by CMS for readmission rates. *Modern Healthcare.* Available via DIALOG. https://www.modernhealthcare.com/safety-quality/coronavirus-outbreak-live-updates-covid-19. Accessed 16 June 2020.

Cavendish, C. (2020). The old are not equally vulnerable to COVID-19. *Financial Times.* Available via DIALOG. https://www.ft.com/content/1daf4e40-9046-11ea-bc44-dbf6756c871a. Accessed 16 June 2020.

Cenziper, D., Jacobs, J., & Mulcahy, S. (2020). Nearly 1 in 10 nursing homes nationwide report Coronavirus cases. *The Washington Post.* Available via DIALOG. https://www.washingtonpost.com/business/2020/04/20/nearly-one-10-nursing-homes-nationwide-report-coronavirus-outbreaks/. Accessed 16 June 2020.

Cenziper, D., Whoriskey, P., Mulcahy, S., & Jacobs, J. (2020). As nursing home residents died, new covid-19 protections shielded companies from lawsuits. Families say that hides the truth.

The Washington Post. https://www.washingtonpost.com/business/2020/06/08/nursing-home-immunity-laws/ Accessed 19 June 2020.

Chaffee, M. (2016). Why giant hospital systems might be getting it wrong. https://www.linkedin.com/pulse/why-giant-hospital-systems-might-getting-wrong-michelle-chaffee. Accessed 19 June 2020.

Chant, B. J. (2019). Nursing home abuse. Lawyers.com. Available via DIALOG. https://blogs.lawyers.com/attorney/personal-injury/nursing-home-abuse-4-52562/. Accessed 1 Feb 2019.

Cherney, E. (2020). DePaul students demand refunds. *Chicago Tribune*. Available via DIALOG. https://www.chicagotribune.com/coronavirus/ct-coronavirus-illinois-depaul-lawsuit-tuition-20200514-33ktvf6rm5eztjxromo4mrspaa-story.html. Accessed 17 June 2020.

Chicago Tribune Editorial Board. (2020a). A nursing assistant strike. *Chicago Tribune*. Available via DIALOG. https://www.chicagotribune.com/opinion/editorials/ct-editorial-coronavirus-nursing-homes-strike-threat-20200429-3hw3fi6py5fitc2notv76t274a-story.html. Accessed 16 June 2020.

Chicago Tribune Editorial Board. (2020b). Blaming politicians for nursing home deaths? Big picture required. *Chicago Tribune*. Available via DIALOG. https://www.chicagotribune.com/opinion/editorials/ct-editorial-nursing-homes-illinois-covid-20200520-3ms3d2i4xvfjjad7tof4cur2jm-story.html. Accessed 16 June 2020.

Coley, C. M., & Wolfe, S. M. (Eds.). (1981). *Pills that don't work: A consumers' and doctor's guide to over 600 prescription drugs that lack evidence of effectiveness*. Chicago, IL: Grand Central Publishing.

Commonwealth Fund. (2019). *Pharmacy benefit managers and their role in drug spending*. https://www.commonwealthfund.org/publications/explainer/2019/apr/pharmacy-benefit-managers-and-their-role-drug-spending. Accessed 12 Oct 2020.

Cookson, C. (2018). Cutting-edge treatment heralds era of cancer genetics. *Financial Times*. Available via DIALOG. https://www.ft.com/content/a020c084-4a3e-11e8-8c77-ff51caedcde6. Accessed 4 Sept 2019.

Coyne, M. (2020). Report: Chicago's cook county jail home to the largest Coronavirus cluster outbreak in the U.S. *Forbes*. Available via DIALOG. https://www.forbes.com/sites/marley-coyne/2020/04/08/report-chicagos-cook-county-jail-home-to-the-largest-coronavirus-cluster-outbreak-in-the-us/#289dd96a1bac. Accessed 16 June 2020.

Cramer, M. (2020). Philadelphia hospital to stay closed after owner requests nearly $1 million a month. https://www.nytimes.com/2020/03/27/us/coronavirus-philadelphia-hahnemann-hospital.html. Accessed 19 June 2020.

Crow, D. (2018). *Billionaire Sackler family owns second opioid drugmaker*. Available at: https://www.ft.com/content/2d21cf1a-b2bc-11e8-99ca-68cf89602132. Accessed 11 Oct 2020.

Cubanski, J., Neuman, T., & Freed, M. (2019). *The facts on medicare spending and financing*. Available at: https://www.kff.org/medicare/issue-brief/the-facts-on-medicare-spending-and-financing/. Accessed 11 Oct 2020.

Cunningham, P. W. (2019). *The Health 202: Trump and Pelosi are still working on a drug pricing deal despite impeachment drama*. Available at: https://www.washingtonpost.com/news/powerpost/paloma/the-health-202/2019/10/23/the-health-202-10232019-health202/5daf1b5a602ff10cf14f969f/. Accessed 11 Oct 2020.

Davenport, C. (2018). Scott Pruitt, Trump's rule-cutting E.P.A. chief, plots his political future. https://www.nytimes.com/2018/03/17/climate/scott-pruitt-political-ambitions.html. Accessed 20 June 2020.

Dayen, D. (2019). Betsy Devos quietly making it easier for dying for-profit schools to rip off a few more students on the way out. https://theintercept.com/2019/04/12/betsy-devos-for-profit-colleges/. Accessed 19 June 2020.

Deloitte. (2018a). Life sciences- Interjective guidance on going concern. *Deloitte*. Available via DIALOG. https://www2.deloitte.com/us/en/pages/audit/articles/life-sciences-accounting-and-financial-reporting-update-including-interpretive-guidance.html. Accessed 9 July 2018.

Deloitte. (2018b). 2018 life sciences accounting and financial reporting update. *Deloitte*. Available via DIALOG. https://www2.deloitte.com/us/en/pages/audit/articles/life-sciences-accounting-and-financial-reporting-update-including-interpretive-guidance.html. Accessed 9 July 2018.

Diamond, F. (2018). Opioid deaths among women not getting the attention they warrant. *Managed Care*. Available via DIALOG. https://www.managedcaremag.com/archives/2018/4/opioid-deaths-among-women-not-getting-attention-they-warrant. Accessed 26 Apr 2019.

Duhigg, C. (2007). At many homes, more profit and less nursing. *The New York Times*. Available via DIALOG. https://www.nytimes.com/2007/09/23/business/23nursing.html. Accessed 20 July 2020.

Duhigg, C. (2018). The case against Google. *The New York Times*. Available via DIALOG. https://www.nytimes.com/2018/02/20/magazine/the-case-against-google.html. Accessed 24 Aug 2018.

Dusetzina, S. B., Keating, N. L., & Huskamp, H. A. (2019). Proposals to redesign medicare part D — easing the burden of rising drug prices. *The New England Journal of Medicine*, 381, 1401–1404.

Edelweiss. (2019). *Pharmacovigilance and pharmacoepidemiology*. Edelweiss Publications. Available via DIALOG. http://edelweisspublications.com/journals/33/Pharmacovigilance-and-Pharmacoepidemiology. Accessed 18 Nov 2019.

Edlavitch, S. A., & Salmon, J. W. (2006). Drug safety within drug use. *Disease Management, 9*(5), 259–265.

Eilperin, J., Dennis, B., & Dawsey, J. (2018). Scott Pruitt's job in jeopardy amid expanding ethics issues. *The Washington Post*. Available via DIALOG. https://www.washingtonpost.com/news/energy-environment/wp/2018/04/05/top-epa-ethics-official-says-he-lacked-key-facts-about-pruitts-condo-rental/?noredirect=on&utm_term=.0db5c3eec1cb. Accessed 9 July 2018.

Ellison, A. (2019). Tower health points to Epic install costs for operating loss. *Becker's Hospital Review*. Available via DIALOG. https://www.beckershospitalreview.com/finance/tower-health-points-to-epic-install-costs-for-operating-loss-021319.html. Accessed 28 Feb 2019.

Evans, M. (2016a). Community health systems retrenches. https://www.wsj.com/articles/community-health-systems-retrenches-1476091800. Accessed 19 June 2020.

Evans, M. (2016b). Nonprofit hospitals adjust strategy to draw investors. https://www.wsj.com/articles/nonprofit-hospitals-adjust-to-attract-investors-1463563802. Accessed 19 June 2020.

Facher, L. (2020). Pharma is showering congress with cash, even as drug makers race to fight the coronavirus. Available at: https://www.statnews.com/feature/prescription-politics/prescription-politics/. Accessed 11 Oct 2020.

Fein, A. J. (2017). Exclusive: Preferred pharmacy networks will dominate 2018 Medicare part D plans (Plus: We review the top plan sponsors). *Drug Channels*. Available via DIALOG. https://www.drugchannels.net/2017/10/exclusive-preferred-pharmacy-networks.html. Accessed 1 Feb 2019.

Feinglass, J., & Salmon, J. W. (1994). The use of medical management information systems to increase the clinical productivity of physicians. In J. W. Salmon (Ed.), *The corporate transformation of health care: Perspective & implications*. Amityville, NY: Baywood.

Fields, R. (2010). "God help you. You're on Dialysis." *The Atlantic*. Available via DIALOG. https://www.theatlantic.com/magazine/archive/2010/12/-god-help-you-youre-on-dialysis/308308/. Accessed 1 Feb 2019.

Financial Times. (2017). CVS/Aetna: Vertically challenged. *Financial Times*. Available via DIALOG. https://www.ft.com/content/7bf82588-d911-11e7-a039-c64b1c09b482. Accessed 6 Aug 2018.

Fincham, J. E., & Wertheimer, A. I. (1991). *Pharmacy and the U.S. healthcare system*. Binghamton, NY: Pharmaceutical Products.

Flaccus, G., & Gecker, J. (2020). 'I just can't do this' some overwhelmed parents are opting to abandon pandemic homeschooling. *Flipboard*. Available via DIALOG. https://flipboard.com/article/i-just-can-t-do-this-some-overwhelmed-parents-are-opting-to-abandon-pandemic-h/a-p8Qq-epuTjaua50lMDmNDA%3Aa%3A3195429-a4427b8445%2Ftime.com. Accessed 16 June 2020.

Flessner, D. (2019). *These are the top nursing home chains in the U.S.* Available at: https://www.timesfreepress.com/news/edge/story/2019/apr/01/these-are-top-nursing-home-chains-us/491406/. Accessed 12 Oct 2020.

Fortune. (2020). *Fortune 500 list.* Available at: https://fortune.com/fortune500/2020/search/. Accessed 11 Oct 2020.

Gittlen, S. (2017). Survey snapshot: Deep frustration with the current payment system. *NEJM Catalyst.* Available via DIALOG. https://catalyst.nejm.org/deep-frustration-current-payment-system/. Accessed 5 Apr 2018.

Global Reports Store. (2019). Global biosimilars market is estimated to grow at a CAGR +6% by 2025. *Globe News Wire.* Available via DIALOG. https://www.globenewswire.com/news-release/2019/07/05/1878827/0/en/Global-Biosimilars-Market-Is-Estimated-to-Grow-at-a-CAGR-of-6-by-2025-Top-Companies-are-Pfizer-Sandoz-Teva-Pharmaceuticals-Amgen-Biocon-Dr-Reddy-s-Laboratories-Celltrion.html. Accessed 18 Nov 2019.

Goldstein, M., Silver-Greenberg, J., & Gebeloff, R. (2020). Setting aside quality care for profit. *The New York Times.* Available via DIALOG. https://www.nytimes.com/2020/05/07/business/coronavirus-nursing-homes.html. Accessed 16 June 2020.

Gooch, K. (2015). Top 10 trends shaping the health industry in 2016. *Becker's Hospital Review.* Available via DIALOG. https://www.beckershospitalreview.com/hospital-management-administration/top-10-trends-shaping-the-health-industry-in-2016.html. Accessed 5 Apr 2018.

Gooch, K. (2020). 14 hospital, health system CEO moves. *Becker's Hospital Review.* Available via DIALOG https://www.beckershospitalreview.com/hospital-executive-moves/13-hospital-health-system-ceo-moves.html. Accessed 20 July 2020.

Gotsch, K., & Basti, V. (2018). Capitalizing on mass incarceration U.S. growth in private prisons. *The Sentencing Project.* Available via DIALOG. https://www.sentencingproject.org/publications/capitalizing-on-mass-incarceration-u-s-growth-in-private-prisons/. Accessed 17 June 2020.

Grant, C. (2017). Drug price squeeze is driving CVS and Aetna talks. *The Wall Street Journal.* Available via DIALOG. https://www.wsj.com/articles/drug-price-squeeze-is-driving-cvs-and-aetna-talks-1509054691. Accessed 1 Feb 2019.

Green, E. L. (2020a). U.S. officials ease rules on student aid as colleges close down campuses. *The New York Times.* Available via DIALOG. https://www.nytimes.com/2020/03/10/us/politics/coronavirus-colleges.html. Accessed 16 June 2020.

Green, E. L. (2020b). DeVos funnels coronavirus relief funds to favored private and religious schools https://www.nytimes.com/2020/05/15/us/politics/betsy-devos-coronavirus-religious-schools.html?auth=login-email&login=email. Accessed 19 June 2020.

Grocer, S. (2019). *Big pharma's hunt for new drugs is pushing up cost of deals.* Available at: https://www.nytimes.com/2019/02/28/business/dealbook/pharmaceutical-biotech-acquisitions.html. Accessed 11 Oct 2020.

Haefner, M. (2017a). Aetna CEO: Talking on Apple's business model a 'real deal'. *Becker's Hospital Review.* Available via DIALOG. https://www.beckershospitalreview.com/payer-issues/aetna-ceo-taking-on-apple-s-business-model-a-real-deal.html. Accessed 6 Aug 2018.

Haefner, M. (2017b). Anthem launches in-house pharmacy business with CVS health after express scripts fallout. *The New York Times.* Available via DIALOG. https://www.nytimes.com/2017/10/18/health/anthem-cvs-pharmacy.html. Accessed 1 Feb 2019.

Haefner, M. (2017c). CVS Health to pay Aetna $2.1B if deal fails: 3 things to know. *Becker's Hospital Review.* Available via DIALOG. https://www.beckershospitalreview.com/payer-issues/cvs-health-to-pay-aetna-2-1b-if-deal-fails-3-things-to-know.html. Accessed 6 Aug 2018.

Haefner, M. (2018). With 8k more physicians than Kaiser, Optum is 'scaring the crap out of hospitals'. *Becker's Hospital Review.* Available via DIALOG. https://www.beckershospitalreview.com/payer-issues/with-8k-more-physicians-than-kaiser-optum-is-scaring-the-crap-out-of-hospitals.html. Accessed 9 July 2018.

Healy, J., Richtel, M., & Baker, M. (2020). New guideline as virus devastates nursing homes: No more visitors. *The New York Times*. Available via DIALOG. https://www.nytimes.com/2020/03/10/us/coronavirus-nursing-homes-washington-seattle.html.   Accessed 16 June 2020.

Himmelstein, D. U., & Woolhandler, S. (2016). Public health's falling share of US health spending. American Journal of Public Health, 106(1), 56–57.

Himmelstein, D. U., Woolhandler, S., Almberg, M., & Fauke, C. (2018). The ongoing U.S health care crisis: A data update. https://pubmed.ncbi.nlm.nih.gov/29566642/. Accessed 19 June 2020.

Hoffman, J. (2019). *Johnson & Johnson's sinking PR from its opioid involvement*. Available at: https://www.nytimes.com/2019/08/26/health/oklahoma-opioids-johnson-and-johnson.html. Accessed 11 Oct 2020.

Hoy, E. W., & Gray, B. H. (1986). *For profit enterprise in health care*. Washington, DC: National Academy Press.

Hubler, S. (2020). At colleges this fall, a patchwork of plans, but will students be there? *The New York Times*. https://www.nytimes.com/2020/05/14/us/college-coronavirus-fall.html. Accessed 17 June 2020.

Illich, I. (1976). *Medical nemesis: The expropriation of health*. London, England.

Inserro, A. (2018a). By 2026, national health spending will climb to 19.7% of economy, report says. AJM.com. Available via DIALOG. http://www.ajmc.com/newsroom/by-2026-national-health-spending-will-climb-to-197-of-economy-report-says-. Accessed 5 Apr 2018.

Inserro, A. (2018b). Americans used less care in 2016 but healthcare costs still soared, report says. *AJMC*. Available via DIALOG. https://www.ajmc.com/newsroom/americans-used-less-care-in-2016-but-healthcare-costs-still-soared-report-says. Accessed 19 July 2020.

IQVIA. (2018a). U.S. nursing home market summary. *IMS Health & Quintiles are now IQVIA*. Available via DIALOG. http://www.skainfo.com/reports/u.s.-elder-care-market-summary. Accessed 1 Feb 2018.

IQVIA. (2018b). Top 50 medical group parents. *IMS Health & Quintiles are now IQVIA*. Available via DIALOG. http://www.skainfo.com/reports/top-50-medical-group-parents. Accessed 1 Feb 2018.

Ivory, D. (2020). 'We are not a hospital': Inside a prison on edge. *The New York Times*. Available via DIALOG. https://www.nytimes.com/2020/03/17/us/coronavirus-prisons-jails.html. Accessed 16 June 2020.

Ivory, D., Protess, B., & Palmer, G. (2016). In American towns, pumping private profit from public works. *The New York Times*. Available via DIALOG. https://www.nytimes.com/2016/12/24/business/dealbook/private-equity-water.html. Accessed 1 Feb 2019.

Ivory, D., & Williams, T. (2020). Jail in Chicago is top U.S. hot spot with more than 350 confirmed cases. The New York Times. Available via DIALOG. https://www.nytimes.com/2020/04/08/us/coronavirus-cook-county-jail-chicago.html. Accessed 16 June 2020

Jack, A., & Smyth, J. (2020). Universities face harsh pandemic lesson. *Financial Times*. https://www.ft.com/content/0ae1c300-7fee-11ea-82f6-150830b3b99a. Accessed 16 June 2020.

Jackson, D., & Ariza, M. (2019). Nursing Home Mogul Philip Esformes sentenced to 20 years for $1.3 billion Medicaid Fraud. https://www.chicagotribune.com/investigations/ct-philip-esformes-sentenced-nursing-home-fraud-20190912-cumxa7wwb5do7iekg32h2o5thy-story.html. Accessed 20 July 2020.

Japsen, B. (2018). Urgent care industry hits $18 billion as big players drive growth. *Forbes Pharma and Healthcare*. Available via DIALOG. https://www.forbes.com/sites/bruce-japsen/2018/02/23/urgent-care-industry-hits-18b-as-big-players-drive-growth/#3f4cc2f54d89. Accessed 9 July 2018.

Johnson, C. K. (2016). Study: 7 of 10 most profitable hospitals are nonprofits. https://apnews.com/8867beb032c049378e4a83d150cb8bc3/study-7-10-most-profitable-us-hospitals-are-non-profits. Accessed 19 June 2020.

Johnson, C. Y. (2017). Why CVS Health would want to buy Aetna. *The Washington Post*. Available via DIALOG. https://www.washingtonpost.com/news/wonk/wp/2017/10/26/why-cvs-health-would-want-to-buy-aetna/?utm_term=.2ea24c95e1d1. Accessed 6 Aug 2018.

Johnson, W. C., Brennan, N., Rodriquez, S., & Hargraves, J. (2018). *Consistently high turnover in the group of top health care spenders*. Health Care Cost Institute. Available via DIALOG. https://catalyst.nejm.org/high-turnover-top-health-care-spenders/. Accessed 5 Apr 2018.

Kacik, A. (2017a). Emerging integrated PBM model could pose threat to hospitals. *Modern HealthCare*. Available via DIALOG. http://www.modernhealthcare.com/article/20171102/NEWS/171109974. Accessed 6 Aug 2018.

Kacik, A. (2017b). Tenet to cut regional management layer in reorganization. https://www.modernhealthcare.com/article/20171006/NEWS/171009938/tenet-to-cut-regional-management-layer-in-reorganization. Accessed 19 June 2020.

Kacik, A. (2017c). C-suite pay raises target transformational healthcare leaders. *Modern Healthcare*. Available via DIALOG. https://www.modernhealthcare.com/article/20170814/NEWS/170819972/c-suite-pay-raises-target-transformational-healthcare-leaders. Accessed 20 July 2020.

Kacik, A. (2019). *New nursing home payment model kicks in next month*. Available at: https://www.modernhealthcare.com/providers/new-nursing-home-payment-model-kicks-in-next-month. Accessed 12 Oct 2020.

Kacik, A. (2020a). Scope-of-practice bills stoke debate over caregivers' roles. *Modern HealthCare*. Available via DIALOG. https://www.modernhealthcare.com/operations/scope-practice-bills-stoke-debate-over-caregivers-roles. Accessed 3 Apr 2020.

Kacik, A. (2020b). Pandemic proves to be pivotal moment for senor care. https://www.modernhealthcare.com/post-acute-care/pandemic-proves-be-pivotal-moment-senior-care. Accessed 19 June 2020.

Kacik, A., & Livingston, S. (2018). Disrupted: American healthcare has reached its tipping point. *Modern Healthcare*. Available via DIALOG. http://www.modernhealthcare.com/article/20180203/NEWS/180209961. Accessed 9 July 2018.

Kalish, B. M. (2017). The year in healthcare: A focus on cost management. *Employee Benefit News*. Available via DIALOG. https://www.benefitnews.com/news/the-year-in-healthcare-a-focus-on-cost-management. Accessed 12 Apr 2018.

Kamp, J. (2020). Coronavirus deaths in U.S nursing, long-term-care facilities top 50,000. *The Wall Street Journal*. Available via DIALOG. https://www.foxbusiness.com/healthcare/coronavirus-deaths-in-u-s-nursing-long-term-care-facilities-top-50000. Accessed 16 June 2020.

Kamp, J., & Mathews, A. W. (2020). Coronavirus deaths in U.S. nursing, long-term care facilities top 10,000. *The Wall Street Journal*. Available via DIALOG. https://www.wsj.com/articles/coronavirus-deaths-in-u-s-nursing-long-term-care-facilities-top-10-000-11587586237. Accessed 16 June 2020.

Kelman, S. (1975). The social nature of the definition problem in health. https://journals.sagepub.com/doi/10.2190/X5H6-TC5W-D36T-K7KY. Accessed 19 June 2020.

Kim, T. (2018). Walgreens, CVS and Rite-Aid lose $11 billion in value after Amazon buys Online Pharmacy PillPack. https://www.cnbc.com/2018/06/28/walgreens-cvs-shares-tank-after-amazon-buys-online-pharmacy-pillpack.html. Accessed 20 July 2020.

Klein, N. (2020). Under cover of mass death, Andrew Cuomo calls in the billionaires to build a high-tech dystopia. https://theintercept.com/2020/05/08/andrew-cuomo-eric-schmidt-coronavirus-tech-shock-doctrine/. Accessed 19 June 2020.

Kolodner, M., & Burtrymowicz, S. (2020). *Could the online, for-profit college industry be "a winner in this crisis"?* Available at: https://hechingerreport.org/could-the-online-for-profit-college-industry-by-a-winner-in-this-crisis/. Accessed 12 Oct 2020.

Lauerman, J., Ring, S., & Hammond, E. (2020). AstraZeneca eyes Gilead in big pharma's move beyond Covid. *Bloomberg*. Available via DIALOG. https://www.bloomberg.com/news/articles/2020-06-07/big-pharma-looks-beyond-covid-with-astrazeneca-eyeing-gilead. Accessed 16 June 2020.

Liu, F., & Salmon, J. W. (2010). Comparison of herbal medicines regulation between China, Germany, and the United States. *Integrative Medicine: A Clinician's Journal, 9*(6), 42–49.

Livingston, S. (2020). COVID-19 may end up boosting value-based payment. https://www.modernhealthcare.com/insurance/covid-19-may-end-up-boosting-value-based-payment. Accessed 19 June 2020.

Love, J. (2019). Why didn't nonprofits and the NIH require 'reasonable' pricing for Zolgensma? That may happen in France. *Stat News*. Available via DIALOG. https://www.statnews.com/2019/09/18/zolgensma-reasonable-pricing-france/. Accessed 18 Nov 2019.

Lovrien, L. C., & Peterson, L. C. (2016a). Creating market relevance: Six steps to build first touch strategies. *Becker's Hospital Review*, pp. 1–2 https://www.beckershospitalreview.com/hr/creating-market-relevance-6-tips-to-build-1st-touch-strategies.html. Accessed 20 June 2020.

Lovrien, L. C., & Peterson, L. C. (2016b). Five tips to build urgent care and fulfill your populations' needs. *Urgent Care Partners*, pp. 1–6 https://www.beckershospitalreview.com/hospital-physician-relationships/5-tips-to-build-urgent-care-and-fulfill-your-populations-needs.html. Accessed 20 June 2020.

Mancini, D.P., Cocco, F., & Shubber, K. (2020) Prisons worldwide braced for surge in cases. *Financial Times*. Available via DIALOG. https://www.ft.com/content/23611814-6ac1-11ea-800d-da70cff6e4d3. Accessed 16 June 2020.

Martino, W. (2017). Ready or not, Amazon is coming. *MM &M*. Available via DIALOG. https://www.mmm-online.com/home/channel/technology/ready-or-not-amazon-is-coming/. Accessed 1 Feb 2019.

Massoudi, A., Fonatanella-Khan, J., & Kuchler, H. (2019). Roche to buy Spark Therapeutics in 63 billion deal. *Financial Times*. Available at: https://www.ft.com/content/282dc5e4-38d2-11e9-b72b-2c7f526ca5d0. Accessed at: October 11, 2020

Master, R. (2017). Marketplace forces can't fix broken health care system. *The Express-Times*. Available via DIALOG. https://www.lehighvalleylive.com/opinion/index.ssf/2017/08/marketplace_forces_cant_fix_br.html. Accessed 9 July 2018.

Masterson, L. (2018). Labor, administrative costs drive UD healthcare spending far beyond other nations. *Healthcare Dive*. Available via DIALOG. https://www.healthcaredive.com/news/labor-administrative-costs-drive-us-healthcare-spending-far-beyond-other-n/518994/. Accessed 5 Apr 2018.

Mathews, A. W. (2017). Anthem to launch its own pharmacy-benefit manager. Available at: https://www.wsj.com/articles/anthem-signs-five-year-deal-with-cvs-for-services-to-new-pharmacy-benefit-manager-ingeniorx-1508326194?

Mattioli, D., Terlep, S., & Mathews, A. W. (2017). CVS Makes Blockbuster Aetna Bid. *The Wall Street Journal*. Available via DIALOG. https://www.wsj.com/articles/cvs-health-is-in-talks-to-buy-aetna-sources-1509047642. Accessed 20 July 2020.

Mayer, K. (2018). How a Walmart-Humana deal could shake up the benefits industry. *Benefit News*. Available via DIALOG. https://www.benefitnews.com/news/how-a-walmart-humana-deal-could-shake-up-benefits-industry. Accessed 9 July 2018.

McKeown, T. (1971). A historical appraisal of the medical task. In G. McLachlan & T. McKeown (Eds.), *Medical history and medical care: A symposium of perspectives*. New York: Oxford University Press.

McKinlay, J. (Ed.). (1984). *Issues in the political economy of health*. New York, NY: Tavistock.

McKinlay, J. B., & McKinlay, S. (1977). The questionable contribution of medical measures to the decline of mortality in the United States in the twentieth century https://www.milbank.org/quarterly/articles/the-questionable-contribution-of-medical-measures-to-the-decline-of-mortality-in-the-united-states-in-the-twentieth-century/. Accessed 19 June 2020.

McKinlay, S., & McKinlay, J. B. (1979, November). Examining trends in the nation's health. Paper presented at the American Public Health Association Annual Meeting, New York.

Milani, K. (2019). Pharmaceutical mergers and megamergers stifle innovation. Available via DIALOG. https://www.statnews.com/2019/07/10/pharmaceutical-mergers-stifle-innovation/. Accessed 19 July 2020.

Minhaj, H. (2020, June 15). Is College still worth it? *You Tube*.

Modern Healthcare. (2017). Q&A with Ubi: Accelerate competition to slow drug price increases. *Modern Healthcare*. Available via DIALOG. https://www.modernhealthcare.com/article/20170803/NEWS/170809956/q-a-with-ubl-accelerate-competition-to-slow-drug-price-increases. Accessed 26 Apr 2018.

Modern Healthcare. (2018a). Largest healthcare investment banks. Ranked by the amount of loans underwritten in 2017. *Modern Healthcare*, p.29.

Modern Healthcare. (2018b, March). Largest security breaches of electronic health records: Reported 2017 HER security breach incidents, ranked by number of individuals affected. *Modern Healthcare*, p. 5.

Modern Healthcare. (2018c). 'We don't think the status quo is acceptable.' *Modern Healthcare*. Available via DIALOG. https://www.pressreader.com/usa/modern-healthcare/20180521/281857234192686. Accessed 6 Aug 2018.

Modern Healthcare. (2018d). We're no.1... in healthcare spending. *Modern Health Care*, p. 21.

Modern Healthcare. (2018e). Lower utilization slowed health spending growth in 2017. *Modern Healthcare*. Available via DIALOG. https://www.modernhealthcare.com/article/20181206/NEWS/181209951/lower-utilization-dampened-health-spending-growth-in-2017. Accessed 26 Apr 2019.

Modern Healthcare Systems Financial Database. (2020). Health systems with largest private equity investments. https://www.modernhealthcare.com/hospitals/numbers-health-systems-largest-private-equity-investments-2020. Accessed 19 June 2020.

Morgenson, G. (2017). Defiant, generic drug maker continues to raise prices. *The New York Times*. Available via DIALOG. https://www.nytimes.com/2017/04/14/business/lannett-drug-price-hike-bedrosian.html. Accessed 4 Sept 2019.

MSNBC. (2020). *Transcript: Into coronavirus and the classroom: The biggest online learning experiment ever*. Available at: https://www.msnbc.com/podcast/transcript-coronavirus-classroom-biggest-online-learning-experiment-ever-n1236816. Accessed 12 Oct 2020.

Nash, D. (2018). Ten trends to watch in 2018. *Medpage Today*. Available via DIALOG. https://www.medpagetoday.com/publichealthpolicy/healthpolicy/70421. Accessed 12 Apr 2018.

Newman, S.A. (2019). The biotech-industrial complex gets ready to define what is human. *Counter Punch*. Available via DIALOG. https://www.counterpunch.org/2019/08/16/the-biotech-industrial-complex-gets-ready-to-define-what-is-human/. Accessed 17 Oct 2019.

Office of Public Affairs. (2017). *U.S district court blocks Aetna's acquisition of Humana*. Department of Justice. Available via DIALOG. https://www.justice.gov/opa/pr/us-district-court-blocks-aetna-s-acquisition-humana. Accessed 9 July 2018.

Oliver J. (2017). The danger of "WhatAbout-ism" arguments, last night tonight. *HBO*. https://www.youtube.com/watch?v=RS82JNd0YzQ. Accessed 20 July 2020.

Ollove, M. (2019). To control drug prices, states may have to face off against feds. Available via DIALOG https://www.pewtrusts.org/en/research-and-analysis/blogs/stateline/2019/02/01/to-control-drug-prices-states-may-have-to-face-off-against-feds. Accessed 19 July 2020.

Ornstein, C., & Sanders, T. (2020). Nursing homes violated basic health standards, allowing the Coronavirus to explode. *ProPublica*. Available via DIALOG. https://www.propublica.org/article/nursing-homes-violated-basic-health-standards-allowing-the-coronavirus-to-explode. Accessed 16 June 2020.

Outsourcing Resources 2019. (2019). Advancing development and manufacturing pharmaceutical technology. http://files.alfresco.mjh.group/alfresco_images/pharma//2019/08/12/5ba3e6af-4161-4974-a376-ed29b50c68f2/PharmTech_NA_Outsourcing_Supp2019_wm.pdf. Accessed 19 June 2020.

Paavola, A. (2018). 61% of hospital leaders say single-payer would help lower healthcare costs. *Becker's Hospital Review*. Available via DIALOG. https://www.beckershospitalreview.com/payer-issues/61-of-hospital-leaders-say-single-payer-would-help-lower-healthcare-costs.html. Accessed 15 Mar 2019.

Pear, R. (2018). New law expands Medicare benefits of patients fighting chronic illnesses. *The New York Times National*.

Philippidis, A. (2019). Top 15 best-selling drugs of 2018. *Genetic Engineering & Biotechnology News*. Available via DIALOG. https://www.genengnews.com/a-lists/top-15-best-selling-drugs-of-2018/. Accessed 4 Sept 2019.

Pierson, R., & Banerjee, A. (2016). *Pfizer boosts cancer drug roster with 14 billion Medivation deal*. https://www.reuters.com/article/us-medivation-m-a-pfizer-idUSKCN10W0YG. Accessed October.

Powles, J. (1973). On the limitations of modern medicine. *Science, Medicine, and Man, 1*, 1–30.

PR Newswire. (2020). Active pharmaceutical ingredients (API) market analysis, growth rate, industry drivers & opportunities report, 2028: radiant insights, Inc. https://news.yahoo.com/active-pharmaceutical-ingredients-api-market-085000450.html. Accessed 20 June 2020.

Qato, D., Daviglus, M. L., Wilder, J., Lee, T., Qato, D., & Lambert, B. (2014). 'Pharmacy deserts' are prevalent in Chicago's predominantly minority communities, raising medication access concerns. *Health Affairs, 33*(11), 1958–1965. https://doi.org/10.1377/hlthaff.2013.1397

Rau, J. (2017). Care suffers as more nursing homes feed money into corporate webs. Available via DIALOG. https://khn.org/news/care-suffers-as-more-nursing-homes-feed-money-into-corporate-webs/. Accessed 20 July 2020.

Rau, J. (2018). 'It's almost like a ghost town.' Most nursing homes overstated staffing for years. *The New York Times*. Available via DIALOG. https://www.nytimes.com/2018/07/07/health/nursing-homes-staffing-medicare.html. Accessed 1 Feb 2019.

Reilly, K. (2020). 'There has to be a plan.' For relatives of nursing home residents, anger and worry as the Coronavirus spreads. *TIME*. Available via DIALOG. https://time.com/5799096/coronavirus-nursing-homes-elderly/. Accessed 16 June 2020.

Reuters (2019). FTC requests AbbVie, Allergan for more information on Reuters. Available via DIALOG. https://www.reuters.com/article/us-allergan-m-a-abbvie/ftc-requests-abbvie-allergan-for-more-information-on-63-billion-deal-idUSKBN1WC2DQ. Accessed 18 November 2019

Rockoff, J. D., & Stevens, L. (2017). Amazon's Push into pharmacy business is full of promise and pitfalls. *Wall Street Journal*. Available via DIALOG. https://www.wsj.com/articles/amazons-push-into-pharmacy-business-is-full-of-promise-and-pitfalls-1509188400. Accessed 14 Feb 2020.

Roland, D. (2018). Pfizer, Glaxo to create over-the-counter drug giant. Available at: https://www.wsj.com/articles/glaxo-pfizer-to-combine-consumer-health-care-businesses-in-a-jv-11545205647. Accessed 11 Oct 2020.

Roland, D., & Loftus, P. (2016). Insulin prices soar while drug makers' share stays flat. *The Wall Street Journal*. Available via DIALOG. https://www.wsj.com/articles/insulin-prices-soar-while-drugmakers-share-stays-flat-1475876764. Accessed 16 June 2020.

Rowland, C. (2020). *A race is on to make enough small glass vials to deliver coronavirus vaccine around the world*. Available at: https://www.washingtonpost.com/business/2020/07/13/coronavirus-vaccine-corning-glass/. Accessed 11 Oct 2020.

Salmon, J. W. (1985). Profit and health: Trends in corporatization and proprietarization. *International Journal of Health Services, 15*(4), 395–418.

Salmon, & Gutkin. (2021). In press.

Salmon, J. W. (2017a). Trump on drugs, part 1. *Health Management*, 17(2), 1–10. Available at: https://healthmanagement.org/c/healthmanagement/issuearticle/trump-on-drugs-part-1. Accessed 14 Oct 2020.

Salmon, J. W. (2017b). Trump on drugs, part 2. *Health Management*, 17(2), 1–18. Available at: https://healthmanagement.org/c/healthmanagement/issuearticle/trump-on-drugs-part-2. Accessed 14 Oct 2020.

Scheer, S., & Rabinovitch, A. (2017). *Teva faces weakening prices in the U.S., hurting profits*. Available on: https://www.reuters.com/article/us-teva-pharm-ind-results/teva-faces-weakening-prices-in-the-u-s-hurting-profits-idUSKBN1AJ1L5. Accessed 11 Oct 2020.

Schencker, L. (2018). Walgreens' value plummets by $6B. *Chicago Tribune*. Available via DIALOG. http://digitaledition.chicagotribune.com/tribune/article_popover.aspx?guid=e3df1d 0a-2876-4b5a-8222-2807c43cf98a. Accessed 6 Aug 2018.

Schorsch, K. (2017). Why for-profit hospitals in Chicago are losing. https://www.modernhealth-care.com/article/20171002/NEWS/171009998/why-for-profit-hospitals-in-chicago-are-losing. Accessed 19 June 2020.

Scott, D. (2017). *Drug industry unveils massive new campaign to counter criticism*. Available at: https://www.statnews.com/2017/01/23/phrma-drug-industry-marketing-campaign/. Accessed 11 Oct 2020.

Sharif, R. (2017). Amazon's disruptive move into pharmaceuticals. *LinkedIn*. Available via DIALOG. https://www.linkedin.com/pulse/amazons-disruptive-move-pharmaceuticals-raja-sharif?trk=portfolio_article-card_title. Accessed 1 Feb 2019.

Sidel, V. W., & Sidel, R. (1977). *A healthy state: An international perspective on the crisis in the United States Medical Care*. New York, NY: Pantheon.

Silverman, E. (2017). Pharma gift-giving sways practitioners and physician assistants, too. *Stat News*. Available via DIALOG. https://www.statnews.com/pharmalot/2017/10/25/pharma-gifts-nurse-practitioners-physician-assistants/. Accessed 4 Sept 2019.

Silverman, E. (2019a). Lawmakers ask FTC to scrutinize pharma mergers over antitrust concerns. *Stat News*. Available via DIALOG. https://www.statnews.com/pharmalot/2019/09/17/ffc-anti-trust-pharma-mergers/. 18 Nov 2019.

Silverman, E. (2019b). More countries are banning or restricting sales of Zantac and others heartburn meds. *Stat News*. Available via DIALOG. https://www.statnews.com/pharma-lot/2019/09/23/zantac-ranitidine-fda-ndma-countries/. Accessed 19 Nov 2019.

Silverman, E. (2019c). Mylan pays $30 million to settle charges of misleading investors over probe into EpiPen Medicaid rebates. *STAT*. Available via DIALOG. https://www.statnews.com/phar-malot/2019/09/27/mylan-epipen-medicaid-probe-investors/. Accessed 17 Oct 2019.

Skapinker, M. (2018). EpiPen dearth shows company and regulator failure. *Financial Times*. Available via DIALOG. https://www.ft.com/content/ace14442-c568-11e8-8670-c5353379f7c2. Accessed 16 June 2020.

Sorkin, A. R., De la Merced, M. J., & Tsang, A. (2017). CVS and Aetna talks take place under Amazon's shadow: Dealbook briefing. *The New York Times*. Available via DIALOG. https://www.nytimes.com/2017/10/27/business/dealbook/cvs-aetna-amazon.html. Accessed 1 Feb 2019.

Spitzer, J. (2018c). Push to reduce ED visits leads patients to urgent care, retail clinics- not tele-health. *Becker's Hospital Review*. Available via DIALOG. https://www.beckershospitalreview.com/payer-issues/push-to-reduce-ed-visits-leads-patients-to-urgent-care-retail-clinics-not-telehealth.html. Accessed 15 Mar 2019.

Sweeney, J. F. (2018). Value-based care: It's not going away this year. Medicaleconomics.com. Available via DIALOG. http://medicaleconomics.modernmedicine.com/medical-economics/news/why-value-based-care-not-going-away-year. Accessed 5 Apr 2018.

Talbot, M. (2018, April 2). Dirty politics. Scott Pruitt's E.PA is giving even ostentatious polluters a reprieve. *The New Yorker*.

Terhune, C. (2016). *Consumer group questions role of drug costs in California premium hikes*. Available at: https://khn.org/news/consumer-group-cries-foul-on-premium-hikes-by-major-insurers-in-california/. Accessed 11 Oct 2020.

Terlep, S., Mathews, A. W., & Cimilluca, D. (2017). CVS to buy Aetna for $69 billion, com-bining major health-care players. https://www.wsj.com/articles/cvs-to-buy-aetna-for-69-bil-lion-1512325099. Accessed 20 June 2020.

Thomas, K. (2019). *Novartis hid manipulated data while seeking approval for $2.1 million treat-ment*. Available at: https://www.nytimes.com/2019/08/06/health/novartis-fda-gene-therapy.html. Accessed 17 Apr 2019.

Toich, L. (2017a). Bill introduced in congress seeks to improve pharmacy access in underserved areas. *Specialty Pharmacy Times*. Available via DIALOG. https://www.specialtypharmacy-times.com/news/bill-introduced-in-congress-seeks-to-improve-pharmacy-access-in-under-served-areas. Accessed 6 Aug 2018.

Toich, L. (2017b). Growth in average health care cost per employee driven by specialty drugs. Specialty Pharmacy Times. Available via DIALOG. https://www.specialtypharmacytimes.com/news/growth-in-average-health-care-cost-per-employee-driven-by-specialty-drugs. Accessed 5 Apr 2018.

Tracer, Z., & Hammond, E. (2018). Walmart in talks with Humana for deeper partnership. *Bloomberg*. Available via DIALOG. https://www.bloomberg.com/news/articles/2018-03-29/walmart-is-said-to-be-in-early-talks-with-humana-wsj-reports. Accessed 9 July 2018.

Vela, L. (2019). *Reducing wasteful spending in employers' pharmacy benefit plans*. Available at: https://www.commonwealthfund.org/publications/issue-briefs/2019/aug/reducing-wasteful-spending-employers-pharmacy-benefit-plans. Accessed 11 Oct 2020.

Vogenberg., R., & Smart, M. (2018). Regulatory change versus legislation impacting health care decisions and delivery. https://www.ncbi.nlm.nih.gov/pmc/articles/PMC5737251/. Accessed 20 June 2020.

Weaver, C. (2020). Graduates' dreams lie in tatters as pandemic scars domestic job market. *Financial Times*. Available via DIALOG. https://www.ft.com/content/da1018d4-dfb6-4239-b391-8df74d27ed75. Accessed 16 June 2020.

Wechsler, J. (2018). Pandemic fears stoke calls for new vaccines and global health initiatives. *BioPharm*. Available via DIALOG. http://www.biopharminternational.com/pandemic-fears-stoke-calls-new-vaccines-and-global-health-initiatives. Accessed 9 July 2018.

White, W. D., Salmon, J. W., & Feinglass, J. (1994). The changing doctor-patient relationship and performance monitoring: An agency perspective. In J. W. Salmon (Ed.), *The corporatization of health care: Perspectives an implications*. Amityville, NY: Baywood.

Wu, T. (2017). How to stop price gouging. https://www.nytimes.com/2017/04/20/opinion/how-to-stop-drug-price-gouging.html. Accessed 19 July 2020.

Wynn, M. (2017). By the numbers: Big jump in nursing home complaints. *MedPage Today*. Available via DIALOG. https://www.medpagetoday.com/publichealthpolicy/by-the-numbers/68386. Accessed 1 Feb 2019.

Yin, A. (2020). Effort seeks stricter nursing home regulation. *Chicago Tribune*. Available via DIALOG. https://www.chicagotribune.com/coronavirus/ct-coronavirus-pandemic-chicago-illinois-news-20200506-cfvfioulyrc23pfp3xxpghcmk4-story.html. Accessed 16 June 2020.

Young, L. (2005). A bad case of sticker shock. *Bloomberg Businessweek*. https://www.bloomberg.com/news/articles/2005-10-23/a-bad-case-of-sticker-shock

Young, Q. (1997). *Personal communication with Stephen Thompson*, Interview for Dissertation.

Zola, I. K. (1972). Medicine as an institution of social control. *The Sociological Review*, 20, 487–504.

Chapter 3
Medical Practice: From Cottage Industry to Corporate Practice

The American medical profession faces much alteration in what they do as practicing physicians that has been felt as an impingement upon their professional autonomy. As more and more physicians transition from private practice controlled by them and their colleagues to employment within large healthcare organizations controlled by an administrative class, their discontent over there loss of status has been evident. The discontent in the profession will be reviewed while examining trends in the supply of physicians, income, specialty practices, and the significant change in moving from independent practice to wage-contract conditions as employees. This set of issues will be seen in light of the overall corporatization of medicine with its new structures being put in place by the Affordable Care Act aka Obamacare and private corporate interests. Such alterations in medical practice and its resulting discontent will likely be the prelude to the next medical malpractice insurance crisis.

General Practitioners and the Push to Specialize

Many academics have studied the profession of medicine over time as well as the changes that have occurred over time since the Civil War in the United States. It's interesting to note that in the United States, the field of medicine has been allowed to grow unfettered particularly when it comes to the delineation between what is considered primary care and what is called a specialty. An 1866 report from the AMA Committee on Ethics as well as an 1875 report of a committee of the Medical Society of the State of New York highlights the issue of clinical specialism could be excessively narrow, create a mechanism to accentuate the specific disease that was covered by the specialty, and dismiss the treatment of the general practitioner as being not appropriate (Stevens, 1971). Clearly as time progressed the tension between specialists and general practitioners continued to be debated with resultant outcome of more and more medical school graduates choosing the more lucrative specialty practice over becoming a general practitioner or in today's world a primary

© Springer Nature Switzerland AG 2021   115
J. W. Salmon, S. L. Thompson, *The Corporatization of American Health Care*,
https://doi.org/10.1007/978-3-030-60667-1_3

care physician. As time has progressed, this bifurcation has been exacerbated by the twin phenomenon of great accelerating medical school tuition with subsequent huge increases in medical student debt and a pay differential that made specialty practice much more financially lucrative as well as intellectually challenging for those who also sought academic status where specialists often practiced. The prestige of the specialist was much greater than the general practitioner (GP)/primary care provider (PCP) always.

The Profession Advances

So how did the practice of medicine evolve from what was deemed a cottage industry of a solo practitioner traveling the countryside to attempt to treat the ill? In the 1800s there were no shortage of individuals that passed themselves off as physicians which included people who had been trained in various disciplines including but not limited to homeopaths, naturopaths, osteopaths, and allopaths. The term cottage industry arose from the notion that physicians practiced either in their own home or in their patient's homes. At that time there was no support staff nor need for any capital equipment to treat patients—it was a physician and his senses (Salmon, White, & Feinglass, 1994). As demand for services rose, it became necessary to increase the number of practitioners in the field which attracted all manner of individuals into the field, some appropriate and others not. This led to substandard schools and practices that led one to question the basis of the field as well as its ability to deliver on its promise of curing the sick. In 1910 the *Flexner Report* clamped down on the nature of medical education particularly in the area of who was considered a proper medical school. The report served to provide a detailed exposé of medical education by actually naming schools in attempt to bring attention to the horrible condition of some of these schools (Flexner, 1910). While the primary thrust of the report was to serve notice to the field and in particular the medical schools needed to provide scientific excellence in its training programs, it seems that most of the schools considered substandard and thus slated for closure were those serving African Americans and women. As Stevens points out, as tuition increased, the program became longer, and the night schools disappeared, it became increasingly difficult for those students without means to enter the field and complete a program in medicine (Stevens, 1971). On the other hand, Starr believes that the number of medical schools had begun to decline prior to the *Flexner Report* going from a high of 162 in 1906 to 131 in 1910. He attributes this to the increasing role of state licensure boards which caused the opportunity costs for would-be physicians to increase substantially (Starr, 1982). The outcome was to significantly reduce the number of medical schools and thus the number of physicians who could train in those medical schools to become physicians.

Stevens points out that the curriculum to become a physician had become fairly predictable as determined by the universities providing medical education under the auspices of the AMA Council on Medical Education which mandated a year of internship post-medical school and then state licensure board exams. From there the student had a choice of going into private practice as a general practitioner or continuing their training to become a specialist. While nothing prohibited one from calling themselves a specialist without training as one, it became more common practice to actually continue training through an approved residency that was approved by specialty boards that were outside the AMA's purview (Stevens, 1971). These were felt to be more "professional clubs" and not overseers of medical care quality, nor were they seen as protectors of the public.

With the reduction in available schools and the barriers to entry created by state licensure boards created a situation in which demand for physician services would soon exceed the supply of those eligible to treat patients. During the 1920s and 1930s, the cost rise is partly attributed to that as well as what was termed a rising medical potential which was defined as a chance that a physician could actually cure a patient. This in turn created an increase in the public's expectations of care along with increases in specialists, and the usual culprits of technology and medication. Because of the reduction in supply of physicians coupled with limited options for patients, they had no choice but to acquiesce to the control of the physician and do what was prescribed no matter the cost (Stevens, 1971). And with physicians increasing authority came the ability to both stimulate and restrict the market for medical services. With authority and market control, the discussion began to center around physicians' authority over the practice of medicine and what it meant for the rest of us. Starr defines two types of authority in the practice of medicine: social and cultural. The social authority was the power of the physician to get others (nurses, etc.) to do what they ordered to happen. It also includes getting patients to do as they are told in respect to the physicians' order. On the other hand, cultural authority was the acceptance of physicians as the one being able to make binding judgments concerning what constitutes sickness, whether a person is physically and mentally fit to work, and whether or not a person is disabled and to pronounce whether or not a person has died (Starr, 1982). To that end the medical profession has historically enjoyed exclusive authority over judgments about the quality and cost-effectiveness of diagnostic and therapeutic services initiated under physician orders (Feinglass & Salmon, 1994).

The downside to these authorities was that the practice of medicine had become more and more reliant on access to capital equipment through hospitals and other organizations which ultimately make them vulnerable to those who supply the capital (Starr, 1982). At the same time, both types of authority changed somewhat as we entered the twentieth century as the fundamental physician-patient relationship was superseded by the need to hold the "necessary credentials and institutional affiliations" (Starr, 1982). Both the practice and outcomes of medicine had become prescribed for more so than any time previously as a result of actions taken by the professional society, the American Medical Association, and the state through licensure boards.

The need for physicians to affiliate with a hospital became more and more acute as the science of medicine advanced in the 1930s. As a result, physician hegemony began to weaken as hospital administration began to exert authority over their organizations, especially beginning with Blue Cross financing. As Starr points out, the split between administrative and clinical oversight became more pronounced with the main difference being that physicians continued to see hospitals as adjuncts to their private office practices, while administrators began to see that they were part of a larger community and beholden to the public interest in providing health services to that community (Starr, 1982). As Stevens points out, this role conflict was a push for professional independence at a time when the demand for "increasing institutionalism, group payments, and the provision of service through specialists and teams" was becoming the norm in these organizations (Stevens, 1971). And costs continued to escalate as a result of the increasing complexity of practice and organization.

As Stevens saw it, the conflict boiled continued to boil down to a demand for professional autonomy and the "privilege of a responsible profession to regulate its members and to dictate its destiny, as indeed it did in the educational area." Arrayed against this concept of professionalism was the public's right to intervene in the provision of that service versus how much authority and responsibility should be ceded to physicians in carrying out the public's interest (Stevens, 1971). Rather than change their approach to physician practice to accommodate the changing organizational realities, the AMA instead sought to block any and all attempts that emanated outside their ranks (Stevens, 1971). As the concept of private practice remained mostly intact through the 1950s and 1960s, the public and outside interests were beginning to mobilize to bring the profession of medicine into compliance with what was more needed to serve the public's interest and/or as was emerging the larger corporate interests.

But different interpretations of the evolution of medicine emerged. Vicente Navarro states that "the evolution of medicine (including its recent corporatization) is viewed as the outcome of power relations defined not by the majority of Americans but by a series of conflicts between classes, races, genders, and other power groupings, within a matrix of dominant-dominated relations, in which dominance is reproduced by coercion and repression, and not merely by persuasion" (Navarro, 1984). Events since 1984 seem to bear that out with several developments occurring that have challenged physicians' traditional authority. They are deprofessionalization, proletarianization, and corporatization (Light & Levine, 1994). Deprofessionalization is the loss of control over the conception and execution of their work, meaning they no longer retain authority over what gets done and when it gets done. Proletarianization is the process of moving from self-employment to employee status, and corporatization brings the practice of medicine under the control of corporate ownership or oversight. To that end, Strobeck believes that increasing bureaucratization of physician practice has allowed their work to be commoditized just like every other healthcare professional in the organization (Strobeck, 1990).

This corporate capture of the medical profession has led to what Braverman described as the separation of conception from execution. Back when physicians were solo or part of small group practices, they decided what to do and how to do it. As more and more physicians have been captured as employees within healthcare organizations, their ability to fully conceive their work has been usurped by corporate interests which have always valued the bottom line first and foremost. Their ability to execute has always been limited by standard operating procedures and clinical guidelines and checklists. Physicians have become highly paid technicians within a larger structure that seeks to minimize their ability to practice medicine freely without constraint (Braverman, 1974). Stoeckle goes on to reinforce that notion stating that "medical practice is now more commercial, competitive and corporatized, with physicians hired as employees to provide services, a trend fostered by a larger supply of physicians than in the past. More treatment is being used with more physicians' work becoming only technical in nature, 'deskilled,' and no longer a mix of science and art. Lastly, more of the doctor's decision making is being standardized and monitored, and is no longer discretionary and personal" (Stoeckle, 1994). Of course, the profession has not gone quietly as physicians have long resisted attempts to standardize health care, claiming the profession is too complex to make things like practice guidelines practically for anything but the most rudimentary issues (Salmon, White, & Feinglass, 1994). The mystery of medicine or the concept of medicine as an art has always been used to allow physicians to stay independent much longer than might have been predicted 50 years ago.

What Is a Professional?

The field of medicine and physicians specifically are often looked at as the quintessential profession and professional. The concept of noblesse oblige, which is nobility that extends beyond mere entitlements to fulfill social obligations natural to their position, seems appropriate here. Clearly physicians have held a special place in society and that remains true today. But what are the more specific tenants of what a professional is? Kirk has defined these as possessing the following characteristics (Kirk, 2007):

- Member of a special group after obtaining advance or specialized training.
- Possesses skills based upon theoretical knowledge, education, and training.
- Competency is assured through the passing of examination.
- A specific ethical code of conduct exists.
- Active professional association which furthers the profession in the political arena and the organization's professional practice to protect professional turf.
- Seeks recognition from his peers.
- Controls over conception and execution of job responsibilities.
- Licensure through states allows for control of both entry and practice and who can call themselves a physician in exchange for acting on as an agent for the patient's best interests in a market that has huge information inequality between buyers and sellers.

As Dean Baker states, the state medical societies' control over licensure boards as well as supply of physicians in states particularly flies in the face of the notion of a free market for physician labor. He cites the economic protectionism that increases physician salaries in some cases twice what they are in other first-world countries. He states that "Under current rules, foreign doctors would get arrested for practicing in the United States unless they complete a U.S. residency program." This protectionism costs us around $100 billion a year in higher healthcare costs. And he ironically points out that these physicians also pay higher costs to obtain care for themselves and their families (Baker, 2017). Elton Rayack said as much 50 years ago when he pointed out the seeming contradiction of a professional organizations desired to maintain quality standards of practice while at the same time further and improve the economic conditions of practice (Rayack, 1967). This dual role allows the profession to restrict the supply of all manner of professional services while increasing the income of those authorized to practice. This can lead to behaviors that one would associate with monopoly rent seeking. While organized medicine has the power to set professional standards for physicians to ostensibly protect the public over time, they have been shown to have abused that trust in pursuing an agenda that works to increase the "incomes, power and prestige of its members" (Rayack, 1967).

In typical market transactions, both buyer and seller of any goods or service possess near equal amounts of information of what they are exchanging. Health care and in particular medicine possess an asymmetry of information available to buyers and sellers of these services, and as a result the state licenses these professionals to act in the best interest of their patients in terms of quality care rather than their own economic interests in running up the bill. The notion of occupational licensure as a way to protect us the public from substandard practitioners is a quaint one. As the licensure boards have shown over and over, they are there to engage in restricting entry into the profession as well as restrict who can call themselves a physician and perform procedures and duties that have been left solely to those who call themselves physicians (Rayack, 1967). Friedman goes on to state that "Licensure is the key to A.M.A. power." While the profession would argue that only physicians should sit on licensure boards and in judgment over other physicians, what has happened over time is protectionist behaviors and too few doctors ever losing their licenses for behaviors unbecoming of a physician. While physicians as a whole are considered to be rather conservative politically, they would never think to subject themselves to conservative Milton Friedman's cure which is to do away with occupational licensure and let the market decide who the competent practitioners are in the community (Friedman, 1962). One of the prime reasons for physician licensure was to protect the patient-consumer in any transaction with a physician because of information asymmetry which has been slightly reduced over time due to patient activation as well as a number of sources (mostly online) that act to inform patients of their options regarding treatment from their physicians.

Physician Supply

For many years prior to the 1960s, the AMA through its medical education oversight attempted to keep the number of medical students low to suppress the supply of physicians in an attempt to provide decent incomes for existing physicians (Rayack, Professional Power And American Medicine: The Economics Of The American Medical Association, 1967; Friedman, 1962). Beginning in the mid-1960s, the AMA's ability to limit entry into the profession was challenged by a competitive fringe, i.e., the number of US medical students and foreign medical graduates (FMGs) began to increase the overall supply of physicians (Noether, 1986). Fast-forward to the present, and we see a 30 percent increase in first-year medical school slots with most of that growth occurring in the public sector (62%) and most of that occurring in the Southern United States (44%) (Association of American Medical Colleges, 2014). The growth in public medical school enrollment might lead one to believe that those graduates could theoretically pursue careers in primary care or fields with lower salaries as a result of not having the same debt load upon graduation (Washko, Snyder, & Zangaro, 2015).

But the primary care shortage continues to persist such because there is no national healthcare plan for staffing this vital role in the system. Given the rather large debt that most medical school graduates incur, there is a financial incentive to practice specialty medicine because of the higher pay. Some solutions that have been proposed to alleviate the primary care shortage include increasing the salaries of primary care physicians. Angelis likens the current situation as follows:

> If the health needs of the population were to be shown on a triangle, the base and upward would be for primary care, the middle for secondary (subspecialty) care, and the apex for tertiary care. However, if that same triangle were to display the salaries of those providing the care, it would be turned upside down. While subspecialists deserve higher salaries, a two- to three-fold difference is simply neither fair nor sustainable, as the consequences for primary care needs have shown. If the reimbursement issue were resolved, the problems of lifestyle and prestige would likely be mitigated. (Angelis, 2016)

An increasing number of medical school graduates who opt for specialization have done one thing that the market could not do, and that is they have weakened the AMA since most specialists identify with their professional organizations rather than the generalist AMA. The AMA has become much more of a diffuse power as more and more physicians opt out of AMA membership. This in turn has lessened their political clout as the AMA represents fewer and fewer doctors over time which in turn has caused a relative deterioration in physicians' social and economic positions. That deterioration may cause a newly minted physician to reassess their self-interests and upon the corporate interests assailing the profession with more concern (Feinglass, Physicians As Employees: Stanley Wohl And The Medical Industrial Complex, 1990).

Threats to Physician Professionalism and Autonomy: Rise of the Healthcare Super-Administrator and Other Dissatisfactions

As previously mentioned threats to the field of medicine have been going on for at least the last 70 years or more and until recently have been successfully defended from any and all comers. But as time progressed, the money in the healthcare sector became more and more significant. This in turn brought increasing pressure on physicians to acquiesce financial authority over health care which created threats to their professional sovereignty as well as a loss of professional autonomy. These threats centered around three main areas:

- Economic alienation when they made the transition from independent practitioners to employees with a change in loyalty from the profession to that of the organization that now employed them
- Organizational alienation which included the administrative oversight of physicians within the hierarchy that centered around improving productivity and efficiency
- Technical alienation which caused them to lose their ability to decide diagnosis and treatment options for their patients (Haug, 1976)

In reality, physicians' patients were no longer "their" patients. Patients or covered lives were controlled by the patient's insurance company and/or the healthcare organization that contracted with that insurance company to care for their clients. The physician has merely become an adjunct to that contractual obligation and care.

Friedberg et al. found eight significant findings in his physician satisfaction survey that centered on what physicians are satisfied with and what they are dissatisfied with (Friedberg et al., 2013):

- Quality of care
- Electronic health records
- Autonomy and work control
- Work quantity and pace
- Work content, allied health professionals, and support staff
- Payment, income, and practice finances
- Regulatory and professional liability concerns
- Health reform

Since this study was done after the passing of the Affordable Care Act but prior to its implementation, one could infer that physicians just didn't know what the ultimate effect would be. But administrative emergence, rise, and oversight with its huge cost and perceived waste are at the heart of a lot of physician complaints. Morra et al. quantifies this as follows:

- The United States spends roughly $82,975 per physician per year dealing with payers, compared with $22,205 per physician per year in Ontario, Canada.

- If US physicians were spending what the Ontario physicians were spending dealing with payers, the total savings would be around $27.6 billion per year.
- US nurses and medical assistants spent 20.6 h per physician per week dealing with health plan administration vs. 2.5 h by Canadian nurses and medical assistants. Of that 20.6 h, US nurses and medical assistants spent around 13.1 h per physician per week obtaining prior authorizations.
- Time spent submitting quality time was minimal in both the United States and Canada (Morra et al., 2011).

One should note that administrative oversight issue is not necessarily a United States-only issue. Physicians in the United Kingdom have seen what has been termed a "striking transformation in the last decade"—increasing market pressures along with increasing public oversight which has fundamentally changed the practice of medicine from what was termed a "state-sanctioned collegial self-regulated" profession to one that is a "state-directed bureaucratic regulation" (Waring, Dixon-Woods, & Yeung, 2010).

Movement of Physicians from Independent and/or Small Group Practices to Employees: The Separation of Conception from Execution

The demise of the independent and small group practice has been going on for many years now with an acceleration of the movement of physicians from independent practitioners outside of the organizations they controlled to employees of those organizations with the loss of autonomy and professionalism that goes with that shift. In 2007, a Center for Studying Health System Change study found that the number of physicians in solo or two-physician practices decreased from 40.7 to 32.5 percent of practices between 1996 and 2005 (Liebhaber & Grossman, 2007). The trend was most definitely toward employment and seemed more marked for specialists and older physicians. At that time the movement away from 2-doctors-or-fewer practices was toward specialty groups of 6 to 50 physicians. So the term employee in this context by and large meant working in a larger physician practice owned by another physician or group. By 2016 the number of small group practices continued their decline with the number of practices with 9 or fewer doctors dropped from 40.1 percent in 2013 to 35.3 percent 2 years later, while even larger groups of 100 or more increased from 29.6 percent to 35.1 percent (Muhlestein & Smith, 2016).

One of the prime drivers behind this phenomenon was the increasing costs associated with administering a practice. As was discussed in the previous section, modern medical practice not only includes increasing clinical requirements but also more and more administrative requirements fueled by insurance companies and government. This results in squeezed practice margins which makes it less economically feasible to practice in a solo or small group practice. At the same time, large group practices and hospital ownership of practices have increased by 86% since

2012. In 2012, roughly 14% of physician practices were owned by hospitals, but by 2015 that number had increased to around 25% of practices (Physicians Advocacy Institute, 2016). The Physicians Advocacy Institute confirmed these trends when it stated that "hospital ownership of practice has increased by 86% in the past three years" (Physicians Advocacy Institute, 2016). The numbers go from 1 in 7 practices that were owned by hospitals in 2012 to 1 in 4 in mid-2015 for what they said was a total of 67,000 hospital-owned physician practices (Physicians Advocacy Institute, 2016).

While issues with insurance can consume quite a lot of hours to process, quality measures as mandated by various organizations and the CMS are beginning to consume more and more resources and time. Casalino et al. state that physician practices in four common specialties take up around 785 h per physician per year and consume more than $15.4 billion in processing claims (Casalino et al., 2015). Woolhandler and Himmelstein take this a step further when they quantified how much time physicians spend on administrative tasks and then related it to their career satisfaction (Woolhandler & Himmelstein, 2014). They found that the average doctor spends 8.7 h per week (out of a 52 h average work week) or 16.6% on administrative tasks. Psychiatrists were found to spend the most time (20.3%), followed by internists, family/general practitioners (17.3%), and pediatricians (14.1%). They found that those physicians who worked in large practices, hospital-owned practices, and those who possessed financial incentives to reduce services spent the most time on administrative work and that increased usage of electronic health records was associated with a greater administrative burden. Lastly they found that this increased administrative burden tended to lower physician career satisfaction, even when controlling for income and other factors.

Organizations should take notice of the administrative burdens they put on their physicians to make sure that they are not spending time in areas that they are not equipped to handle, could be handled by other personnel, and most importantly detract from the clinical practice that most physicians entered the profession to do.

Physician Burnout

Sexton et al. and Vincent et al. have stated that the increasing pressures on physicians to provide high-quality health care as resources continue to decline will cause more and more stress on practitioners and reduce overall satisfaction in their profession (Sexton, Thomas, & Helmreich, 2000; Vincent, Moorthy, Sarker, Chang, & Darzi, 2004). Of course these pressures strike directly at the heart of a profession that has always enjoyed near complete autonomy. It is those restrictions that, coupled with a myriad of changes that are mostly out of the control of the average physician, have led to conditions described as physician burnout. A recent survey of 17,236 physicians by the Physicians Foundation found several troubling trends that may bolster the argument that physicians are indeed burning out at a higher than expected rate (The Physicians Foundation, 2016). The highlights of this report are:

- 54% of physicians rate their morale as somewhat or very negative.
- Only 37% describe their feelings about the future of the medical profession as positive.
- 49% often or always experience feelings of burnout.
- 49% would not recommend medicine as a career to their children.
- 80% of physicians are overextended or at capacity, with no time to see additional patients.
- 72% indicate that external factors such as third-party authorizations significantly detract from the quality of care they are able to provide.
- 20% of physicians practice in groups of 101 doctors or more, up from 12% in 2012.
- 17% of physicians are in solo practice, down from 25% in 2012. 48% of physicians plan to cut back on hours, retire, take a non-clinical job, switch to "concierge" medicine, or take other steps limiting patient access to their practices.
- Only 44% of physicians believe hospital employment of doctors is a positive trend.
- Only 11% of physicians say electronic health records (EHRs) have improved patient interaction, while 60% say they have detracted from patient interaction.
- 71% of physicians describe "patient relationships" as the most satisfying aspect of medical practice, while 58% say "regulatory/paperwork burdens" are the least satisfying.

These numbers seemed to have grown worse in several areas since a similar survey done in 2014 (*Health Affairs*, 2016). The data above seem to indicate that the profession may be in crisis, but one does wonder if physicians will make good on their threats to respond to this "professional burnout" by actually leaving the practice of medicine to pursue other opportunities. Given the amount of time, money, and energy that physicians have invested in their profession, it seems highly unlikely that those skills are transferrable to any other profession, particularly one that pays as much as medicine does. So what can be done? A couple of issues related to the concepts of practitioner resilience seems to be key in how well practitioners respond to loss of autonomy and other stressors (Gittell, 2016). Waddimba found that "more resilient practitioners experience frequent satisfaction, relational needs gratification, better uncertainty tolerance, lighter workloads and practiced on units with more colleagues" (Waddimba et al., 2016).

On the flipside it appears that those physicians who are burned out and depressed with issues of poor self-care have a higher association with being more dissatisfied with the profession. There remain many factors contributing to burnout, and the phenomenon varies among the different segments of the profession. Generally, the dysfunctional healthcare system and its increasing bureaucratization, including EHRs, has most to do with the changing nature of doctoring (Bendix & Lutton, 2020). Loss of autonomy, erosion of trust, and moral injury also come into play. This can lead to "diminished physician concentration, effort, empathy, and professionalism. This results in misdiagnoses and other medical errors, a higher rate of inappropriate referrals and prescriptions, lower patient satisfaction and adherence to physician recommendations, and worse physician performance in areas not observed by others" (Casalino & Crosson, Physician Satisfaction and Physician Well-Being: Should Anyone Care?, 2015). Blumenthal and Squires believe that several factors are causing physician burnout issues.

Demands from many stakeholders for cost and quality data, health system complexity including many different reimbursement schemes, and the poor implementation of electronic health records seem to be contributing to physician dissatisfaction and burnout (Blumenthal & Squires, 2016). However, Tarcan et al. seem to think that while there are unclear factors causing physician burnout, there does appear to be a significant relationship to job satisfaction, that is, those who were satisfied with the job were not at risk of burning out. They found that annual income and household economic well-being were positively associated with job satisfaction while gender, age, education, and marital status showed little association with it. They also found that emotional exhaustion significantly predicted job satisfaction but that the concept of deprofessionalization did not (Tarcan, Hikmet, Schooley, Top, & Tarcan, 2017).

Shanafelt et al. have documented a trend in physician burnout that is an increasing trend over the years from 2011 to 2014. Their survey used the Maslach Burnout Inventory (Maslach, Jackson, & Leiter, 1997). They found that in 2014 54.4% of their sample reported at least one symptom of burnout as compared with 45.5% in 2011 while work-life balance satisfaction declined from 48.5% to 40.9% in that time period. They compared these findings using probability samples of US working adults and found that physicians are experiencing more significant symptoms of burnout as compared to this more general population. Their conclusion is that physician burnout is a serious issue and is increasing over time (Shanafelt et al., 2015).

The Affordable Care Act and the Influx of New Patients

A survey published by the Commonwealth Foundation, about physicians who are seeing new patients recently insured under ACA and including those insured under the Medicaid expansion, found that they were able to deliver the same level of high-quality care as they did prior to the Act. Of those physicians who served Medicaid patients prior to ACA, many continue to keep their practices open to new enrollees. The survey found that a large majority of primary care doctors were satisfied with their medical practices although many seemed pessimistic about the future of their work (Hamel et al., 2015). More troubling in some respects was that many primary care doctors were not well informed about what the ACA actually does and like the general public tend to view the law through the same political lens. With the recent push to repeal and replace the Affordable Care Act, the AMA sent a letter to Congressional leaders stating that they continued to "embrace the primary goal of the law—to make high quality, affordable health care coverage accessible to all

Americans" (Madara, 2017). Their view is that any replacement should "make coverage more affordable, provide greater choice, and increase the number of those insured." One can say with fair certainty that the coming changes to the Affordable Care Act and what has been deemed Trumpcare otherwise known as the American Health Care Act (House bill) will not lessen physicians' stress, nor will it reduce their uncertainty. The AMA has stated its opposition to the House bill stating that refundable tax credits are the preferred method for assisting individuals in obtaining private health coverage.

They go on to state that they do not support:

- The proposed rollback of Medicaid expansions
- Repeal of the Prevention and Public Health Fund
- Elimination of the ability of patients to choose and receive their care from qualified providers
- Elimination of federal support for Planned Parenthood Federation of America (American Medical Association, 2017)

The AMA's overriding concern was to ensure that those that now have coverage do not lose that coverage in any repeal and replace efforts. This position is at odds with the new Secretary of Health and Human Services, a former conservative congressman from Georgia and orthopedic surgeon who has continuously advocated for repeal. While the AMA House of Delegates voted to reaffirm its support for ACA, it was not without controversy (Graham, 2016).

The Internet Generation and the Activated Patient

Coupled with the influx of new patients comes a more activated patient population that regularly consults the Internet to evaluate doctors' ratings on a wide variety of sites, the value of which is not clearly known. Clearly the notion of physicians possessing the bulk of information in a typical physician-patient interaction may be on the wane as patients arm themselves with all sorts of information about their health needs and what the physician ought to do for them during any interaction. Some interesting data is emerging on why patients pick certain doctors and more importantly why they may leave a doctor. Reasons why a patient may select a specific doctor may revolve around their empathy and bedside manner, their experience with patients, and how convenient it is to see them (Beaulieu-Volk, 3 Recurring Themes In How Patients Pick Doctors, 2013b; American Osteopathic Association, 2013). What cause patients to leave physicians typically revolves around communication issues, e.g., unclear or dismissive, the physicians' insistence that they are right, and lastly physicians who misrepresent their expertise and more importantly their credentials (Gerencher, 2013; Beaulieu-Volk, 2013a, 2013b).

MACRA: Medicare Access and CHIP Reauthorization Act of 2015

Deloitte explored the subject of whether or not physician practices were ready for the law and whether or not those practices had adapted their behaviors in response to the new law. What they found was an overall level of little to no knowledge of the law or its requirements. Of these physicians they surveyed, 50% had not heard of it, while 32% recognized the name but did not know what it entailed. More self-employed/independent physicians (21%) knew of the law compared to those employed by hospitals (9%). The upshot of this survey is primarily that physicians by and large prefer fee-for-service or salary-based compensation as opposed to payment models based on value. Most do not believe that compensation should be tied to quality, and most of the sample (58%) said they would rather join a larger organization to avail themselves of support and resources rather than expose themselves to financial risk (Deloitte Center for Health Solutions, 2016). But fee-for-service remains a resistant form of payment as Zuvekas and Cohn found. Roughly 95% of all physician office visits made in 2013 were reimbursed this way although that is prior to the MACRA, so perhaps there is significant change coming in the way that physicians are paid (Zuvekas & Cohen, 2015). Either way it appears that this kind of change will not be welcomed by most practitioners.

Physician Supply/Demand Issues for the Future and the Use of Physician Substitutes

While it appears that American's appetite for health care continues unabated and expects to keep growing given the overall aging of the population, the numbers appear to be sobering for whether or not the supply of physicians can keep up with the demand. According to the Association of American Medical Colleges, a couple of ominous trends are presenting themselves:

- A projected shortfall of physicians is expected in 2025 to be around 61,700 to 94,700.
- Primary care shortfalls will range from 14,900 to 35,600 by 2025, while non-primary care doctors will be short by 37,400 to 60,300.
- Physician retirements are projected to have the most impact on physician supply, and roughly 33% of all currently active physicians will be over 65 in the next decade.
- Because of reduced population projections by the Census Bureau, there will be a similar reduction in demand for physicians in relation to the reduced population.
- ACA-related influx of new patients can be expected to increase demand for physicians particularly on the primary care physicians, but current plans in Congress to repeal and replace ACA will reduce the number of Americans covered under

the most optimistic assessment of any plan currently put forth (IHS Inc., 2016). All of these estimates appear to be increased from a study the year before on the same subject (Dall, West, Chakrabarti, & Iacobucci, 2015).

So the question becomes if medical schools cannot produce physicians fast enough to meet the perceived demand as outlined above, then what can and will fill the void? The concept of labor substitutes is instructive here as there are practitioners particularly on the primary care side that can and will step up to fill the void. The Commonwealth Fund published an interesting piece on the use of community health workers providing primary care in Brazil (Wadge et al., 2016). As the authors pointed out, the key to safe and effective care was recruiting individuals with knowledge of both the community and ways to build trust with those in the community.

Challenges remain, namely, how do we ensure that this level of care can reduce more expensive secondary and tertiary care, and how are these workers integrated into the current health system dominated by physicians and nurses? And even if we just use currently trained practitioners, how do we get physicians to let go of the notion that they and they alone are uniquely qualified to provide this care to patients in the United States. The AMA has clearly rejected the use of nurse practitioners to fill the void stating that they lack the breadth of training and education (Donelan, DesRoches, Dittus, & Buerhaus, Perspectives of Physicians and Nurse Practitioners on Primary Care Practice, 2013). The other side of this argument is what the Center for Economic and Policy Research calls an economic cartel (Center For Economic and Policy Research, 2016). It's pretty clear cut once one cuts through all the rules set up to protect who can be licensed in the United States as a physician. There is effectively no competition to providing physicians outside of those that come from US residency programs so that supply can be increased or decreased by one element in the chain of supply of labor. The control over labor supply can only cause salaries to rise for this profession unless there are more robust substitutes or foreign medical graduates allowed to practice without the constraints that are currently imposed upon them to practice in the United States.

Streeter et al. state that there are 37 states that are projected to have primary care physician shortages in 2025 and 9 of those states are also projected to have a shortage of physician assistants, as well. No states are projected to have a shortage of nurse practitioners in 2025 (Streeter, Zangaro, & Chattopadhyay, 2017) which brings us back to the use of substitutes or, in this case, nurse practitioners. What do we know of their use and their effectiveness in providing primary care? Muench et al. found a slight increase in healthcare costs (1–4%) in two of three patient cohorts studied, but provider prices for primary care fell about the same amount following the implementations of standard operating procedures for nurse practitioners (Muench, Coffman, & Spetz, 2016). Years earlier Goodman et al. had recommended a national workforce commission in order to direct training funds toward high-need clinicians, i.e., primary care practitioners, but it's clear that that intervention hasn't happened (Goodman, Fisher, & Bronner, Hospital And Physician Capacity Update – A Brief Report From the Dartmouth Atlas Of Health Care, 2009). Even earlier Goodman et al. had described the twin problems of too many specialists/not enough primary care doctors and new physicians not settling in areas where need is the greatest. This continues today with a maldistribution of both physician type and the amount in any given area leaving some populations overserved and others underserved (Goodman & Fisher, Physician Workforce Crisis? Wrong Diagnosis, Wrong Prescription, 2008). Four years earlier he had described the increase in physician supply from 1979 to 1999 and found that specialists grew at 118% per capita while primary care practitioners grew by 45% per capita and the trend of physicians to settle in areas where supply is already high continues with four out of five settling in these regions (Goodman, Twenty-year Trends in Regional Variations in the US Physician Workforce, 2004).

Several observers have denoted what is termed a primary care crisis in the United States. The opinion is based upon patients getting shorter and shorter appointment times with their PCP, which has been pegged at around 8–12 min with the first interruption coming 18 s into the appointment and a sense that physicians are not really listening to them (Schimpff, 2017). As the primary care practitioner shortage becomes more acute, there seems to be several ways to address the problem. One is to train more medical students to go into primary care and perhaps entice them with some sort of economic package that might include increased pay and/or forgiveness of student loans.

One way to address this issue is to employ more physician substitutes, e.g., nurse practitioners and physician assistants, who could be employed to do a significant amount of the workload of primary care work that is routine in nature. But this notion is certainly controversial between physicians and nonphysicians. Donelan has looked at the perspectives from both sides of this controversy, and the results are fairly predictable from a historical perspective. They found that "70% of physicians and 90% of nurse practitioners" agreed that nurse practitioner should practice to the "full extent of their education and training," and most NPs thought that they were doing it so in their jobs. But the difference of opinion arises over what the role should actually be and even more so over the issue of equal pay for equal work. But the difference of opinion arises over what the role should actually be and even more so over the issue of equal pay for equal work. Physicians routinely oppose the concept that nurse practitioners should be paid the same as a primary care physician. They routinely state that physicians should be paid more because they provide a higher quality of care based on their lengthier and more theoretical level of training vs. nurse practitioners. Nurse practitioners argue that physicians do not provide any higher quality of care and therefore their point is without merit. Lastly the physicians do not believe that increasing the supply of nurse practitioners will have any positive effect on the cost or effectiveness of care. Naturally NPs believe the opposite (Donelan, DesRoches, Dittus, & Buerhaus, Perspectives of Physicians and Nurse Practitioners on Primary Care Practice, 2013).

But the results of this research are suspect because it does not look at actual evidence related to costs of care or effectiveness in relation to the two types of practitioners. As Schimpff points out, primary care is not just for the "simple stuff," but rather PCPs dealing with rather complex situations including managing patients with many chronic conditions like diabetes and heart failure. As such the cure would be to increase reimbursements and allow them to oversee lesser amounts of patients for longer periods of time. He states that each day an average PCP takes 24 phone calls, reads 17 emails, deals with 12 prescription refills, and reviews more than 40 diagnostic reports. And then there is the time spent dealing with billing, electronic health records, and any quality indicators necessitated by payers as well as the organization they work for (Schimpff, 2017). Outside of a huge workload and an overtaxed workforce, our problem with primary care most revolves around the dismissal of primary care as an honored career track for graduating medical students. Medical school graduates who seek meaningful work and income that helps to pay off their crushing student debt almost mandate that they pursue specialty practice in academic medical centers.

This focus on specialty practice has made our system less efficient than other healthcare systems which we have known for many years now. Efforts to change that have gone unheeded as evidenced by a 2008 GAO report that pointed this out and advocated for a new emphasis on primary care services (Government Accounting Office, 2008). Complicating matters a bit more, the rise of a primary care practitioner called the hospitalist has further splintered the practice of primary care into those who work with inpatients in hospital settings and those whose practice primarily in office settings. The rationale behind the divide was an acknowledgment that it was becoming much too difficult for one doctor to manage both outpatients in their office and inpatients in the hospital. Availability of physicians to be able to respond to their patients on a more routine basis drove this change. Of course, this leads toward further fragmentation of an already fragmented system and provides more opportunities for communication between physicians to break down (Sadick, 2016).

As physicians and nurses argue overcompensation, it is important to note that they both consume a large portion of healthcare compensation. According to Glied et al., "The compensation of physicians and nurses alone, which accounted for 42 percent of total sector labor compensation across the sectors and 1.24 percent of overall US GDP in 1997, rose to 46 percent of total labor compensation and 1.56 percent of GDP by 2012. This group's rising share suggests that, overall, technological changes in the sector to date have favored, rather than substituted for, those with high skills" (Glied, Ma, & Solis-Roman, 2015). This clearly seems to point out that highly skilled healthcare labor, e.g., physicians, nurses, etc., will continue to be paid more and more to work in this field for some time to come.

How much do physicians currently earn? Hamblin provides the answer: for specialties it ranges from a low of $157,394 for pediatric endocrinologists to a high of $609,639 for neurosurgeons, with the average being $313,990. For primary care doctors, pediatrics is on the low end of the salary range at $205,610 to $227,541 for family medicine doctors, with the average among all primary care physicians being $226,835 (Hamblin, 2015). One can see that the average of the salaries is $87,000 higher for specialty practice than primary care practice.

Physicians in Training: Harbinger of Things to Come?

On the training front, physicians continue to struggle with resident work hours and recent limitations that have been imposed on the number of hours that resident physicians or physicians in training can work during a given time period. There are those physicians who state that long hours and a grueling training regimen properly prepare these individuals to go out on their own and practice without oversight. But the rhetoric rarely matches the reality as sleep-deprived residents made more errors than their non-sleep-deprived colleagues (Van Dongen, Maislin, Mullington, & Dinges, 2002).

Interestingly, it was a lawsuit that changed the situation and began the process of limiting resident physicians' work hours. The Libby Zion case where an attorney's daughter died within 24 h of admission began the process of policy change to limit what overtired residents and interns could do (Lerner, 2006). This arduous training ritual in which physicians in training are assigned via match and must accept that assignment with no ability to bargain over working conditions seems to be glorified indentured servitude. Resident physicians had sued back in 2002 in federal court that the National Residency Match Program that was run by the American Council for Graduate Medical Education violated the Sherman Antitrust Act by allowing universities and hospitals to act in collusion to restrain job mobility as well as salary and working conditions. Physicians in training must accept the assignment they are matched to, or they will not be allowed to practice their specialty or be eligible for licensing as a physician (Jung v. Association of American Medical Colleges, 2002). The suit was effectively rendered moot in 2004 when President George W. Bush signed into law the Pension Fund Equity Act of 2004, which allowed graduate medical education residency match programs to be exempt from the Sherman Anti-Trust Statute (15 U.S.C. Section 37b (Confirmation of Antitrust Status of Graduate Medical Resident Matching Programs), 2004). The ruling left resident physicians beholden to a system that is anti-competitive and leaves them with little recourse to bargain over their wages and terms of employment. Resident and intern unions have changed that dynamic somewhat, but that will be discussed more fully in Chap. 6. While some senior attending physicians, who made it through the professional hazing known as a residency, continues to believe that we should return to that method of training because it limits caregiver transitions and increases continuity of care because the resident physician never leaves the hospital. It is clear that limitations on work hours in an effort to reduce mistakes made by overtired physicians may be reduced. One study found the reductions didn't appear to affect their ability to take care of patients as new attending physicians with no change in hospital mortality or length of stay when compared to physicians who worked with no hour restrictions (Jena, Schoemaker, & Bhattacharya, 2014). Another study found no significant differences in 30-day mortality rates of 30-day all-cause readmission rates for those hospitalized in the year after the 2011 ACGME duty hour limitations as compared to those hospitalized 2 years prior to the duty hour limitations (Patel et al., 2014). In short, the hour limitations do not appear to have impacted patient care at all. It appears that enough time has elapsed that once again there is renewed pressure on ACGME to increase the consecutive hour limitations that residents can work from 16 to 28. And naturally the predominant voices missing in that debate are the resident physicians and the patients they treat (Aguirre, 2016).

The Changing Landscape

The PWC Health Research Institute listed five forces that are causing change with health care and medicine in particular (PWC, 2016). They are:

- The rise in consumerism which includes more market incentives to share information, costs, prices, and shopping around for value
- More value and less volume, with reimbursement schemes and other performance incentives being tied to outcomes rather than quantity
- Increasing technology and the digitization of medicine which means broader use of electronic health records, 3D printing, and other technological advances
- Decentralization of care away from hospitals and physician offices along with remote monitoring and sharing of data among all stakeholders including patients
- Increased focus on wellness from both the patient as well as the employer and the insurance companies

Clearly many of these items have been predicted for years prior to now, but it seems that more and more focus is on increasing patient responsibility for their own health as well as ensuring that whatever health care they consume is cost-effective and of high quality. And where does that leave the physician? As an adjunct to the patient to maximize their ability to focus on wellness. The role of the physician has clearly changed from one of a benevolent paternalistic figure who told us what to do for our own good to one of working with us or maybe more accurately for us to maintain our lifestyle and our health. Again the physician is becoming a hired hand to help us negotiate our health and illnesses, a position for which many are not prepared.

References

15 U.S.C. Section 37b (Confirmation of Antitrust Status of Graduate Medical Resident Matching Programs). (2004).

Aguirre, J. (2016, December 13). A vote to reimagine residency. *Health Affairs Blog*. Retrieved from http://healthaffairs.org/blog/2016/12/13/avotetoreimagineresidency/

American Medical Association. (2017, March 8). AMA says American health care act is critically flawed. Retrieved from American Medical Association. https://www.ama-assn.org/ama-says-american-health-care-act-critically-flawed

American Osteopathic Association. (2013, September). Finding Dr. *Right*. Retrieved from American Osteopathic Association. www.osteopathic.org/FindingDrRight

Angelis, C. D. (2016). Where have all the primary care doctors gone? *Milbank Quarterly, 94*, 246–250.

Association of American Medical Colleges. (2014, March). Results of the 2013 Medical School Enrollment Survey. Retrieved from Center For Workforce Studies - Association of American Medical Colleges. https://members.aamc.org/eweb/upload/13-239%20Enrollment%20 Survey%20201310.pdf

Baker, D. (2017, January 9). Think of the money physicians' families would save on health care costs if we ended protectionism for doctors. Retrieved from Beat The Press. https://cepr.net/ think-of-the-money-physicians-families-would-save-on-health-care-costs-if-we-ended-protec-tionism-for-doctors/

Beaulieu-Volk, D. (2013a, July 2). 3 reasons patients leave their doctor. Retrieved from Fierce Healthcare. http://www.fiercehealthcare.com/practices/3-reasons-patients-leave-their-doctors

Beaulieu-Volk, D. (2013b, November 5). 3 recurring themes in how patients pick doctors. Retrieved from FierceHealthcare. http://www.fiercehealthcare.com/ practices/3-recurring-themes-how-patients-pick-doctors

Bendix, J., & Lutton, L. (2020, June 30). Why do physicians experience burnout? *Medical Economics*.

Blumenthal, D., & Squires, D. (2016, December 13). Physician dissatisfaction: Diagnosis and treat-ment. Retrieved from Commonwealth Fund. http://www.commonwealthfund.org/publications/ blog/2016/dec/physician-dissatisfaction

Braverman, H. (1974). *Labor and monopoly capital - The degradation of work in the twentieth century*. New York: Monthly Review Press.

Casalino, L. P., & Crosson, F. J. (2015). Physician satisfaction and physician well-being: Should anyone care? *Professions & Professionalism, 5*, 1–12.

Casalino, L. P., Gans, D., Weber, R., Cea, M., Tuchovsky, A., Bishop, T. F., … Evenson, T. B. (2015). US physician practices spend more than $15.4 billion annually to report quality measures. *Health Affairs, 35*, 401–406.

Center For Economic and Policy Research. (2016, December 31). Economists, doc-tors' cartels, and uber. Retrieved from cepr.net. http://cepr.net/blogs/beat-the-press/ economists-doctors-cartels-and-uber

Dall, T., West, T., Chakrabarti, R., & Iacobucci, W. (2015, March). The complexities of physician supply and demand: Projections from 2013 to 2025. Retrieved from American Association of Medical Colleges. https://www.aamc.org/download/426242/data/ihsreportdownload.pdf

Deloitte Center for Health Solutions. (2016, July 13). Are physicians ready for MACRA and its changes? Perspectives from the Deloitte Center for Health Solutions 2016 Survey of US Physicians. Retrieved from Deloitte Center for Health Solutions. https://www2.deloitte.com/ content/dam/Deloitte/us/Documents/life-sciences-health-care/us-lshc-are-physicians-ready-MACRA.pdf

Donelan, K., DesRoches, C. M., Dittus, R. S., & Buerhaus, P. (2013). Perspectives of physicians and nurse practitioners on primary care practice. *New England Journal of Medicine, 368*, 1898–1906.

Feinglass, J. (1990). Physicians as employees: Stanley Wohl and the medical industrial complex. In J. W. Salmon (Ed.), *The corporate transformation of health care - Issues & directions* (p. 245). Amityville, NY: Baywood.

Feinglass, J., & Salmon, J. W. (1994). The use of medical management information systems to increase the clinical productivity of physicians. In J. W. Salmon (Ed.), *The corporate transfor-mation of health care: Perspective & implications* (p. 144). Amityville, NY: Baywood.

Flexner, A. (1910). *Medical education in the United States and Canada - A report to the Carnegie Foundation*, bulletin no. 4 for the advancement of teaching. New York: Carnegie Foundation.

Friedberg, M. W., Chen, P. G., Van Busum, K. R., Aunon, F., Pham, C., Caloyeras, J. P., … Tutty, M. (2013). *Factors affecting physician professional satisfaction and their implications for patient care, health systems, and health policy*. Santa Monica, CA: Rand Corporation.

Friedman, M. (1962). *Capitalism and freedom*. Chicago: University of Chicago Press.

Gerencher, K. (2013, June 29). When should you fire your doctor? *Wall Street Journal*. Retrieved from http://www.wsj.com/articles/SB10001424127887324328204578571640215952804

Gittell, J. H. (2016). Rethinking autonomy: Relationships as a source of resilience in a changing healthcare system. *Health Services Research, 51*, 1701–1705.

Glied, S., Ma, S., & Solis-Roman, C. (2015, July). Where the money goes: The evolving expenses of the US health care system. *Health Affairs, 35*, 1197–1203.

Goodman, D. C. (2004). *Twenty-year trends in regional variations in the US physician workforce*. Health Affairs, Supplement/Web Exclusives, VAR90–VAR97.

Goodman, D. C., & Fisher, E. S. (2008). Physician workforce crisis? Wrong diagnosis, wrong prescription. *New England Journal of Medicine, 358*, 1658–1661.

Goodman, D. C., Fisher, E. S., & Bronner, K. K. (2009, March 30). Hospital and physician capacity update - A brief report from the Dartmouth Atlas of health care. Retrieved from Dartmouth Atlas: http://www.dartmouthatlas.org/downloads/reports/Capacity_Report_2009.pdf

Government Accounting Office. (2008, February 12). *Primary care professionals: Recent supply trends, projections, and valuation of services*. Retrieved from Government Accounting Office. http://www.gao.gov/products/GAO-08-472T

Graham, J. (2016, December 22). *'Like a slap in the face': Dissent roils the AMA, the nation's largest doctor's group*. Retrieved from Statnews.com: https://www.statnews.com/2016/12/22/americanmedicalassociationdivisions/

Hamblin, J. (2015, January 27). *What doctors make - Variations in salary are drastic and opaque*. Retrieved from Theatlantic.com. https://www.theatlantic.com/health/archive/2015/01/physician-salaries/384846/

Hamel, L., Doty, M. M., Norton, M., Ryan, J., Brodie, M., Abrams, M. K., ... Audet, A.-M. J. (2015, June 18). Experiences and attitudes of primary care providers under the first year of ACA coverage expansion. Retrieved from Commonwealth Fund. http://www.commonwealthfund.org/publications/issue-briefs/2015/jun/primary-care-providers-first-year-aca

Haug, M. R. (1976). The erosion of professional authority: A cross-cultural inquiry in the case of the physician. *Milbank Memorial Fund Quarterly, 54*, 83–106.

Health Affairs. (2016). The landscape of physician practice. *Health Affairs, 35*, 388–389.

IHS Inc. (2016, April 5). The complexities of physician supply and demand: Projections from 2014 to 2015 (2016 update). Retrieved from aamc.org. https://www.aamc.org/download/458082/data/2016_complexities_of_supply_and_demand_projections.pdf

Jena, A. B., Schoemaker, L., & Bhattacharya, J. (2014). Exposing physicians to reduced residency work hours did not adversely affect patient outcomes after residency. *Health Affairs, 33*, 1832–1840.

Jung v. Association of American Medical Colleges, 300 F. Supp. 2d 119 (D.D.C. May 7, 2002).

Kirk, L. M. (2007). Professionalism in medicine: Definitions and considerations for teaching. *Baylor University Medical Center Proceedings, 20*, 13–16.

Lerner, B. H. (2006, November 28). A case that shook medicine - How one man's rage over his Daughter's death Sped reform of doctor training. *Washington Post*, p. HE01. Retrieved from http://www.washingtonpost.com/wp-dyn/content/article/2006/11/24/AR2006112400985.html

Liebhaber, A., & Grossman, J. M. (2007). *Physicians moving to mid-sized, single-specialty practices*. Washington, DC: Center For Studying Health System Change.

Light, D., & Levine, S. (1994). The changing character of the medical profession: A theoretical overview. In J. W. Salmon (Ed.), *The corporate transformation of health care: Perspectives & implications* (p. 164). Amityville, NY: Baywood.

Madara, J. L. (2017, January 3). AMA letter to congressional leaders on reform of health care system. Retrieved from American Medical Association. https://www.ama-assn.org/ama-letter-congressional-leaders-reform-health-care-system

Maslach, C., Jackson, S. E., & Leiter, M. (1997). The Maslach Burnout Inventory manual. In C. P. Zalaquett & R. J. Wood (Eds.), *Evaluating stress: A book of resources* (pp. 191–218). Lanham, MD: The Scarecrow Press.

Morra, D., Nicholson, S., Levinson, W., Gans, D. N., Hammons, T., & Casalino, L. P. (2011). US physician practices versus Canadians: Spending nearly four times as much money interacting with payers. *Health Affairs, 30*, 1443–1450.

Muench, U., Coffman, J., & Spetz, J. (2016, February 25). Does independent scope of practice affect prescribing outcomes, healthcare costs, and utilization? Retrieved from Health Care Costs Institute. http://www.healthcostinstitute.org/files/HCCI-Issue-Brief-Independent-Prescribing-Outcomes.pdf

Muhlestein, D. B., & Smith, N. J. (2016). Physician consolidation: Rapid movement from small to large group practices, 2013-15. *Health Affairs, 35*, 1638–1642.

Navarro, V. (1984). Medical history as justification rather than explanation: A critique of Starr's The Social Transformation of American Medicine. *International Journal of Health Services, 14*, 511–528.

Noether, M. (1986). The effect of government policy changes on the supply of physicians: Expansion of a competitive fringe. *Journal of Law and Economics, 29*, 231–262.

Patel, M. S., Volpp, K. G., Small, D. S., Hill, A. S., Even-Shoshan, O., Rosenbaum, L., … Silber, J. H. (2014). Association of the 2011 ACGME resident duty hour reforms with mortality and readmissions with mortality and readmissions. *JAMA, 312*, 2364–2373.

Physicians Advocacy Institute. (2016, September). Physician practice acquisition study: National and regional employment changes. Retrieved from Physicians Advocacy Institute. http://www.physiciansadvocacyinstitute.org/Portals/0/PAI-Physician-Employment-Study.pdf

PWC. (2016, September). Surviving seismic change: Winning a piece of the $5 trillion US health ecosystem. Retrieved from PWC Health Research Institute. http://www.pwc.com/us/en/health-industries/health-research-institute/publications/health-industry-changes.html

Rayack, E. (1967). *Professional power and American medicine: The economics of the American Medical Association*. Cleveland/New York: World Publishing Company.

Sadick, B. (2016, August 23). A look at the growing specialty of hospitalist. *Chicago Tribune*. Retrieved from http://www.chicagotribune.com/lifestyles/health/sc-hospitalists-profile-health-0824-20160823-story.html

Salmon, J. W., White, W. D., & Feinglass, J. (1994). The futures of physicians: Agency and autonomy reconsidered. In J. W. Salmon (Ed.), *The corporate transformation of health care: Perspectives & implications* (p. 126). Amityville, NY: Baywood.

Schimpff, S. C. (2017, January 7). *Here is the PCP crisis solution and it's simple*. Retrieved from Medicaleconomics.com. http://medicaleconomics.modernmedicine.com/medical-economics/news/here-pcp-crisis-solution-and-its-simple

Sexton, J. B., Thomas, E. J., & Helmreich, R. L. (2000). Error, stress, and teamwork in medicine and aviation. *British Medical Journal, 320*, 745–749.

Shanafelt, T. D., Hasan, O., Dyrbye, L. N., Sinsky, C., Satele, D., Sloan, J., & West, C. P. (2015). Changes in burnout and satisfaction with work-life balance in physicians and the general US working population between 2011 and 2014. *Mayo Clinic Proceedings, 90*, 1600–1613.

Starr, P. (1982). *The social transformation of American medicine*. New York: Basic Books.

Stevens, R. (1971). *American medicine and the public interest*. New Haven, CT: Yale University Press.

Stoeckle, J. D. (1994). Reflections on modern doctoring. In J. W. Salmon (Ed.), *The corporate transformation of health care - Perspectives & implications* (p. 118). Amityville, NY: Baywood.

Streeter, R. G., Zangaro, G. A., & Chattopadhyay, A. (2017). Perspectives: Using results from HRSAs health workforce simulation model to examine the geography of primary care. *Health Services Research, 52*, 481–507.

Strobeck, J. A. (1990). Mindbend against a corporate intrusion into health care. In J. W. Salmon (Ed.), *The corporate transformation of health care* (p. 266). Amityville, NY: Baywood.

Tarcan, M., Hikmet, N., Schooley, B., Top, M., & Tarcan, G. Y. (2017). An analysis of the relationship between burnout, socio-demographic and workplace factors and job satisfaction among emergency department health professionals. *Applied Nursing Research, 34*, 40–47.

The Physicians Foundation. (2016, September 21). 2016 survey of America's physicians - Practice patterns & perspectives. Retrieved from Physiciansfoundation.org: http://www.physicians-foundation.org/healthcare-research/physician-survey/

Van Dongen, H. P., Maislin, G., Mullington, J. M., & Dinges, D. F. (2002). The cumulative cost of additional wakefulness: Dose-response effects on neurobehavioral functions and sleep physiology from chronic sleep restriction and total sleep deprivation. *Sleep, 26*, 117–126.

Vincent, C. K., Moorthy, S. K., Sarker, A., Chang, A., & Darzi, A. W. (2004). Systems approaches to surgical quality and safety. *Annals of Surgery, 239*, 475–482.

Waddimba, A. C., Scribani, M., Hasbrouck, M. A., Krupa, N., Jenkins, P., & May, J. J. (2016). Resilience among employed physicians and mid-level practitioners in upstate New York. *Health Services Research, 51*, 1706–1734.

Wadge, H., Bhatti, Y., Carter, A., Harris, M., Parston, G., & Darzi, A. (2016, December). Brazil's family health strategy: Using. Retrieved from Commonwealth Fund. http://www.commonwealthfund.org/publications/case-studies/2016/dec/~/media/files/publications/case-study/2016/dec/1914_wadge_brazil_family_hlt_strategy_frugal_case_study_v2.pdf

Waring, J., Dixon-Woods, M., & Yeung, K. (2010). Modernising medical regulation: Where are we now? *Journal of Health Organization and Management, 24*, 540–555.

Washko, M. M., Snyder, J. E., & Zangaro, G. (2015). Where do physicians train? Investigating public and private institutional pipelines. *Health Affairs, 34*, 852–856.

Woolhandler, S., & Himmelstein, D. U. (2014). Administrative work consumes one-sixth of U.S. physicians' working hours and lowers their career satisfaction. *International Journal of Health Services, 44*, 635–642.

Zuvekas, S. H., & Cohen, J. W. (2015, March). Fee-for-service, while much maligned, remains the dominant payment method for physician visits. *Health Affairs, 35*, 411–414.

Chapter 4
Medical Malpractice Crisis: Oversight of the Practice of Medicine

Introduction

Medical malpractice results from any errors that practitioners make in caring for patients, which naturally has been both helped and made worse by *increasing use of technology* and the burgeoning bureaucratization inherent in complex health organizations; thus, unintentional mistakes typically occur due to *dysfunctional system issues*. These errors are often made much worse by the failure to evaluate errors in an open and transparent manner for learning and, more importantly, for preventing reoccurrence.

As we will discover in this chapter, there are certain systemic issues that will predispose an organization and its practitioners to making mistakes. For example, Tawfik et al. found that the rate of medical errors tripled if physicians in the unit reported high levels of burnout independent of how safely rated the facilities were that they worked in (Tawfik et al., 2018). While stress and burnout (mentioned in an earlier chapter) are significant and climbing in physician practices, it could be made safer by "emphasizing information systems, promoting a culture of quality and improving the hectic environment" (Linzer et al., 2005).

Starting with the Institute of Medicine report in 1998, the number of Americans killed by avoidable medical errors was estimated to be between 44,000 and 98,000. Yet both physicians, policymakers, and members of the public often underestimate the severity of the problem, or certainly don't agree on any solutions to fix it (Blendon et al., 2002). The number of Americans killed by medical errors has subsequently and unfortunately been revised upward since 1998 with recent estimates ranging from 210,000 to 400,000 Americans per year 3 years ago (James, 2013). Makary and Daniel now estimate that medical error is the *third leading cause of death in the United States* and as such requires much more attention that it currently gets (Makary & Daniel, 2016). And while we are yet to fully grasp the enormity of costs both in lives lost, human suffering, and damages, policymakers continue to attempt policy solutions that don't address the real problem of reducing harm caused by practitioner error.

© Springer Nature Switzerland AG 2021
J. W. Salmon, S. L. Thompson, *The Corporatization of American Health Care*,
https://doi.org/10.1007/978-3-030-60667-1_4

Instead, the medical profession insists that the real issue isn't one of medical errors or patients dying needlessly from preventable mistakes, but rather overzealous trial attorneys and families seeking retribution for a loved one's death through the legal system due to our litigious society. State and national medical societies constantly complain that a "crisis" in rising medical malpractice premiums paid by various doctors is somehow tied to outrageous jury awards to those allegedly harmed by physicians.

The medical profession at both state and national levels has fought back consistently, often not seeming to understand the underlying economic issues of medical malpractice insurance rate setting. It turns out that the past few malpractice insurance crises and premium spikes are more a function of "hard markets" rather than large unpredictable awards made by juries (Hunter & Doroshow, 2011). Some studies have indicated that the rates of return by insurance companies more so dictate the increased premiums they charge doctors during periods of economic downturn and not related to award settlements and payouts (Baker, 2005). Despite evidence to the contrary, state medical societies continue to regularly lobby their legislators in a variety of measures designed to limit their exposure to punitive/non-economic damages that does nothing to fix the actual problem and clearly doesn't benefit the public's health. The object is to limit the punitive or non-economic damages to a specific and predictable amount like $250,000 no matter how egregious the physician conduct is.

Kessler and McClellan (1996) compared treatments for cardiology treatments in non-cap states with cap states and found that patients received more care (e.g., stents, etc.) in non-cap states but the outcomes for those patients were no better. The thinking here is that physicians in non-cap states order more tests and perform more procedures than physicians in cap states, but it would seem that performing more procedures, especially risky and invasive ones would enhance one's risk of a malpractice suit rather than mitigate it. To answer that question more definitively, we will look at various states to see what is happening in regard to malpractice awards and patient safety relative to whether or not tort reform, or the use of non-economic damage caps, has improved patient access, malpractice premium increases, and, most importantly, patient safety.

These soft and hard markets create boom and bust cycles in the insurance market. When markets are in boom mode (premiums and investment income far outpace insurance claims and payouts), insurance can be found at reasonable prices, which can continue this way until claims outpace both premiums and investment incomes, thus ushering in a "medical malpractice crisis." When bottom lines are threatened, insurance companies will increase premiums substantially to boost their reserves. Physicians may be unable to find insurance coverage at any price, and even if they could find it, they may not be able to afford the premium.

Beider and Elliott (2003) describe the efficiency of the current tort system by how well it compensates victims for their injuries caused by medical malpractice (Beider & Elliott, 2003). Costs that get figured into whether or not the system is equitable include the costs of the injury, the costs associated with attempting to prevent or avoid injuries, the costs of administering the system (including courts and attorney costs), and any externalities borne by those not a party to the injury such as bankruptcies and plant closings.

Chapter Purpose

Medical malpractice has been one of the most misunderstood American policy debates over the past 40 years. This chapter will explore the concept of medical malpractice, what is currently discussed as policy alternatives, and some possible ways to address the real crisis, which is not too many physicians getting sued. Rather it is that too many patients are being harmed in healthcare settings!

It is our belief that such altering the focus from liability avoidance and defensive medicine to patient safety, harm reduction, and transparency in documenting, discussing, and fixing systemic issues that cause medical errors to occur can result in better and safer patient care, as well as much improved quality at a lower overall system cost.

What Is Malpractice Insurance and Why Is It So Different from Other Insurance Markets?

Medical malpractice insurance is a very small niche market provided mostly to the roughly 950,000 practicing physicians across the United States (Young et al., 2017). Insurance typically works when predictable amounts of claims occur in real times and the cost is spread over many more policy holders through the payment of premiums to mitigate their risk of some calamitous event.

In the case of home or car insurance, the risk of filing a claim is pretty well-known to the underwriters at the various companies that write policies in these areas. Claims are often made and paid in a relatively short period of time, and the matter is often resolved quickly in very predictable patterns, basically actuarial science. Most people who insure their homes or autos may never file a claim so they will subsidize those who may occasionally do file claims. Health insurance is slightly different in that sooner or later most people who buy coverage will file a claim in any given year, especially as they age. But health insurance, like home and auto insurance, will subsidize those who file claims from the many more who do not, but still pay premiums; the outlays over time become fairly predictable and paid in a certain short time frame.

But medical malpractice as an insurance market is much different; it fails on a number of fronts. The first is that it's difficult to spread the risk over a larger risk pool as there are only so many physicians in a given market, so the amount of premiums that must be collected fall on a rather shallow pool of policy holders. Second, claims under medical malpractice insurance can be made months or even years after the fact, making risk adjustment and premium setting exceptionally hard to do. Insurance companies in this market typically can set higher rates to cover larger than expected losses but risk losing business to another insurer who charges lower rates and who also may underestimate actual risk to attract new premiums.

So the main questions this chapter seeks to ask are: Will medical malpractice insurance companies raise premiums substantially during the next economic downturn independent of any actual malpractice claims data? It is the authors' contention that an upsurge in insurance premiums, which the medical profession continues to assert, is due to "out of control" jury awards—not the frequency of mistakes, nor the ebb and flow of the business cycle, will manufacture a "crisis." As a policy issue, the noise over medical malpractice costs garners much more attention than the 2–3% of the total US health expenditures they currently consume (Mello, Chandra, Gawande, & Studdert, 2010). Van Den Bos et al. estimated the total cost of measurable medical errors at $17.1 billion in 2008 with the most frequent adverse events caused by drugs followed by pressure ulcers (Van Den Bos et al., 2011). They go on to state that most of these medical errors are caused by "common and relatively straightforward medical services" and not from complex procedures or procedures involving complex medical technology.

Medical malpractice, like general negligence, requires four conditions to be met. They are:

- The physician had a duty.
- The physician breached that duty.
- There was harm to the patient.
- The harm to the patient was caused by the physician's breach of duty.

But even if all four conditions are met, there are mitigating circumstances that could be used in a court of law to exonerate a physician, such as Good Samaritan act or sudden emergency. As for defenses that physicians can take in response to a malpractice suit, Hudson and Moore found eight different defenses (Hudson & Moore, 2012). Table 4.1 lists those defenses and their definitions.

So if an individual sues a physician, the case goes to court, and the physician is found to be liable for malpractice, what happens next? Actual awards are often different and less than what is reported when a verdict is made. Hyman et al. reviewed medical malpractice claims in Texas from 1988 to 2003 in which the plaintiff received at least $25,000 (in 1988 dollars) from a jury. Seventy-five percent received an award less than verdict awarded, 20 percent received the verdict amount (+2 percent) and 5 percent received more than the verdict (Hyman, Black, Zeiler, Silver, & Sage, 2007). The larger the verdict, the more likely the amount would be reduced. These findings underscore the rhetoric thrown around about "out of control" jury awards and a broken malpractice system when only the original award is published.

Table 4.1 Special defense arguments against malpractice claims (Hudson & Moore, 2012)

Special defense	Definition
Assumption of the risk	A plaintiff's implied or expressed agreement (consent) absolves the defendant from responsibility
Good Samaritan	A physician who in good faith and without prior notice provides emergency medical care without a fee to a person is not liable for damages secondary to their acts or omissions except in the case of gross negligence
Contributory negligence	Conduct on the part of the plaintiff that falls below the standard to which he should conform for his own protection and which is a legally contributing cause cooperating with the negligence of the defendant in bringing about the plaintiff's harm. Allows no recovery of damages
Comparative fault	The same definition of contributory negligence; however, damages are awarded based on the amount of negligence on the part of the plaintiff compared to the amount of negligence on the part of the defendant. Allows some recovery of damages
Sudden emergency	A defendant completed an inappropriate action against the plaintiff; however, it was done in the setting of a sudden unexpected emergency, which caused actions that would not have otherwise been taken if it were not a sudden emergency
Respectable minority	A defendant fails to practice within the standard of care of the majority; however, this is excusable if it is shown that a respectable minority of physicians approve of the course of action
Two schools of thought	The treatment or procedure undertaken by the defendant has been approved by one group of medical experts even though there is an alternate school of thought that recommends another approach
Clinical innovation	Use of clinical knowledge to perform a procedure or treatment that varies from the standard care in situations in which the standard treatment cannot be used

Source: Reprinted from Hudson and Moore (2012), Copyright (2012), with permission from Elsevier

Malpractice, Not Malpractice Jury Awards, Are the Real Issue

Illich describes a significant transition in the practice of medicine from an ethical issue into a technical problem. He believes that what had formerly been considered "an abuse of confidence and a moral fault can now be rationalized into the occasional breakdown of equipment and operators." Negligence therefore becomes "random human error or system breakdown," and incompetence becomes "a lack of specialized equipment" (Illich, 2002). In a large study, Tehrani et al. found that diagnostic errors were the leading cause of malpractice claims and accounted for over a third of payments (Tehrani et al., 2012). While they found more diagnostic errors in the outpatient setting, the inpatient errors were found to be more lethal.

In the policy arena, there are generally thought to be five myths of medical negligence that get passed around as truth (American Association for Justice, 2009). They are:

- There are too many "frivolous" malpractice lawsuits.
- Malpractice claims drive up healthcare costs.

- Doctors are fleeing states with no caps to states with caps.
- Malpractice claims drive up doctors' malpractice insurance premiums.
- Tort reform will lower insurance rates.

The data simply does not support point number 1. As several studies have pointed out, the number of filings has decreased over time. Lee and LaFountain found the number of medical malpractice filings fell 18 percent from 2000 to 2009 in the seven states they surveyed. In five of the seven states, filings fell between 18 and 42 percent (Lee & LaFountain, 2011). This was borne out by the National Center for State Courts Study on Tort Reforms and the Center for Justice & Democracy at New York Law School (Center for Justice & Democracy at New York Law School, 2012). Studdert et al. make two general conclusions regarding point 1. The first is that the malpractice system is *not* full of frivolous litigation. Of the cases they examined that contained errors, most went unpaid. The second is that the system does a good job in separating claims that have merit from those that do not. But all claims, frivolous or not, cost significant amounts of money, time, and acrimony for all parties involved. Delays in resolution, as well as the administrative costs, typically add up to approximately 54 percent of the compensation that is eventually paid out (Studdert et al., 2006). While the actual costs may be less than what the physician side would argue, the psychic costs of a malpractice claim are not minimal. The time away from work, stress, and reputational damage are significant and ongoing (Carmen, 2011). Waterman et al. reported that physicians do report anxiety, loss of confidence, sleeping difficulties, reduced job satisfaction, and harm to their reputation following errors (Waterman et al., 2007). This will require more attention to supporting frontline medical personnel in the prevention of errors, as well as the fallout caused by an error.

On point number 2 above, there has been some recent data that significantly pokes holes in the narrative being proffered that malpractice is a prime driver of healthcare cost increases over time. Public Citizen has written several pieces on this myth in that payments fell 11.9 percent, while at the same time healthcare spending increased 96.7% (Lincoln, 2011). Texas, which implemented stringent malpractice caps in 2003 for the purpose of directly reducing healthcare costs, has found out that healthcare costs have risen faster in Texas than the national average, thus refuting one of the major reasons to implement caps to control healthcare costs.

Point 3, doctors are not fleeing from states with no malpractice caps to states that have malpractice caps. The evidence from either side of the debate is not clear and the "net effect of medical malpractice reform in one state vs. another is theoretically ambiguous" (Klick & Stratmann, Does Malpractice Reform Help States Retain Physicians and Does It Matter? 2005). It would appear that the economic barriers to making a move for this reason are rather insurmountable given the enormous task of closing up a practice in one location and moving to a completely different location in a different state, which would include obtaining a license to practice in that new state, as well as building whole practice relationships, the barriers might seem rather insurmountable, but not impossible.

As to point 4, Baicker and Chandra (2005) have found that "increases in malpractice payments made on behalf of physicians do not seem to be the driving force behind increases in premiums." Lastly, tort reform has not been shown that it has any measurable effect on lowering malpractice insurance rates. Typically, any savings as the result of lower payouts is not passed along to physicians in the form of lower premiums, and they certainly never get passed on to patients or health insurers with lower bills for services rendered (American Association for Justice, 2009).

And lastly to point 5, the insurance industry does argue that they incur huge losses from malpractice suits which of course justifies the large premiums that providers pay. But a study by the Foundation for Taxpayer and Consumer Rights found that the insurance industry overstated their losses by 30 percent for each of the 9 years on the report (Starkman, 2005). Bixenstine et al. (2013) found that catastrophic payouts (those $1 million or over) represent roughly 8% of all paid claims. These catastrophic awards were most often associated with patient age of less than 1 year; quadriplegia, brain damage, lifeline care, and anesthesia mishaps. They also found out that settlements were often associated with decreased odds of a catastrophic payment vs. court judgments. They estimated that total catastrophic payouts averaged $1.4 billion per year or 0.05% of US health expenditures, meaning that jury verdicts get exaggerated to make a political point about outrageous awards bankrupting doctors. Hyman et al. explain that actual payouts are vastly different from verdicts. Defendant physicians rarely make out-of-pocket payments and rarely pay what the jury awards to plaintiffs. So studies based on jury awards typically don't mirror the reality of what malpractice awards are actually costing (Hyman, Black, Zeiler, Silver, & Sage, 2007).

Naturally physicians will counter with anecdotes of what it is like to have to defend oneself against a malpractice lawsuit. They feel especially vulnerable due to stories of physicians being sued for a bad result that occurred while practicing within the standards of care. Clearly the medical profession wants protection against unwarranted malpractice suits for bad outcomes that occur when practicing cost-effective care using clinically appropriate guidelines. Policy reform should focus on protecting those physicians acting within guidelines who make every attempt to treat their patients in good faith (Bishop, Federman, & Keyhani, 2010). But the use of guidelines is not without its own risks as physicians must ensure that they are current and revised according to the latest evidence of best practice (Brennan, 1991).

Because of the anecdotal horror stories told of "innocent physicians" being sued for outrageous sums of money, some state legislatures have been lobbied to enact caps on non-economic and punitive damages. The idea, of course, is to limit that part of the award designed to punish the physician for their error. Non-economic damage caps are also seen as a way to stop the supposed movement of doctors from states without caps to states with caps. In Illinois (a state currently without a cap), it is believed that doctors are fleeing for Wisconsin (a state with a cap) because of the high cost of malpractice insurance. But the data does not appear to support the argument that this is indeed occurring on an aggregate scale. Zhao found evidence that caps on total awards had some impact on the provision of obstetric services at the local county level but did not find much of any difference, while non-economic and punitive damage caps had little effect on the provision of services (Zhao, 2005). Donohue and Ho (2007) have shown that caps have not altered the number or awards or settlements. And in states that have enacted caps, Sharkey has shown that attorneys will ramp up their economic damages to cover what is capped on the non-economic side (Sharkey, 2005). The lesson is that whatever policy is enacted, people will find a way around it.

A lot of "remedies" for the malpractice insurance crisis have been offered over the last two decades. Whether government health insurance (e.g., Medicare and/or Medicaid) will cover injured persons' medical costs (thus negating some motivation for bringing suit) and whether universal health coverage ever gets around to improving health outcomes, to lessen injury to fewer people, both remain to be seen perhaps in the far future. In the mid-1970s, the California Hospital and Medical Associations sponsored a study they hoped would support their tort reform efforts by showing how out of control the system was. What they found instead was that malpractice injured many thousands of patients each year and that despite the common perception, few of them ever sued. Because the study refuted their well-known position of an out-of-control tort system, they buried it (Baker, 2005). As Baker points out the problem isn't too much litigation but too much malpractice. This was borne out by the 20-year-old Institute of Medicine (IOM) report *To Err is Human*, which estimates that close to 100,000 Americans die every year as a result of medical malpractice (Kohn, Corrigan, & Donaldson, 1999). That surprising estimate has unfortunately been revised significantly upward to 210,000 to 400,000 lives lost per year due to preventable medical errors (James, 2013). As Baker points out, the real costs of medical malpractice are lost lives, extra medical expenses, and time away from work, along with pain and suffering. Twenty years later Bates and Singh found that the implementation and practice of effective solutions to improve patient safety have been inconsistent including the continuing occurrence of "never events" such as surgery on the wrong patient or wrong site (Bates & Singh, 2018).

So what types of errors are being made that lead to lawsuits? The large physician-owned medical malpractice insurer, Doctor's Company, analyzed 464 closed claims of Hospitalists between 2007 and 2014 and found that the bulk of claims were diagnosis related (36%), improper management of treatment (31%), medication errors (11%), improper performance or delay in treatment or procedure (5%), failure to treat (3%), and failure to monitor psychological status (3%) (Ranum, Troxel, & Diamond, Hospitalist Closed Claims Study, 2016). In terms of medication errors, opioids lead the list of errors tied to medication in that physicians continue to be lax in monitoring whether or not the medication has improved the patient's symptoms (Lowes, 2017).

A tangle of motives lies behind a patient or family's decision to take legal action following medical injury, and money is only one of them. These motives, which all can be considered to represent a demand for some form of "accountability," generally fit into four themes: (1) restoration, including financial compensation or some other intervention to "make the patient whole again"; (2) correction, such as a system change or competence review to protect future patients; (3) communication, which may include an explanation, expression of responsibility, or apology; and (4) sanction, including professional discipline or some other form of punitive action (Vincent, Young, & Phillips, 1994).

According to Danzon, the purpose of professional liability or more specifically medical malpractice liability is to provide for two basic goals. Number one is to provide compensation to those injured as a result of the negligence of their physicians. Number two is to impose sanctions on those found negligent in such a manner as to act as a deterrence to those actions (Danzon, 1983). Baker goes a bit further as to why malpractice lawsuits continue to be needed. These include promoting patient safety by identifying dangerous conditions and providing an incentive for patient safety. Access to the courts to be made whole as a result of a medical mistake is a traditional American value and one which malpractice lawsuits promote (Baker, 2005).

How often do patients and/or families sue their healthcare providers? Although the available data didn't permit Saks to calculate an exact figure for rates of lumping and claiming outside the tort law system, he did determine that, of all the victims in cases classified by experts as actionable medical errors, only 4 percent hired lawyers and only 2 percent filed lawsuits (Saks, 1992). This seems to counter the oft-heard rhetoric that patients and/or their families sue physicians every chance they get.

Engel found that there are several reasons that patients do not sue their physicians. Injuries can disable one to the point of self-isolation and blame so that patients do not seem to look to find external answers to their predicament. Couple that with negative social views of those who are victims of injuries, and there is a negative incentive to sue one's physician. The predominant social value does not appear to support the claim of causality in injuries, and they may be viewed as a bad outcome or unavoidable, or worse, caused by the victim themselves. The physician may be looked at as incapable of causing a foreseeable injury to a patient under their care (Engel, 2016).

So how many physicians get sued, and how often are they getting sued? Studdert et al. have some interesting data on that matter, and they point to a rather troubling trend. Approximately 1% of physicians were responsible for 32% of paid claims (Studdert, Bismark, Mello, Singh, & Spittal, 2016). Of those who had paid claims against them, 84% had one, 16% had two, and 4% had at least three or more against them. When they compared those with three or more claims to those with just one, they found that their risk of further claims increased substantially. They also found that certain specialties had a greater risk than others; neurosurgeons have a four times greater risk than psychiatrists, which makes sense on its face. Bixenstine et al. (2013) found that catastrophic payouts ($1 million or more) represented 7.9% of all paid claims from the National Practitioner Data Bank over the period of 2004–2010. They found that the factors most often associated with these payouts were patients less than 1 year of age, quadriplegia, brain damage, and injuries that required life-long care. They did not find any relationship between years a physician was in practice nor any previous paid claims history. In another study by Studdert et al.

(2019), they found that malpractice prone physicians were "no more likely to relocate geographically than those without claims, but they were more likely to stop practicing medicine or switch to smaller practice settings." If the medical profession can find a way to police the profession in such a way to sufficiently discipline these repeat offenders, they could significantly reduce the number of medical malpractice claims and payouts.

Malpractice Crises and Market Cycles

There have been three reported crises in medical malpractice insurance over the past 40 years. This is defined as "a period of volatility in the malpractice insurance market characterized by above-average increases in premiums, contractions in the supply of insurance and deterioration in the financial health of insurance carriers. In a crisis, medical specialties at high risk for claims, such as obstetrics and orthopedic surgery, experience the largest premium increases" (Mello, 2006).

When these conditions manifest themselves, the term "hard market" is used to describe the squeeze that physicians feel trying to keep covered. The basic mechanism is that the business cycle offers either many competitors or few. When there are many competitors, downward pressure on premiums occurs in an attempt to lure new customers. These lower premiums eventually lead to insufficient monies to pay claims which starts a push upward in premiums; some insurers begin to realize that the market isn't as lucrative as it might seem so they leave the market. Given that the medical malpractice market is small to begin with, coupled with long lag times between injury and any payout, it becomes very difficult to estimate premium levels that are sufficient to meet claims that could be made in the distant future.

The current policy rhetoric around these "malpractice crises" never mentions business cycles at all, but rather attempts to push for tort reform and blame "so-called" greedy, litigious patients to mitigate exposure and risk for the insurer. None of this does anything to rein in huge premium spikes caused by a downturn in the business cycle and a hard market for their product (Hunter & Doroshow, 2011). One study has highlighted a portion of this phenomenon pointing out "medical malpractice insurers have historically inflated their loss projections and then revised their reported losses downward in subsequent years. The 'incurred losses' that medical malpractice insurance companies initially reported for policies in effect in each of the years examined were, on average, 46% higher than the amount the insurers actually paid out on those policies" (Rosenfield & Balber, 2005).

It is widely agreed that the periods of 1975–1978, 1984–1987, and 2001–2004 were considered hard market years and as such constituted a crisis in the medical malpractice insurance industry (Posner, 1986). That is, there were fewer sellers of insurance, and they were all charging higher premiums than previously. Clearly physicians have to pay much more for the same or less coverage in a hard market, and they complained to their state legislatures loudly for relief. But it is difficult to lobby for the repeal of a hard market in insurance, particularly when the predominant political paradigm in American medicine is staunchly conservative and pro-free market. So physicians cast about for a plausible policy remedy and arrived upon tort reform and limiting payouts for non-economic damages, which most physicians came to believe are out of control and unwarranted. The other response is to protect themselves by practicing defensive medicine, which is to order additional tests and procedures which may or may not help the patient but is perceived by the doctor to allay the fears that he has not done everything possible to treat the patient (Nahed, Babu, Smith, & Heary, 2012).

Kessler and McClellan (1996) compared cardiology treatment in states that had capped malpractice payments vs. those that had not. They found that in states without caps, physicians were providing more aggressive treatments, such as stenting, but their outcomes were no better than those states that were capped and were not performing those procedures as often. In addition to performing unnecessary procedures, some practitioners in high-risk specialties like neurosurgery have resorted to eliminating certain high-risk procedures from their practice, which can limit healthcare access to some patients in need (Japsen, 2003).

If one looks at this from the perspective of boom and bust cycles, it becomes evident that what happens in the regular insurance industry also happens in the market for medical malpractice insurance. In a boom cycle, the premiums for insurance do not rise as fast and that those in the sales side of the operation fight to keep them low so that their product is more competitive in the marketplace. As claims start to mount, it becomes evident that premiums were not set high enough to cover losses and the actuaries in the claims department begin to hold sway on premiums such that the company's reserves are built up, which means higher premiums until the next cycle.

As Baker notes, there are basically three problems that occur as a result of an insurance crisis. The first is access, some doctors find it very hard to get insurance at any price. The second is some doctors in certain specialties are stuck with much higher bills than others and thus carry an unequal burden. Third, unpredictable and rapid increases in premiums cause huge disruption in small medical offices who do not have the margin to absorb such costs (Baker, 2005).

Too Many Lawsuits or Too Much Malpractice?

What is happening is a bigger cause for concern and that is the epidemic of medical errors that occur each year and that number has unfortunately been increased substantially upward from the 1998 IOM number of 44,000 to 100,000 to a much higher 200,000 to 400,000 per year (James, 2013). While 35% of physicians do report that they or a family member has suffered from a medical error, they believe that no systematic changes need be made; instead we should work to sanction those individuals who are responsible for the bulk of the more serious errors (Blendon et al., 2002).

Medicare recently decided to require hospitals to publicly report nine different measures related to medical errors (Centers for Medicare & Medicaid Services, 2006). These were:

- Foreign object retained after surgery
- Air embolism
- Pressure ulcers, Stage 3 and 4
- Trauma and falls
- Collapsed lung due to medical treatment
- Breathing failure after surgery
- Postoperative PE/DVT (a preventable and often deadly blood clot)
- Wound split open after surgery
- Accidental cuts or tears from medical treatment

The idea was to inform the public on which hospitals had a greater incidence of making deadly mistakes and which were not.

Naturally the American Hospital Association did not share the belief that this information should become public because it was felt that the public would misinterpret those results (Binder, 2013). Patient knowledge of healthcare costs and outcomes would be a necessary condition for a functioning market in health care, but it is apparent we will not see data on either, because it is believed the public wouldn't be able to make sense of it enough to make an informed decision about their care. They would prefer we leave the decision-making up to healthcare professionals who are bound to act as our agents as to what is right and proper care; and patients pay whatever they deem fit to charge for those services. The bottom line is that the fear and silence are the responses the public gets when they seek to find out what happened to themselves or a loved one; preventing litigation takes precedence over seeking out the truth and working to prevent errors (Coylewright, 2007).

To reiterate the real problem is not medical malpractice lawsuits and awards but rather inadequate patient safety. Coulombe and Boughton found that 5.3 percent of physicians nationally are responsible for 56 percent of medical malpractice payouts nationally. They found that each of those physicians had multiple malpractice claims with 2 percent having three or more claims against them that accounted for 30.9 percent of all payouts. More importantly they found that 83.2 percent of doctors had never made a malpractice payout (Coulombe & Boughton, 2004). More importantly, according to the National Practitioner Data Base, only 11.1 percent of those who had three or more malpractice payouts among them faced disciplinary action taken against them by their state medical boards, while that number increased only slightly to 14.4 percent and 17.2 percent of physicians who had four and five payouts made. And that is when medical malpractice payments get reported to the National Practitioner Data Base. According to Public Citizen (a non-profit consumer advocacy organization), HHS failed to report 63% of medical malpractice payment reports to the database which of course undermines the utility of the database in tracking malpractice (PublicCitizen, 2019).

One study looked at over 700,000 patient safety events that occurred in over 40 million Medicare hospitalizations from 2007 to 2009. Roughly 1–2 percent experienced one or more of 13 patient safety events. Of those that experienced one or more patient safety events had a 12.5% chance of dying from those events; this resulted in close to 80,000 in-hospital deaths during that time period. And then there is the cost of these patient safety events. Reed and May (2011) found those 13 patient safety events cost the United States about $7.3 billion dollars over those 2 years measured and 2 of the 13 (pressure ulcers and post-operative respiratory failure) accounted for over 50% of that money.

Obviously the fear of malpractice litigation is real; it does alter the practice of medicine such that physicians would order extra and, some would say, unnecessary tests to protect themselves against what they see as an out of control malpractice litigation environment. Studdert et al. (2005) surveyed 824 physicians in high-risk specialties, and nearly all of those who completed the survey reported practicing "defensive" medicine. Some of these practitioners have reported limiting their performance of high-risk or complex procedures that were believed to lead to bad outcomes and litigation. The belief is that if physicians increase their use of defensive medicine because of the fear of litigation, patient access to care and increased costs of that care will result (Nahed, Babu, Smith, & Heary, 2012). And it is not just the high-risk professions that perceive this risk of malpractice suits. Physicians in lower liability risk areas, such as primary care, show as much concern over malpractice as those in high-risk areas (Bishop, Federman, & Keyhani, 2010). Carrier et al. evaluated physicians' perceptions of malpractice concern across various states and found that policies that seek to control malpractice costs have limited effect on those concerns regardless of tort reforms take (Carrier, Reschovsky, Mello, Mayrell, & Katz, 2010). Frakes and Gruber (2019) found an interesting natural experiment comparing based on active duty physicians treating active duty personnel and thus immune from malpractice lawsuits. They compared the healthcare service intensity of that population that couldn't sue with their other patients that could and found that the active duty personnel were "treated with less intensity" and had no adverse health outcome consequences. The notion of defensive medicine (no pun intended) is real, and while patients may believe they received more and perhaps better care, there is no evidence to support the notion that more is better when it comes to healthcare services.

The question remains as to how big a problem this really is, particularly when compared to rather large healthcare expenditures that are now over 3 trillion dollars a year in the United States. People that promote the notion of tort reform as the answer to reducing the practice of defensive medicine and keep litigious patients and attorneys at bay seem to believe that if these costs were reduced or eliminated, those healthcare costs in the United States would substantially decline. Thomas et al. found that while defensive medicine practices are prevalent, their impact on medical costs are small. While this study relies on hypothetical situations to make its case, the evidence points to putting tort reforms in place such as caps on non-economic damages that does little to nothing to reduce overall healthcare costs but suggests that caps may still be a worthwhile thing to enact even given its minimal effect on costs (Thomas, Ziller, & Thayer, 2010).

Tort Reforms Commonly Adapted by States

The evidence between tort reform and lower malpractice premiums is rather mixed. In three states (Texas, West Virginia, and Ohio) that enacted tort reform legislation, physicians have seen lower liability premiums and/or less steep premium increases. This, in turn, has led to more insurers entering the market and more physicians setting up practice in those states (Norbut, 2005). But for Texas, which enacted reforms in 2003 (a $250,000 non-economic damage cap), the effect was short-lived and did not have any long-term effect on health insurance markets and costs (Born, Karl, & Viscusi, 2017). Public Citizen has found that while malpractice payments for Texas doctors have decreased almost 65%, insurance rates and Medicare spending have actually increased more than the national average (Lincoln, 2011). Arkush et al. state that Texas has one of the worst healthcare systems in the United States on almost every measure. Costs for services have increased, the number of uninsured has gone up, the cost of health insurance has gone up, the growth of doctors per capita has slowed, and more importantly the number serving in underserved rural areas has dropped (Arkush, Gosselar, Hines, & Lincoln, 2009). Paik et al. found some evidence that physician spending did increase somewhat in Medicare patients, thus refuting the argument that tort reform will reduce healthcare spending because the need for defensive medicine is much less (Paik, Black, Hyman, & Silver, 2012).

California was the first state to implement medical malpractice caps with the passage of the Medical Injury Compensation Reform Act in 1975. It did not limit economic damages for actual cost of care for someone hurt from a medical mistake, but it did limit attorney fees to no more than 15 percent or $600,000 total. Malpractice attorneys said that the law had a chilling effect on them taking cases because the cost of doing so would far outweigh any award they would receive for their efforts (Lohr, 2005). The main effects of this legislation has been a modest decrease in medical malpractice premiums for physicians, but that came after the state adopted price controls in 1988. More telling is the reduction in malpractice victims receiving a just settlement for their justifiable claims (The Henry J. Kaiser Family Foundation, 2009). Its impact on healthcare costs was not found to be very much if at all, thus undercutting one of the arguments for having the caps in the first place.

Massachusetts took a different route in 2012, when they enacted legislation that was referred to as a policy of Disclosure, Apology, and Offer (DA&O). This legislation was designed to "promote healing for all parties involved – and prevent recurrence of mistakes" (Beaulieu, 2012). Rather than a reactive and adversarial form of liability system shrouded in a wall of silence and blaming others, a DA&O system is thought to be proactive, where physicians can help in the recovery process as well. The more important feature of this besides working with the patient is to evaluate the error that caused the medical harm and work to prevent recurrences, in other words, to learn from one's mistakes in an open and transparent fashion. But the debate over high malpractice premiums continued on. Massachusetts had enacted a $500,000 cap on non-economic damages, but it was rarely enforced, and as a result, physicians believed that malpractice premiums had increased over 50%

in the years 2001 to 2004; blame was placed either on greedy insurance companies or a non-enforcement of the cap on non-economic damages (The Henry J. Kaiser Family Foundation, 2006).

More interesting in this discussion is that approach the Board of Registration took in regard to physicians who have made three or more malpractice payments as a result of legal action against them. Nancy Achin-Audesse, executive director of the Board, said at least three malpractice award payments were the number that made a physician subject to disciplinary action by both hospitals and the medical board itself: in the 10 years from 1995 to 2005, 0.25% of all doctors in the state caused about 13% of all malpractice payments which amounted to about $134 million (Pear, 2005). It seems that the approach of disclosure, apology, and offer in conjunction with oversight of those physicians who are most subject to malpractice verdicts and judgments holds a great deal of promise in significantly reducing errors as well as the burden those errors have on patients and their families who suffer from them.

Oregon is attempting to implement a more novel approach that seeks to cut down on medical malpractice lawsuits and at the same time improve patient safety. The approach was designed to allow physicians to learn from errors, compensate those injured as a result of those errors, and reduce the overhead of administering the medical liability system (Levine, 2012). One other incentive that came out of Oregon was malpractice premium discounts for doctors who used electronic health records and secure email to communicate with patients. The *use of disclosure of medical errors for learning purposes and to improve patient safety* is a novel approach because it allows an admission of error without worrying that it will be used in a malpractice suit against the provider. The state would set up a patient safety commission that would receive voluntary reports of adverse events from providers, patients, and/or families. The parties involved in the matter would be encouraged to sit down and discuss the event with the purpose of learning what caused the event as well as how to prevent its recurrence. The process is confidential and cannot be used in a court nor are any claims report to the National Practitioner Data Base or state licensure agencies (Wojcieszak, 2013). One might expect that such legislation would change the current dynamic of blame and cover up that occurs in most.

Illinois had passed tort reform in the form of capping non-economic damages at $500,000 in cases against physicians and $1 million against hospitals. The Illinois Supreme Court struck down the law saying that the law allowed the legislature to interfere improperly with a jury's right to determine damages (Japsen & Sachdev, 2010); see also Lebron v. Gottlieb Memorial Hospital (2010). Of note the ISMIE Mutual Insurance, the largest malpractice insurer in the state, had paid out about $150.4 million to settle claims in 2004, which was down 10% from 2003; nevertheless, the premiums charged to doctors were higher than that to cover unexpected losses; however that surplus grew 5.4% to $212.5 million, which reinforced the notion that insurance companies were charging higher than necessary premiums (Klein, 2005). Of note, ISMIE put a moratorium on any new policyholders in 2003 because of lower than expected stock market performance, healthcare inflation, and larger compensatory awards (Japsen, 2007).

Another argument that gets made a lot in favor of non-economic caps in Illinois is the belief that physicians are fleeing the state for states with caps, e.g., Wisconsin. The record during the last malpractice crisis does not support this argument in that in 2004 there were more than 9000 more physicians licensed to practice medicine in Illinois than 10 years previously (Parsons & Japsen, 2004). Back in 2005 Chase found that Illinois registered 3% more neurosurgeons and 2% more OB-GYN over the previous year with neighboring states with caps registering about the same increase (Chase, 2005). But the *fear* of losing physicians unless states adopt malpractice reforms is very real. And for some "high-risk" specialties, there may be some movement of physicians to states with non-economic damage caps (Klick & Stratmann, 2007). But for other lower-risk specialties, there is no correlation between the place where they practice and non-economic tort reforms (Klick & Stratmann, 2007).

One of the areas in Illinois often cited as an epicenter of the malpractice crisis is Madison County. President George W. Bush dubbed Madison County a "judicial hellhole" for the volume of malpractice lawsuits filed in the county (Silva, 2005). An analysis of Madison, as well as neighboring St. Clair County, found that there was no evidence to support the rhetoric that awards were more frequent or larger than anywhere else (Vidmar & Robinson II, 2005). Vidmar and Robinson found that from 1992 through 2004, only 11 jury verdicts found in favor of the plaintiff, and only 2 of those verdicts exceeded $1 million dollars (Vidmar & Robinson II, 2005). They also found that there is no evidence that supports the claims that physicians are leaving Illinois because of a perceived malpractice crisis, but rather there has been an increase in total physicians in Illinois including the at-risk specialties of OB/GYN and neurosurgery (Vidmar & Robinson II, 2005). This was confirmed by an American Board of Medical Specialty study that showed an increase in both OB/GYNs and neurosurgeons (Chase, 2005).

The Policy Discussion

To reiterate in a different way, policy discussions that focus on correcting the unsafe and poor-quality health care that many Americans receive go nowhere in the current policy debates. For years healthcare providers were under little incentive to make sure that patients would not be readmitted to the hospital for foreseeable and preventable issues related to their care. Under the Affordable Care Act, Medicare has begun to address this issue of the preventable readmission of payments by withholding reimbursement for those events (Rau, 2012). Meanwhile, the consumer-directed healthcare ideology continues to talk about "empowering patients" with patients and families making choices over their health insurance benefits and care processes based on cost and quality information that simply is *not* yet available to the general consuming public. In addition, data that would help state licensure boards and the general public determine how safe a particular practitioner is available to states on a rather prohibitive fee structure and not available at all to the general public (USA

Today Editorial Board, 2018). By making the data unavailable, it becomes most difficult for patients to knowledgably negotiate the medical care system and determine who the best practitioners may be based on quality.

What is not being discussed in this arena are the elements of how "free markets" work and do not work in health care. In order for health care to work as a truly free market, both patients and physicians must have access to the same cost and quality information on procedures in order to make an informed choice on care direction. Healthcare cost and quality data are not now available, nor has it ever been available to the healthcare-consuming public. At the same time, the profession of medicine must come to grips with how changing existent practice patterns to encompass patient input may mean hurting provider incomes, as well as interfering in physician autonomy and hegemony all while continuing to leave patients and their loved ones at the mercy of a system that has a high probability of hurting and/or killing them.

This chapter raises the issue of how malpractice may come to be redefined in which the focus becomes providing safer, less lethal care to patients rather than protecting professionals who make avoidable mistakes, that is, what are "mistakes" or "errors," or what is merely not holding to "good standards" or "best practices." Costs will be a determining factor at the hands of provider management.

So we return to the notion of why is there focus on malpractice suits and awards as the primary problem and not medical mistakes and malpractice itself. Like a lot of policy discussions, this policy direction is one built on perception and protecting oneself in the pursuit of correcting what is deemed to be professional priorities. Peters examined the notion of the perception of jury verdicts and awards characterized as unfair by looking at three decades of data. What he found was that physicians won half of those cases examined that expert reviewers believe they should have lost. The bottom line is that physician defendants and their expert witnesses were more successful than plaintiffs and their expert witnesses at swaying juries in a manner that contradicted outside independent reviews of the cases (Peters, 2007).

Possible Solutions

Physicians Healing Themselves One of the more interesting stories of a physician specialty that saw the problem squarely for what it was then transformed their practice into something safer and less risky for all of us. In 1985, anesthesiologists came to the conclusion that it was in their best interests to improve patient safety rather than protecting themselves against lawsuits by using devices and technology that alert physicians to potentially fatal mistakes made in the operating room (Hallinan, 2005). They worked with nurses, insurance companies, and medical product companies to take a hard look at why people were being injured and killed as a result of the use of anesthesia. Most of their preventable mistakes involved human error, e.g., ventilator disconnections, changes in gas flow, and drug administration problems. While equipment failure was not found in many cases, the design was part of the problem in exacerbating the human error. Other issues that contributed included poor communication, inexperience and not being familiar with equipment, and/or procedures (Cooper, Newbower, Long, & McPeek, 2002). By investigating recurring problems that could be fixed, they were able to develop new standards of practice to provide guidance on safe practice. They found that as they adhered to these standards, their malpractice liability dropped, malpractice premiums dropped, and more importantly the number of medical errors declined (Eisenbrey, 2005). The proof is borne out in the numbers of reduced lawsuits and claims from before. In 1972, anesthesiologists accounted for 7.9 percent of all medical malpractice claims, but by 2001 that number had dropped in half to 3.8 percent of all claims (Coulombe & Boughton, 2004).

So why don't more physician practices and specialties learn from what anesthesia did in response to what it saw as a crisis? Patient safety events or the occurrence of preventable errors were found to have occurred 708,642 times out of 40,348,218 acute care Medicare hospitalizations from 2007 through 2009. It affected 667,828 unique individuals (Reed & May, 2011). There were some patients that had multiple safety events occur to them which increased their chances of dying as a result, the phenomena of cascade iatrogenesis (Potts et al., 1993). And the cost of dealing with these events cost around $7.3 billion for the 2 years studied (Reed & May, 2011). Wachter cited four main forces that continue to cause patient safety issues in health care. They are:

- Healthcare systems that are not responsible for errors caused.
- Errors are viewed as single incidents and rarely discussed openly.
- A reimbursement system that is based on services performed, not results and outcomes and certainly not safe care delivered.
- A structure that separates the physician from the rest of the healthcare enterprise which creates different financial incentives (Wachter, 2004).

Caps on Non-economic Damages Several states have enacted caps on tort reform, and, as previously stated, these tend to limit injured patients from seeking redress for malpractice committed against them, as well as not really fixing the issue at hand which is malpractice, not malpractice awards or insurance premiums. Weiss et al. found that in states with caps, the median payout was 15.7% lower in states with caps vs. states without caps and payouts increased only 83.3% vs. 127.9%, but premiums went up regardless in both (Weiss, Gannon, & Eakins, 2008). In states with caps, median annual premiums went up 48.2% vs. 35.9% in non-cap states.

This data points toward some other driving variables to increasing premiums for medical malpractice insurance. Other more important variables related to the increasing premiums include the insurance business cycle, the need to increase reserves, the underperformance of investment income, and supply and demand of insurance providers in the market (Weiss, Gannon, & Eakins, 2008). Studdert et al. state that the real issue on whether or not a state implements caps is how society values the stabilization of the medical malpractice insurance markets and its relationship to allowing juries to determine the appropriate amounts of non-economic damages in any particular case (Studdert, Yang, & Mello, 2004). It is also unclear whether or not damage caps have any impact on if services are performed in specific areas where tort reform has not occurred (Zhao, 2005).

Caps on Attorney Contingency Fees By capping what an attorney can charge on any given malpractice case, it would make these cases less financially attractive to lawyers and thus make it more difficult to file malpractice suits because there is little financial incentive for attorneys to take such cases. While this may in effect reduce malpractice suit filings, it also reduces the truly injured patients from seeking redress for their grievances in a court of law for want of finding any attorney to take the case. Attorneys typically charge up to 40% mostly on contingency and often based their representation on the likelihood of a winning case, not on a patient's need for restitution.

Enterprise Liability In the 1970s, this was defined as "institutional licensure"; this notion was proposed in the Clinton health plan in 1993 in an attempt to shift liability from physicians to health plans and other organizations; the thought was that physicians would work for one or two health plans rather than the many they often do work for. As health plan consolidation didn't occur under the Clinton proposal, as increasing numbers of physicians have later moved into employment status, they become accountable to the organization in which they work and would not have as much personal professional exposure. The enterprise is better at overseeing physician performance and as a trade-off for covering physicians would have better control over physician behaviors that would lead toward better control over liability exposure for the organization (Danzon, 1991). At the same time, physicians are not held responsible for errors caused by system failures within the organization itself (Baker, 2005; O'Neill et al., 2014).

Safe Harbors One possible solution for malpractice involves providing practitioner protection when they follow designated guidelines. Kachalia et al. looked at the potential effects of a safe harbor law by evaluating closed claims in the state of Oregon. They found that the outcomes would have changed in favor of the defendant physician in only 1 percent of 266 claims from 2002 to 2009 (Kachalia, Little, Isavoran, Crider, & Smith, 2014). Karls (2009) found similar findings when he examined safe harbors in the state of Maine. Aside from the underwhelming evidence on safe harbors, one must question who is developing the guidelines for clinical practice and how are the outcomes for following those guidelines measured in terms of safety and quality. It is also important to note that not all malpractice results in a lawsuit. The Institute of Medicine developed guidelines in 2011 on how these guidelines should be developed. They must be based on a complete review of the existing evidence, developed by experts representing key groups in the field; be considerate of patient preferences where appropriate, based on explicit and transparent processes; and be revised when appropriate (Graham et al., 2011). Bovbjerg and Berenson delineated the challenges of guidelines as hard and expensive in terms of both development and implementation. Resistance to them can be significant and ongoing, and most importantly they are not foolproof (Bovbjerg & Berenson, 2012).

Revocation of Practitioner Licenses   Very few physicians have been disciplined by State Regulatory and Licensing Boards with sanctions. According to a ProPublica story in August of 2011, more than 700 physicians in California were sanctioned by healthcare organizations and yet faced no discipline from the Medical Board (Wang, 2011). As Adams states, even when physicians are disciplined in one state, they can move and set up a practice in another state (Adams, 2007). There is no effective national oversight of physicians, a serious negligence of the profession as a whole. Levine and Wolfe state that while state medical boards may provide information on identifying those physicians who commit malpractice over and over, they found a more disturbing pattern of non-discipline by the boards vested in overseeing clinical practice (Levine & Wolfe, 2009). And if practitioners do the right thing and report errors and mistakes through a good faith effort to correct the problem and make the patient whole again through disclosure and apology, they should not be punished with sanctions and license revocation (Wojcieszak, 2012).

What is clear in the current set up is that state licensure boards are subject to regulatory capture by the very individuals they are supposed to be overseeing and that by and large they do an ineffective job in sanctioning bad physicians (Levine, Oshel, & Wolfe, 2011). As Rayack pointed out over 50 years ago, "Occupational licensing is the fundamental technique for maintaining acceptable standards, and authority over licensing is vested in the fifty-five state or territorial boards of medical examiners." However, as we have shown operationally, the boards are little more than extensions of organized medicine, i.e., control over standards is in fact exercised by the American Medical Association. And its de facto control over standards is the seminal source of the A.M.A.'s power to engage in economic restrictionism. As Friedman has pointed out "Licensure is the key to A.M.A. power" (Rayack, 1967).

Acknowledgment of Errors and Disclosure Programs   One of the most misunderstood notions in this whole discussion is the concept of admitting mistakes and disclosing them to the patients impacted by that mistake. Mazor studied the concept of full disclosure and found that it addresses the patients' expectations of care and honesty, as well as enhancing the physician-patient relationship—but may not completely prevent litigation for medical malpractice (Mazor et al., 2004). What seems clear for the last 20 years is that most patients "desire an acknowledgment from their physicians of even minor errors and doing so may actually reduce the risk of punitive actions" aka malpractice lawsuits (Witman, Park, & Hardin, 1996). One of the best examples of this type of program is called Sorry Works run by Doug Wojcieszak who launched this coalition after losing his brother to medical error. His program flew in the face of a traditional response to a medical error, which was to hide it, never discuss it in public, and, most troublesome, never discuss and fix the system problems that may have contributed to the error. The outcome of a silent wall campaign in which families and patients are told nothing is amply illustrated in an August 2018 Narrative Matters piece in the journal *Health Affairs* (Hemmelgarn, 2018). She describes the wall of silence that arose after her 9-year-old daughter died rather suddenly after a diagnosis of leukemia. As she states so eloquently, "No one in the organization where Alyssa died came to work with the intent of harming her.

She was a small piece in a complex health care system, where holes aligned and mistakes slipped through. While it is difficult to understand how this happens, the trauma becomes even more egregious when silence is all you receive from the organization in the aftermath." While the hospital and caregivers may be knowledgeable about what happened, it is imperative that patients and their families are brought into the discussion to obtain reasons to what happened and in most cases closure.

The way the program worked was fairly simple, the practitioner requests a review if they suspect a medical error has occurred. A team of outside experts reviews the particular case looking to make sure that standards of care have been met. The patient's family is advised to get an attorney, and if a medical error is determined to occur, the parties will work out a fair settlement between them (McAree, 2005; Wojcieszak, Saxton, & Finkelstein, 2007). The notion behind this approach centers on the concept of an apology being a healing restoration of damaged relationships as well as strengthening currently satisfactory relationships (Lazare, 2006).

Michael Woods speaks to the 4 R's of apology, which are:

- Recognition of when an apology is necessary
- Regret when the practitioner responds with empathy
- Responsibility where the practitioner owns up to what's happened
- Remedy or making it right to the patient (Woods, 2007)

Kaldjian et al. (2007) noticed several differences between physician attitudes and how they responded to error disclosure. They found that a "willingness to disclose errors was associated with higher training level and a variety of patient centered attitudes, and it was not lessened by previous exposure to malpractice litigation."

Gallagher et al. (2006) conducted an interesting study on physicians and how they would respond to various clinical scenarios involving medical errors. They found that 56% of respondents chose statements that mention the outcome of the error, but not the error itself. 42% would mention both the outcome of the error and the error itself. Respondents disclosed more information if they had engaged in this behavior before and had had a positive experience with it, and they were Canadian.

One of the main problems with adopting this apology approach is a practitioner's belief that disclosing and apologizing will be used against the physician in a malpractice trial. It is a tough task to get practitioners on board with this direction when they've been immersed in a "defend and deny" environment that denied that no adverse event occurred, let alone any error that resulted in that event. But slowly over time that position may be eroding. The University of Michigan Health System was one of the first major medical centers to adopt disclosure and apology as a policy. They found that the number of pre-suit claims and lawsuits dropped from 260 in July 2001 to 100 after enactment of the policy (Landro, 2007). Since Michigan adopted this program, lawsuits have decreased, and legal defense costs have declined 61 percent (Kalb, 2010). Once implemented, key stakeholders in this institution got strongly behind it. The evidence appears to support this approach, but as always, more research is needed (Bell et al., 2012). The University of Illinois Health Systems also adopted a disclosure and apology program in 2006, and they have seen malpractice filings drop by half since implementation. The hospital has acknowledged preventable error and apologized in 37 different cases, and only 1 patient has filed suit (Sack, 2008). Kachalia et al. (2018) found that "implementing a communication-and-resolution program does *not* expand liability risk and may, in fact, improve some liability outcomes."

Maintaining the old "deny and defend" policy was found to increase the chances of patients seeking legal advice and created a more negative emotional response in all that were involved (Mazor et al., 2006). In these endeavors it's very important to have buy in to the policy from the very top of the organization to create a safe environment for others to come forward and get past their shame in admitting their mistakes (Ofri, 2013). Mello et al. studied six such programs and looked at both challenges and lessons learned in implementation (Mello et al., 2014). They found that program success was based on having "a strong institutional champion, invested in building and marketing the program to skeptical clinicians, and making it clear that the results of such transformative change will take time" (Mello et al., 2014). One of the bigger turning points in this area came in the VA hospital in Lexington, Kentucky, in 1999. They had lost two major suits in the 1980s and changed their approach to a disclosure and apology policy, that is, all the medical errors would be communicated fully and immediately to patients and their families, and they would also discuss ways to prevent recurrence of those errors (Zimmerman, 2004). It was thought that this type of policy would lead to more lawsuits and higher payouts, but that was not the case. Transparency in this area can also help healthcare organizations and practitioners to regain the public's trust. In order for us to move forward, we must learn from our mistakes (Makary, 2012).

The Veteran's Administration adopted a system-wide disclosure policy in 1995 and JCAHO followed suit in 2002 requiring disclosure to patients for specific events. That was the year the University of Michigan adopted its Disclosure, Apology, and Compensation policy, which cut litigation costs by $2 million a year and new claims by over 40%. Other organizations have since joined in adopting these policies, and so far the results have been positive in reducing costs associated with medical errors (O'Reilly, 2010).

States that have passed apology laws have done so to accomplish several policy outcomes. Typically, these laws would exclude any statement of apology from any subsequent malpractice trial, thus alleviating one of physician and risk manager fears about the process. The idea of the laws is to facilitate communication between practitioner and patient to resolve the error as well as fixing those issues that led to the error. McMichael et al. did study this issue by examining a dataset of malpractice claims across the United States (McMichael, Van Horn, & Viscusi, 2016). They found that physicians who do not regularly perform surgery may face increased probability of a malpractice lawsuit and a higher than average payout to resolve that claim. Surgeons did not see much of any change in their malpractice lawsuit cases nor their average payouts. Their conclusion was that apology laws do not effectively limit medical malpractice liability risks for physicians (McMichael, Van Horn, & Viscusi, 2016).

So why do practitioners still seek to conceal medical errors? The first is what Banja refers to as resolving cognitive dissonance, that is, concealing the error is not "morally or professionally wrong" (Banja, 2005). Physicians may use a variety of techniques to obscure the error that helps them to resolve their moral quandary, such as euphemistic language, comparing the error to something far worse and therefore not as bad, displacement and/or diffusion of responsibility to others, or outright blaming others for the error. The second is referred to as Daniel Goleman's Model of Moral Attentiveness (Watson, Hickman, Morris, Milliron, & Whiting, 1995). By rationalizing the error, the practitioner can move their moral attentiveness away from the very uncomfortable truth of the error to a more morally problematic option that feels more comfortable and allows for a reinterpretation of the event to something less threatening. This leads to the concept of medical narcissists and their role in perpetuating errors rather than admit they are fallible and make mistakes. Watson et al. describe three characteristics of medical narcissists that include emotional disengagement, ideological rigidity, and compulsiveness (Watson, Hickman, Morris, Milliron, & Whiting, 1995).

So how do we change the culture of medical training and practice to change the culture of medicine so that disclosure of medical errors to patients and families is the only reasonable and moral option. White et al. conclude that while disclosure is happening, physicians are still not receiving any formal training in how to do it (White et al., 2008). This is important at the beginning of physician training as that is the time when errors occur more often and a time to teach how to correctly respond to them (Haller, Myles, Taffe, Perneger, & Wu, 2009). Kirch and Boysen (2010) list five changes to medical education that would change the culture around the response to medical errors. They are:

- Making patient safety top priority
- Routing morbidity and mortality conferences
- Offering safety course electives to any physician in training
- Using simulations of specific error situations
- Creating an environment of teamwork with all healthcare professions so that all can be empowered to identify and report medical errors

Disclosure of medical errors has theoretical support among physicians with one survey stating that 77 percent of clinicians believing that when a mistake is made, patients should be notified (Mazor, Simon, & Gurwitz, 2004). But the reality is often different when confronted with an actual error.

Readmission Restrictions and Penalties Several years ago, Medicare laid out new rules that would penalize hospitals for high readmission rates in attempt to incentivize better and more efficient care (Rau, 2012). Naturally health insurers, like Aetna and WellPoint, are following suit in not paying for care related to preventable medical errors. Items not being reimbursed included bed sores, falls, and a variety of other preventable injuries that occur in hospitals. The change is based on the belief that stopping the monetary incentive of added treatment resulting from error seems to reward those who fail to provide quality and efficient care. By not paying for the extra care required to fix outcomes related to an error, it is believed that hospitals will have a financial incentive to fix those situations that cause errors in the first place (Fuhrmans, 2008).

So after all that, why can we not get a handle on fixing the issues that lead to mistakes? One physician describes the atmosphere that leads to mistakes that centers around the complexity of caring for patients in today's healthcare settings, the sheer volume of patients that practitioners oversee care on and the number of distractions that occur that draw their attention away from the task at hand, as well as our belief that one individual can be responsible for fixing all that ails us (Allen, 2013). All of these values are part of the corporatization strategy to maximize throughput of patients through the physicians' office, and healthcare complexes can maximize labor while minimizing expenses. Leape addresses this in his call to improve working conditions at hospitals by utilizing appropriate nurse to patient ratios, appropriate physician workload, and limiting work hours to ensure that practitioners are not operating on little to no sleep (Leape, 2004).

As Igel states, it is not the practitioner's fault so much as it is the system in which they work and the environment, and predicaments that management puts practitioners in that drive the current situation. He goes on to state that "it is often soon-forgotten that lapses in the delivery of quality care are not so much a failure of medicine than a failure of management's task to efficiently and effectively place the right people where they need to be at a particular time." By extension, physicians who become preoccupied with the prevention of malpractice suits cannot concentrate fully on the tasks and activities in which they employ their strengths, which means their skills become less and less organized. This, in due course, disrupts the doctor/patient relationship. For better and worse, so too do the snowflakes of information available on the World Wide Web that have emboldened patients to perform self-diagnosis and self-treatment, as do the television dramas that examine the medical decisions and procedures made by physicians and lay bare their personal life decisions and activities (Igel, 2010).

Perednia clarifies several steps that can minimize medical errors that primarily result from poor communication and/or system failures. They are eliminating and minimizing the number of steps in any healthcare transaction wherever possible, emphasizing electronic systems that capture transactions and make sure that all software is connected and able to communicate with each other, implement unique and universal identifiers for system users, and most important given what was said above allow more time for communications and interactions between practitioners and patients as well as practitioner to practitioner (Perednia, 2011).

Electronic Health Records What is the role of the electronic health records (EHR) in identifying systemic issues that lead to errors and medical mistakes? Virapongse et al. found that physicians who used electronic health records were less likely to have a paid malpractice claim than those who did not (Virapongse et al., 2008). Quinn et al. found that using EHR improved patient safety and found less paid claims against physicians who used EHR than those who did not (Quinn, Kats, Kleinman, Bates, & Simon, 2012). The reason for this decrease in medical errors and improvement in patient safety was based on the use of checklists, alerts, and predictive tools embedded in the EHR. More accurate prescribing and test ordering processes enhanced patient safety and reduced redundancy brought about by mis-communication (Quinn, Kats, Kleinman, Bates, & Simon, 2012). Unfortunately, EHR use can lead to new problems that can lead to malpractice claims which include practitioners who copy/paste information from one patient to another, auto-population of erroneous or outdated clinical information into a patient's chart, entry error caused by selection of the wrong item in a drop-down menu, and letting the computer the physician is using to enter information positioned such that the physician has to turn their back on the patient to enter data, thus interfering in the physician-patient connection during the exam (Ranum, 2019).

Limiting Hours of Work Especially for Resident Physicians

One of the issues related to medical errors has to do with the number of hours that physicians-in-training work in their training program. The American Council for Graduate Medical Education (ACGME) approved new work-hour standards for residency programs back in 2002 (Philibert, Friedmann, & Williams, 2002). The hours' limitation was brought about by the death of Libby Zion in a New York Hospital allegedly due to mistakes made by overtired physicians in training who misdiagnosed her in 1984. The case brought about a change in the rule that physicians in training could work over 100 hours per week. The impact of sleep deprivation on impairing judgment was brought up as a policy issue that needed to be addressed (Beck, 1988). Poulose et al. (2005) found that contrary to popular belief, there was no association between resident work hours and improvements in patient safety. But Landrigan et al. (2004) found that interns made more medical errors when working shifts greater than 24 h than when working less. While common sense might suppose a link between sleep deprivation and the probability of committing errors, the evidence appears to be more mixed with some studies saying there is no reduction in mortality, while others stating that patient safety is improved. The sense is that hours may not be so much the issue as errors in communication that lead to disruptions in care (Borman, Jones, & Shea, 2012). Most studies focus on the length of time that a physician in training spends on task without taking a break. Desai et al. (2013) found that depression rates and sleep length were not improved, and error rates increased with shorter shifts. ACGME responded to the controversy by developing Common Work Hour Standards (Accreditation Council for Graduate Medical Education, 2017). In this document, they affirmed the 80-hour weekly limit, as well as continuous work-hour limit of 16 hours for first-year residents. Work done at home in support of their clinical training is included in that 80-hour limit. While much work needs to be done to gauge the effect of sleepiness on physician performance, it seems clear that this issue will continue to be considered when attempting to reduce medical errors. One other area that seems to be warranting a further look is depression in medical providers and the increased risk of committing medical errors as a result of suffering from depression (Pereira-Lima et al., 2019).

Specialty Health Courts

One of the complaints physicians have had with the current malpractice tort system is that non-physicians often sit in judgment of them and the type of care they provided. The idea as Common Good saw it would have judges that were dedicated to working full time on healthcare issues and those judges would provide rulings based on proper standards of care. These rulings would provide guidance to both practitioners and patients as to what standards of care should be and provide predictability and fairness (Common Good, 2012). This model has several characteristics which would include trained judges with expertise in medical matters and would be able to consult with neutral experts on medical injuries. These judges would use that information to issue rulings independent of the jury system. The proceedings would be both expedited and evidence-based and revolve around how the event in question occurred and whether or not the error could have been prevented. The standard utilized for compensation would be avoidability, rather than negligence which gets away from the issue of fault. They would operate off of a schedule of awards related to both non-economic and economic damages providing fairness, and, most importantly, the findings would be published and used to prevent reoccurrence of the same event (Barringer, 2006)

It sounds too good to be true, and in some cases, it is because any humanly created system will fall prey at some point to human frailties. Widman (2006) does an excellent job of countering the major points of setting up separate health courts. The major downside is that the law was never intended to have separate courts for all facets of the law even though they may differ considerably in scope. Our system is designed to handle all manner of cases, and the realization that judges, as well as attorneys, are not specialty based like medicine drives home the concept that tort law and malpractice is part of common law since the beginning of the Republic. Our system is generalistic in nature and legal principles are deemed more important than subject/specialty areas. As such the precedents built into common law are what makes up the core of our judicial system. The belief is that these types of courts may be found to be unconstitutional in that they may deny those harmed by medical malpractice access to redress of their grievances in a court of law. By pointing to programs such as worker's compensation and product liability arbitration clauses, we are allowed to see that these specialty courts could work, but those programs have been problematic and have been shown over time to foster corporate America's desire to reduce and eliminate the average person's access to the courts for injuries caused by negligence and unsafe practices (Widman, 2006).

There is also a feeling that a specialized health court would fall prey to "capture" by the more powerful players in that venue and therefore might be even more heavily weighted toward physicians and healthcare organizations than the current jury system. There is a sense that a jury would be more representative of the public at large and may be more impartial in seeing both sides to a particular case (Peters, 2008).

New York State began a program of "judge-directed negotiation" and at its core uses something similar to a health court in that a judge with "expertise" in medical matters runs the case and brings the parties together to effect a settlement if possible. Since one judge instead of multiple judges oversees the case, procedural meetings can proceed apace, and parties are always up to speed on what is happening throughout. The object is to have the judge facilitate settlements but not dictate them, and if the parties don't agree, they have the option to go to trial like they have always done. While malpractice cases can typically take upward of 3 years or more, to complete these types of cases, if settled it can be done in 6–9 months (Kaiser Daily Health Policy Report, 2011).

Other Nations Offer a Path Forward

One solution might be to look at what other nations' health systems are doing to minimize errors and improve patient safety. Clearly the American way of health care is not to look elsewhere for solutions that would benefit us, because we believe we possess the greatest healthcare system in the world in addition to our belief in American Exceptionalism and our individualistic mindset. But if we do look to other nations for some kind of roadmap to be helpful, there are a few useful examples that might provide direction to a better and safer future for all of us.

New Zealand uses a no-fault system to compensate victims who sustain medical injuries that are not part of a "necessary and ordinary" part of treatment independent of whether negligence is involved. Physicians submit claims on the patient's behalf, and those claims are decided by a panel comprised of clinicians who typically resolve most claims within 7 months of filing. While the actual payout may be lower than what a US patient may receive in a standard malpractice case, it's important to note that citizens of New Zealand enjoy universal health coverage and therefore don't incur costs of care due to the injury that are not covered (Bismark & Paterson, 2006). The payments received are "ongoing and cover items like lost income, childcare, medical expenses, housing modifications and social and vocational rehabilitation." One benefit of using such a centralized system is to track incidents and determine both causative elements of the errors, as well as ways to fix those elements to prevent recurrence.

Sweden uses a different system in a public insurance company which covers all public healthcare providers and any private providers who work for the government. All other private providers are required to have liability insurance through private providers. Sweden uses an avoidability standard to determine whether an injury qualifies for payment in that providers had a less risky option available. This is a less strict standard than negligence. Claims are submitted by patients and are reviewed by claim handlers in the company along with provider consultants; most claims are completed within 8 months (Johanssen, 2010). The Claims Company does use the information from such incidents to improve patient safety.

Denmark uses something slightly similar to the above countries but uses an independent organization governed by the Patient Insurance Association or PIA. Patients or their providers file a claim with the PIA, and they use the same avoidability standard instead of the higher standard of negligence. Claims can take upward of

7 months to complete, and compensation is determined by things like the cost of treatment, loss of earnings, and the inability to work again. The Danish Liability for Damages Act controls what payments are made including any costs associated with "pain and suffering." Like New Zealand and Sweden, the data compiled is often used to drive patient safety efforts to prevent recurrence of the same medical errors.

As for developing countries, Cortez argues "that it is particularly important for patients to have realistic avenues to redress their medical grievances." Cortez (2011) compares Mexico to India and states that Mexico is superior because it "eliminates the requirement that patients carry the burden of proof by securing medical records and expert testimony from reluctant parties" and appears to be less adversarial which may suit the realities in these countries.

Lastly, the United Kingdom is waging a campaign to strengthen transparency by requiring hospitals to inform their patients that their safety has been threatened, but as far as learning from these errors and not repeating them, there is no current duty to do so, although one might suspect that it would make the most sense if you're collecting this data on a national level to determine causation and work to prevent recurrence across the National Health Service (GOV.UK, 2012).

Looking to the Future

Lucien Leape believes that we need to focus on the "fundamental deficiencies and dysfunctions in our health care system" (Leape, 2004). He believes that we need to focus on implementing EHR, improving working conditions with appropriate nurse staffing ratios and physician's workloads with reasonable working hours enforced, implementing a full disclosure policy that informs patients when errors occur and an enterprise liability system that focuses on compensation for medical injuries and not blame. His last recommendation was to create a Federal Health Safety Agency that would do for health care what the FAA does for aviation and would set and enforce national standards for patient safety (Leape, 2004).

Hyman and Silver believe that we should look at the incentives that continue to be misaligned to safe and effective health care (Hyman & Silver, Medical Malpractice Litigation And Tort Reform: It's The Incentives Stupid, 2006). They propose the following improvements:

- Tying practitioner compensation to measureable improvements in care outcomes that would allow the market to determine who the superior performers are.
- When mistakes become expensive to make, then practitioners will have an incentive to stop making them and take the necessary measures to keep patients from being injured. Malpractice premiums should be based on experience and that doctors who commit malpractice should pay more in premiums than those who do not.
- Using non-economic damage caps to reward those who report errors and punish those who cover up or not report errors.

- Strengthen reporting of faulty delivery systems and whistleblower protections for healthcare workers who report errors and defective systems and processes.
- Repeat offenders must undergo quality audits, and results of those audits must be made public. Bad actors must either change their behaviors or leave the profession.
- Repeal tort reforms that have not been found to enhance public safety, including all laws in states who implemented caps on non-economic damages.
- Research of additional solutions must expand so that we can continue to identify systems and processes that cause patient harm.

"The medical liability system is broken and failing all key stakeholders: physicians, patients, and the health care system. It is costly, inefficient, and the process of compensating injuries related to medical errors is imprecise. For the past 40 years, reforms to the tort system have met with variable success, partly due to tepid political enthusiasm and partly due to equivocal cost-control and patient safety outcomes. Increasingly partisan political climates have made advancing additional tort reforms difficult, especially on the federal level. The time has come for a paradigm shift in our strategy for addressing medical liability from simple tort reform focused on cost-containment to a patient-centered approach that prioritizes patient safety and preserves the doctor-patient relationship" (O'Neill, et al., 2014). What clinicians need to realize is that medical errors are not inevitable, so steps must be taken to prevent errors, rather than react to them once they occur (Yurkiewicz, 2018). While physicians may genuinely lament medical errors that cause harm and death to their patients, one recent editorial strongly advises that physicians not see themselves as victim or second victims (Clarkson, Haskell, Hemmelgarn, & Skolnik, 2019). The sense is that it takes attention away from the true victims of medical errors, the patients and their families, but more importantly it "subtly promote the belief that patient harm is random, caused by bad luck, and simply not preventable." Clearly, given the discussion in this chapter, most, but not all, medical errors can be predicted and perhaps prevented.

Several themes emerge from this review of malpractice: malpractice occurs much more often than it should and that policymakers, practitioners, and the general public grasp at "solutions" that don't fix the underlying problems; in fact, proposed solutions may worsen the actual situation by limiting patient's ability to seek redress in the courts. By limiting access to the courts and limiting non-economic damages, providers can continue to perform more and more procedures with little concern for clinical outcomes—whether or not anyone is hurt in the process of performing those procedures. Under current reimbursement schemes, both providers and healthcare organizations can enhance their bottom lines by performing more procedures, more complex procedures, and riskier procedures without much risk of backlash from patients, most of whom are not paying the bill directly.

The medical-industrial complex stays intact with little outside authorities questioning its motivations or intents because the practice of modern medicine remains a complex and expensive undertaking that only few, if any, individuals completely can understand. Corporate forces are formulating their own "solutions" to quality problems that may or may not address these malpractice and malpractice insurance issues. In any case, the medical profession must come to grips with their atavistic past reactions to this set of critical systems problems.

References

Accreditation Council for Graduate Medical Education. (2017). The 2017 ACGME common work hour standards: Promoting physician learning and professional development in a safe, human environment. *Journal of Graduate Medical Education, 9*, 692–696.

Adams, D. (2007, May 21). Alerts foil state-jumping by disciplined doctors. Retrieved from *American Medical News*. http://www.ama-assn.org/amednews/2007/05/21/prl20521.htm

Albers, J. (2010, July 13). Minnesota nurses strike advances debate on hospital safety, quality fundamental health care system change needed. *Twin Cities Daily Planet*.

Allen, M. (2013, January 9). What a new doctor learned about medical mistakes from her mom's death. *ProPublica*.

American Association for Justice. (2009, November). *Five myths about medical negligence.* Retrieved from American Association for Justice. http://www.justice.org/clips/Five_Myths_About_Medical_Negligence.pdf

Angoff, J. (2005, July). *Falling claims and rising premiums in the medical malpractice industry.* Retrieved from Center for Justice & Democracy. http://centerjd.org/content/study-falling-claims-and-rising-premiums-medical-malpractice-insurance-industry

Arkush, D., Gosselar, P., Hines, C., & Lincoln, T. (2009). *Liability limits in Texas fail to curb medical costs.* Washington, DC: Public Citizen.

Aronowitz, S. (1998). *From the ashes of the old - American labor and America's future.* Boston, MA: Hougton-Mifflin.

Auerbach, D. I., Buerhaus, P. I., & Staiger, D. O. (2020). Implications of the rapid growth of the nurse practitioner workforce in the US. *Health Affairs, 39*, 273–279.

Baicker, K., & Chandra, A. (2005, Fall). *Defensive medicine and disappearing doctors?* Retrieved from Cato Institute: https://www.cato.org/sites/cato.org/files/serials/files/regulation/2005/9/v28n3-4.pdf

Bailey, M. (2020, February 4). Beyond burnout: Docs decry 'moral injury' From financial pressures of care. *Kaiser Health News*, pp. 1–6.

Baker, T. (2005). *The medical malpractice myth.* Chicago, IL: University of Chicago Press.

Banja, J. (2005). *Medical errors and medical narcissism.* Sudbury, MA: Jones & Bartlett.

Barbash, J. (1984). *The elements of industrial relations.* Madison, WI: University of Wisconsin Press.

Barringer, P. (2006). *Windows of opportunity.* Brooklyn, NY: Common Good.

Basu, S., Berkowitz, S. A., Phillips, R. L., Bitton, A., Landon, B. E., & Phillips, R. S. (2019). Association of primary care physician supply with population mortality in the United States, 2005-2015. *JAMA Internal Medicine, 179*, 506–514.

Bates, D. W., & Singh, H. (2018). Two decades since to err is human: An assessment of progress and emerging priorities in patient safety. *Health Affairs, 37*, 1736–1743.

Beaulieu, D. (2012, June). *Disclosure, apology and offer: A new approach to medical liability.* Boston, MA. Retrieved from http://www.massmed.org/News-and-Publications/Vital-Signs/Back-Issues/Disclosure,-Apology-and-Offer%2D%2DA-New-Approach-to-Medical-Liability/#.WzUxT9VKjIU

Beck, J. (1988, March 24). Meet Libby Zion, victim of a tired hospital resident. *Chicago Tribune*.

Beider, P., & Elliott, C. (2003, October). *The economics of U.S. Tort liability: A primer.* Retrieved from Congressional Budget Office. http://cbo.gov/sites/default/files/cbofiles/ftpdocs/46xx/doc4641/10-22-tortreform-study.pdf

Bell, S. K., Smulowitz, P. B., Woodward, A. C., Mello, M. M., Duva, A. M., Boothman, R. C., & Sands, K. (2012). Disclosure, apology, and offer programs: Stakeholders' views of barriers to and strategies for broad implementation. *Milbank Quarterly, 90*, 682–705.

Berenson, R. A. (1991). A physician's view of managed care. *Health Affairs, 10*, 106–119.

Binder, L. (2013, July 15). *Bone-chilling mistakes hospitals make and why they don't want you to know.* Retrieved from Forbes.com. http://www.forbes.com/sites/leahbinder/2013/07/15/bone-chilling-mistakes-hospitals-make-and-why-they-dont-want-you-to-know/

Bishop, T. F., Federman, A. D., & Keyhani, S. (2010). Physicians' views on defensive medicine: A national survey. *Archives of Internal Medicine, 170*, 1081–1083.

Bismark, M., & Paterson, R. (2006, January/February). No-fault compensation in New Zealand: Harmonizing injury compensation, provider accountability, and patient safety. *Health Affairs, 25*, 278–283. Retrieved from Commonwealth Fund.

Bivens, J., Engdahl, L., Gould, E., Kroeger, T., McNicholas, C., Mishel, L., … Zipperer, B. (2017, August 24). *How today's unions help working people.* Retrieved from Economic Policy Institute. https://www.epi.org/publication/how-todays-unions-help-working-people-giving-workers-the-power-to-improve-their-jobs-and-unrig-the-economy/

Bixenstine, P. J., Shore, A. D., Mehtsu, W. T., Ibrahim, A. M., Freischlag, J. A., & Makary, M. A. (2013). Catastrophic medical malpractice payouts in the United States. *Journal of Healthcare Quality.* https://doi.org/10.1111/jhq.12011.

Black, S. E. (2012). Economic credentialing of physicians by insurance companies and headache medicine. *Headache, 52*, 1073–1040.

Blendon, R. J., DesRoches, C. M., Brodie, M., Benson, J. M., Rosen, A. B., Schneider, E., … Steffenson, A. E. (2002). Views of practicing physicians and the public on medical errors. *The New England Journal of Medicine, 347*, 1933–1940.

Borman, K. R., Jones, A. T., & Shea, J. A. (2012). Duty hours, quality of care, and patient safety: General surgery resident perceptions. *Journal of the American College of Surgeons, 215*, 70–77.

Born, P. H., Karl, J. B., & Viscusi, W. K. (2017). The net effects of medical malpractice tort reform on health insurance losses: The Texas experience. *Health Economics Review, 7*, 42–58.

Bovbjerg, R. R., & Berenson, R. A. (2012). *The value of clinical practice guidelines as malpractice "safe harbors".* Princeton, NJ: Robert Wood Johnson Foundation & the Urban Institute.

Braverman, H. (1974). *Labor and monopoly capital.* New York: Monthly Review Press.

Brennan, T. A. (1991). Practice guidelines and malpractice litigation: Collision or cohesion? *Journal of Health Politics, Policy and Law, 16*, 67–85.

Brenner, M. (2011, June 24). *California strike highlights hospitals' skewed priorities.* Retrieved from Labor Notes. http://labornotes.org/2011/06/california-strike-highlights-hospitals-skewed-priorities

Breslin, E. M. (1987, August). The moral costs of the Ontario physicians' strike. *Hastings Center Report*, pp. 11–14.

Breunig, E. (2015, May 1). Even conservative millennials support unions. *The New Republic.* Retrieved from https://newrepublic.com/article/121688/pew-releases-new-labor-survey-millennials-supports-unions

Brewbaker, W. S., III. (2000). Physician unions and the future of competition in the health care sector. *UC Davis Law Journal, 33*, 545–600.

Brunton, M., & Sayers, J. G. (2011). Jostling for the ethical high ground during a junior doctors' strike. *Australian Journal of Communication, 38*, 69–87.

Bucknor, C. (2016, August). *Black workers, unions, and inequality.* Retrieved from Center for Economic and Policy Research. http://cepr.net/images/stories/reports/black-workers-unions-2016-08.pdf?v=2

Bureau of Labor Statistics. (2020, January 22). *Union members - 2019.* Retrieved from Bureau of Labor Statistics: https://www.bls.gov/news.release/union2.nr0.htm

Bureau of Labor Statistics, U.S. Department of Labor. (2019, July 24). *Annual work stoppages involving 1,000 or more workers, 1947-2018.* Retrieved from Bureau of Labor Statistics. https://www.bls.gov/web/wkstp/annual-listing.htm#annual_listing.xlsx.f.3

Bureau of Labor Statistics, United States Department of Labor. (2019, July 29). *Annual work stoppages involving 1,000 or more workers, 1947–2018*. Retrieved from Bureau of Labor Statistics. https://www.bls.gov/web/wkstp/annual-listing.htm

Capps, C., Dranove, D., & Ody, C. (2017). Physician practice consolidation driven by small acquisitions, so antitrust agencies have few tools to intervene. *Health Affairs, 36*, 1556–1563.

Carmen, D. (2011). The frequency and severity of medical malpractice claims: High risk and low risk specialities. *Maedica, 6*, 230–231.

Caroll, J. (2007). Convenient care clinics inconvenience the AMA. *Managed Care*, p. 8.

Carrier, E. R., Reschovsky, J. D., Mello, M. M., Mayrell, R. C., & Katz, D. (2010). Physicians' fears of malpractice lawsuits are not assuaged by tort reform. *Health Affairs, 29*, 1585–1592.

Carr-Saunders, A. M., & Wilson, P. A. (1933). *The professions*. Oxford, UK: Clarendon Press.

Casalino, L. P. (2017). The Medicare access and CHIP reauthorization act and the corporate transformation of American medicine. *Health Affairs, 36*, 865–869.

Casalino, L. P., Ramsay, P., Baker, L. C., Pesko, M. F., & Shortell, S. M. (2018). Medical group characteristics and the cost and quality of care for medicare beneficiaries. *Health Services Research, 53*, 4970–4996.

Castellucci, M. (2019, September 28). Low unemployment emboldening healthcare workers to strike. *Modern Healthcare*. Retrieved from https://www.modernhealthcare.com/labor/low-unemployment-emboldening-healthcare-workers-strike?utm_source=modern-healthcare-am&utm_medi%E2%80%A6

Center for Justice & Democracy at New York Law School. (2012). *The truth about medical malpractice litigation*. New York: Center for Justice & Democracy at New York Law School.

Centers for Medicare & Medicaid Services. (2006, May 18). *Eliminating serious, preventable, and costly medical errors - Never events*. Retrieved from CMS: https://www.cms.gov/newsroom/fact-sheets/eliminating-serious-preventable-and-costly-medical-errors-never-events

Chapman, C. (2006). Doctors' strike blamed for patient's death in Germany. *The Lancet, 368*, 189.

Chase, B. (2005, September 12). Number of licensed doctors growing. *Crain's Chicago Business*.

Chima, S. C. (2013). Global medicine: Is it ethical or morally justifiable for doctors and other healthcare workers to go on strike? *BMC Medical Ethics, 14*, S5–S15.

Clarkson, M. D., Haskell, H., Hemmelgarn, C., & Skolnik, P. J. (2019). Abandon the term "second victim". *BMJ, 364*, 1233.

Collins, J. (2019, November). *Future outlook: Retail clinics in store healthcare market 2025 with business opportunities, challenges, market share and company profile*. Retrieved from Wheel Chronicle: https://wheelchronicle.com/2019/11/19/future-outlook-retail-clinics-in-store-healthcare-market-2025-with-business-oppourunities-challenges-market-share-and-company-profile-access-health-ama-atlanticare/

Common Good. (2012, March 26). *Health courts continue to gain bipartisan support from 2012 presidential candidates*. Retrieved from PRNewswire. http://www.prnewswire.com/news-releases/health-courts-continue-to-gain-bipartisan-support-from-2012-presidential-candidates-144266955.html

Cooper, J. B., Newbower, R. S., Long, C. D., & McPeek, B. (2002). Preventable anesthesia mishaps: A study of human factors. *Quality & Safety of Health Care, 11*, 277–283.

Cortez, N. (2011). A medical malpractice model for developing countries. *Drexel Law Review, 4*, 217–241.

Coulombe, S., & Boughton, B. (2004, March). *The facts about medical malpractice in Pennsylvania*. Retrieved from Public Citizen: http://www.citizen.org/documents/PA_MedMal_Exec.pdf

Coylewright, J. (2007). No fault, no worries… Combining a no-fault medical malpractice act with national single-payer health insurance plan. *Indiana Health Law Review, 4*, 29–58.

Cunningham, S. A., Mitchell, K., Venkat Narayan, K. M., & Yusuf, S. (2008). Doctors' strike and mortality: A review. *Social Science & Medicine, 67*, 1784–1788.

Dallet, B. (1994). Economic credentialing: Your money or your life! *Health Matrix: Journal of Law-Medicine, 4*, 325–363.

Dampier, C. (2019, October 25). Chicago's striking teachers helped spark a new wave of teacher activists. Here's why teacher activism is on the rise. *Chicago Tribune*.

Danzon, P. M. (1983). An economic analysis of the medical malpractice system. *Behavioral Sciences & the Law*, 39–54.

Danzon, P. M. (1991). Liability for medical malpractice. *Journal of Economic Perspectives, 5*, 51–69.

Demanuelle-Hall, J., & DiMaggio, D. (2019, December 20). *2019 year in review: Workers strike back.* Retrieved from portside.org: https://portside.org/2019-12-21/2019-year-review-workers-strike-back

Desai, S. V., Friedman, L., Brown, L., Dezube, R., Yeh, H.-C., Punjabi, N., ... Confrancesco, J. (2013). Effect of the 2011 vs 2003 duty hour regulation–compliant models on sleep duration, trainee education, and continuity of patient care among internal medicine house staff a randomized trial. *JAMA Internal Medicine, 173*, 649–655.

DiSalvo, D. (2019, February 14). *Public-sector unions after janus: An update.* Retrieved from Manhattan Institute. https://www.manhattan-institute.org/public-sector-unions-after-janus

Dobkin, J. (1975). Housestaff strike - Immoral or inevitable? *New York State Journal of Medicine, 75*, 1785–1786.

Donohue, J. J., III, & Ho, D. E. (2007). The impact of damage caps on malpractice claims: Randomization inference with differences-in-differences. *Journal of Empirical Legal Studies, 4*(1), 69–102.

Eisenbrey, R. (2005, August 2). Malpractice made perfect. *The American Prospect.* Retrieved from http://prospect.org/article/malpractice-made-perfect

Engel, D. M. (2016). *The myth of the litigious society - Why we don't sue.* Chicago, IL: University of Chicago Press.

Fiester, A. (2004). Physicians and strikes: Can a walkout over the malpractice crisis be ethically justified? *The American Journal of Bioethics, 4*, W12–W16.

Frakes, M., & Gruber, J. (2019). Defensive medicine: Evidence from military immunity. *American Economic Journal: Economic Policy, 11*, 197–231.

Freeman, R. B. (1979). *Labor economics.* Englewood Cliffs, NJ: Prentice-Hall.

Freeman, R. B., & Medoff, J. L. (1984). *What do unions do?* New York City: Basic Books.

Fuhrmans, V. (2008, January 15). Insurers stop paying for care linked to errors. *Wall Street Journal*.

Furnivall, D., Bottle, A., & Aylin, P. (2018, February 8). Retrospective analysis of the national impact of industrial action by English junior doctors in 2016. Retrieved from *BMJ Open.* https://bmjopen.bmj.com/content/bmjopen/8/1/e019319.full.pdf

Gallagher, T. H., Garbutt, J. M., Waterman, A. D., Flum, D. R., Larson, E. B., Waterman, B. M., ... Levinson, W. (2006). Choosing your words carefully - How physicians would disclose harmful medical errors to patients. *Archives of Internal Medicine, 166*, 1585–1593.

Glick, S. M. (1986). Health workers' strikes: A further rejoinder. *Journal of Medical Ethics, 12*, 43–44.

Goldstein, D. (2019, October 25). It's more than pay: Striking teachers demand counselors and nurses. *New York Times*, p. A12.

Gooch, K. (2016, September 6). 8 latest developments on Allina Health's dispute with nurses. Retrieved from *Becker's Hospital Review*: http://www.beckershospitalreview.com/human-capital-and-risk/8-latest-developments-on-the-allina-health-nurse-dispute.html

Gorman, G., & Westing, C. (2013). Nursing, unionization, and caste: The lessons of local 6456. *Advances in Nursing Science, 36*, 258–264.

GOV.UK. (2012, December 4). *NHS will have to admit to patient safety failures.* Retrieved from Inside Government: http://mediacentre.dh.gov.uk/2012/12/04/nhs-will-have-to-admit-to-patient-safety-failures/

Graham, R., Mancher, M., Wolman, D. M., Greenfield, S., & Steinberg, E. (Eds.). (2011). *Clinical practice guidelines we can trust.* Washington, DC: The National Academies Press.

Greenwood, E. (1957). Attributes of a profession. *Social Work, 2*, 44–55.

Grosskopf, I., Buckman, G., & Garty, M. (1985). Ethical dilemmas of the doctors' strike in Israel. *Journal of Medical Ethics, 11*, 70–71.

Guwande, A. (2018, November 5). Why doctors hate their computers. Retrieved from *The New Yorker*. https://www.newyorker.com/magazine/2018/11/12/why-doctors-hate-their-computers

Hadley, J., & Mitchell, J. M. (1997). Effects of HMO market penetration on physicians' work effort and satisfaction. *Health Affairs, 16*, 99–111.

Hagedorn, J., Paras, C. A., Greenwich, H., & Hagopian, A. (2016). The role of labor unions in creating working conditions that promote public health. *American Journal of Public Health, 106*, 989–995.

Haller, G., Myles, P. S., Taffe, P., Perneger, T. V., & Wu, C. L. (2009). Rate of undesirable events at beginning of academic year: Retrospective cohort study. *British Medical Journal, 339*, 3974–3982.

Hallinan, J. T. (2005, June 21). Once seen as risky, one group of doctors changes its ways. *Wall Street Journal*.

Han, S., Shanafelt, T. D., Sinsky, C. A., Awad, K. M., Dyrbye, L. N., Fiscus, L. C., … Goh, J. (2019). Estimating the attributable cost of physician burnout in the United States. *Annals of Internal Medicine, 170*, 784–790.

Harmon, R. G. (1978). Intern and resident organizations in the United States: 1937-1977. *Milbank Memorial Fund Quarterly*, pp. 500–530.

Hemmelgarn, C. (2018). Seeking answers, hearing silence. *Health Affairs, 37*, 1332–1334.

Hibberd, J. M., & Norris, J. (1991). Strikes by nurses: Perceptions of colleagues coping with fallout. *The Canadian Journal of Nursing Research, 23*, 43–54.

Hirschman, A. O. (1970). *Exit, voice and loyalty - Response to decline in firms, organizations, and states*. Cambridge, MA: Harvard University Press.

Ho, C. (2019, April 11). Nurses authorize strike at Stanford, Lucile Packard Children's Hospital. Retrieved from *San Francisco Chronicle*. https://www.sfchronicle.com/business/article/Nurses-authorize-strike-at-Stanford-Lucile-13760829.php?psid=frG5a

Housestaff win patient care improvements: Freedman's hospital. (1975). *The New Physician, 24*, 17.

Hsu, J., Vogeli, C., Price, M., Brand, R., Chernew, M. E., Mohta, N., … Ferris, T. G. (2017). Substantial physician turnover and beneficiary 'churn' in a large Pioneer ACO. *Health Affairs, 36*, 640–648.

Hudson, M. J., & Moore, G. P. (2012). Defenses to malpractice - What every emergency physicians should know. *Journal of Emergency Medicine, 41*, 598–606.

Hunter, J. R., & Doroshow, J. (2011, December 15). *Insurance industry creates insurance crisis harming their policyholders*. Retrieved from Americans for Insurance Reform: http://www.insurance-reform.org/studies/Repeat_OffendersFinal.pdf

Hyman, D. A., Black, B., Zeiler, K., Silver, C., & Sage, W. M. (2007). Do defendants pay what juries award? Post-verdict haircuts in Texas medical malpractice cases, 1988-2003. *Journal of Empirical Legal Studies, 4*, 3–68.

Hyman, D. A., & Silver, C. (2006). Medical malpractice litigation and tort reform: It's the incentives stupid. *Vanderbilt Law Review, 59*, 1085–1136.

Igel, L. H. (2010). The forgotten hysteria over malpractice. *Society, 47*, 525–528.

Illich, I. (2002). *Limits to medicine - Medical nemesis: The expropriation of health*. New York: Marion Boyars Publishers LTD.

James, J. J. (1979). Impacts of the medical malpractice slowdown in Los Angeles County: January 1976. *American Journal of Public Health, 69*, 437–334.

James, J. T. (2013). A new, evidence-based estimate of patient harms associated with hospital care. *Journal of Patient Safety, 9*, 122–128.

Japsen, B. (2003, February 16). Doctors curtail practices to fight insurance costs. *Chicago Tribune*. Retrieved from http://articles.chicagotribune.com/2003-02-16/business/0302160243_1_malpractice-coverage-brain-surgery-malpractice-premiums

Japsen, B. (2007, January 16). Doctors' insurer to ease freeze. Retrieved from *Chicago Tribune*. http://articles.chicagotribune.com/2007-01-16/business/0701160189_1_medical-malpractice-stock-market-insuranc

Japsen, B., & Sachdev, A. (2010, February 4). Illinois supreme court strikes down medical malpractice law. Retrieved from *Chicago Tribune*. www.chicagotribune.com/business/ct-biz-0205-malpractice-doctors-20100204,0,1406171.story

Johanssen, H. (2010). The Swedish system for compensation of patient injuries. *Upsala Journal of Medical Sciences, 115*, 88–90.

Johnson, L. A. (2019a, April 27). CSO strike is over as trustees and musicians approve new five-year contract. Retrieved from *Chicago Classical Review*. https://chicagoclassicalreview.com/2019/04/trustees-approve-new-five-year-contract-cso-strike-is-over/

Johnson, S. R. (2019b, July 22). Physician pay rebounds in 2018 after flat 2017. *Modern Healthcare*, pp. 22–26.

Jones, J. M. (2019, August 28). *As labor day turns 125, union approval near 50-year high*. Retrieved from Gallup: https://news.gallup.com/poll/265916/labor-day-turns-125-union-approval-near-year-high.aspx

Jones, T. (2003, January 4). Surgeons' strike over insurance splits W. Va. *Chicago Tribune*.

Kachalia, A., Little, A., Isavoran, M., Crider, L.-M., & Smith, J. (2014). Greatest impact of safe harbor rule May be to improve patient safety, not reduce liability claims paid by physicians. *Health Affairs, 33*, 59–66.

Kachalia, A., Sands, K., Van Niel, M., Dodson, S., Roche, S., Novack, V., ... Mello, M. M. (2018). Effects of a communication-and-resolution program on hospitals' malpractice claims and costs. *Health Affairs, 37*, 1836–1844.

Kaiser Daily Health Policy Report. (2011, November 21). N.Y. malpractice program may offer model for medical liability cases. *Kaiser Daily Health Policy Report*.

Kalb, C. (2010, September 27). Do No Harm. *Newsweek*.

Kaldjian, L. C., Jones, E. W., Wu, B. J., Forman-Hoffman, V. L., Levi, B. H., & Rosenthal, G. E. (2007). Disclosing medical errors to patients: Attitudes and practices of physicians and trainees. *Journal of General Internal Medicine, 22*, 988–996.

Kanter, G. P., Polsky, D., & Werner, R. M. (2019). Changes in physician consolidation with the spread of accountable care organizations. *Health Affairs, 38*, 1936–1943.

Karls, C. C. (2009, September). *Retooling medical professional liability*. Retrieved from Milliman Health Reform Briefing Paper: http://publications.milliman.com/publications/healthreform/pdfs/retooling-medical-professional-liability.pdf

Kessler, D. P., & McClellan, M. (1996). *Do doctors practice defensive medicine?* Cambridge, MA: National Bureau of Economic Research.

Khazan, O. (2020, February 25). The opposite of socialized medicine. *The Atlantic*, pp. 1–9.

Kirch, D. G., & Boysen, P. G. (2010). Changing the culture in medical education to teach patient safety. *Health Affairs, 29*, 1600–1604.

Klein, S. A. (2005, March 14). Doc insurer's payouts dip. *Crain's Chicago Business*, pp. 1, 8.

Klick, J., & Stratmann, T. (2005, November 3). *Does malpractice reform help states retain physicians and does it matter?* Retrieved from USC FBE Applied Economics Workshop: https://pdfs.semanticscholar.org/a581/b927b13f1504280987ff5ab371d9de3524aa.pdf

Klick, J., & Stratmann, T. (2007). Medical malpractice reform and physicians in high-risk specialties. *Journal of Legal Studies, 36*, S121–S142.

Kohn, L. T., Corrigan, J. M., & Donaldson, M. S. (1999). *To err is human: Building a safer health system*. Washington, DC: National Academies Press.

Krause, E. A. (1996). *Death of the guilds: Professions, states, and the advance of capitalism, 1930 to the present*. New Haven, CT: Yale University Press.

Landrigan, C. P., Rothschild, J. M., Cronin, J. W., Kaushal, R., Burdick, E., Katz, J. T., ... Czeisler, C. A. (2004). Effect of reducing interns' work hours on serious medical errors in intensive care units. *New England Journal of Medicine, 351*, 1838–1848.

Landro, L. (2007, January 24). Doctors learn to say 'I'm sorry'. *Wall Street Journal*, p. D5.

Lazare, A. (2006). Apology in medical practice - An emerging clinical skill. *JAMA, 296*(11), 1401–1404.

Leape, L. L. (2004a). *Learning from mistakes: Toward error-free medicine*. New Brunswick, NJ: The Robert Wood Johnson Foundation.

Lebron v. Gottlieb Memorial Hospital, 930 N.E.2d 895, 237 Ill.2d 217 (Supreme Court of the State of Illinois February 4, 2010).

Lee, C. G., & LaFountain, R. C. (2011). *Medical malpractice litigation in state courts*. National Center for State Courts. Retrieved from http://www.courtstatistics.org/~/media/Microsites/Files/CSP/Highlights/18_1_Medical_Malpractice_In_State_Courts.ashx

Levine, A., Oshel, R., & Wolfe, S. (2011). *State medical boards fail to discipline doctors with hospital actions against them*. Washington, DC: Public Citizen. Retrieved from http://www.citizen.org/documents/1937.pdf

Levine, A., & Wolfe, S. (2009). *Hospitals drop the ball on physician oversight*. Public Citizen. Retrieved from www.citizen.org/hrg

Levine, D. (2012, September 25). *2 states try to tackle medical malpractice reform*. Retrieved from Governing.com: http://www.governing.com/columns/col-states-tackles-medical-malpractice-reform.html

Lincoln, T. (2011). *A failed experiment - Health care in Texas has worsened in key respects since state instituted liability caps in 2003*. Washington, DC: Public Citizen. Retrieved from http://www.citizen.org/documents/a-failed-experiment-report.pdf

Linn, R. (1987). Moral reasoning and behavior of striking physicians in Israel. *Psychological Reports, 60*, 443–453.

Linzer, M., Manwell, L. B., Mundt, M., Williams, E., Maguire, A., McMurray, J., & Plane, M. B. (2005, February). *Organizational climate, stress, and error in primary care: The MEMO study*. Retrieved from NCBI. https://www.ncbi.nlm.nih.gov/books/NBK20448/

Linzer, M., Sinsky, C. A., Poplau, S., Brown, R., & Williams, E. (2017). Joy in medical practice: Clinician satisfaction in the healthy work place trial. *Health Affairs, 36*, 1808–1814.

Liu, F., & Salmon, J. W. (2010). Comparison of herbal medicines regulation between China, Germany and the United States. *Integrative Medicine, 9*, 42–49.

Lohr, S. (2005, February 27). Bush's next target: Malpractice lawyers. Retrieved from *New York Times*. http://www.nytimes.com/2005/02/27/business/yourmoney/27mal.html

Lowes, R. (2017, October 16). Opioids top list of malpractice claims linked to medications. *Mescape*.

Magali, L. (1977). *The rise of professionalism*. Berkely/Los Angeles, CA: University of California Press.

Makary, M. (2012, September 21). How to stop hospitals from killing us. *The Wall Street Journal*, p. C1.

Makary, M. A., & Daniel, M. (2016). Medical error - The third leading cause of death in the US. *British Medical Journal, 353*, i2139.

Malinowski, B., Minkler, M., & Stock, L. (2015). Labor unions: A public health institution. *American Journal of Public Health, 105*, 261–271.

Manthous, C. A. (2012). Hippocrates as hospital employee: Balancing beneficence and contractual duty. *American Journal of Critical Care, 21*, 60–66.

Marjoribanks, T., Good, M.-J. D., Lawthers, A. G., & Peterson, L. M. (1996). Physicians' discourses on malpractice and the meaning of medical malpractice. *Journal of Health and Social Behavior, 37*, 163–178.

Mazor, K. M., Reed, G. W., Yood, R. A., Fischer, M. A., Baril, J., & Gurwitz, J. H. (2006). Disclosure of medical errors - What factors influence how patients respond? *Journal of General Internal Medicine, 21*, 705–710.

Mazor, K. M., Simon, S. R., & Gurwitz, J. H. (2004a). Communicating with patients about medical errors. *Archives of Internal Medicine, 164*, 1690–1697.

Mazor, K. M., Simon, S. R., Yood, R. A., Martinson, B. C., Gunter, M. J., Reed, G. W., & Gurwitz, J. H. (2004b). Health plan members' views about disclosure of medical errors. *Annals of Internal Medicine, 140*, 409–418.

McAree, D. (2005, April 25). *A med-mal litigation antidote: "I'm sorry" under proposal, doctors would apologize to their patients-the arbitrate.* Retrieved from Law.com. http://www.law.com/jsp/nlj/PubArticleNLJ.jsp?id=900005427742

McGeehan, P. (2019a, April 10). New York hospitals reach a landmark deal on nurse staffing. *New York Times* , p. A25.

McGeehan, P. (2019b, March 2019). Nurses in large hospital systems threaten to strike over staffing. *New York Times*, p. A23.

McKinlay, J. B., & Stoeckle, J. D. (1988). Corporatization and the social transformation of doctoring. *International Journal of Health Services, 18*, 191–205.

McMichael, B. J., Van Horn, R. L., & Viscusi, W. K. (2016, December 10). *Sorry is never enough: The effect of state apology laws on medical malpractice liability risk.* Retrieved from ssrn.com. https://papers.ssrn.com/sol3/papers.cfm?abstract_id=2883693

Mechanic, D. (1989). Doctor strikes and other signs of discontent. *American Journal of Public Health, 79*, 1218–1219.

Mehrota, A., Ray, K., Brockmeyer, D. M., Barnett, M. L., & Bender, J. A. (2020). Rapidly converting to "virtual practices": Outpatient care in the era of COVID-19. *NEJM Catalyst, 1*, 1–9.

Mello, M. M. (2006). *Understanding medical malpractice insurance: A primer.* Princeton, NJ: The Robert Wood Johnson Foundation.

Mello, M. M., Boothman, R. C., McDonald, T., Driver, J., Lembitz, A., Bouwmeester, D., … Gallagher, T. (2014). Communication-and-resolution programs: The challenges and lessons learned from six early adopters. *Health Affairs, 33*, 20–29.

Mello, M. M., Chandra, A., Gawande, A. A., & Studdert, D. M. (2010). National costs of the medical liability system. *Health Affairs, 29*(9), 1569–1577.

Metcalfe, D., Chowdhury, R., & Salim, A. (2015, November 25). What are the consequences when doctors strike? Retrieved from *BMJ*. https://www.bmj.com/content/351/bmj.h6231

Miller, P., Thrall, T. H., & Norbeck, T. (2010, October 23). *Health reform and the decline of physician private practice.* Retrieved from The Physicians Foundation. https://physiciansfoundation.org/research-insights/health-reform-and-the-decline-of-physician-private-practice-2010/

Mondore, S., & Tivisonmo, J. G. (2015, July 9). *The new costs of unionization in healthcare union elections and representation: Lower HCAHPS scores and increase readmission rates.* Retrieved from IRI Analytics: http://www.fha.org/files/education/acrobat/2015Feb_LaborTrends_WhitePaper.pdf

Nahed, B. V., Babu, M. A., Smith, T. R., & Heary, R. F. (2012). Malpractice liability and defensive medicine: A national survey of neurosurgeons. *PLoS One, 7*, 1–7.

Norbut, M. (2005, March 28). Three crisis states show improvement since tort reform. *American Medical News*. Retrieved from www.amednews.com/2005/prl10328

O'Neill, K. M., Raykar, N., Bush, C., Murthy, S., Coffron, M., Armstrong, J. H., … Selzer, D. (2014). *Surgeons and medical liability: A guide to understanding medical liability reform.* Chicago, IL: American College of Surgeons.

Ofri, D. (2013, May 28). My near miss. *New York Times*.

Olson, J. (2016, June 26). Twin cities nurses' strike is over; dispute with Allina is not. Retrieved from *Minneapolis Star-Tribune*. http://www.startribune.com/twin-cities-nurses-strike-is-over-but-not-their-dispute-with-allina/384401821/

Ong'ayo, G., Wang'ondu, R., Bottomley, C., Nyaguara, A., Tsofa, B. K., Williams, T. N., … Etyang, A. O. (2019, May 22). Effect of strikes by health workers on mortality between 2010 and 2016 in Kilifi, Kenya: A population-based cohort analysis. Retrieved from *The Lancet Global Health*. https://www.thelancet.com/journals/langlo/article/PIIS2214-109X(19)30188-3/fulltext

O'Reilly, K. B. (2010, February 1). "I'm sorry": Why is that so hard for doctors to say? *Amednews*.

Page, L. (2016, August 17). *Would unions really help doctors get what they want?* Retrieved from Medscape.com. https://www.medscape.com/viewarticle/866869

Paik, M., Black, B. S., Hyman, D. A., & Silver, C. (2012). Will tort reform bend the cost curve? Evidence from Texas. *Journal of Empirical Legal Studies, 9*, 173–216.

Parsons, C., & Japsen, B. (2004, July 16). Physician count clouds malpractice argument - State data show increase in doctors. *Chicago Tribune*.

Pear, R. (2005, January 5). Panel seeks better disciplining of doctors. *New York Times*.

Penfield, R. (2018). Why junior doctors need more autonomy. *British Medical Journal, 363*, k4525.

Pensa P, (2007, August 24). Medical mistake caps put to the test. Florida Sun-Sentinel. https://www.sun-sentinel.com/news/fl-xpm-2007-08-24-0708240001-story.html

Perednia, D. A. (2011). *Overhauling America's healthcare machine - Stop the bleeding and save trillions*. Upper Saddle, River, NJ: FT Press.

Pereira-Lima, K., Mata, D. A., Loureiro, S. R., Crippa, J. A., Bolsoni, L. M., & Sen, S. (2019). Association between physician depressive symptoms and medical errors: A systematic review and meta-analysis. *JAMA Network Open*. https://doi.org/10.1001/jamanetworkopen.2019.16097.

Peters, J. P. (2008). Health courts? *Boston University Law Review, 88*, 227–289.

Peters, Jr., P. G. (2007, May). Doctors & juries. *Michigan Law Review*, pp. 1453–1495.

Philibert, I., Friedmann, P., & Williams, W. T. (2002). New requirements for resident duty hours. *JAMA, 288*, 1112–1114.

Piascik, A. (2019, April 22). Grocery store workers take on billion dollar multinational. Retrieved from *Counterpunch*. https://www.counterpunch.org/2019/04/22/grocery-store-workers-take-on-billion-dollar-multinational/

Posner, J. R. (1986). Trends in medical malpractice insurance, 1970-1985. *Law and Contemporary Problems, 49*, 37–56.

Potts, S., Feinglass, J., Lefevere, F., Kadah, H., Branson, C., & Webster, J. (1993). A quality-of-care analysis of cascade iatrogenesis in frail elderly hospital patients. *Quality Review Bulletin, 19*, 199–205.

Poulose, B. K., Ray, W. A., Abrogast, P. G., Needleman, J., Buerhaus, P. I., Griffin, M. R., … Holzman, M. D. (2005). Resident work hour limits and patient safety. *Annals of Surgery, 241*, 847–860.

PublicCitizen. (2019, July 16). *HHS has failed to report nearly two-thirds of its medical malpractice payments to National Data Bank, new analysis shows*. Retrieved from Public Citizen. https://www.citizen.org/news/hhs-has-failed-to-report-nearly-two-thirds-of-its-medical-malpractice-payments-to-national-data-bank-new-analysis-shows/

Quinn, E. (2013, October 8). Irish doctors strike to protest work hours amid austerity. Retrieved from *Wall Street Journal*. https://www.wsj.com/articles/no-headline-available-1381217911?tesla=y

Quinn, M. A., Kats, A. M., Kleinman, K., Bates, D. W., & Simon, S. R. (2012). The relationship between electronic health records and malpractice claims. *Archives of Internal Medicine, 172*, 1187–1189.

Rama, A. (2019). *Physician practice benchmark survey*. Chicago, IL: American Medical Association. Retrieved from https://www.ama-assn.org/system/files/2019-09/prp-care-delivery-payment-models-2018.pdf

Ranum, D. (2019, August). *Electronic health records continue to lead to medical malpractice suits*. Retrieved from The Doctors Company: https://www.thedoctors.com/articles/electronic-health-records-continue-to-lead-to-medical-malpractice-suits/

Ranum, D., Troxel, D. B., & Diamond, R. (2016, March 3). *Hospitalist closed claims study*. Retrieved from The Doctors. http://www.thedoctors.com/KnowledgeCenter/PatientSafety/articles/Hospitalist-Closed-Claims-Study?refId=HOSPITALISTSTUDY

Rau, J. (2012, April 24). Medicare to add hospital efficiency, patient safety to payment formula. *Kaiser Daily Health Policy Report Blog*.

Rayack, E. (1967). *Professional power and American medicine: The economics of the AMA*. Cleveland, OH: World Publishing.

Rayback, J. G. (1966). *A history of American labor*. New York: The Free Press.

Reed, K., & May, R. (2011). *HealthGrades patient safety in American hospitals study*. Denver, CO: Health Grades, Inc.

Reich, H. (2019, March 11). CSO musicians picket in front of Orchestra Hall after announcing strike. Retrieved from *Chicago Tribune*. https://www.chicagotribune.com/entertainment/music/howard-reich/ct-ent-cso-musicians-union-0311-story.html#nws=true

Rho, H. J., & Brown, H. (2019, March 6). *Union membership byte 2019.* Retrieved from Center for Economic and Policy Research: http://cepr.net/data-bytes/union-membership-bytes/union-byte-2019-01

Rhodes, D. (2019, May 28). 'Because we know strikes work': College unions leverage publicity in touch contract battles. Retrieved from *Chicago Tribune*. https://www.chicagotribune.com/news/breaking/ct-met-college-university-labor-unions-strikes-20190523-story.html

Roberts, E. T., Mehrotra, A., & McWilliams, J. M. (2017). High-Price and low-Price physician practices do not differ significantly on care quality or efficiency. *Health Affairs, 36*, 855–864.

Rosato, D. (2020, May). More choice, more power. *Consumer Reports*, pp. 35–45.

Rosenfeld, J., Denice, P., & Laird, J. (2016, August 30). *Union decline lowers wages of nonunion workers.* Retrieved from Economic Policy Institute. https://www.epi.org/publication/union-decline-lowers-wages-of-nonunion-workers-the-overlooked-reason-why-wages-are-stuck-and-inequality-is-growing/

Rosenfield, H., & Balber, C. (2005, December 29). *False accounting: How medical malpractice insurance companies inflate losses to justify sudden surges in rates and tort reform.* Retrieved from Consumer Watchdog: http://www.consumerwatchdog.org/resources/falseaccounting-medmalstudy.pdf

Rosenthal, E. (2014a, February 14). Apprehensive, many doctors shift to jobs with salaries. *New York Times*, p. A14.

Rosenthal, E. (2014b, February 13). Apprehensive, many doctors shift to jobs with salaries. Retrieved from *New York Times*. http://www.nytimes.com/2014/02/14/us/salaried-doctors-may-not-lead-to-cheaper-health-care.html?emc=eta1&_r=0

Ross, M. (2019). 2019 retail clinics in store healthcare market: Key players. *OpenPR, Report Hive Research*.

Sack, K. (2008, May 18). Doctors say 'I'm sorry' before 'see you in court'. *New York Times*, p. A1.

Saks, M. J. (1992). Do we really know anything about the behavior of the tort litigation system-and why not? *University of Pennsylvania Law Review, 140*, 1147–1292.

Scheffler, R. M. (1999). Physician collective bargaining: A turning point in U.S. medicine. *Journal of Health Politics Policy and Law, 24*, 1071–1076.

Scheiber, N. (2016, January 9). Doctors unionize to resist the medical machine. *New York Times*, p. BU 1.

Schencker, L. (2019, September 20). Hospital strike: 2,200 University of Chicago Medical Center Nurses walk off the job. *Chicago Tribune*. Retrieved from https://www.chicagotribune.com/business/ct-biz-university-of-chicago-hospital-nurse-strike-20190920-7ddk2jacgbgsxea47k-qwp6delu-story.html

Schmitt, J. (2009, April). *Unions and upward mobility for service-sector workers.* Retrieved from Center for Economic and Policy Research: http://cepr.net/documents/publications/unions-service-2009-04.pdf

Scott, D. (2019, June 12). The nation's most prominent doctors group almost dropped its opposition to medicare-for-all. Retrieved from *Vox*. https://www.vox.com/policy-and-politics/2019/6/12/18662722/ama-medicare-for-all-single-payer-vote-2020

Scott, W. R. (1966). *Professionalization.* (H. M. Vollmer, & D. L. Mills, Eds.). Englewood Cliffs, NJ: Prentice-Hall.

Sharkey, C. M. (2005). Unintended consequence of medical malpractice damages caps. *New York University Law Review, 80*, 391–512.

Shierholz, H., & Poydock, M. (2020, February 11). *Continued surge in strike activity signals worker dissatisfaction with wage growth.* Retrieved from Economic Policy Institute. https://www.epi.org/publication/continued-surge-in-strike-activity/

Silva, M. (2005, January 3). Bush's tort reform efforts to start at 'judicial hellhole'. *Chicago Tribune*.

Smith, K. (1980). Competing ethical values in medicine. *New England Journal of Medicine, 303*, 1482.

Starkman, D. (2005, December 29). Calculating malpractice claims. Retrieved from *Washington Post*. http://www.consumerwatchdog.org/story/calculating-malpractice-claims

Statistics, U. B. (2020, February 11). *Major work stoppages (annual) news release*. Washington, DC: U.S. Bureau of Labor Statistics. Retrieved from https://www.bls.gov/news.release/wkstp.htm

Stockman, F., & Baker, M. (2020, March 6). Nurses battling coronavirus beg for protective gear and better planning. *New York Times*, p. A10.

Studdert, D. M., Bismark, M. M., Mello, M. M., Singh, H., & Spittal, M. J. (2016). Prevalence and characteristics of physicians prone to malpractice claims. *New England Journal of Medicine, 374*, 354–362.

Studdert, D. M., Mello, M. M., Gawande, A. A., Gandhi, T. K., Kachalia, A., Yoon, C., … Brennan, T. A. (2006). Claims, errors, and compensation payments in medical malpractice litigation. *The New England Journal of Medicine, 354*, 2024–2033.

Studdert, D. M., Mello, M. M., Sage, W. M., DesRoches, C. M., Peugh, J., Zapert, K., & Brennan, T. A. (2005). Defensive medicine among high-risk specialist physicians in a volatile malpractice environment. *JAMA, 293*, 2609–2617.

Studdert, D. M., Spittal, M. J., Zhang, Y., Wilkinson, D. S., Singh, H., & Mello, M. M. (2019). Changes in practice among physicians with malpractice claims. *New England Journal of Medicine, 380*, 47–55.

Studdert, D. M., Yang, Y. T., & Mello, M. M. (2004). Are damages caps regressive? A study of malpractice jury verdicts in California. *Health Affairs, 23*(4), 54–67.

Su-Ting, L. T., Srinvasan, M., Der-Martirosian, C., Kravitz, R. L., & Wilkes, M. S. (2011). Developing personal values: Trainees' attitudes toward strikes by health care providers. *Academic Medicine, 86*, 580–585.

Sweeney, B. (2017, March 1). Can the national labor relations board drag advocate to the bargaining table. Retrieved from *Crain's Chicago Business*. https://www.chicagobusiness.com/article/20170301/NEWS03/170309978/can-the-national-labor-relations-board-drag-advocate-health-care-to-the-bargaining-table#utm_medium=email&utm%E2%80%A6

Ta-Seale, M., Dillon, E. C., Yang, Y., Nordgren, R., Steinberg, R. L., Nauenberg, T., … Li, J. (2019). Physicians' well-being linked to in-basket messages generated by algorithms in electronic health records. *Health Affairs, 38*, 1073–1078.

Tawfik, D. S., Profit, J., Morgenthaler, T. I., Satele, D. V., Sinsky, C. A., Dyrbye, L. N., … Shanafelt, T. D. (2018). Physician burnout; Well-being and work unit safety grades in relationship to reported medical errors. In *Mayo Clinic Proceedings*, pp. 1–10. Elsevier.

Tehrani, A. S., Lee, H., Mathews, S. C., Shore, A., Makary, M. A., Pronovost, P. J., & Newman-Toker, D. E. (2012). 25-year summary of US malpractice claims for diagnostic errors 1986-2010: An analysis from the National Practitioner Data Base. *BMJ Quality & Safety*, p. 22. Retrieved from http://qualitysafety.bmj.com/content/early/2013/03/27/bmjqs-2012-001550

The Henry J. Kaiser Family Foundation. (2006, January 13). Kaiser Daily Health Policy Report examines developments related to malpractice in two states. *Kaiser Daily Health Policy Report*.

The Henry J. Kaiser Family Foundation. (2009, September 21). Malpractice reform in spotlight, earns mixed reviews. *Kaiser Daily Health Policy Report*.

The Physicians Foundation. (2018a, September 18). 2018 survey of America's physicians - Practice patterns & perspectives. Retrieved from *The Physicians Foundation*. https://physiciansfoundation.org/wp-content/uploads/2018/09/physicians-survey-results-final-2018.pdf

The Physicians Foundation. (2018b, September 18). The Physicians Foundation 2018 physician survey. Retrieved from *The Physicans Foundation*. https://physiciansfoundation.org/research-insights/the-physicians-foundation-2018-physician-survey/

Thomas, J. W., Ziller, E. C., & Thayer, D. A. (2010). Low costs of defensive medicine, small savings from tort reform. *Health Affairs, 29*(9), 1578–1584.

Thompson, P. (1983). *The nature of work - An introduction to debates on the labour process.* London, UK: Macmillan Press.

Thompson, S. L., & Salmon, J. W. (2014). Physician strikes. *Chest, 146,* 1369–1374.

Thorpe, K. E. (2004). The medical malpractice 'crisis': Recent trends and the impact of state tort reforms. *Health Affairs, w4,* w20–w30.

USA Today Editorial Board. (2018, March 14). How dangerous doctors escape despite data bank. *USA Today.*

Van Den Bos, J., Rustagi, K., Gray, T., Halford, M., Ziemkiewicz, E., & Shreve, J. (2011). The $17.1 billion problem: The annual cost of measurable medical errors. *Health Affairs, 30*(4), 595–603.

Vidmar, N., & Robinson II, R. M. (2005). *Medical malpractice and the tort system in Illinois.* Durham, NC: Duke University Law School. Retrieved from http://scholarship.law.duke.edu/faculty_scholarship/1125

Vincent, C., Young, M., & Phillips, A. (1994). Why do people sue doctors? A study of patients and relatives taking legal action. *The Lancet, 343,* 1609–1613.

Virapongse, A., Bates, D. W., Shi, P., Jenter, C. A., Volk, L. A., Kleinman, K., … Simon, S. R. (2008). Electronic health records and malpractice claims in office practice. *Archives of Internal Medicine, 168*(21), 2362–2367.

Wachter, R. M. (2004). The end of the beginning: Patient safety five years after 'To err is human'. *Health Affairs, 23,* W4-534.

Waitzkin, H. (2016, May 20). *Doctor-workers: Unite!* Retrieved from Medscape.com. https://www.medscape.com/viewarticle/863297

Wang, M. (2011). *As side effect of fiscal constraints, dangerous docs go undisciplined in California.* ProPublica.com.

Waterman, A. D., Garbutt, J., Hazel, E., Dunagan, W. C., Levinson, W., Fraser, V. J., & Gallagher, T. H. (2007, August). The emotional impact of medical errors on practicing physicians in the United States and Canada. *Joint Commission Journal on Quality and Patient Safety, 33,* 467–476.

Watson, P. J., Hickman, S. E., Morris, R. J., Milliron, J. T., & Whiting, L. (1995). Narcissism, self-esteem, and parental nurturance. *The Journal of Psychology, 129,* 61–73.

Weber, M. (1978). *Economy and Society* (G. Roth, & K. Wittich, Eds.). Berkeley: University of California Press.

Weiss, M. D., Gannon, M., & Eakins, S. (2008). *Medical malpractice caps - The impact of non-economic damage caps on physician premiums, claims payout levels, and availability of coverage.* Palm Beach Gardens, FL: Weiss Ratings, Inc.

White, A. A., Gallagher, T. H., Krauss, M. J., Garbutt, J., Waterman, A. D., Dunagan, W. C., … Larson, E. B. (2008). The attitudes and experiences of trainees regarding disclosing medical errors to patients. *Academic Medicine, 83*(3), 250–256.

Widman, A. (2006). Why health courts are unconstitutional. *Pace Law Review, 27,* 55–88.

Witman, A. B., Park, D. M., & Hardin, S. B. (1996). How do patients want physicians to handle mistakes? *Archives of Internal Medicine, 156,* 2565–2569.

Wojcieszak, D. (2012, May). *Reforming state licensure boards & the national practitioner data bank.* Retrieved from Sorry Works. http://sorryworkssite.bondwaresite.com/what-is-the-problem%2D%2Dcms-44

Wojcieszak, D. (2013, January 31). Oregon's disclosure plan includes reporting changes to licensure boards, NPDB. *Sorry Works! E-Newsletter.*

Wojcieszak, D., Saxton, J. W., & Finkelstein, M. M. (2007). *Sorry works! - Disclosure, apology, and relationships prevent medical malpractice claims.* Bloomington, IN: Author House.

Wolfe, S. (1979). Strikes by health workers: A look at the concept, ethics, and impacts. *American Journal of Public Health, 69,* 431–433.

Wolinsky, F. D. (1988). The professional dominance perspective, revisited. *The Milbank Quarterly, 66,* 33–47.

Wong, A. (2019, January 22). America's teachers are furious. Retrieved from *The Atlantic*. https://
    www.theatlantic.com/education/archive/2019/01/teachers-are-launching-a-rebellion/580975/
Woods, M. S. (2007). *Healing words: The power of apology in medicine*. Oakbrook Terrace, IL:
    Joint Commission Resources.
Xu, R. (2018, May 11). The burnout crisis in American medicine. *The Atlantic*, pp. 1–9.
Yates, C. A. (2009). In defence of the right to strike. *University of New Brunswick Law Journal,
    59*, 128–137.
Yee, D. (2007, November 12). Some medical centers open facilities to complete. *Minneapolis Star
    Tribune*.
Young, A., Chaudhry, H. J., Pei, X., Arnhart, K., Dugan, M., & Snyder, G. B. (2017). A cen-
    sus of actively licensed physicians in the United States, 2016. *Journal of Medical Regulation,
    103*, 7–21.
Young, S. G., Gruca, T. S., & Nelson, G. C. (2020). Impact of nonphysician providers on spatial
    accessibility to primary care in Iowa. *Health Services Research*, 1–10.
Yurkiewicz, I. (2018). Complicated: Medical missteps are not inevitable. *Health Affairs, 37*,
    1178–1181.
Zhao, L. (2005, July 27). *The impact of medical malpractice reforms on hospital-based obstetric
    services*. College Park, MD: Digital Repository at the University of Maryland. Retrieved from
    http://hdl.handle.net/1903/2896
Zimmerman, R. (2004, May 18). Doctors' new tool to fight lawsuits: Saying 'I'm sorry'. Retrieved
    from *Wall Street Journal*. http://www.valuemd.com/relaxing-lounge/17935-doctors-tool-fight-
    lawsuits.html

Chapter 5
Big Data: Information Technology as Control over the Profession of Medicine

Introduction

All across the globe, there are promises for practical technological solutions to critical issues confronting societies, from artificial intelligence (AI) detecting sensors in at-risk flood areas to snow melting sensors on glacier disappearance, smart grids to power up after blackouts, autonomous cars (which may require AI traffic control), lamps on Wi-Fi for crime prevention, connected "smart cities" (Huber, 2020), surveillance over tree thieves in rain forests (Ives, 2019), a substantial variety of business applications (Using Artificial intelligence to power better business decisions, 2019), and many more. These practical improvements hold great potential for saving lives and the environment, as well as for property. Health sector applications have also been zooming with a greater number of applications on the horizon promised.

Yet, the technology of artificial intelligence (AI) holds significant dangers, especially in the hands of politicians with varying objectives of maintaining social control over populations; Kendall-Taylor, Frantz, and Wright (2020) explain how technology strengthens autocracy by enabling surveillance tabs on virtually every aspect of citizens' lives. AI in the hands of corporate managements bent on extracting huge profit streams moves forward without being subject to either regulatory oversight or ethical considerations.

Historically, it has been well reported that the embrace of new technologies has profoundly altered societies and the entire world: from the radio and television to the Internet and smartphones, and now AI and 5G. A post-embrace analysis of any one of the above technologies would reveal unforeseen social implications. Therefore, what can we as a society now assess before AI, 5G, and more technology comes to occupy our daily lives with multiple unforeseen implications?

As artificial intelligence engulfs more of our American society—and as the giant IT firms encircle the healthcare system in significant ways—it might be worthwhile

© Springer Nature Switzerland AG 2021
J. W. Salmon, S. L. Thompson, *The Corporatization of American Health Care*,
https://doi.org/10.1007/978-3-030-60667-1_5

to urge more than a modicum of caution from medical professionals to keep watch over their future. This is crucial in that both healthcare issues and the COVID-19 crisis are being framed within information technology and Big Data "solutions" and these will not be neutral.

Chapter Purpose

This chapter will describe how information technology solutions are becoming widespread in the healthcare system to address cost, quality, and accountability issues. As medical decision-making is increasingly scrutinized, opportunities for small and giant IT firms are opening, as well as for other for-profit entries with sweeping private investment in health care. The chapter will examine beginning efforts by the powerful and pervasive *FAANG* entities (the acronym used to describe Facebook, Apple, Amazon, Netflix, and Google), plus numerous other corporate groups, that collectively amounts to rather significant healthcare involvement. The following descriptions of several firms with this preliminary analysis point to some implication with potential sources of danger. Beyond this summary analysis, greater attention is now warranted. These cautionary notes should be carefully observed over the coming months and years since the pace of movement among IT firms goes amazingly fast, especially given the post-COVID-19 pandemic which has inspired many new activities. Multiple opportunities are being carved out by these cash-rich companies.

The degree that the American healthcare sector comes under tighter corporate profit-making is a major threat today; it remains unclear how or whether this marketplace grip will ever serve the public's health. While the summary here may be brief in terms of its complicated, multi-faceted directions, the chapter's purpose is to delineate issues that health professionals and policymakers may want to know and follow. The current IT investments and the huge resource base of these Silicon Valley behemoths in cash and expertise suggest that what is at stake is not easily predicted at this stage. As with the current corporatization of health care described in Chap. 2, the key question will be "who benefits?" Investors or the public's health?

Artificial Intelligence Concerns

In a *New York Times* special section on artificial intelligence in October 2018, a panel of industry experts were interviewed to discuss the ramifications of a data-informed world (Behar, Five Voices on Artificial Intelligence, 2018, p. F2). Behar (2018) believes that our thinking on AI might not be broad enough in that it could be used to monitor the health of individuals currently in need of greater oversight, e.g., patients with needing care titrated on a moment-to-moment basis. Anderson (2018) thinks that AI can alter our perceptions of what humans are and what they can be, personalizing our medical treatments and improving both our mental and physical capabilities, which creates moral dilemmas about how much is too much. Five Artificial Intelligence Insiders in Their Own Words (2018) postulates that AI can perpetuate biased systems and societal distributions in a way that heightens current inequities and thus only serve to justify the existence of those who preside over society now. Haenssle (2018) makes the point that AI using algorithms can improve diagnosis of certain skin cancers over that of experienced dermatologists. Lastly, Ibrahim (2018) makes the case that AI can vastly improve our lives and lifespans but at the same time we must be wary of the moral ramifications brought about by consequences neither seen nor predicted at the outset of implementation. Behar (2018) feels thinking about AI only for search, security, and social media is limited; its potentials should be seen in new contexts, especially for its healthcare promise. Anderson (2018) sees radically new personalized medicine, but it may require broader conversation beyond merely scientists and engineers, which Five Artificial Intelligence Insiders in Their Own Words (2018) identifies as an insular subset of society (code writers) making the rules. Will their decisions be biased? Beyond practical applications and awareness of unintended consequences, is there sufficient urgency about the risks of AI (Ibrahim, 2018)?

How will societies reckon the mounting issues of AI *when they go unexplored, and untested, until they are well embedded across industries, in addition to our work and daily life?* Upon us now are significant displacements in the labor force and a completely redesigned nature of work. Automation here at home, as well as flight of multinational capital abroad, was responsible for America's deindustrialization and the resultant huge job loss since the 1960s. When the unemployed are finally called back to jobs post-COVID-19, will they be there for them? And how will firms "going Lean" and intensifying automation efforts now post-virus outbreak come to affect the nature of work?

For health care, we must ponder how AI may impact all facets of the nature of doctoring, along with costs, quality, and finally our population's health status, while it is ongoing now.

Siegele (2018) in a special report in the *Economist* was forthright in stating that the Internet—now 50 years of age—turned out to be much less decentralized as promised and certainly not always an uplifting and hopeful presence in our lives, as if one couldn't have found that out by scanning Facebook, Twitter, and Instagram to ascertain how much social media, and the Internet in general, has taken on a rather cesspool character.

While many folks celebrate technological progress, Henry Kissinger (former Secretary of State under Presidents Nixon and Ford) saw AI systems in flux with certain upheavals in many quarters, as well as doubts about its awe-inspiring promises (Kissinger, 2018). There remains questionable impact from self-learning machines that acquire new knowledge through their own processes. It is not yet well understood in various applications how machines interpret goals within search engine algorithms (like reducing medical care costs). If managers seek a higher ROI next year, what changes in care patterns may be automatically instituted without clinicians' thorough review?

Kissinger noted that the Internet can amplify and distort knowledge by being able to capture the huge amount of data and use it to further one's particular end. At that end is becoming less about us as individuals and more about us as data points; the use of that data, especially when taken out of context, can overwhelm moral decision-makers (Kissinger, 2018).

Reflecting on Kissinger's notions above for healthcare applications, professionals might want to note that *not* much knowledge nor critique is currently being given to the overall health information technology (HIT) trend; most if not all HIT is being seemingly heralded in all quarters; technology's wonders are praised while objections are more often personal or argumentative, rather than analytical. There are, of course, occasional luddites writing across the media, but it should be pointed out that objections rarely explore deeper ethical transformations currently underway; there is a great absence to counter the mere marketplace advancement being its leading force. Many people eagerly succumb to tech consumption. In health care, a real and present danger with profound implications may be witnessed earlier than professionals may think. Pay careful attention to the rapid march toward utilization management and performance monitoring (Feinglass & Salmon, 1990).

Thus, when AI implementation is ill conceived, and systems are poorly executed (as according to many physicians when electronic health records began), how can we be assured that serious political and ethical concerns will be considered before being built into ongoing AI applications? What might be considered reasonable applications, and for whom, beyond their corporate sponsors and players seeking higher returns on investment?

The corporate domination of the IT industry with its phenomenal growth and size, as well as its political and cultural power, is sweeping into the US healthcare system with alacrity. *Financial Times Intelligent Business* had a special section that heralded that AI ushers in an era for business that will use Big Data to become faster, bigger, safer, and more efficient, which will fundamentally change the way we do business and not necessarily for the better (Sen Gupta, 2019, p. 3).

Blockchain is extolled for tackling supply chain inefficiencies to regulating city transport companies, and consumers are beginning to see the effect for themselves beyond the Bitcoin fascination (Bennett, 2020). Changes are starting to blur the lines between professional services (including medicine, law firms, and consultancies), with 160 blockchain-based proof of concept projects underway. Software companies are muscling into a variety of service firms to make services more efficient and secure with blockchains. Other examples are given where IBM Global Business Services works with counties on a variety of projects to coordinate care for vulnerable people in local communities. Cloud-based apps are provided that bring about better public services (2019, p. 4). Other examples are provided as case studies in new technology applications.

Wariness over Technology Introduced in the 1990s
The American public was ushered into the advanced technological age with Stanley Kubrick's movie *2001: A Space Odyssey*. A spacecraft carried a crew of astronauts who were removed from commanding the vessel when HAL, an AI computer, deemed human decision-making to be inadequate as HAL saw itself in ways superior to human minds. AI is known to make improvements to itself from strategic judgments based on the premises built into the system (the purpose of the flight Hal was commanding *must be preserved* over the frailties he considered among the astronauts). Therefore, he killed the crew! In the future, potential human dilemmas from AI installations must be considered beforehand and then accounted for. Kubrick's dramatic warning came from early cinema!

Artificial Intelligence (AI) to the Rescue?

As the tech industry encircles not just health care but also numerous sectors of the American economy, and worldwide, artificial intelligence (AI) is being blasted across the business and popular press as the salvation for companies tackling their concept of "Big Data." *Machine learning* has great significance in numerous applications as an increasingly useful tool for business. *Algorithms* aid *computer learning* to replace humans to improve efficiency and enhance quality and with much less error. Evidence of this abounds with new *software* beating humans on complicated video and board games, through *reinforcement learning*.

Computer vision allows facial recognition, as well as self-driving cars, which allows for safer transactions, as well as safer driving. *Neural networks* sift through data to identify patterns, and when mixed with machine learning, it makes for *deep learning*, which can calculate and crunch enormous amounts of data and help humans detect obscure patterns and meaning. Finally, and more importantly, *natural language processing* allows computers to understand and react to human speech, which has been improving quickly to lessen errors and misunderstandings (Harper, 2018).

Fortune's (2019) CEO survey found 60% of firms using AI to improve efficiency and to reduce costs. Twenty-two percent of firms were reported using AI to create new products and services (Murray, 2019). *Financial Times* projected growth in an army of data labelers for AI, mostly workers underpaid in areas in need of upgrading *ethical supply chains* from countries like Kenya, India, and the Philippines (Murgia, 2019). Meanwhile, worldwide spending on virtual reality (VR) and augmented reality (AR) technologies are expected to be larger than $20 billion in 2019, up to 69% from the previous year; both VR and AR are rapidly spreading into enterprises (Torchia & Shirer, 2018).

Marcus and Davis (2019) writing in the *New York Times* state that AI has a trust problem, and it hasn't yet earned our confidence in terms of time, space, and causality, which are significant theoretical and practical challenges. These authors argue the need to look at AI differently so that we can develop devices that will understand the context in which they operate well enough that we will not have to fear any unintended consequences (2019, p. A23).

AI in Health Care

Applications in health care are being widely touted in the literature (Adamson, 2015). This surge combines many Silicon Valley entities making substantial investments, along with smaller proprietary firms developing some capabilities; many such players are hoping to find a niche inroad to lead to an absorption from the larger IT firms. M&A has been prevalent among IT firms across their history, so extensions into the health ventures are merely how they will expand into another lucrative market. Amazon recently added a new division to focus on health and wellness. Google is obviously planning to use AI in its insurance venture with JP Morgan Chase and Berkshire Hathaway (Scott, 2018). Dozens of other firm positionings regarding their benefit reorganization can be found in the business news. The vast data warehouses by the pharmacy benefit managers have been ripe for AI once the insurance company mergers are consummated for the combined clinical and drug data amalgamations; potentials were never actually explored in the PBM industry for public health improvements (Salmon & Dedhiya, 1998).

Clinical variation is said to be a significant contributor to health care's multibillion-dollar overuse problem, which could be as high as 20% of clinical care spending (Frakt, 2019; Shrank, Rogstad, & Parekh, 2019). Thus, AI is being touted to reduce clinical variation (Cohen, 2019a, 2019b) in efforts to standardize care and eliminate unnecessary services, which drive up costs and create additional clinical complications. For providers under value-based care, this creates a tremendous market for artificial intelligence, but hopefully with decent data analytics under professional guidance. Without such, AI is also being proffered to prevent the widespread physician burnout. This burnout issue among physicians (thought to be as high as 68%) has been framed as a crisis; nevertheless, its dimensions are much broader than a mere tech solution (Mazzolini, 2019). Rosenfeld (2019, p. 1) believes that record physician burnout is being caused by electronic health records (EHR) that are being used to administrative and regulatory oversight.

While numerous businesses may march forward toward AI, how prepared are health providers for machine learning, given that most applications remain in the research stage (Wilson, 2019)? Much of the heterogeneity of data is institution specific, as many in the field are coming to realize. Pilot testing is necessary to assess how each application works in the actual provider to avoid mishaps, which not only slows down implementation but remains quite costly. Sophisticated expertise on site is usually required, which is rarely found and expensive. Care must be taken to evaluate the sales pitches of vendors.

Computers with AI capabilities can be trained to analyze patterns in large swaths of data. Applications to improve the workflow of radiologists are expanding widely (Wilson, 2019). Virtual cardiac rehabilitation is being explored (Funahashi, Borgo, & Joshi, 2019). Medical academicians and clinicians are trying to leverage AI for decision support in several specialties with a bullish hope for greater meaning to doctors and doctoring through teamwork (Shah & Lee, 2019). Physicians get to do more of what they are trained to do, that is actually more "conception" tasks and less tedious "execution" tasks.

Tackling some routine chronic disease care problems is also on the horizon, for example, the care of diabetics is also being flagged as being vastly improved by new technologies, by assisting patients with lifestyle changes through self-management, education, and support (Kent, 2020). Platforms for remote patient monitoring have potentials for ambulatory and home care services, including web-based care coordination and use of mobile apps focused on the patient experience. A variety of providers are implementing these with databases being created that can be explored by AI-powered systems.

Five Safeway grocery stores in Phoenix have launched virtual health clinics to improve access to care in certain neighborhoods to leverage AI and augmented reality for patient guidance through the entire diagnostic process. CVS Health also has retail stores turning into healthcare hubs in some communities it serves (Japsen, 2019). In addition to finding ways to engage consumers onto "better health pathways," acute care venues continue to provide low acuity conditions where phenomenal wastage from overutilization and fraud and abuse is really one of the best potentials for AI applications. With the rise of urgent care centers, retail clinics, telemedicine, and the like, trends in utilization of newer care venues and emergency departments of hospitals provide for much opportunity for decreasing care, thus saving money for insurers, or for payers (Poon, Schuur, & Mehrotra, 2018).

Advances in artificial intelligence within health care will be significantly contributing to the projected $15.7 trillion economic boost related to machine learning, according to Price Waterhouse Cooper (PWC) Consultants (www.pwc.com, 2019). This will give rise predictably to a 14.5% increase in North America's GDP by 2030, driven by the increasing efficiencies and ability to make decisions of AI (Bresnick, 2018a). The report maintains that all of health care will be effected by change including payers, providers, Big Pharma, and consumers as artificial intelligence is meshed into their lives. Preparation for deeper integration of AI is underway in many quarters, but certain entities surely will lag behind (Kent, 2019).

In addition, retail, logistics, and financial services are immediately finding obvious automation, but without the stricter privacy and security regulations that health care may surely need. Usually played down are the job losses that are going to come from this improved "efficiency" and for corporate leanness. The introduction of clinical decision support will require slow and carefully planned introductions in order to overcome resistance and encourage greater adoption. Physicians will be mindful of the difficulties during Electronic Health Records (EHR) implementations, and this will give rise to conflicts and slow down processes. Will they be skeptical of decisions being automatically made by algorithms, maybe not for routine services, but for the more complicated procedures and by specialists? Nevertheless, AI will be able to automate administrative tasks and financial transactions; these areas are getting significant attention by administrators in revenue cycle management, so issues of surveillance and speedup may generate conflict issues.

As the phrase goes, "The train has already left the station," and PWC (www.pwc.com, 2019) has said that AI can alter the healthcare landscape in such a way to fundamentally alter what are considered well-established businesses and business models and render them obsolete. So, the multitude of cheerleaders for AI are lining up to "transform medicine." The main thrust is on the side of administrative bodies who intend on reducing waste, standardizing services, and eliminating inefficiencies.

Lewin and Balser maintain that the exponential ongoing growth of computational power and datasets create the potential for AI to impact health care widely, meaning that we will invest in building infrastructure, competencies, and collaborations so that we can become reliant on the help of AI to look at available options, determine the best course of action, and then proceed with that plan (Lewin & Balser, 2019, p. 27).

Will AI restore the doctor-patient relationship (Inserro, 2019)? A visit to the doctor these days involves many of the same prompts, but instead of the doctor jotting down notes in a paper chart, he/she is typing into a EHR interface. This makes the data available to anyone who has access to the organizational EHR which and increase the risk of privacy breaches which can negate security guarantees. Coupled with the very fact that most AI algorithms cannot be fully explained, each new AI inroad will likely worsen disarray and expose a host of ethical quandaries (O'Connor, 2019).

One major question is how patients will accept the coming AI in medicine? If properly informed, patients may come to appreciate AI's reduction of repetitive error-prone tasks, as well as use of new massive amounts of data being analyzed by healthcare teams to discover optimal treatments for individuals and populations, e.g., making sure that physicians don't prescribe a potentially lethal drug that would interact with other medications the patient is already on. AI could also be welcomed by consumers to improve hospital operations, which could improve scheduling, costs, billing, and insurance issues. Nevertheless, if assembly line cultures result— and, in fact, are deepened—consumers are likely to rebel in a variety of ways, particularly if technology change gets interpreted as means for just enhancing provider and payer profits and not actually improve care in any meaningful way (The AI Will See You Now, 2019).

Era of Big Data

In the 1980s, the *Age* of the Internet—now 50 years old—gave rise to a plethora of dot.com entities that yielded several powerhouses in Silicon Valley and Seattle, with the subsequent decade viewing the dot.com tech bubble for Wall Street and the economy. The larger surviving firms set off a consumer buying rage for the latest tech innovation and propelled computer science programs within colleges.

The miniaturization of the computer to palm-sized smartphones with the advance of microchips propelled people's wonderment on how technology could "improve" their lives. As the industry produced search engines, now dominated by Google and Microsoft's Bing, ever refining search programs have been "perfected" to serve different business and consumer bases. Stern (2019, p. 1) reports that the smartphone changed over time, while it was changing us. A *New York Times Magazine* article stated that Google has succeeded in global domination where others have failed (Duhigg, 2018). Though estimates may vary by region, the company now accounts for an estimated 87% of online searches worldwide. It processes trillions of queries each year, which work out to at least 5.5 billion a day, 6300 a second (Duhigg, 2018).

Today microchips run everything from iPhones to ATMs and now with the Internet of Things (IoT) for everyday life. Each wave of chip advancement has given a reboot to the Internet to transform American society (Karlgaard, 2018). Of the current IT giants, which ones will find the potential and financial position to jump new social and economic hurdles?

Many have said that Big Data is rapidly transforming medicine, promising greater transparency, improved efficiency, and new ways of delivering care (Glorikian & Branca, 2017). A plethora of news reports appeared in 2018–2019 extolling AI applications in health care: algorithms for cancer detection (Towers-Clark, 2019); reducing medication risks (Grissinger, 2019); AI diagnostic diabetic retinopathy matching specialists (Wise, 2018; Frellick, 2018); monitoring brain attacks (Mirtskulava, 2018); predicting sepsis (Chettipally, 2018); and numerous applications in the pharmaceutical industry (Wince, 2018).

Software systems are advancing rapidly with "Digiceuticals" catching the eye of Big Pharma (Sweeney, 2018). The former US Food and Drug Administration (FDA) chief supported quick review of AI, and the agency has approved its first autonomous AI diagnostic system (Murtha, 2018) plus an FDA-approved AI diagnosis tool (Arndt, 2018a, 2018b). An *AI in Medicine* journal is now being published (AIMED, 2018).

Within this surge of both interest, investigation, and applications, AI, Big Data, and IoT will attract opportunities for growth across health care. Bresnick (2018a) sums up opportunities for vendors, developers, and their clients: the $3.62 billion segment of computer visions was predicted to reach $25.32 billion by 2023. The IoT sector will grow to $60 billion of smart appliances, manufacturing of sensors, and security cameras, in addition to healthcare industry areas to zoom 70% by 2025 to $40 billion. Amazon now offers more than a dozen devices for its Alexa voice assistant which can sate any problem or need the user may or may not know they had (Weise, 2020a, p. B1). Wearable sensors are poised for major growth also, smart watches that will perform fitness tracking, in addition to multiple health functions to climb to a billion dollars by 2025. The insurance analytics market is predicted for a 12.5% surge to $6.63 billion by 2023 to integrate Big Data from multiple sources. Analytics are intended to equip payors with tools for making improved decision-making during uncertain times (Bresnick, 2018a, p. 4). Allen states that everything that is out on the Internet about you will be used to determine your health insurance rates (Allen, 2018, p. 2).

All of this necessitates great carefulness that must be heeded over such future direct to consumer sales to order to keep track of the parties who are supposedly keeping track of yours and the public's health.

Beyond the widespread concern for privacy of patients' medical data, the burgeoning area of genetic explorations poses another problem that exemplifies how fast technological changes are taking place with apparently wide consumer acceptance. How far behind are any regulatory actions, let alone concerning insight and respective solutions for what to remedy? Millions of Americans have willingly given over their genetic information to two prominent commercial outfits, which made it collectively a valuable commodity sold to numerous parties, and we would like to wish, de-identified. Medical providers, pharmaceutical companies, and information technology companies are now engaging in widespread search to identify disease-causing genetic variants to aid the discovery of new drug targets; thus, compound issues of genetic data privacy are important to consider for discussion in public policy forums, and not left to the private marketplace. Berger et al. listed 38 studies using data that had varying degrees of criticality in what might (should) be considered for tighter privacy (Berger & Cho, 2019).

Cryptographic techniques are being used to secure data analyses if individuals choose to contribute their genomes to scientific studies. Yet, should the researcher be able to share data across the scientific community without safeguards, nor no knowledge of the subjects? Are protocols needed in this area? More importantly, investigations into cold case crimes use DNA matches for law enforcement purposes, so can these be trusted? Do consumers and patients realize their data has been commercialized and became property of a corporate entity to use whatever way it desires? Beyond personal privacy, security over genetic data requires much greater public oversight. Hacking is still all too commonplace of late with the ransomware shutting down several large computer networks leading to compromised personal information as well as large ransom payments for those users who don't regularly back up their systems. The threat of hacking and ransomware has led to a new market for cyber liability coverage. Insurance companies have arisen to specialize in this area given the huge number of cyberattacks and continual ransomware in the health sector over the last decade. While digital privacy and security concerns have become paramount amidst revelations of outside surveillance, incidents have become highly publicized, embarrassing, and costly. Precautionary IT systems have fended off hackers, but not to the degree that may be necessary, with hackers getting more adroit at getting at data and circumventing cybersecurity. Such sophisticated technology is adopted often with *security as an afterthought*, with many health providers now trying to speedily construct cyber defense plans.

Regulation of the IT Industry

The beginnings of regulatory attention to Big Tech had much to do with outsized company political clout and power within the economy, and throughout the society. In October 2019, five investigations into Big Tech led the *Financial Times* to claim the corporate power of Google, Facebook, Amazon, and Apple was threatened in US antitrust probes (Stacey & Shubber, 2019). Was this the beginning of a new front in US antitrust enforcement, and how would Big Tech change as a result (Stacey & Shubber, 2019, p. 4; Condliffe, 2019)? The Department of Justice, the Federal Trade Commission, Congress, and several states' attorney generals (Stacey et al., 2019) all seem to have an overbearing concern for the concentration of corporate power that may have been leading to consumer harm.

Investors are constantly searching for overperforming stocks (Wigglesworth, 2018). This constant pressure for stock market performance and return on investment (ROI), along with congressional regulation talk, has led to a lot of market uncertainty and surely affects the overall economy. Increased antitrust investigations are only going to lead to more investor angst and increasing market volatility (Stacey, Shubber et al., 2019). Meanwhile Britain, Australia, and the European Union (Condliffe, 2019) have legislated controls on social media; each nation is looking for stricter legal interpretations, particularly with an eye toward a more "ethical AI."

It is important to point out that other corporate entities across the US economy are reported to voice a large increase in the number of complaints against Big Tech monopolies, (Stoller, 2019) where the smaller-sized seek market freedom according to a writer in the *Wall Street Journal*. Regulatory talk has emerged as a *bipartisan critique of IT reflecting public sentiments* about Google's 90% of the search market and Facebook's advertising market under its social networking. With market power concentrated in few large firms, they have become the go-to source for all of our more important needs (Stoller, 2019, p. C3), thus making it more difficult for so many smaller businesses to survive let alone grow. Critics have maintained that the huge fines against these behemoths are not enough to remedy ingrained behaviors (Condliffe, 2019). Facebook settled a $5 billion fine with the Federal Trade Commission in July 2019 over its mishandling of user data, but the settlement did not change any privacy practices that would have ensured users' data privacy (Condliffe, 2019, p. B5). It remains difficult to prosecute companies that provide "free services," or low-cost cheaper services, than historic antitrust investigations have targeted. Nevertheless, the Department of Justice may examine multiple fronts of different firms to investigate based on market-based competition.

An editorial in the *New York Times* advocated for "the Internet bill of rights" which would protect individuals against data breaches and not give technology companies immunity from bad behavior. The notion that social media is free must be countered with the message that our information on these "free" platforms is being used to sell us stuff, attack us, and steal from us (Swisher, 2018, p. 9).

When one realizes the pharmaceutical industry's solid grip on Congressmen, documented K Street annual lobbying by the IT industry for 2018 to win influence inside the beltway reveals a flood of cash, according to the Center for Responsible Politics: Alphabet spent $21.7 million, Amazon spent $14.4 million, Facebook spent $12.6 million, Microsoft spent $9.6 million, and Apple spent $6.7 million (Tech Does K Street, 2019, p. 100). In all for the industry, $428.8 million was spent on lobbying, with one of the largest industries increases per year. The current Speaker of the House, Nancy Pelosi, said that she will push to get the industry in line, but she has been obviously distracted by action against the President over his quid pro quo with Ukraine. Like reigning in drug prices, this set of issues will tarry after 2021, if even then. Bad behaviors are very difficult to correct, and self-regulation or regulatory capture by the companies themselves have not helped. While Facebook has lost considerable market value in July 2018 (Eavis, 2018), they were being punished for bad financial performance and not bad intentions or behavior. And what appears to be a free service to consumers is quickly found out to be a way to gather data on subscribers in order to sell them more stuff. Instead of changing their behaviors, they blame the victims instead, telling them to disconnect from the service (Eavis, 2018).

Expecting *marketplace discipline* for keeping IT bad behaviors minimal is clearly insufficient in fixing the problem. As more health sector insiders grasp future possibilities from the IT firm invasion, their recent embrace may temper amidst a greater crescendo of voiced criticisms.

Threats to Health Sector

Since the Reagan Administration-imposed market-oriented standards of economic efficiency have been foisted on the health sector which stimulated price and product competition rather than access expansion, it did little to rein in health costs. Twenty years after the Institute of Medicine (IOM) publication of *To Err is Human (2000)*, the estimated number of Americans dying from medical care (98,000 annually) seemed to shock the public; but unfortunately the flurry of provider response was clearly insufficient to improve quality of care across the nation. In 2012, the IOM (2013) estimated $750 billion of annual healthcare spending was wasted; more recently an article in the *Journal of the American Medical Association* (Shrank et al., 2019) plugged the figure between $760 and $935 billion that can be deemed as waste. This amount includes unnecessary services, excessive administrative costs, fraud and abuse, inefficiently delivered services, and built-in system missed opportunities for prevention and earlier treatments. Reports indicate a few health systems are attempting to voluntarily remove services that don't add value for the patient ahead of perhaps some regulation; yet, the group is avoiding tackling prices and administrative costs, which are typically the source of most waste in the system (Castellucci, 2020, p. 19).

Such a legacy of built-in system waste essentially means that rationalization of medical care is highly necessary for cost control and quality improvement, but should *not* necessitate service cutbacks to more vulnerable population cohorts; nevertheless, the variety of means for this rationalization to be pursued are apparently still up for grabs. Feinglass and Salmon (1990) wrote more than two decades ago:

> To be effective in boosting profitability and market share, these interventions will have to penetrate deeply into the clinical settings where most of the providers' variable costs are generated, and where research on medical practice variations…has revealed gross examples of waste and overutilization by physicians. Just as the corporate business sector has fostered a "computer literate" culture in other industries, large numbers of health care employees are now obtaining the requisite training and experience to advance computer applications for medical records and medical decision making. This advance of personnel and firms in the health information technology segment of the industry has moved forward phenomenally in the last 26 years. There has been a virtual explosion of IT firms, personnel, and applications that have marched forward rapidly and taken root in the beginning transformation of providers. While much is in the administrative realm for addressing areas where costs can be shaved, much of this is taking root in new ways aimed at medical practice variations and medical ineffectiveness. (1990, p. 236)

Apparent policy directions influenced by market forces are value-based reimbursement for services, evidenced-based solutions, integration of care models under combined larger organizational units, reduction of administrative burdens, and, foremost, information technology to promote exchange of information.

It should be remembered that technology costs a lot in terms of software and hardware purchases, but many organizations find that the implementation costs much more than originally projected and unforeseen mistakes pile up during implementation and usage. Thus, management remains more intent on not wanting to lose control as processes move forward regardless of whether or not EHR operates as intended in improving quality and reducing error.

The acronym *FAANG* (Fernando, 2020) includes Facebook, Apple, Amazon, Netflix, and Google—the biggest titans of 2020s American capitalism—but oddly enough does not include former tech goliaths Microsoft, IBM, Huawei, Samsung, and several more. Nicas, Weise, and Issac (2019) assess the administrations of Big Tech that has attracted government scrutiny in Washington and Brussels over using their corporate size and wealth to squash competition and expand their respective domains; too much power lies in the hands of too few companies! Several state investigations are underway, as well as the House Antitrust Subcommittee for Amazon favoring its own products over third-party vendors and Apple's control over the App Store to get more spent on Apple itself. Facebook has the Federal Trade Commission (FTC) investigating its policy of acquiring its competitors in social media such as Instagram; Facebook has bought over 70 competitors over 15 years. Google's search (90% of the market) dominance is a target of antitrust regulators as it stands accused over how it presents its search results, as well as other anti-competitive behaviors, in that Google makes most of its money from ads and can target algorithms to highlight paid advertisements at the top of any search list. In addition, regulators are considering whether Google unfairly leverages Android software on over 75% of the world's smartphones (Nicas, 2018, p. B2).

With the IT industry now staking out the healthcare sector, the United States may be on the verge of an upswing in corporate takeovers. Several giants are already deep into health care, along with perhaps thousands of small upstarts tinkering in modifying electronic health records (EHRs), revenue cycle management, analytics, and a variety of other areas. These diverse information technology ventures may predictably be brought together by the more powerful resources, ingenuity, and general "making a market" by the Silicon Valley mega-corps. M&A fervor in 2018 witnessed a substantial new corporate development, not fully assessed here, but left to the dynamics and likelihood of their significant desired advancement.

Notwithstanding monopolistic behaviors, IT firms do aggressively compete against each other for market share in specific areas, as well as for public favor. Often personality rivalries among billionaire founders and CEO egos play a role in the publicized media disputes.

Americans' dependence on social media, its pervasiveness in everyday life, with a lack of controls over the firms, has forced social media into the political spotlight, particularly given the Russian influence over the Presidential election, according to all government intelligence sources. The Internet promised so much, but today, loss of privacy, hackers, cyberattacks of large companies, and selling personal data now fill new stories. From the social media addictions and echo chambers created by Facebook, Instagram, and Twitter to the incredible reach of Amazon, the technology behemoths have combined revenues of over $500 billion dollars annually (Duhigg, 2018, p. 37).

As the IT industry recognizes its new healthcare market, will firms pose themselves as saviors to rationalize the sector for greater efficiency? The premises and promises of Big Data may deserve and require examination: the individual companies will warrant a closer watch over time. Microsoft, Amazon, Google, and Apple have reached the $1 trillion market capitalizations, now each with spectacular resources to spend and significant unparalleled expertise, in addition to their pervasive influence over society. Some have argued that the online world is so fast moving that antitrust laws cannot ever keep pace; others recognize the dearth in policymaking circles of folks sufficiently knowledgeable to address industry issues. Nowadays even the biggest titan can be challenged by a tiny innovative startup, called unicorns, if the newcomer has better ideas, faster tech, and ample financial backing to last. Giants typically absorb startups in this industry. Thus, antitrust lawsuits, some digital executives may say, aren't needed anymore.

It is far from certain what the entry and implications of Amazon, Apple, IBM, and other IT firms will mean to the existing playing field in the healthcare sector. As we later examine the cooperation of Warren *Buffett*, *Amazon* (Jeff Bezos), and Jaime *Dimon* (Morgan Stanley Chase)—now to be referred to as *BAD*—for their employees, it is further unclear whether the *overall direct contracting by employers* moves portend a *nascent beginning for a new wave of corporate class reorganization of the American healthcare system,* as seen when the Carnegie and Rockefeller Foundations reorganized medical education in the 1920s (Berliner, 1977; Brown, 1975) (see Chap. 1).

Will Big Data through AI, 5G, and newer tech introductions finally come to rationalize and/or rescue purchasers, providers, and payers in some positive ways? Or will Big Data dramatically change their historic roles beyond recognition 10 or more years out?

Several colossal technology firms are already deep into health care, along with perhaps thousands of small upstarts that have been modifying EHRs, revenue cycle management, data analytics, cloud computing, and a variety of other IT tinkering. These diverse information technology forays may predictably be brought together by the powerful resources, ingenuity, and general "expanding a market" by select Silicon Valley and Seattle firms. M&A fervor in 2018 witnessed substantial new corporate heights, not fully assessed here, but left to the dynamics and likelihood of their significant desired combinations for rapid advancements.

The following narratives on several IT giants likely add to the readers' current knowledge of these companies which have for the most part become household names. Their brief descriptions on healthcare activities are intended to convey a sense of the individual firm, besides introducing several issues surrounding the IT industry, in general. It is hoped that the objective of informing on various issues prepares the reader to think about the future of health care under possibly new auspices. It is strongly suggested that the documented referencing be examined to discover the actual descriptions by the expert journalists who intensely follow this complex industry. A few firms will be examined.

International Business Machines (IBM)

One of the earliest computer manufacturers for business then later personal desktops, IBM has invested in several health projects, a few resulting in costly business failures (Ross, 2019). In 2019 the company invested $2 billion into an AI research hub in New York partnering with businesses to address several chronic diseases, including cancer, and for mitigating climate change. IBM Data Science seeks to achieve AI-driven insights for proven tools and resources. Such nascent R&D aiming at many firms is for scaling up its AI capabilities and applications (Janakiram, 2018). IBM is also aiding pharma firms with blockchain for supply chain technology (IBM targets pharmaceuticals, 2017). IBM's new CEO Arvind Krishna will build upon its quantum computing, blockchain, and other technical areas he has led to please investors in this tight competitive turnaround. IBM is also partnering with Pfizer on advanced immune-oncology drug discovery (Japsen, 2016). An entire set of issues seems up for grabs in such new uncharted territory, as policymaking falls sway to corporate pressures for little or no federal oversight. IBM has successively fought against regulatory oversight of health software, spending $26.4 million lobbying in 2013–2017. What makes software actually a medical device requires more precise definition perhaps dependent upon its intended use (When is software a medical device? 2019). In healthcare circles, IBM is most notably known for its Watson Health Division, which has encountered operational difficulties with its supercomputer developed in conjunction with Memorial Sloan Kettering Cancer Center that was intended to meld human expertise for personalized treatment advice (Ross & Swetlitz, 2017a, 2017b).

Watson has generated some erroneous cancer treatments (Ross & Swetlitz, 2017b), indicating that such medical software projects may require longer periods of evaluation prior to being brought to market. IBM Watson is partnering with TEVA, the Israeli generics firm, to develop a systematic approach for "drug repurposing" and "data-driven" pro-active "chronic disease management." Yet, the 21st Century Cures Act, bolstered by former Vice President Joe Biden, grants exemptions so that "clinical decision support" systems will be able to use Big Data in the private hands of IT firms' machines.

In a surprise move after a lengthy transition, IBM replaced its CEO with a 30-year veteran technologist to change direction toward cloud computing in order to directly compete with Microsoft, Google, and Amazon (Waters, 2020; Lohr, 2020; Rosenberg & Fried, 2020a, 2020b). The company's previous software acquisition of Red Hat for $34 billion, which enables customers to pursue a "multi-cloud market," is an important new front in the area of cloud computing, and they are attempting to do so by drawing more developers to improve on its technology (Waters, 2020a, 2020b, p. 12).

The Digital Transformation of Healthcare (Contreras, 2019) identifies a worldwide market for cost reduction in health care to promote "ecosystem transitions" from a value-based care to new point-of-care models enabled by digital tools. The intersections of medical technology with the IT industry, moreover, are off and running with a variety of pharma firms also. While the healthcare market may be highly appealing at this juncture on its surface, IT firms are used to making monster profits, and their individual stock market stake will have investors insistent on keeping those high margins and consistent dividends. The international arena of healthcare systems is *not* to be overlooked, for over the coming decade, many nations will await the infusions of funding by IT firms. Tech firms must then adapt to what more rudimentary health systems may have already installed (as many domestic hospitals here), so IBM's approach seems to be moving in a calculated direction.

Microsoft

With its $125.8 billion of 2019 revenues, Microsoft's Windows software dominates worldwide computers today. This firm is having its strongest annual growth in over a decade, mainly from its cloud operations. A *New York Times* article has highlighted Microsoft's attempt to become a moral leader as compared to both Facebook's and Google's technologies which can spread misinformation, as well as

Donald Trump's regular targeting of Amazon's market power, while Apple's pioneered smartphone is viewed as addicting (Wingfield, 2018, p. B3).

Microsoft is no longer seen as the bully running roughshod over its competitors like a few decades ago with antitrust battles (Stacey et al., 2019); it is interesting to note that they issued a book cautioning about artificial intelligence (AI), which appears to be at the forefront of the IT industry. This firm's growth expansion is in cloud services, maybe being the biggest cloud platform among a small oligopoly to dominate a large slice of the IT industry (Wingfield, 2018, p. B3). The key factor is the sheer scale of spending needed to compete in cloud computing.

Morgan Stanley predicted aggregate capital spending by 14 of the biggest cloud groups to jump 29% in 2018 alone, with 3/4 of that growth coming from Microsoft, Google, Facebook, and Amazon. The $135 billion video game market depends on cloud computing, so Sony and Microsoft joined forces going up against Google, Amazon, and Apple (Bradshaw & Lewis, 2019). All this could eventually lead to more takeovers, with the biggest platforms observing the suppliers of main applications that run in the cloud—a remorseless process of consolidation that has happened as other areas as corporate computing mature (Waters, 2018a, 2018b, 2018c, 2018d, p. 14). Microsoft and Amazon are estimated to account for 70% of this highly concentrated cloud market in the future, perhaps a provocation for regulatory attention (Waters, 2018a, 2018b, 2018c, 2018d).

Microsoft had a $1.06 trillion capitalization in July 2019. While Apple was the first to join the trillion-dollar market cap club, Amazon, Google, and Microsoft are bouncing up and down for that top slot depending on their weekly performance in the stock market. Likely due to its past run-ins with the feds, it has been dodging the bullets its peers are currently attracting (Condliffe, 2019). The *Financial Times* editorialized for investors to beware of the growing $1T tech club for the risks of concentration, their core business revenue growth rates maturing and that these firms' stock prices surely have great impact on the market and the overall economy (Financial Times, 2020c). Periodically, analysts caution about gyrations among tech stocks and question if the "tech sector is running out of steam" (NPR, 2018; Larson, 2018). Sommer (2018) cautions against the "magical thinking" about the value of tech stocks staying high. In past years, the tech giants lifted the stock market to historic highs, but by Fall 2018, the bull market was led down by the FAANG group leading the market down around Thanksgiving (Larson, 2018). Multiple factors, beyond company and industry dynamics, influence gyrations in the market's ups and downs.

Duhigg (2018, p. 39) wrote that while the US Government spent a bulk of the 1990s suing Microsoft for antitrust violations, Chief Executive Bill Gates termed it a waste of time and money and predicted that nothing would change what Microsoft did or how they would go about their business. One can assume that the same might hold true for its cloud-based services as it goes after less tech-sophisticated businesses.

Since Microsoft excels in retrofitting legacy systems, commonly found in hospitals, healthcare systems, and physician practices (Bass, 2018), and given its vast cloud capabilities, Microsoft seeks to bring medical device data to EHRs in competition to the more advanced Apple foray into EHRs (Microsoft, Hill-Rom team to bring, Davis J, 2019).

Besides EHRs' unpopularity with segments of the medical profession on feasibility of use, these electronic records on patients have been rankled with security breaches in office and hospitals. In 2019, Optum was the largest with over 11.5 million individuals affected, with millions more listed by *Modern Healthcare* (largest security breaches of electronic health records, 2020). This was before the intended transfer of health records to smartphones.

Elsewhere in health care, Microsoft Genomics is a set of cloud-based processing tools for clinicians and scientists pursuing genomics research, part of Microsoft's Healthcare NExT to integrate AI and cloud computing. The parent firm just jumped into open source software with a $7.5 billion acquisition of an online code-sharing platform, GitHub. The move brings to Microsoft a new audience of developers with skills to forge new arenas in health care (Waters, Kuchler, & Waters, 2018; Cohen J, 2018; Cohen JK, 2018a, 2018b, 2018c, 2018d). Sponsored IT conferences woo business partners, inspire users, recruit loyal developers, and attract programming talent (tech companies use huge conferences to battle for developer attention (2019)).

Bloomberg Technology maintained that GitHub will be a place for app developers to develop and show their work. It is host to 27 million programmers with 80 million repositories of code, which has increased in the last 5 years from 10 million (Wooing Developers, Developers, Developers, 2018).

On the Pharmacy front, Microsoft manages Walgreen's data storage with its pharmacy leveraging the IT firm's AI platform (Kim, 2018) by launching "health corners" in pharmacies to facilitate patient talks with pharmacists over medications and health-tech devices.

Microsoft's employees—somewhat a liberal workforce—petitioned its CEO with 300,000 names to cancel a contract with the US Immigrant, Customs, Enforcement (ICE) due to objections over the federal agency's punishment of families at the Mexican border (Frenkel, 2018). Other IT firms are finding employee activism over certain company business decisions. In *Bloomberg Businessweek*, Brustein and Bergen (2019) delineate tech employee resistance toward their firms' military contracts, AI contracts with China, use of technologies against immigrants, and general surveillance programs (like face recognition), even though executives still pursue such high-profit contracts. It has been noted that Presidential candidate Bernie Sanders raised more money from Big Tech employees than anyone else as of early February, even with his critique of the companies (Schleifer, 2020). To the firm's credit, once the outbreak of the COVID-19 became clear just miles from its headquarter campus, Microsoft management early on approved work at home and has taken other steps to shield its valuable workforce from the disease that has ransacked the Seattle area (Weise, 2020b). Managerial and highly skilled technical employees are immensely valued since replacements of sick or deceased staff is highly disruptive and costly.

Perhaps to its credit, Microsoft has litigated four lawsuits against the government over the past 5 years to defend customers' privacy rights. CEO Satya Nadella routinely refers to George Orwell's novel *1984* and Aldous Huxley's *Brave New World* in his speeches in an effort to ensure that technology doesn't create a dystopian future that none of us want.

Notwithstanding such occasional warnings, the IT industry contains the most powerful corporations the world has ever seen; IT firms use their resources to fend off scrutiny over their policies and, for certain, they fight regulation, even if and when federal policymakers will be able to know enough to figure out what regulatory actions might be judicious and worthwhile.

Microsoft still dominates the PC software market worldwide with the Windows operating system. IT firms have essentially remained unregulated to date. However, new recent public concerns from late 2017 have surpassed a serious level of concern relative to the IT industry's power and influence, especially for certain individual firms, like Facebook. IT firms have become so gigantic that a firm's sheer size and dominance defeats challengers, except when an occasional upstart may get attention for an innovation, but the enormity of existing firms usually prohibits much possibility that challengers might ever arise, but if they do, they can be bought and absorbed.

Apple

Apple is the first corporation in history to reach a trillion dollars in capitalization but at the same time has experienced a very rapid growth of its debt level (Foroohar, 2018). This *Financial Times* author cautions that historically this might predict a crisis for an individual firm, or collectively for the industry and larger economy. In 2018 the corporate bond market ballooned with the easy money economy, and it goes on. Corporate debt nears $10 trillion at the end of 2019 (47% of the entire economy), which the *Washington Post* reports the weakest firms accounting for most of the debt growth, much of it speculative and not much better than junk (Lynch, 2019, p. 1). Health insurers have soared their debt over the last decade also (Livingston, 2019). Nine firms calculate $115.5 billion debt in 2018 compared with $24.8 billion in 2009, much related to M&A wars. Could several firms be vulnerable since they need sufficient profits for debt payments if interest rates in the society should climb?

Portside considers the $19 trillion in corporate debt that could sink the global economy (Horowitz, 2020), compounded by the coronavirus touching off a plunge in the energy sector and the collapse of the travel, hospitality, and restaurant industries. Federal bailouts of industries along with a consumer cash benefit also doesn't do much for the federal debt picture either.

After reaching its trillion-dollar capitalization (Bradshaw, 2018a, 2018b, 2018c, 2018d) and the Trump tax cut was signed, Apple used its second quarter profit of $13.8 billion plus ample cash reserves to buy back $100 billion of its stock and paid shareholders a 16% larger dividend (Haefner, 2017). Apple's revenue ($229 billion) comes mainly from iPhone sales (greater than 60%), which Wall Street has started to doubt funding its future (Bradshaw, 2018a, 2018b, 2018c, 2018d).

Apple has historically had very rapid growth but has financed that growth with hardware sales. Phillips has cautioned that the 9-year bull market (which has somewhat become a bear market recently as a result of the coronavirus pandemic) was usually led by the likes of Amazon, Apple, Facebook, and Google all leading to a new constellation of firms toward more antitrust concerns. Is this trend toward consolidation and large growth in profits responsible for the socioeconomic issues of slow wage growth, income disparities, and the ever-shrinking middle class in America? Given their sway over multiple political levers, one wonders who will step forward to rein in their excessive power and influence (Phillips, 2018).

Consider that the health sector is ripe for new investment, if not for a further corporate takeover. Will the gigantic IT involvement actually lower care costs, or explode overall healthcare costs, more? With the COVID-19 crisis, numerous opportunities have also emerged for greater IT firm entries, from analytical assistance to governmental agencies through consumer contact tracing apps.

Apple has played not only a vital role in the stock market but also in the larger economy, but more importantly, its products have profoundly influenced American culture; Apple products have acquired a devoted cult-like consumer following. Becoming the first corporation in the world to ever reach a trillion-dollar capitalization (Bradshaw, 2018a, 2018b, 2018c, 2018d), after the Trump tax bill was signed, Apple used its second quarter profits of $13.8 billion to buy back $100 billion of its stock and paid shareholders a 16% larger dividend (Haefner, 2017). Stock price gains offer the executive suite a great boost in their quarterly bonuses and further endear the institutions which are huge investors.

The firm's revenue ($229 billion) comes mainly from technology hardware (iPhones hold over 62% of the US smartphone market with their sales greater than 60% of Apple's total annual revenue), a situation Wall Street fears will level off in the future mainly since people only buy one iPhone at a time and given its cost they hold on to it for several years (Bradshaw, 2018a, 2018b, 2018c, 2018d). Growth at some point will level off once the market is saturated with smartphones, and not many new customers can be swayed to join the Apple cult. In light of those realities, the firm has been slowly moving into services, the business strategy of health care being prime for growth, along with Apple TV, Apple PAY, and gaming branching out. The promise of double-digit returns after outlays from new services may be longer term.

Gaming

As far as gaming, the fast-growing entertainment industry (video gaming industry, 2020), it is estimated that 60% of Americans play them daily, with 48% of them being women, and most are adults. The worldwide market (China is the biggest) is growing by leaps and bounds (Gaming's next level, 2020). A single game in popularity can earn over a billion dollars (Perez, 2019), many are branded to movie themes (now shows like Sleep No More get you to accept new realities, 2020). Games have become political too. This segment of IT is undergoing a shakeup as smaller platforms get poached of key streamers in a heated-up war (Liao, 2020). Apple seeks to remain a main player.

The US gaming market in 2015 is estimated to be over $43.4 billion annually and $91.5 billion internationally, mostly played online, with a third using their smartphones. Most gaming is cloud-based, which makes this market contestable. More devices, platforms, and services are present to provide choice to consumers, but constant updating and streaming over the Internet via subscriptions is catapulting old consoles (Needleman, 2019).

FinTech

Just as credit card debt has touched a record with largest proportion of people seriously behind on their payments (Hoffower, 2020), numerous firms are mining the FinTech direction actively trying to find their niche (Galvin et al., 2018). FinTech apps (Venmo, Square Cash, Chime, Coinbase, and more) were key in VISA's acquisition of Plaid for $5.3 billion (Kauflin, 2020). FinTech startups are maturing; the last quarter of 2019 saw 452 deals spreading to emerging and frontier markets; diverse directions covered personal finance, wealth management, real estate, insurance, payments and billing, block chain, and money transfers, besides capital markets, according to CB Insights (The state of Fintech: Investment & sector trends to watch, 2019), which monitors this burgeoning financial sector.

Facebook's Libra has dominated the news with early sign-ups of payments companies, venture capitalists, and ecommerce groups (Murphy, 2019), but this new revenue stream for the firm faces several obstacles in its rollout, including regulators in the Group of Seven nations (Binham, 2019). The threat of significant disruption from digital money wars extends way beyond the Bitcoin craze; cryptocurrency obscures monitoring by governments (Vigna, 2019). As the nature of money changes, central bankers around the world are considering adoption of digital currencies; China is close, but should the United States commit (Bagnara, 2020)?

Armstrong and Megaw (2020) note the onslaught of FinTech mergers over just the past few years. Global FinTech deals topped $8.9 billion in the 3rd quarter of 2019, a quarterly record, with India and China battling over Asia's top FinTech hub. Financial services companies in China are quickly capturing consumers (Guastella, 2020). Amazon has also deeply plunged into financial services to be discussed in a following section.

It will be difficult to predict many of the implications of this rapidly moving trend, and how Apple will fare in its FinTech venture is unknown at this time; however changes in the way we pay for services, as well as engage in financial transactions of any kind, will most certainly change in the next few years.

Streaming

More than merely exploring new services to replace falling revenues from hardware sales with services, Apple has yet to find solid profitable streams. Apple entered a very tough competitive fight over the future of American and worldwide entertainment. Disney, ATT, Netflix, Hulu, Amazon, Google, Comcast, HBO, Quibi, and others are vigorously staking out the market for streaming services with a vengeance; big name investors and celebrities are active in designing old and new content to win in the competition to solidify their customer base (Chmielewski, 2019). Fights over intellectual property may become more commonplace (Jha, 2019). Chen (2020a, 2020b) cautions consumers about subscription overload as people subscribe to multiple platforms with monthly automated payments made which will wind up costing consumers a lot. During the COVID-19 pandemic, streaming has become the go-to entertainment sources as movie theaters and all other forms of out of the house entertainment venues closed. Whether this old form ever rebounded remains to be seen as the virus hangs on.

Becoming a streaming colossal and staying on top will be mighty expensive. The media conglomerate Disney has a big jump ahead with a roster of studios and much experience in entertainment with ABC TV and Hulu (Barnes, 2019). It claimed 26.5 million paid subscribers by February 2020 since its November startup (Allen, 2020). Yet, Disney reported a 60% decline in quarterly profits in November 2019, the result of digging deep in its pockets for Disney Plus. A Netflix style movie and TV service will arrive in 2020. Its streaming service captured roughly 16 million more sub-scribers in less than 3 months (Lee, 2020). Amazon streaming recently reached 55 million (Nicolaou, 2020a, 2020b, 2020c) out of its 150 million Prime subscribers, surpassing Netflix's 139 million subscribers (Stat du jour, 2020). Netflix spent lav-ishly hyping its 24 nominees for Oscars (up from 13 in 2019), in order to sustain its subscriber base against new competition, but it proves very costly (Barnes & Sperling, 2020). Streaming TV time exploded as consumers subscribed to two or more services to get the content they desired (Watson, 2020). Thus, marketing and production costs will be high, sustainability in the competition will get even tougher, and how Apple can secure a desired profit stream from streaming seems an uphill climb.

Apple has new shows rolling out on its Apple TV Plus (Hsu, 2019) utilizing its smartphones and tablets to build its huge market to hopefully develop a fast sub-scriber base, with likely 5G devices needing to be upgraded, given such 5G net-works now being established by telephone firms. Nevertheless, content-related costs will require significant investment by Apple, and the fight to win *an increasing market share* will be costly, but Disney is betting strongly that this trend will con-tinue (Epstein, 2019). As major media firms reported earnings this past November, new concerns emerged about cord cutting with cable and satellite hookups being cancelled at an accelerating rate (Barnes & Sperling, 2019). As with FinTech, the streaming wars will be disruptive and surely depend on if and when consumers decide to spend in a recessionary economy.

While Apple may play the underdog for a while, the entertainment horse race will be exciting—and eventually far more newsworthy than the Presidential cam-paign of 2020. Each giant competitor will differ in its strategy to secure millions of subscribers and stay able to maintain them over time (Power to the People, 2019). Netflix, the pioneer producing company and current industry leader, garnered 34 Golden Globes nominations in 2019, indicating the intensity in the streaming com-petition (Barnes & Sperling, 2020). Due to its strong favored content, Netflix keeps adding subscribers (8.8 million 4th quarter of 2019), even since Apple and Disney announced their entries (Associated Press, 2020).

Apple's nascent advantage is its 1.5 billion smart iPhone users globally (Gurman & Wittenstein, 2020), who may need, along with all platforms, dedicated subscribers to get 5G smartphones to derive the greatest benefit. As an IT conglomerate reaching out on several new business lines, who will get burnt in the ensuing cost spiral?

Again, a phenomenal effect of the COVID-19 pandemic came with the *Financial Times* reporting on the binge watching and playing online games becoming global pastimes, as profits rolled in. More than 780 million people stuck at home in China given lockdown travel restrictions became great for gaming giants Tencent and peer NetEase. It was noted that Chinese phone owners downloaded a record number of games from the App store as the coronavirus and their government kept them in their homes, to boost the $150 billion global games industry. Gaming exceeded education, entertainment, and photo and video apps in China, offering fine opportunities for these gaming companies (Lewis, 2020).

Domestically streaming (Poniewozik, 2019) also ballooned with several state lockdowns, perhaps killing movie and live theaters forever. Subscriptions to various competitors along with the complete Hollywood shutdown in California makes a comeback for theaters awfully hard to predict with social distancing in place, or consumers' fears of gatherings. A few direct to streaming movies, mainly animation, may be the future for Hollywood to return but not necessarily to its heyday. Will Americans go back to theaters, who knows? A few states now "opening their economies" may give some evidence to this, but watching the film with a mask and eating popcorn while sipping a coke may keep folks in their living rooms.

Netflix and MTV made their marks in the 1980s with strong consumer followings on TVs. Today billions of profits are in play with a variety of IT firms coming into gaming and music, too. The cultural prominence of the past led to purchases of consoles for gaming, including Nintendo, Sony's PlayStation, and Xbox by Microsoft. All are hyping new offerings (Faber, 2020) along with new fancy hardware being designed. Partnerships with brand fashion retailers are seeking to attract and aiming to keep new subscribers (Faber, 2020). Similarly, virtual auctions in the art market seek new viewers, who may not have been used to being online (Gerlis, 2020) noting again the digitalization of more of the old economy. Yet, Sony and Nintendo, which are dependent on greater hardware sales, in China did not do as well due to supply chain disruption with closed-console factories (Lewis, 2020). From 1993 on, piped in Muzak may not have as large an audience with all the closed retail stores and restaurants today and in the future, but online content delivery gives multiple choices over a dozen popular mediums for consumers through their phones and TVs (From Muzak to Netflix, 2019).

COVID-19's arrival with gaming popularity zooming with lockdowns, price gouging seems like the American way of business in many arenas. Numerous articles have been written about issues in the supply line disruptions that have given entrepreneurs and corporate entities new opportunities to profit, along with the political corruption yet to be fully exposed. Nintendo consoles faced a significant shortage in the growing demands under the circumstances. Despite eBay and Amazon's policies to dissuade such practices, they only apply to essential items.

The global demand given many supply chain issues, resulted in price gouging (Khalid, 2020) as with many common examples of this market dynamic in America. Another related opportunity for profit-making related to streaming comes from ad-supported video services being attached to streaming services (Rizzo et al., 2020). Fox and Comcast are advancing an estimated $500 million deal as a service to the entertainment giants who may be offering free or lower-cost alternatives to consumers who do not want to pay so high for subscriptions. Such streaming services have programming choices that consumers may like for their attractive content, but also for variance in pricing. During lockdowns, multiple subscriptions were likely to be chosen, so reassessments may lead to perhaps more conscious choices post-COVID-19 (Consumer Reports, The Programs and the Prices, 2020).

Netflix had 150 million people on board in January 2020 and was predicted to remain a blockbuster hit beyond the current crisis, based on its appeal to "hearts and minds" (Schumpter, 2020). First quarter subscribers rose by 15.8 million, now reaching 183 million worldwide, with new releases being planned for 2020. Nevertheless, competitors may refuse to sell new shows (Disney) or license old shows (Warner Media, owned by AT&T's HBO Max). All of the industry, including Comcast-owned NBC Universal which started Peacock, may face a dwindling base or even further "cable cutting" when the coming recession gets deeply felt. This entire market will remain unstable as noted that Netflix and Disney shares fell when Apple unveiled its $4.99 streaming service per month, which beats out HBO at $14.90, Amazon $12.99, Netflix $12.99, and Disney $6.99. New iPhone buyers get it at this $4.99 price point (Klebnikov, 2019). Content choices may be confusing at first, but many consumers will engage in back and forth decision-making over time depending on their content preferences. Thus it can be seen that any IT firm may be actually gambling on a huge revenue and profit flow out of streaming services.

It is uncertain how the streaming wars will play out, and if Apple can finagle success against several formidable competitors. Clearly since the stay-at-home orders necessitated from the COVID-19 pandemic, it appears that streaming services are enjoying wide popularity (Barney, 2020). How badly do many Americans need to escape Trump's society?

Whither Apple in All of This Diversification?

Historically, Apple's business and stock performance has been truly remarkable, so it remains one of the most sought after and studied listings on Wall Street. A lot of investors made a great deal of money from this firm's stock; its large institutional investment base expects the same future performance. However, this may be problematic as iPhone and other hardware sales have slowed dramatically. Nevertheless, its strategy change toward services has been underway for this company best known for its technical innovation and its large consumer following with nearly a billion iPhones available to download its many apps and direct followers to its new services. A *New York Times* piece details the startling snooping on people's daily habits that has grown increasingly more intrusive (Valentino-DeVries et al., 2020); concerns over vulnerability to hacking are discussed over the hordes of apps folks download, not to mention the concept of using the phone to trace the whereabouts of their users by the telecom giants in virus tracing.

The firm lowered prices on iPhone 11 making $51 billion last quarter 2019, but its Airpods and Watch wearables may sustain earnings, along with $46 billion in services for 2019 for a new bullish outlook (McGee, 2020a, 2020b); however, in China with much of its content blocked, it is not clear how Apple will be able to expand its business there (McGee, 2020a, 2020b, p. 6).

Thus, the historical role that Apple has played in the economy and the culture renders corporate objectives to influence how the firm embarks on its healthcare activities, amidst its substantial diversification. These larger pressures will change Apple's strategy over its emphasis on services and apps with content-based work rather than hardware. Such a turnaround indicates a significant organizational cultural change; it will also be a far different outlook economically for the firm. The cultural change may likely be disruptive to its current workforce and demand careful management along the way.

Then again in business activities, unanticipated events can disrupt a company in a disastrous way: the coronavirus epidemic that arose in China and swept the world within weeks (Global emergency: It is an emergency, 2020). With lagging sales in China already, Apple abruptly shut 42 retail stores and other corporate locations in the country (McGee, 2020a, 2020b) that combined with more multinationals pulling up stakes with the economy (Sheikh, Watkins, Wu, & Grondahl, 2020). The China lockdown of cities due to the COVID-19 spread, its resulting economic downturn and falling trade, will be a heavy jolt on Chinese consumers and eventually spread to the rest of the world just as COVID-19 has done.

In connection to China's recent COVID-19 epidemic, it has been mentioned that the stock market crash of February 2020 should cause retrenchment in these companies that have not experienced a significant bear market for at least 10 years, and most are not prepared to weather the storm (Heath & Bogage, 2020, p. 2). These companies have become so reliant on international demand to sustain their business model that will be severely tested by closed borders and shut down societies that have occurred in the COVID-19 pandemic (Fried, 2020, p. 3).

Apple's performance and its needed growth by investors quivers the stock market when things do not go well, as has been the historical legacy (Wigglesworth, Waters, & Bradshaw, 2019, p. 1). Maintaining year-after-year stock price increases is *not* the only finance issue the company faces. The firm is fighting a $14.3 billion tax bill with the European Union, which comes on top of a tussle over a tax deal with Ireland in 2016 that is being disputed (Apple Can't Win Its $14.3 Billion Tax Battle, 2019). Apple had an average tax rate of only 5% overseas, which results in accusations that Apple is not paying its fair share in taxes.

Most if not all IT firms are international, which complicates the time management must spend due to much different playing fields in each arena. Apple's disappointing hardware sales were not just with US consumers, even given resorting to promo deals and trade-ins to boost iPhone sales (Gurman, 2018).

Chinese consumers are also shortening the cycle for phone replacements (Rocco, 2018), and competing firms there are challenging Apple's innovations and building in other incentives for greater sales. While the lockdown of cities over the rise of the coronavirus infections may have spurred Internet usage, Tim Cook, Apple's CEO, noted that quarterly earnings estimates will be missed due to the coronavirus (Fried, 2020). It is unknown if many Chinese will have future incomes and willingness to buy new hardware once normality comes back, but how soon and when?

Disappointing hardware sales with US consumers, as well as internationally, may indicate that smartphones had earlier reached a saturation point worldwide. Trump's trade war with China had begun to shake Apple's future, not just due to its manufacturing hubs there, but also to his imposed tariffs of up to 25% (Bradshaw, 2018a, 2018b, 2018c, 2018d). Samsung ($205.6 billion revenues) has stepped up its challenge to iPhones as well, domestically and internationally. Samsung, South Korea's biggest company, produced one of the first 5G Android phones in 2019, again a firm to be affected by this nation's COVID-19 spread. Apple's streaming will be available through Samsung TVs in a new partnership. Chinese firms (Huawei, Xiaomi, among several others) are also targeting the broader Asian market, beyond China's consumers (Zhong, 2019). Such demand dynamics on the international level raise doubts about Apple's future in the largest smartphone market of China. Chinese firms are challenging pricey iPhones, and Samsung is stepping up competition, while this firm is moving toward cloud-based services (White, 2019). India has become the second largest smartphone market of late (NewsGram Desk, 2020). Such demand dynamics on the international level raise doubts about Apple's future, in the largest smartphone market of China.

Still, by the beginning of 2020, Apple shares topped a record $300 a share, with 2019 gaining 86% its best year in a decade (Gurman & Wittenstein, 2020). The company has an obvious track record in both consumer engagement and customer loyalty. Now with over 62% of the US phone market, customers don't necessarily talk on their iPhones, but regularly download apps, including many health-related, for multiple activities, including streaming—as Steve Jobs had likely planned (Fowler, 2019). The firm is producing lots of patented health apps now creating revenues and opportunities for data mining (Fung, 2020).

In sum, Apple is venturing into several new areas for growth, each which will require significant investment along new learning curves amidst the competitive landscapes. Leaving behind the highly lucrative hardware business growth worries investors since the streaming, FinTech, gaming, and healthcare lines necessitate a corporate cultural adaptation amidst demanding a new different workforce. For success, the changing of a corporate culture goes well beyond coming up with the best products; it requires the executive suite consistently treating both workers and customers ethically (Creating the right culture in a business, 2019). Prospects for its new health foray appear quite good as Apple assesses the sector for several ways to make its indelible mark by using its hardware.

Health Care

One can easily grasp the IT industry, as rich and powerful as its firms are, is moving into many new arenas, only one being health care. A few may do well but others may not. Apple has devoted the firm toward a huge stake in health care, apparently becoming influential.

It should be noted that Apple's entry into health care was at first gradual, then suddenly building upon its hardware prominence jumped onto a fast learning curve. It plans to keep its large and loyal customer base. Literally, a huge number of iPhone and Mac users do sales work for the firm's products to family and friends; it will be likely that health apps get pushed with the same vigor by its devoted fans.

In October 2017, the firm explored buying a medical clinic startup as part of a big push into health care (Farr, 2017). Two system takeovers were explored. AC Wellness, a launch of operational medical clinics to serve Apple's employees, is now enabled by advanced technology. Health care is considered a "build out" on Apple's retail (Miller, 2017). Its worldwide network of more than 300 retail stores has captured "consumer delight" (Farr, 2018a, 2018b), with the Apple Watch taking off for personal health functions. The firm has hired a cadre of health professionals and experts for its significant health foray, including involvement with the FDA and clinical trials, and using the iPhone for reporting personal health data to their providers.

Apple's entry into EHRs may open up a "growing marketplace of applications" with its hardware already in the hands of consumers. Thus, a "user-friendly mobile health portal" will likely become widely accepted. Its health records section apparently conquers interoperability that proprietary EHR vendors have competitively squandered over time (Spitzer, 2018a, 2018b). A positive outcome then becomes medical record portability, where existing vendors (EPIC, Cerner, Allscripts, and others) procrastinated on correcting the serious problem of communication and portability between their EHR systems. Finally, CMS and the Office of the National Coordinator for Health Information Technology have unveiled final versions to supposedly make it easier for providers, insurers, and patients to exchange health data by adopting standardized program interfaces (HHS releases final interoperability rules, 2020). Patients will be permitted to use smartphones for their medical records (Schulte & Fry, 2020).

Apple's relationship with Stanford Health Care had the firm involved in the building of the new $2.1 billion hospital. While in bed, the patient can direct entertainment, room temperature, window blinds, and interface with medical records, as well as communicate with medical and nursing staff. This is all due to the built-in Apple robotics, sensors, to create efficiency and convenience.

While Apple's use of its technology may make some consumers more health conscious by allowing consumers to monitor their disease conditions in more careful ways, recent criticisms over social media and computerized devices are that they provide, and entice people, for screen addiction (or in this case, health narcissism obsessed with their clinical indicators). Apple is developing an app for addiction and excess screen time to make individuals aware that such habits may be deleterious to their well-being. It is not clear to what extent people take advantage of that information to cut back on their device usage. Google with its Android operating system has also come under pressure from shareholders and health campaigners to deal with the constant distraction of people to their phones and computers with compulsive behavior associated with mobile device addiction.

AC Wellness, an operational launch of medical clinics to serve Apple's employees, is enabled by advanced technology. CEO Tim Cook described the healthcare industry as an area where the company could make significant inroads and impact. Bambrough (2018) goes on to say while health care remains a lucrative field for companies to enter, it appears the entry costs are significant enough to limit entry to the tech giants already in place.

Cook has been forward-thinking about regulations for the tech industry being unavoidable, even embracing it when the market is not working well (Kuchler, 2019). Apple holds many patents that suggest a whole new platform for personal health technology for monitoring clinical signs and symptoms (Edwards & Edwards, 2018). Apple Health Records works with existing EHR vendors for piloting in over 40 health systems across the United States. It records personal health information (including data from apps) to grant increased consumer access to their health information. Apple apps can combine medical information from their notable provider systems and organize the data so patients can share it with any future provider.

In a *New England Journal of Medicine* "Mobile Devices and Health," Sim (2019) noted that 81% of North American adults own a smartphone that have revolutionize society and changed history and just witness recording police killings and other brutality, as well as how social media enables the massive protests of Spring and Summer 2020. Active and passive sensors, functional assessments, and digital biomarkers and diagnostics hold great potential for integrating with clinical care, but much remains to be determined in the direction of this $8.1 billion market growth from 2018, including the potential of harm.

Wearable Technology

Fitbit was the pioneer in wearable fitness technology, and it became somewhat of a pop culture accessory from basic tracking of activities, such as running, cycling, and swimming, heart rates, and sleep patterns to now gathering a greater share of health data for the consumer. Currently, there are 28 million online active users worldwide with over 100 million devices sold (O'Brien, 2019) now under the control of Google.

Apple is also launching studies on its watch's ability to monitor hearing, mobility, and women's health to bolster its medical research potential (Robbins, 2019). Medical grade wearables are now becoming reimbursable, which is helping doctors to accept them if they get paid to spend time trying to interpret remote data transmitted to the provider (Al-Siddiq, 2019). Apple and Google's Fitbit will eventually be backed by advanced biometrics to promote this real-time monitoring that is expected to spur sales significantly both of the devices and the apps that will upload information to the cloud for use by physicians and others.

Digital medicine is zooming ahead with personable wearables beyond the Apple Watch and Google's Fitbit. The latest wearables are able to monitor signs and symptoms and then call your doctor if potentially serious problems may arise, such as atrial fibrillation (AF). This is being studied at Stanford University (New England Journal of Medicine, 2019) with watch-notifying the patient to call for help if vulnerable data presents. This appears to be a useful function of many devices coming up under IoT, some going directly to the provider (glucose monitoring, CPAP sleep machines, compliance with pharmaceuticals, etc.). In the case of the AF data, Apple owns it—not the patient or provider—which causes some concern over privacy (Park, 2019).

Apple is also launching studies on its watch's ability to monitor hearing, mobility, and women's health to bolster its medical research potential (Robbins, 2019). A larger UK insurer has followed the car insurance utilization model of the black box to invoke loss aversion as a preventive medicine intervention in the NHS (Neville & Atkins, 2018). Data from 400,000 people were compiled from watches to find increased activity for calorie burn, which may mean "extra life years." Medical grade wearables are now becoming reimbursable, which is helping doctors to accept them if they get paid to spend time trying to interpret remote data transmitted to the provider (Al-Siddiq, 2019). Apple and Google's Fitbit will eventually be backed by advanced biometrics to promote this real-time monitoring that is expected to spur sales significantly.

In recognition of this market for sales, as well as its massive data repository, Google swept in to pay $2.1 billion for the Fitbit company when its financials were not doing so well. An alarm was raised (Feibus, 2019) over privacy of the personal data and what it would mean in terms of higher costs now under the Google auspice. The new owner's analytic capabilities could lay the groundwork for better insights from the stream of data from wearables. It is not as though Fitbit owners made the choice that Google should be the keeper of their health data as Feibus mentioned in *USA Today*. Feibus went on to say that privacy of one's data is a fungible asset that can be collected and used without consent, while at the same time that we're being assured that these companies take our privacy seriously (2019, p. 3b).

And if people are unhappy with one provider changing to another, it will not be easy as one's data will not be transferable or available unless one continues to pay the monthly fee. Apple and Samsung are obviously scrambling to make the migration from Google's Fitbit as easy as possible.

While numerous employers have purchased Fitbits for their employees to track their performance, the push for wellness perhaps has gone a little too far with a program called "a Fitbit for the brain." Several employers are buying this idea to understand and monitor the mental health of their employees, who often are not performing at peak levels in the office. The program will measure things like memory, focus, and decision-making, crucial variables for worker productivity. If Total Brain feels an individual may have a mental disorder, it can refer them to an employee assistance program or a licensed professional who can provide a deeper analysis of what the issue might be, or fire the worker. The opportunities for employers to have all sorts of personal health data and use them for all sorts of reasons such as promotions, and worse discipline and terminations, will be unlimited.

As Wall Street and tech insiders are figuring out the implications of Google's purchase of Fitbit and lining up hardware products, Robbins and Herper (2019) also questioned the implications for health and privacy from the acquisition. In the meanwhile, with the 40 million people who have smart watches or fitness trackers that are supposedly monitoring their heartbeats, one study showed that some people of color may be at risk for getting inaccurate readings. Hailu (2019) writes in STAT about the inaccuracy in tracking heart rates that this issue gets almost no media attention even as the smart watches and fitness tracker market has grown exponentially. The potential inaccuracies have broad implications for the scientific research that is being conducted on these wearables, raising the suggestion that existing biases in medicine now have a new overleaf beyond what doctors and providers already display. Any number of employers has been collecting information from their employees' wearable devices, and it is unclear what actions they do in the realm of human resources that rely upon this flawed data (Hailu, 2019).

In recognition of a whole new territory of data collection related to medical records, the FDA is trying to figure out how to regulate mobile health software and products that use AI (Ross, 2019). Beyond watches, a large amount of voice-activated devices (Chen, 2019, p. 1) are being pitched at consumers. Voice-controlled devices, like robot vacuums, alarm clocks, refrigerators, and other accessories, can be directed from Google's Assistant (Home) and Amazon's Alexa and Echo. A *Financial Times* special report on the growing cyber security issues over IoT spoke to remote hijacking, such as the risk for aircraft and refrigerators. It has been found that lasers shown through a window can hack Alexa and other voice command devices to shut off security systems in order to open doors and windows. As we become more reliant on the Internet to run our affairs and our homes, we also become more vulnerable to those being hacked and controlled by others. While these devices are constantly updated to close vulnerabilities, new ones pop up over time so the cycle continues.

While overly optimistic technology is constantly hyped in the market, much is becoming available, with consumers buying as early adopters. This author has friends who become unpaid salespeople for products once they purchase it. Shortcomings in the safety and use of the technology become noted with voice-assisted hardware, which are just in their infancy today. IoT has newer cutting-edge devices that can perform, extract, transform, and load functions on data gathered locally (Gal, 2019). As folks find themselves surrounded by such devices, it presents challenges to federal consumer protection agencies as well as social scientists to delve into how all this technology changes our lives, and what it means for everyday life in our culture.

Therefore, the Apple firm has been moving into services, the business strategy of health care being thought prime for growth. In October 2017, the firm explored operating clinics as a bigger push into health care (Farr, 2017). Health care is considered a "build out" on Apple's retail (Miller, 2017). AC Wellness' operational medical clinics serving Apple's employees is a kind of industrial medicine control over employees, to make "meaningful impact" (Bambrough, 2018).

Apple is on a fast learning curve in health care building on its track record in both consumer engagement and customer loyalty, which its services ventures wish to capitalize upon, now with 62% of the US phone market. Apple holds patents to engage a new platform for personal health technology (Edwards & Edwards, 2018). Apple Health Records works with existing EHR vendors to record personal health information for increased consumer access to their health information. The Apple app can combine medical information from prestigious institutions and organize it so patients can share it with any provider.

So if your spouse, kids, and coworkers do not listen to you anymore, you can be assured that your personal assistants clearly are—listening to you all the time so they will now give you news broadcasts, even if you are not sure where they get the content, what gets chosen to be sent, and what political affiliation may be there (Krotoski, 2020). Voice-driven gadgets will be advancing even more with voice recognition technology, though *Fortune* magazine suggested that it still has a way to go for multiple applications. Even the Apple Watch, introduced in 2015, now allows a kind of Flash Gordon experience with a wearable, with significant expenditure for wearable accessories and all the expensive apps for these devices.

It has been reported that Amazon's Ring and Google's Nest are aiding Americans to normalize surveillance, as well as turn us into a nation of voyeurs (Harwell, 2020). The camera in the doorbell is sold for a neighborhood watch so that anyone around the world can enjoy the view from one's front door. Yet, they have been found to be hackable.

Amazon

Amazon thus may be considered one of the biggest disruptive forces on the planet. In a very short while, the online bookstore of Amazon morphed into a huge supplier—across several different industries. Amazon quickly learned how, as a corporation, to control the infrastructural speed of development. It knows its customers *very well* through their purchases and its Alexa voice-assisted technology that listens and records. It is a global corporation bigger than Australia. A CNN special report, *The Age of Amazon* on August 16, 2019, reported that 50% of online commerce is handled by this firm. Many small manufacturers *must use* Amazon's platform to sell their products since Amazon's logistics give each a phenomenal advantage in the online marketplace, which has increasingly left out bricks and mortar establishments.

Indeed, the retail industry has been transformed in a short period of time as Amazon warehouses have mushroomed across the nation; their automation in filling a purchase, and through its Prime function for next day delivery, has been remarkable and very appreciated by consumers. It is leading in building fulfillment centers, and creating jobs, in communities across the nation (Diakantonis, 2020)—even during the coronavirus pandemic. As Walmart had plummeted away thousands of mom-and-pop stores and pharmacies nationwide in the 1990s with its huge expansion, Amazon has eliminated many retailers, even large ones like Sears, Sports Authority, Toys R Us, and more.

Even though Amazon pays absolutely no taxes to the federal government because of its lobby for corporate tax breaks, it has been deemed as the second most trusted institution after the military in American society. The firm is starting its four-star stores with consumer-rated local products like a walk-in website (Wingfield, 2018). Since antitrust policies are weak and the market is not competitive (though big IT firms vie with each other and do fight at times), the business practices of Amazon can move forward at a quick speed as it enters retail food and now pharmaceutical distribution. Another implication of the COVID-19 pandemic was the emptying of face masks, hand sanitizer, and other demanded items from its inventory until the firm curbed its warehouse shipments of nonessential goods in March (Lee, 2018).

The main function of Amazon is mining data from its customers and data on their extensive market of manufacturers who use their site. Third-party sellers allow Amazon to analyze their data to assess their businesses. Independent retailers know Amazon's impact on small businesses, but they have truly little alternative than to cooperate with this powerhouse.

It is still deeply unclear how people's privacy is currently being violated, and when it constantly occurs on social media and purchases, where do ads come from, how are they being targeted, who pays for them, and whether data is generated where people have never given their permission nor very likely do not know their data was seized in the first place.

The McKinsey Global Institute led off a report "Navigating a World of Disruption" with the following paragraph:

> We live in an era of disruption in which powerful global forces are changing how we live and work. The rise of China, India, and other emerging economies; the rapid spread of digital technology; the growing challenges of globalization; and, in some countries, the splintering of long-held social contracts are all roiling business, the economy, and society. These and other global trends offer considerable new opportunities to companies, sectors, countries, and individuals that embrace them successfully—but the downside for those who cannot keep up has also grown disproportionally. For business leaders, policy makers, and individual, figuring out how to navigate these skewed times may require some radical rethinking. (Bughin & Woetzel, 2019)

This report noted that disruption is intensifying; the gulf between those embracing change and those falling behind is growing. Disruption is the word that is constantly used to characterize the Amazon corporation, in several areas where it has forged new businesses, particularly alarming in health care. When Amazon released that is was thinking of entering pharmaceutical distribution, even though it was just selling drugs to hospitals, it put a major scare into the retail pharmacy chains. When it finally decided to become its own pharmacy benefit manager with the takeover of PillPack, it caused reverberations all across the healthcare system.

Within the global economy, the dynamism of the high-growth "outperformers" has gone hand in hand with the rise of highly competitive emerging market companies. By several standards, many of these companies are already more innovative, nimble, and competitive than several Western rivals. This results in something different than the previous decade's financial overseas flight of US and European multinationals that went with globalization.

Today globalization patterns are changing with the rapid growth in data flows, but we can still witness stressed fluidity within the global economy, which has shifted gears to become much more data driven, according to Bughin and Woetzel (2019). These authors note that global value chains continue to evolve over time, reshaped in part by technology, including automation, which could amplify the shift toward more localized production of goods near consumer markets.

When considering China, India, and other emerging markets, this holds many implications for American multinationals. Businesses are benefiting from IoT, and those in the forefront will be able to reap greater benefits utilizing artificial intelligence, but McKinsey points out that "These technologies still have limitations." This global management consulting firm still hopes that AI could contribute to tackling pressing societal challenges, which we will wait to see (Amazon vs. The Left, 2019). Despite all the anti-Amazon fervor, there are surely places across the country who love the jobs that are created, as well as the love by massive consumer pockets for provided product services.

According to historian Gabriel Kolko, there has been no breakup of large corporations in the United States since the Progressive Era under Theodore Roosevelt; but even then reforms did not lessen the domination of Capital over Labor in this society very much (Kolko, 1963). While the federal government treads softly and will very unlikely ever force a breakup of any American company again, the European Union continues to investigate a host of issues of IT firms and their lack of competition, along with virtually no market entry by anyone else even predicted. Looking below the surface, Amazon has so many partnerships for abundant leverage in policymaking; for example, JPMorgan Chase and Amazon are credit card partners. Most of the IT firms have forged vital business relationships, solid enough to yield great support politically, but the sheer puzzling complexity of this IT industry, particularly as it applies to health care, remains a challenge to both politicians and bureaucrats. Ahead of domestic regulators, the EU has been probing Amazon's online commerce and its knowing exactly what people want to buy (Bond, 2018). In 2017 more than half of all items sold on its platform came from third-party vendors, and the use of this information to gain market leverage is at the heart of the inquiry by the European Union (EU) (Bond, 2018). The firm's deeper understanding of why consumers do, or do not, buy things underpins its expansion into private label goods that compete with outside brands and sellers. Data, analyzed for greater sales, drives this firm's huge growth.

Brick-and-mortar stores cannot compete, and newer generations of Americans prefer an online presence for convenience and price comparison. Every grocery store and other firms followed suit with delivery locally assisted by Uber, Grubhub, and Lyft. Prepared meal delivery has zoomed with the "stay-in-place" orders in several states. In grocery food delivery, logistics can be difficult with time limits on item availability and perishability that limits the range of what can be sold, so many hybrid models have persisted in the market, segmented highly by generational preferences. Young professionals engage in greater activities outside of grocery shopping, while an older generation views a trip to the supermarket as a social event by the postwar generation. The younger generation has price points to opt for consumer service that they calculate against their time value. Again, with the COVID-19 pandemic, the massive disruption to supply chains, whether in food, pharmaceuticals, or dry goods, and the fallout for the next evolution will be determined over time, but Amazon's warehouse expansions underway are set to grow with long-term plans now being formulated based upon its overwhelming knowledge of the whole country and its consumer preferences.

But that service and ability to serve the entire nation on a same day or overnight service model comes at a cost. Amazon has been widely criticized for the cutthroat work environment at its filling stations with tough physical quotas imposed upon their workforces. Warehouse workers are disgruntled even with their recent wage rise to $15 an hour, but safety concerns over working in close proximity to others during the COVID-19 pandemic have driven further doubts about Amazon's ability to continue its market dominance at the expense of the people who work there.

It is interesting to compare Amazon's US nonunion workforce's ability to effect change in addressing safety concerns vs. Amazon's French workforce which is unionized. The latter led to a walkout on its French operations (Alderman & Satariano, 2020). Amazon fought back by putting 10,000 employees on paid furlough, and the case went before the French Supreme Court after a lower court ordered the company to stop delivering nonessential items; that was when Amazon locked down warehouses and told employees to stay home (Alderman & Satariano, 2020). The court's decisions will challenge Amazon's ability to sidestep the demands of workers for safer working space (Alderman & Satariano, 2020). Generally known as a major disruptor, Amazon, along with other tech platforms, may be ripening for a major disruption of their operations because of the COVID-19 pandemic (Alderman & Satariano, 2020).

Weise and Conger speak to the anger as the coronavirus spread to more than 50 Amazon facilities employing over 400,000 workers (Weise & Conger, 2020). Because regular brick-and-mortar retailers were closed due to the pandemic, there was a crushing demand for goods during the lockdown and stay-at-home policies. Apparently America's insatiable demand for stuff can carry on uninterrupted by a global pandemic even though we have no place to go and nothing to do if we could get there.

Bezos' personality and his management philosophy guides the company. His leadership principles are laminated and posted throughout his plants to supposedly induce greater productivity. Duhigg (2019) explores nuances of this weird corporate culture around Bezos. Workers are digitally tracked and evaluated in all fulfillment centers to spot employees who may fall behind, with reprimands often given. Some workers feel that this truly is "surveillance capitalism." Yet, the company justifies the very intense work environment so that it can provide free one-day delivery to its customers. Customers who by and large could wait an extra day or two for their order but have been swayed to pay an extra yearly fee to be Amazon Prime members to gain access to their stuff quicker all shipped for free.

Amazon's Rekognition service was developed for police use as a tool to assess dangers through facial screening, but accuracy was an issue, and suspicions of misuse with little or no accountability were raised. There is no regulatory oversight of such technologies and how they are used especially by the Government. There are Democrats, as well as Republicans, who would like to see Amazon's monopoly of 50% of online sales in the United States broken up, even though they do have minor competitors; the same may go for Apple's 50% of smartphone sales, Microsoft's 77% use of Windows software, Facebook's 2.4 million users a month, and Google reaching 87% of searches. Amazon Web Service has grabbed 33% of the $100 billion cloud computing market. In short, each firm's market power seems formidable (Richter, 2020).

Amazon's impact on the environment will remain significant, and its treatment of workers over the COVID-19 safety issue, as well as the regular abuse heaped on them, will be disputed for a while. Other folks do not like Amazon's contracts with ICE and the US Department of Defense. It also has dealings with the Veterans Administration and New York City, so its extensive variety of "partners" who like its services and depend upon them may very well aid in resistance to regulatory oversight, let alone lead to an antitrust regulatory breakup.

Streitfeld (2020), an antitrust lawyer, had her convictions strengthened when the COVID-19 outbreak made Amazon more essential to households, but also more vulnerable. Its visibility has been heightened by its treatment of its workers and other decisions made by management. More resistance will likely follow.

The company had gone through a year-long competition for its HQ2, a second headquarters taking it to New York and Virginia. Stiff community opposition canceled the New York location, but Amazon came away from the exercise with access to huge data files from 200 other cities across the country, who were bidding to get the headquarters put in their place. This bountiful information the company gathered (it is a firm striving for and thriving by information) will be mined for amazing future investments; for sure, it will be used in multiple ways for further growth of the firm. Amazon is keen on lobbying, and with Bezos' ownership of the *Washington Post*, which President Trump calls "fake news," the company stands solid in looking at its future despite bountiful criticism.

Frontline's Amazon Empire: The Rise and Reign of Jeff Bezos (PBS, 2020) examined the global impact of Amazon and Jeff Bezos' fantasy of colonizing the moon for the future of humanity. It pointed out deep-set fears over Amazon's size and aspects of its business operations. Wall Street saw in Bezos' early book selling that *data provided an untapped potential in the digital landscape*. His futuristic bookstore, positioned for the world in July 1995, was characterized as "Napoleonic ambition," but it actually came to be the mainstay of bookselling for the consumer market.

Amazon is considered the second most trusted corporation in America because of its consumer-centric value. Nevertheless, the company is really a massive data collection organization that has turned data into a commodity, whereby consumer behavior is studied in order *to sell more*. Wall Street went along with Bezos before Amazon turned a profit, because there were those who believed in the long term for Amazon to gain greater market share. Stock traders still seem to admire the fact that Amazon does not pay American taxes. One factor that allowed it to monopolize the book selling market was that customers pay no sales tax on their purchases from Amazon with free delivery on Prime, which gives it an advantage over brick-and-mortar retail stores although that is changing as states begin to impose sales tax on any merchandise purchase and sent to an address in that state. It was also noted that many smaller businesses have little choice but to adhere to the Amazon retail platform so that they can gain business growth even though they have to pay to ship any goods as Prime customers get free shipping and Amazon merely passes that cost onto the vendor to deal with.

With the rise of this firm in the 1990s, e-commerce soared and took over a large share of book publishers. Outside sellers criticized its "tough tactics" to pay the percentage kickbacks to have their list of books distributed by Amazon. Kindle, a book reading electronic device manufactured by Amazon, allowed for the digital takeover of actual printed books disrupting the industry even further. Publishers saw their long-held business model dramatically changed and their business diminish significantly overnight. In 2005 with Amazon creating its Prime 2-day delivery, there are now 150 million sign-ups; people kept on buying, which was the whole idea. Warehouses, or what Amazon calls fulfillment centers, were scattered around the country creating jobs. Almost every state in the country today has a fulfillment center. They are automated for a punishingly fast pace for nonunionized workers. The Occupational Safety and Health Administration hears many complaints, but Amazon's job creation over last decade's economy remains valued by most communities (Evans, 2019). Increased rates of productivity are often objected to by workers, along with the camera surveillance for all the data gathered on keeping up the grueling pace of their tracked work. Safety rules are usually ignored or compromised, according to *Frontline*, with the automation of workers creating a good deal of stress (PBS, 2020).

Amazon's philosophy of becoming the biggest is built upon a set of ideals coming from Bezos' management team. In developing the Prime subscriber base for the services consumers supposedly wanted, Amazon established a network of independent contractors to rival UPS and Federal Express so that delivery could be given promptly to satisfy consumer demand. On this group of independent businesses, there is performance pressure; there have been contractor crashes trying for faster deliveries. There have been reportedly no safety records kept. Now Prime subscribers can get one-day delivery so demands upon drivers have intensified.

It has also been criticized that there are no safety standards on sold products, so it is alleged that unsafe products from Chinese firms were selling on the platform. Sixty percent of what is sold comes from third parties, but Amazon does not assume any responsibility for products; it's up to each manufacturer, so the history of dangerous products delineated on *Frontline* does not necessarily impact customer commitment to the site.

Amazon's obtaining strong consumer-centric services tends to avoid the traditional legal antitrust critique since it is usually pursued against a company driving down prices against competitors. This monopolization, on the other hand, can be an issue since 40% of all new books go through this Amazon gatekeeper. 100 million Prime subscribers make Amazon their main retail outlet. Outside vendors are increasingly being charged higher fees on their businesses; they have little choice since Amazon maintains monopolistic control of this ecommerce.

Nevertheless, Amazon managers' obsession for maintaining the upper hand focuses on "market segment share" in order to grow. Thus, the latest concern is the monopoly power that the firm exhibits. Additionally, Bezos has purchased the *Washington Post*, a staunch enemy of Donald Trump, which results in part of his attacks on "fake news" that affects dynamics within the D.C. government arena where the firm does considerable business. Amazon Web Services (AWS) plays an important role in the federal contracting. The President has routinely held the US Postal Service hostage over Amazon's shipping practices (O'Brien, 2020).

For a variety of reasons, a powerful corporation headed by the richest man in the world is bound to attract criticism. Amazon's enemies for whatever are numerous, beginning with its own employees some who are upset about climate change. Delivering goods under Prime using gas-powered vehicles leaves a huge carbon footprint, plus Amazon helps the oil and gas industry with cloud computing services. Certain employees have begun using their stock votes they receive to agitate for corporate change revealing their own names. Other employees protested over how the firm handled sexual harassment claims.

Competition has become more bothersome. Google is seeking shippers to build its online commerce. Google Express and Google Pay allow for digital ordering, which has been beefed up assisted by its databases to target consumers (Wakabayashi, 2020). Oracle's financials have not been living up to Wall Street expectations with his autonomous database coming out against Amazon Web Services, but industry rivals are taking steps competitively (Wheatley, 2019).

But it was Amazon's decision to find two new headquarters that brought about more trenchant critique, along with additional scrutiny over the firm's tactics. Cities across America offered up substantial financial incentives or what some analysts called them bribes to the company as they turned over huge amounts of data to entice this corporate giant to build in their towns. Amazon, which is a data mining firm, now can digest all of this for its future growth.

Once deciding upon New York City, Democratic US Representative Alexandra Ocasio-Cortez, known as AOC, engineered a populist triumph over this relocation, along with the Democrat-leaning state Senate objecting to the incentive package (Goodman, 2019). The company was promised $2.2 billion in subsidies to relocate its HQ2 to New York City. The company was promised $2.2 billion in subsidies to relocate its HQ2 to New York City, however, they received another promise by Northern Virginia, where it finally settled after the NYC fallout. Additional investment may go to Nashville, Tennessee (McGee, 2019), but it's becoming more apparent that Amazon may be mortal after all (Ovide, 2019). It is important to note that the left-wing opposition coalesced for New York City in a different way than the Seattle-based activists have critiqued Amazon's political role with many activist groups concerned about all the money they are *not* paying in taxes, while seeking huge state and local incentives for their operations can lead to further economic inequalities as they become net takers from any community they settle in. Seattle activists were pushing for company contributions to build affordable housing for the homeless (Zakrzewski, 2019).

Bezos, the richest man in the world, gets attention for more than just his role over his Amazon empire. His public affairs department has built his image, and there are many Prime subscribers who are interested in all the company's new developments. Besides there are a variety of journalists, Wall Street analysts, and paparazzi that follow his routines, one scandalous run-in was with the National Enquirer over his affair and his subsequent divorce ($36.7 billion in the settlement) (Alexander & Tindera, 2020). This series of events became quite newsworthy for over a few months, letting him pursue some international travel with his mistress and tinkering in his billion-dollar investment in his space venture, Blue Origin. His arch-rival Elon Musk beat him out on the space station docking in May. Nevertheless, the COVID-19 epidemic brought him back for more hands-on involvement with the company, when the virus offered Amazon multiple financial benefits from the crisis (Weise, 2020b). Seattle's early virus outbreak was cited as a need to address working conditions in his home city and nationwide in its warehouses. Criticisms later came in management's delay to announce actions as the firm was gearing up its logistics, changing its website, delaying Prime Day, and moving to distributing just "essential items"—all seemingly important for a sales upsurge. Testing employees was under discussion, but the warehouse infections erupted and safety concerns at more than 50 facilities went viral.

Bezos' "outsized" presence in the Washington, D.C. arena extends well beyond his ownership of the *Washington Post* with huge government contracts by AWS for technology and cloud services and his warehouses providing many goods to government agencies (Foer, 2019). Trump's personal animosity of Bezos brings a watchful eye to these interactions in D.C. A *Fortune* magazine article "What's Behind the Great Big Billionaire Backlash" notes harboring mixed feelings about the ultra-wealthy, where they no longer seem to be admired as much by the public as in past decades (Colvin, 2019). Inequality seen in the wealthiest 1% of US households now accounts for more than half of the value of equities (Wigglesworth, 2020).

Health Care

Amazon has become bent upon revolutionizing health care according to Diakantonis (2020). Early in 2018, Amazon saw its distribution efforts could easily find application in the healthcare sector with its technological expertise in cloud computing and data analytics easily finding willing partners. Announcing its potential for entering pharmaceutical distribution shook up traditional health sector parties, first to the hospital market, then direct to consumers gaining wholesale pharmacy licensing with the PillPack purchase (Farr, 2019).

The company's expertise in streamlining supply chains (Kacik, 2018) saw a ready market in hospital procurement to be automated for easy delivery from Amazon warehouses. The firm's service reputation enabled trimming hospital vendor portfolios and lowering supply chain expenses, which tend to be the second highest outlay after hospital labor. Hospitals could use its Alexa for decentralized ordering of medical supplies and pharmaceuticals. Group purchasing organizations (GPOs) have played a historic role in the hospital industry, along with several large corporate distributors (like Cardinal), but Amazon brings its superior automation and preferred services capabilities (e.g., demand-forecasting) that can be key to improving hospital efficiency; the company has many other new tools besides offering office supplies and numerous other products that hospitals consume.

Amazon Business has forged numerous relationships in the healthcare system (Beth Israel Deaconess teams with Amazon to boost efficiency, 2019). This article speaks to AI support for various projects, and as they are implemented, Amazon studies them in order to take improved programs to other clients. The idea was to disrupt and improve the supply chain in such a way to deal with all recalls on alerts on medical products (Kacik, 2018, p. 14) quotes one hospital spokesperson.

Amazon also uses its Alexa technology for physicians providing a medical transcription service, another area of branching out into the health sector. Diakantonis (2019) highlights the use of the ability to capture patient/physician interactions and then digitize them into the patient's medical record. Clearly this makes the healthcare provider's job much easier, but current transcription software leaves much to be desired in terms of accuracy.

All these areas represent extensive branching out from the Amazon core business to find niches for learning and further developing *the market for health care intrusion*. For its warehousing function, the company received HIPAA eligibility utilizing its AI capabilities for rendering products. Prime customers can use Health Savings Account dollars to purchase eligible items on the Amazon site, a further move into the healthcare space to likely boost HSA favorability among employers and employees (Vivero, 2019). Following the lead of Apple, Amazon has established a virtual medical clinic for its Seattle employees (Pifer, 2019). The company is developing Amazon Care to oversee this virtual medical clinic in an industrial medicine model, which will be testing telemedicine to enter that market, which is expected to become $130 billion by 2025. Telemedicine has gotten a burst of interest given the impact of the COVID-19 pandemic of late (Hollander & Carr, 2020; Dorsey & Topol, 2016).

Amazon's purchase of PillPack (Farr, 2019) and its new media advertising for this pharmacy benefit manager shook up the PBM industry, as well as chain drug stores. For example, upon Amazon's entry, CVS, Walgreens, and other chain drug store stocks plummeted (Ellison, 2018). The company is developing a new pharmacy integration app, which will give it a formidable advantage in this field; it is reported that tackling rising costs is a primary objective (Inserro, 2019). PillPack provides daily packaged prescription drugs for its client in the delivery mode of many other mail order pharmacies. As it develops this PBM area, the company will likely innovate with many changes to achieve improved customer satisfaction; some PBMs are not particularly held in highest favor by their patients. Amazon may likely curry favor with many on drug delivery services and, when stocked up, necessities for preventing drug delivery mishaps, but they will definitely challenge drug stores and other PBMs for business over time.

Meanwhile, Warren Buffet Berkshire Hathaway and Jeffrey Bezos of Amazon joined with Jamie Dimon of JPMorgan Chase, together known here as "BAD," in a joint venture formed Haven, which will be redesigning health benefits for their 1.2 million employees, with potentially grandiose plans for additional employers (Ellison, 2018; Davenport, 2019). Atul Gawande, M.D., appointed CEO, was expected to carry out multiple investigations with profound implications for cost and quality improvement with a focus on primary care and lowering prescription drug costs. His tenure as CEO ended in May 2020 but will instead be the Chair of the Board for Haven Healthcare. These three powerhouse and very wealthy individuals may eventually lead the way in revamping overall corporate employer benefit design to revolutionize the private insurance industry or do away with the industry. They hope other employers will join them.

Another corporate initiative, Health Transformation Alliance, is a consortium of employers from 2016 also trying to lower their healthcare outlays (Davenport, 2019). Such ventures in direct contracting may not sit well with existing health system players, but more importantly, should the billionaire class be trusted from the top down to change the overall healthcare system (Staley, 2018)?

It is difficult to imagine the lives of the billionaires who have circumscribed the lives of Americans around their corporate personas and vast enterprises. For example, Jeff Bezos of Amazon is worth more than $109.7 billion, even after his divorce where he gave a huge chunk of stock to his wife. Mark Zuckerberg of Facebook has a net worth of $72 billion. According to Forbes Magazine, which heralds the extremely wealthy as celebrities, and backed up by their respective public affairs offices, both billionaires come off as the American Dream writ large.

Clearly, this upper class of ruling Americans has a totally different reality than what most people in America and the world face every day. Conditions of living are just impossible to imagine with this kind of great wealth. It is beyond the fact that they are so detached from the lives of the ordinary people, their employees (who help create their wealth), or the consumers of their products and services (who shovel money toward their corporate endeavors). It is often pointed out that the rich get richer, and the middle and working class and poor do not see anywhere near comparable gains in their wealth, what Bernie Sanders laments as the inequalities beyond the top 2%. In fact, quite the opposite over the last couple decades in America has deepened worldwide wealth inequities (Piketty, 2014).

Staley (2018) in a piece, "Our system is so broken, we're turning to billionaires like Bezos to save us" questioned the wealth, power, and influence of their wisdom and the public's loss of faith in the super-rich. He points out the rise of social problems during this huge wealth accumulation. Restructuring our healthcare system based on their ideas (particularly on workers' benefits) may not be judicious.

Direct contracting schemes have been saving costs for some employers for decades. Nevertheless, there are difficulties here, such as growing a good network of providers and obtaining their performance for whom constructing databases and developing analytics based upon ethical studies for good decision-making on costs and quality. Walmart is another firm that engages in direct contracting (Diamond, 2019), but one of the more prominent American corporations to go down this path was General Motors.

Twenty-four thousand of its 180,000 workforce were placed in a 5-year direct contracting program with the Henry Ford Health Care System, circumventing insurance companies. Boeing also contracts in California for its employees. Plans provide discounts to employees who participate, but educating them to choose wisely for the "best doctors" and hospitals can be problematic. Integrating care among the set of providers takes effort, especially if they are not already formed into well-functioning systems.

For 2020, the US Department of Health and Human Services seeks such global feed models to reduce fee-for-service medicine by contracting with physicians who can retain patients based on their satisfaction with their care and their retention of those patients in their practice. It was said that systems should be promoting partnerships with Big Tech companies so the analytics could be developed (Luthi, 2019).

Proven management ideas and methods in the larger corporate trending seem ripe for placing on health care, not always with full consideration that human health and behavior often challenges medicine; dealing with highly educated and highly paid professionals may require a lessened managerial command structure, along with the cost/quality dynamic not being certain.

Moise (2019) asks the question, if Amazon is able to put the customer at the center of its operations and relentlessly drive costs down through efficiency, will this ability also work in health care (Moise, 2019, p. 1)? Many people, from what little has been shared from the Haven venture, are coming to believe that they can indeed do that.

Most large corporations are self-insured and possess the capability of understanding employee health conditions, its relation to productivity, and employee interface with healthcare providers for monitoring both. The rhetoric indicates the trend toward value-based care, utilizing insurance data systems, and the targeting of costly chronic diseases in target and in special programs. Health Transformation Alliance has partnered with CVS and OptumRx, and similar deals are continually being struck in the medical marketplace without much oversight.

For direct contracting to succeed, it definitely requires advanced analytics, with follow through to rein in the costs of climbing employer benefit outlays. An essential question remains: can workers trust their employers to manage their health care, and will they resist? Will they be willing to trade privacy for better services? Or will privacy be violated as the pressure cost reduction wins over quality? What else will be obscured in benefit redesign over time? Employers have historically picked their insurance company and designed benefits since the beginning of employer-based private insurance in the 1930s. Not too long ago, within the HMO movement, doctors agreed to "gag rules" in their contracts, meaning not to mention to their patients, the best care alternatives for serious illnesses if the employer's HMO benefit package did not cover that best alternative. This situation involving a loss of the agency relationship with patients provoked a huge loss of patients' faith in their doctors, let alone when HMOs expelled millions of expensive seniors after the Clinton/Gingrich Balanced Budget Amendments of 1990 which irreparably damaged the sacrosanct doctor-patient relationship (Goold & Lipkin, 1999).

At its January 2018 pronouncement, the Amazon, Berkshire Hathaway, and JP Morgan Chase venture captured the popular and business press, reacting to its formation from favor for the media personalities of Buffett, Dimon, and Bezos to maintaining that it was not a threat or an unwelcomed outside influence, but most commentary centered on the expected coming disruption to health care (Ellison, 2018; Muchmore, Howland, & Byers, 2018).

As an example of the ideological grip regarding health care, an editorial in the *Chicago Tribune* inferred that while the three business leaders have no experience in the complex healthcare sector, so what? It went further in potshots at government and not solving issues but extolled a couple of billionaires and other corporate firms who have stepped in "when government stumbles…" (Chicago Tribune Editorial Board, 2018).

The corporate entities who consult and advise on healthcare benefits may recognize that analytics alone do not provide the best understanding of what medical care is really about. Employees take interest in their benefits, or the lack thereof when they go through periods of illness in their family, or when an epidemic of coronavirus wipes out all their benefits and places them in the uninsured pool.

Artificial intelligence in health care was reportedly $4 billion in 2019, according to CB Insights (Diakantonis, 2020). Amazon Web Services (AWS) has also constructed a cloud-based medical software called Care Cloud, which provides software to manage medical practices, EHRs, and patient experiences. Amazon technical staff are also tinkering with Alexa to become a diagnostic screen for owners based upon the voice pattern of a sick person. Davis mentions:

> AWS Data Exchange is unlocking a number of data sources that have traditionally been locked in silos across multiple organizations, and gives health care stakeholders a scalable and secure service to create new collaborative business models to reimagine how they approach research, clinical trials, pharmacovigilance, population health and reimbursement according to a principal at Deloitte Consulting. The AWS data exchange will provide capability to search, subscribe to, and use third-party data from companies within the cloud. This service "provides integrated cloud-based analytics, knowledge management, and collaboration tools to life sciences and health care organizations". (Davis B, 2019, p. 1)

Bezos and company have been very adroit in building a phenomenally successful enterprise that is also highly profitable based upon consumer service and satisfaction. It is, however, a data gathering analysis engine geared to corporate growth.

Not only did the firm transform the retail industry in America to online sales, but it has also revolutionized distribution of goods in this society toward greater efficiency and profit-taking. In all its entries, its business model offers auxiliary services to gather greater data to champion in the sector over time. It is based upon utilizing its dominance in networking and logistics. So the game plan for health care will likely follow such lines.

Google

Now 50 years old, the Age of the Internet in the 1980s gave rise to a plethora of dot. com entities that yielded the powerhouses in Silicon Valley and Seattle, with the subsequent decade viewing the dot.com tech bubble for Wall Street and the economy. The larger surviving firms set off a consumer buying rage for the latest tech innovations and propelled computer science programs within colleges—from desktops to miniaturization into portables and smartphones and a plethora of IoT devices. As the industry produced search engines (now dominated by Google and Microsoft's Bing), ever-refining search programs have been "perfected" to serve different business and consumer markets and build massive databases. Almost 90% of the world's searches are conducted "free" on Google (Richter, 2020), and it still is trying to penetrate China for its 800,000 smartphone users. The firm's huge revenue comes from targeted advertising to users. A *New York Times Magazine* article remarked that Google dominates the world in a way that many have tried and failed to do before, with trillions of searches performed each year which calculates roughly to 6300 searches per second or 5.5 billion per day (Duhigg, 2018).

Like other IT behemoths, Google is another data gathering operation, in which it turns into selling advertisements on its platform and that accounts for its growth. Its "free" market for searches makes it dominant. Like the other powerhouses in Silicon Valley and Seattle, it gets its share of scrutiny, suspicion, and resentment.

Like all the other tech giants, Google is frequently a target of concern and criticism over its outsized power and influence. Antitrust sentiments against the company are found in both the United States and Europe (Condliffe, 2019). Since most of the firm's income comes from advertisements, its sophisticated algorithms, which had been developed over years, are very suspicious to many. The company has been accused of unfairly leveraging its Android software, which is in operation on over 75% of smartphones (Nicas, 2018). Since it has rich cash reserves similar to other IT firms, it can easily perform public relations feats to quell doubts about it, lobby heavily, and sweep into new markets; it has ventured into Google Express for shipping and in the FinTech area, now Google Pay.

The company is staking out the healthcare sector like the other Big Tech firms. Its past action several years ago in EHRs ended in a wipeout. Now it is well situated in the cloud business in order to organize scattered medical data for easier access and use with adoption of new and emergent technologies in artificial intelligence (AI) and machine learning (Murphy, 2018). Google's Cloud Healthcare API provides the architecture to integrate numerous voice technologies into EHR systems to reduce administrative burdens by digitalization of massive amounts of data. Amazon Web Services and Microsoft Azure are competing to do similar cloud projects (Spitzer, 2018a, 2018b).

This is no small investment by Alphabet, Google's expansive parent company, putting $375 million to start up Oscar (Reints, 2018) through Google's Verily to update infrastructure for its Medicare Advantage program. Google also teamed up with Fitbit, which it bought outright to unite patient-generated data into EHRs, with past Fitbit owners needing to decide if they want Google to own their personal data. Apple is similarly doing this with iPhone customers and its Apple Watch (Arndt, 2018a, 2018b). Both operations are behind closed doors for their future biometric data combinations with no regulations for privacy and use over who owns the personal data and how it gets used.

No longer satisfied to be just a search and advertising company, Google is mounting new organizational directions with DeepMind, Verily, and Calico in analytic health research using its expertise in AI. The firm's trillion-dollar market capitalization is impressive to Wall Street, but its net income is affected by such investment decisions, as well as its costly ongoing operations. YouTube revenues have been good for the company in 2020, and Google Cloud, its computer storage business, is doing well too (Swartz, 2020). Due to the importance of tech behemoths to Wall Street, Google's decisions and directions are constantly examined and future speculated upon, including when its two founders, Larry Page and Sergey Brin, recently left the firm (Turning a Page and a Brin, 2019).

Google is frequently a target of concern and criticism over its size, pervasiveness, and power. Antitrust sentiments against the company are found in both the United States and Europe (Condliffe, 2019). Since most of its income comes from advertisements, its sophisticated algorithms (developed over years) appear very suspicious to many. The company has been accused of unfairly leveraging its Android software, which is in operation in over 75% of smartphones (Nicas, 2018). Since it has bountiful cash reserves and looks for new markets similarly to others, it has ventured into Google Express for shipping and in the FinTech area, Google Pay.

As a data gathering warehouse, Google clearly sees that data protection has risen as a key issue as the European Union uses its new authority under the General Data Protection Regulation in May 2019 to examine US tech firms in more depth (Satariano, 2018). In an article "Google's Android Fine is Not Enough to Change Its Behaviour" (2018), it was noted that the firm received a €4.34 billion fine in 2018 on top of €2.4 billion fine on the previous year (The Economist, 2018). The firm also finds itself in the displeasure of Saudi Arabia in its account of the killing of *Washington* Post writer Jamal Khashoggi along with unrest from employees who do not always agree with top management's decisions for customers (like ICE, the military, or other foreign governments with perhaps nefarious agendas).

Google handles massive amounts of data in its search capacity, Gmail, chats, and location data from Google Maps besides other apps on personal computers and phones that generate data. Google staff have been creative and utilize indirect ways to understand a user's place, movement, and purchasing. Personal data is amassed, and its mechanisms are disputed, but it remains unknown how the data is gathered and used and if the user actually ever knows this is happening or ever gets a chance to give permission (Popken, 2018). The Internet has actually developed an echo web system that the publishing, technology, and retail industries have come to rely upon. Spying from phones and computers is not just a Google issue, but Firefox and Internet Explorer also do surveillance, though it is reportedly less than what Google Chrome does. To remember, people download apps on their phones (social apps, local guides, weather apps), in addition to personal data from retailers and credit card companies. While perhaps thousands of articles have been written to alert consumers to actions, they can take to protect themselves, but the machine grinds on incessantly.

PR pieces on tracking tend to explain a few social benefits, like how Google aids police to be digital dragnets to ensnare criminals (Valentino-DeVries, 2019), and it is not just Google but Amazon that cooperates with the police (Files Not Faces, 2019). Such directions indicate that technology moves far faster than a regulatory apparatus, even if it existed and lawfulness discussions do not normally look at the growing ethical dimensions of this dramatic threat to American democracy.

The company is staking out the healthcare sector like all other Big Tech firms. Its past action in EHRs several years back ended in a wipeout, but now it is well situated in its Google Cloud business in order to seek to organize scattered medical data for easier access and use with adoption of new and emergent technologies in artificial intelligence and machine learning (Murphy, 2018). Google bought the pioneer in wearable fitness technology, Fitbit, after it emerged as a pop culture accessory to track movement activities, to now gather greater health data for the consumer. Online active users number 28 million worldwide with over 100 million devices sold (O'Brien, 2019). Much has yet to emerge for its integration. Google's Cloud Healthcare provides the architecture to integrate numerous voice technologies into EHR systems to reduce administrative burdens by digitalization of massive amounts of data. Amazon Web Services and Microsoft Azure are competing to do similar cloud projects (Spitzer, 2018a, 2018b).

This was no small investment by Alphabet ($375 million) to start up OSCAR (Glazer, Tracy, & Horwitz, 2019) through Google's Verily to update infrastructure for its Medicare Advantage program. Google also teamed up with Fitbit which it bought to unite patient-generated data into EHRs as Apple is seeking to do with iPhone customers and its Apple Watch (Arndt, 2018a, 2018b). Fitbit was the pioneer in wearable fitness technology, and it became somewhat of a pop culture accessory from basic tracking of activities, such as running, cycling, and swimming, heart rates, and sleep patterns to now gathering a greater share of health data for the consumer. Currently, there are 28 million online active users worldwide with over 100 million devices sold (O'Brien, 2019).

No longer satisfied to be just a search and advertising company, Google is mounting new organizational directions with DeepMind, Verily, and Calico in analytic research using its expertise in artificial intelligence. The firm's trillion-dollar market capitalization is impressive to Wall Street, but its net income is affected by its investment decisions as well as its ongoing operations. YouTube revenues have been good for the company in 2020 and Google Cloud, its computer business is doing well of late too (Swartz, 2020). Like the other tech behemoths, Google's decisions and directions are constantly examined and speculated on, including the two founders recently leaving the firm (Turning a Page and a Brin, 2019).

One technology in particular has been given a good deal of emphasis because of its phenomenal spread in use and the host of issues that accompany it. That issue is facial recognition software, now advanced and widely used by governments across the globe and businesses of all stripes. The Google chief has explained that he sees a significant downside here and feels facial recognition is so fraught with risks, he urged a moratorium on its use, while regulators try to create some guidelines (Espinoza & Murgia, 2020). Yet in all these matters, the nascent regulatory and social demands always come up to cost the bottom line (The Economist, 2018).

In "Google's biggest problem? It can never be as transparent as we need it to be?" (Steinmetz, 2018), Steinmetz explains how the firm's unrivaled influence over information consumed by billions of people worldwide: the issue comes down to Trust; the transparency creep may be insufficient, but the question remains what is still hidden? Does Google collect too much data?

In reviewing the general situation above with ongoing perhaps irreconcilable issues, how comfortable should the American public be with unregulated IT firms moving full throttle into the healthcare system? Kirlin (2020) discusses how Google burns cookies into people's personal computers and phones that means will be used for healthcare marketing. By 2022, Google announced a phase out of third-party cookies on its Chrome browser, joining Mozilla, Safari, and Microsoft to render third-party cookies all but extinct. Kirlin was concerned about the implications of user data collection in health care, despite legal mandates and corporate pledges. Already marketers are devising ways to work around any restrictions, striving for cookie preferences. She notes that healthcare marketing will need to adapt by shifting metrics, contextualizing the target, and building first-party strategies that allow drug brands a millisecond advantage to push products.

In sum, Google, as the king of corporate cash piles (Stacey et al., 2019), continues to be scrutinized by investors and others on Wall Street (Wakabayashi, 2018), but like other IT firms, its size, diverse operations, and constant dealings with regulators, dissenting employees, and competitors makes its ventures into health care, like Apple and a couple other firms, potentially precarious on a few levels: whether investors see the healthcare area and the particular Google's action providing sufficient ROI; whether the complexity of healthcare operations with the uncertainties in federal and state financing; the enormity of the population health problems with difficulties to solve some through information technology solutions; and then, in general, how long-term planning actually can be when attempted in a chaotic healthcare system post-Republican rule and the COVID-19 pandemic. The current un-insurance rate in the economy has many middle- and working-class people finding their incomes may not come back to what they enjoyed in early 2020. So, will healthcare return to be the booming sector that was earlier salivated for in the later 2020s?

Moreover, the overall privacy concerns may be required to be tied up before healthcare applications come to roost. In a major article, Google was accused of changing search results to suit its ends and not the user's (Grind, Schnechner, McMillan, & West, 2019). These authors discuss the proprietary algorithms of Google that are presumed to be objective and unbiased but in reality are not. Google's Corporate Mission statement includes the statement "to organize the world's information and make it universally accessible and useful" (Google, 2020). Their advertising ecosystems brought over the years' phenomenal profits as it did with other ad tech companies (DeVynck & Nix, 2019). Google began amassing customer data even while they turned no profit for several years of operations; Wall Street backed them as they did the other IT companies who were amassing mounds of data—it was seen as, and has been, the way forward to advance the economy and build greater and greater revenues and profits. A nation of citizens absorbed in consumption are not as likely to become critics of the economy nor the governmental system, though lately people have come to doubt both concentrations of power against their interests and become deeply concerned over their privacy.

Facebook

Americans' dependence on social media, its pervasiveness in everyday life, and the lack of controls over it have forced social media into the political spotlight, particularly given the Russian interference in Trump's election, according to all government intelligence sources. The Internet promised so much, but today, loss of privacy, hackers, cyberattacks of large companies, and selling personal data now fill new stories. Critics believe that Facebook engages in behaviors that furthers our need to look at it (the addictive impulse) and then engages us in confirmation bias by sucking us into the world's largest echo chamber. Like other large IT firms, it determines what we see and when we see it, and they have all gotten so large that their combined revenues are more than $500 billion annually (Duhigg, 2018).

As the IT industry recognizes its new healthcare market, and other expansions, will firms pose themselves as saviors to rationalize the sector for greater efficiency? The premises and promises of Big Data may deserve and require examination, and the individual companies will warrant a closer examination over time. Microsoft, Google, Amazon, and Apple reached $1 trillion market capitalizations in 2019, each now holding spectacular resources to spend, in addition to their unduly pervasive influence upon society. Some have argued that the online world is so fast moving that antitrust laws can't ever keep pace; others recognize the dearth in policymaking circles of folks sufficiently knowledgeable to address the industry, so lawmakers listen to lobbyists, and staff accept industry-written paragraphs to insert in the regulations. Nowadays even the biggest titan can be challenged by a tiny innovative startup, called unicorns, if the newcomer has better ideas, faster tech, and ample financial backing to last. Silicon Valley IPOs in 2019 fell short of expectations (Bowles & Conger, 2019, p. B5), which may indicate beginning a new era for technology firms of all kinds. Giant firms typically absorb many of the startups in this industry.

Thus, antitrust lawsuits, some digital executives may say, aren't needed anymore. A *New York Times* article (Benner & Kang, 2019) "Antitrust official guided merger of T-Mobile and Sprint telecoms" revealed how the Trump official in the DOJ reversed the earlier Obama rejection of this $26B amalgamation. Politics as it has lately become should provoke skepticism over future IT developments facing much scrutiny.

As we close the writing of this chapter, the news media is ablaze with Mark Zuckerberg's relationship with Donald Trump over the broader dispute with content management on Facebook and other social media. Zuckerberg found himself at odds with a group of his employees over how to handle Trump's posts, while Jack Dorsey at Twitter shielded his message, "When the looting starts, the shooting starts," as a call to violence (Frenkel et al., 2020). Snap Incorporated went further to state Trump's promoting racism and violence in public statements so removed his content (Newton, 2020). In an unprecedented move, Facebook employees staged a virtual walkout against Zuckerberg's disagreement (Frenkel et al., 2020). Kuchler (2019) had reported that Facebook's employees were overwhelmingly Democrats, perhaps why they objected to Zuckerberg's cozying up with Donald Trump.

A 2018 poll found out that the public thinks tech companies should be regulated (Smith, 2018). Facebook and other social media companies have long been promulgating disinformation due to their passive policies. In an attempt to quell the issue, Zuckerberg pledged $10 million to groups working on racial justice after the George Floyd protests (Frenkel, 2020).

But the challenge from within to Zuckerberg was unprecedented, but he stood firm in his position (Issac, Kong, & Frenkel, 2018). The resultant firestorm spread across civil rights groups and others who were chiming in with their comments. The Facebook owner is said to rely upon a small circle of staff and friends for advice (Kuchler, 2019). Grillo, in Axios (2020), maintains he won't compromise on big essential issues, often makes cosmetic gestures, and focuses on influencers. The game is rarely changed by investigations and big record fines.

Back in 2018, 72% of Americans thought Facebook and Twitter had carried political views that brought to light the content management issues over the years (Smith, 2018). Republicans have accused Facebook of censoring right wingers on religious and conservative political content (Rosenfeld, 2019). Yet BBC (2018) questioned whether the platform harbored extremists or even helped create them, based upon violence that broke out in Myanmar (BBC Trending: The country where Facebook posts whipped up hate, 2018; BBC, 2018).

With Facebook the largest and most influential communication platform in the world, Zuckerberg has made controversial decisions on content (e.g., not barring

Holocaust denialism on the site in 2018) (Manjoo, 2018). Extremist recruitment has often been found on Facebook according to Bloomberg Business Week (Silver and Frier (2018). The company has been blamed for slow moves, fixing little, and taking no stand on parts of criticism, but later Facebook did remove an Iran-based network for disinformation (Issac & Frenkel, 2018) and for its attacks on Trump. Several foreign groups had been earlier using Facebook following the 2016 patterning of misinformation tactics triumphed by Russia. The firm has frequently come under fire for how it has handled the speed of fake news spreading and the misinformation that has become prevalent on the site (Brody & Simon, 2018). In 2019 Facebook said it was removing more hate speech, seven million instances (Perrigo, 2019). Here is where its capabilities in artificial intelligence have advanced and will find usefulness.

There is an important issue here: private corporations making content decisions arouses free speech advocates. Fact-checking may be worthwhile by social media firms, but should they be forums for free speech from hate groups and allow interfering with American elections? These are difficult issues to navigate for each IT firm while necessarily listening to the broader societal discussion on how to limit false, misleading, and troubling posts while allowing its users the freedom to speak their minds. Hopefully, firms consider taking the public into account. The companies are shielded from legal liability since the content is posted by users; firms are merely platforms they maintain, not publishers.

On the decisions by a few firms to review Trump, he fired back with an executive order that called on the federal government to review Section 230 of the Communications Decency Act of 1996, in essence threatening to take action against social media firms that "restrict speech" including Twitter and Facebook (Twitter and Facebook, 2020). Social media firms face the dilemma of how to stay out of politics, particularly as the 2020 Presidential election campaigns gear up as major sources of revenue (Rogers, 2015). Political campaigns, like the World Cup and other highly viewed events, bring flocks of people to the platforms, and ad revenues blossom. Vice President Biden plans to pour $5 million into Facebook ads as of June (Goldmacher, 2020). His campaign before this spend had dumped staggering sums on Facebook, as the Trump campaign has historically done. Most Democrat and Republican Senators and Congressmen will also be running to the site to buy ads for the Fall election season. Zuckerberg's decision not to change its basic rules on political advertising, unlike Google and Twitter, before the 2020 election seems to have been calculated on this monetary gain (Romm, 2020).

Due to Facebook's size, notoriety, and the sheer dependence of so many of its users for its being their main source of news, this tech giant seems to find and dive into repeated media-discussed scandals. In the 2016 election, the firm ignored Russian influence, as well as the manipulation of its website. Then there was the ugly smearing of left-leaning billionaire George Soros in a negative way, along with a smear against its competitor Apple.

There are no easy corrective steps for any IT giant to rectify compounding circumstances after they pop up as media storms, especially if they stand to monetarily benefit from their laissez faire attitudes. Meanwhile, after his posts were flagged by

Twitter, Trump signed an executive order that seeks to limit liability protections for the social media companies (Sink, Egkolfopoulou, & Fabian, 2020). Trump responded with his usual outrage that he could never be censored, because he sees himself as the ultimate protector of the first amendment and free speech.

Two years of ceaseless controversy followed the Cambridge Analytica scandal that shocked hundreds of millions of Facebook users and brought up the critical issue of Trust (Confessore, 2018). Reportedly, Zuckerberg was criticized along the way in terms of how he personally handled it. Many of the public became disillusioned about the tremendous power that the social media platform had over what we see and hear. As an outsized corporate celebrity, Zuckerberg became the focus of everything that the corporation was about.

Facebook and social media are about making money, and the election of 2016—just for the advertising spent—is supposed to be good (Osnos, 2018). Trump had used Facebook to raise $280 million for his campaign. Zuckerberg has downplayed if ads can change people's vote in his denial of Russian influence on his site. He has been criticized, however, for many blind spots and his excessive optimism while attempting to contain the damage from the fallout. The firm spent $11.5 million on lobbying in 2017, which has increased annually after a series of scandals. Facebook's psychographic techniques to manipulate voters' behavior have been revealed, as the FBI, Security Exchange Commission, Department of Justice, and Federal Trade Commissioners have investigated the Cambridge Analytica case.

The reaction among users were many who struck out at the firm in commentaries and news pieces, or just left the site as users. Osnos' piece (2018) in the New Yorker attempted to provide some personal insights into Zuckerberg's history, experiences, and personality. The other unflattering portrayal came in David Fincher's Oscar-winning movie *The Social Network* in 2010 that traced this Harvard dropout starting the platform and discussed when he discovered the power to affect people's political behavior. Early on Facebook used advertisers and got people's profiles, raising privacy concerns along the way, but his financial drive can be best seen in Zuckerberg's paying a billion dollars for Instagram, the photo sharing app, that now is over a hundred times that value of what he paid. Such allows him, like Gates and a few other tech capitalists, to initiate some charitable gifts with his wife Priscilla Chan, in an attempt at more public relations to limit damage. Like Bezos, Zuckerberg has not been at the forefront of donations from his wealth.

Thus, issues of Trust over this social media Titanic linger. Biddle (2018) describes the artificial intelligence models Facebook is developing to predict consumer behavior. The firm is concerned with suicide prevention using speech recognition, language processing, and other technologies to identify an application, possibly used in preventing suicide among veterans. Facebook has been reported to be obtaining medical records from several healthcare systems so they could analyze it and model bringing in social and economic factors, but these data sharing agreements have been cautiously approached after Cambridge Analytica fiasco in which 87 million users' data may have been shared.

So data privacy in its newfound ventures in health is immediately raised as a deep concern. In an effort to demonstrate a concern in health care, Zuckerberg sold

$13 billion of his stock to help examine major diseases (Spitzer, 2018a, 2018b). Zuckerberg and his number two, Sheryl Sandberg, have become increasingly unpopular within the Silicon Valley crowd, obviously the lesson of Bill Gates and his charitable giving after he left the "despised" Microsoft; he quit to be part of a larger plan to change their waning popularity in the tech world (Madrigal, 2018).

Following the lingering story of Cambridge Analytica, the worst data breach in Facebook history (The Economist, 2018), there was a $5 billion payment to settle data breach according to the FTC (Glazer, 2019). In this agreement, Facebook was seeking broader immunity for past mistakes too, but it got held up in court negotiations. Dispute over Facebook's infrastructure and its privacy practices is a very complex issue debated by hordes of lawyers and the intransigents of the firm harvesting user data for different business purposes. As these breaches, subsequent investigations, and court cases pile up, Trust becomes paramount with Facebook's figuring out what are its obligations of privacy to its users? Facebook was trying to provide in 2018 huge amounts of data to be shared with researchers in response to claims of Russian interference in the election (Frenkel, 2020), but Facebook has failed to deliver at the speed to approved researchers.

Steinmetz (2018) wrote about another news cycle for Facebook, this time 50 million user accounts over a security issue. Attackers had penetrated the Facebook platform with the question of should users trust Facebook after several promises to improve defenses, but not having them work. Facebook staff's devotion to improving such defenses appears to have intensified after warnings from the FTC and Congress for much stricter oversight of user information.

Tough issues raise a key question about Facebook, so even if asked permission to share one's health data, should users be willing to do so? What also are the cryptographic techniques that will guarantee assurance over what is *not* to be hacked, or what disclosures will be used over what data, and for what purposes? In terms of their securing data from several large healthcare systems, Facebook has maintained in 2018 that they are still in the discussion phase (Farr, 2018a, 2018b). In the meanwhile, Zuckerberg has pushed for a campaign to get users to think about organ donation (Tsukayama, (2012). The company continues with other ventures in the health sector also.

The trust issue on multiple levels cannot be removed from big IT tech companies moving into health care, nor can it belie the reality that these cash-rich titans are eager to enlarge by seizing the multiple moments given by the coronavirus pandemic, the economic slump worldwide, and just the fact that they are still unhampered in ways as other parties (especially those currently in health care) appear to be through this 2020 crisis (Isaac, 2020). This *New York Times* reporter speaks to Amazon, Apple, Facebook, Google, and Microsoft sitting on top of $557 billion of cash and looking for a pace of acquisitions and investments like when the economy was humming along in 2019. Facebook was noted as capitalizing on the momentum by bringing forth new products, introducing messenger rooms and group video chat services. Facebook swooped into India, building a stake in Reliance Jio and also secured Giphy to integrate into Instagram and other investments that would keep its international front booming.

As users worldwide become more enmeshed into Facebook's corporate web, it is difficult to figure out the different levels of trust one must put in each of its activities. All tech firms require good faith on the part of customers that their data will not be used without their permission, but so far that faith has not been restored due to multiple data breaches and false promises previously described. However, knowing the purpose these data gathering machines have decided for the realms of personal data that are rendered unto them will help in rebuilding some needed conviction that each firm can be trusted, given regulatory oversight. Unfortunately, whether or not users can ever trust Facebook (or any tech behemoth) again will always be hard to know and understand. There is fear that even de-identified data in the hands of these immense firms can fairly easily be re-identified given the technology each has in place. And if there ever was any doubt about their capabilities, all one has to look at the ads in their social media accounts to know they are continuing in targeting ads to users (Arndt, 2018a, 2018b).

Gandolf (2018) delineates issues in social media for healthcare marketing purposes. Seven hundred million users in 2018 relied upon social networking sites to obtain health ideas from the Internet. This personal data is recognized as a tremendous business benefit for hospitals and other health systems, along with pharmaceutical firms and device manufacturers. Gandolf speaks to Facebook accounts being free, mobilizing groups that vested health firms can look at on its platform to connect and target certain constituencies. Business pages can be established to attract "fans." Facebook can then serve as a mechanism for a firm to listen to "the voice of the consumer" and then send out specialized branding messages to boost visitor traffic to the firm's site where easy ad tools in Facebook's platform can seize new opportunities.

Privacy and Trust

The long developing public's love for technology, however, may be beginning to erode given the abundance of discoveries flooding the popular media. The *Economist* maintains the heart of public disenchantment has much to do with centralization of Internet providers and search engines become too centralized (Siegele, 2018, p. 3), dominated by a few giants who remain suspect of privacy and placing profits ahead of consumers. Other corporate IT shenanigans that the popular media regularly highlight add to the suspicion that firms are not so "consumer-oriented." The consumer-connected world of today is now being seen with several unwelcomed downsides. As platforms such as Facebook monopolize our time, we can be victims of bad algorithms that keep us from hearing genuine voices of those we disagree with and more of individuals and foreign agents and governments' intent on subverting our political way of life through social media manipulation. And then having one country holding a significant amount of our personal data puts us all at greater risk of having that information stolen and used against us (Siegele, 2018, p. 4).

Every year *Bloomberg Businessweek* presents a list of issues of "What We Got Right (and Wrong) in 2019:" In stating what they *got right*, the *first issue was about privacy*: by not protecting users' privacy and leaving enforcement of privacy laws to the individual 50 states, we have set up a system that can be easily circumvented and make us prone to more privacy breaches (Killingsworth, 2019).

Broad concerns over IT firms trampling privacy can be found among the population; media accounts are plentiful and alarming over incidents of harm in extracting personal data without a person's permission or knowledge. Millions of users' data (and often patients' data) have been hacked due to sloppy security and held for ransom; sold by IT giants for uses beyond people's knowledge. Data is a valuable commodity, and databases are easily triangulated to create what the industry calls "personal avatars" and "synthetic communities" that are used in predictive modeling for all sorts of purposes, none of which are transparent or made known to the individuals making up the database.

Given diverse intrusions into health care, furthering the corporate takeover seems evident with these far richer, more resourceful, and much more politically powerful IT firms. Naturally given the IT industries apparent lack of concern for our privacy and their use of our data to sell us stuff, we can expect more data breaches, more ads, and rapid pronouncements about how much they value our privacy and protect our data. Consumer engagement is their means to results, which flies in the face of now privacy issues becoming acute.

Many events led up to the worldwide soaring public concern over privacy. Trolling data without the user's consent, or even knowledge, selling personal data for marketing purposes, or political use, all came to light last decade. Tracking and surveillance programs, along with facial recognition software already widely embedded, and not just by Chinese authorities, permeates businesses and schools (Thompson & Warzel, 2019). The spreading technology is considered invasive and often inaccurate (Editors, Scientific American, 2020). Beyond facial recognition—30+ businesses are doing it (Facial recognition is already here, 2019)—state surveillance is steadily growing across the world using DNA databases (Moreau, 2019). Fowler questions how are we to survive the surveillance apocalypse, even as the COVID-19 pandemic has been burgeoning new uses for technologies for mass surveillance (McGee, 2020). In January before the coronavirus scourge, in a *New York Times* Opinion special section, "One Nation Tracked" (2019), Thompson and Warzel spoke to dozens of companies, largely unregulated, nor scrutinized, amassing data on 12 million phone movements (Thompson & Warzel, 2019). When virus tracing begins, what leap in our citizenry's surveillance will then take place? And the question Thompson and Warzel (2019) raise concerning the erosion of democracy: what happens to dissent when there is no anonymity anymore? Is not just China's technological prowess to worry about?

Foroohar (2018) warns of Big Tech's unhealthy tendencies as monopolistic complex and opaque advertising firms, though both Google and Facebook have felt the outside pressures to change. She notes that even if devoting more resources at content management, they are not very good at it.

This overall situation shows how web-hosting and online payment firms may sometimes get censored by corporate entities, or not: hate posts, human trafficking, dangerous products, and other grievous situations continue, not always often addressed by public regulation. In addition, the corporate-censoring of sites are to the chagrin of free speech advocates, which indicates the issues are mighty complex, and controversial, for public policy to begin to tackle.

Nevertheless, the private marketplace is proudly addressing a few issues, but to whose advantage and whose satisfaction? In a *Financial Times* opinion piece, in "We Are Living in an Age of Unprecedented Risks," Bush's Treasury Secretary Henry Paulson stated that because more and more data are controlled by large, private, and disruptive multinational firms, no nation, not even the most repressive regimes, can be expected to rein in much of anything anymore (Paulson, 2018). This former Bush man worries more about how governments and business may collide with the realm of changing dynamics. But who is articulating the concerns of consumers?

The rise of "surveillance capitalism" is frequently written about with clear warnings (Singer, 2019b). The term was coined by Shoshanna Zuboff, a Harvard Business School professor, in her book, *The Age of Surveillance Capitalism* (2019). She saw how problematic digital services challenging humanity could be, ones that are now being used to predict and influence human behavior; "the stakes could not be higher: a global architecture of behavior modification threatens human nature…just as industrial capitalism disfigured the natural world in the twentieth [century]" (Zuboff, 2019).

More so, the term captures private human experiences to manipulate for buying and selling on the marketplace, but most people remain unaware since their transactions remain generally opaque (Singer, 2019a). A "behavior speculation market" has arisen with general consumer ignorance over the privacy over its format. Individual efforts to protect one's privacy, are generally unknown and it is very difficult discovering how compromised a person has been up to that point.

More importantly, huge amounts of data are already gathered on most Americans: it is just too complicated to undo what's already done without unsurpassed federal regulatory reforms, but what and how? In the absence of the federal government having no basic consumer privacy laws, to soon have effective privacy protection appears a very long shot. The State of California has passed its Consumer Privacy Act (CCPA), coupled with the General Data Protection Regulation (GDPR) instituted in Europe. Both are highly resisted by IT industry forces so these regulations' net effectiveness remains an open question. However, beyond protection over one's personal data is what can be hacked out of existing databases. Another effect of the COVID-19 epidemic is a jump in "active attacks" including ransomware, on hospitals (Cohen, 2020b) since they are facing duress and subject to email scams.

Already beyond the privacy issue (Cohen, 2020b) are the numerous hacking threats to health systems' patient data and the announcements of paying ransomware to keep operations afloat. Hacking threats have grown in sophistication with Fortune 500 entities reporting break-ins (Marriott, Equifax, and more) each with much greater security than most healthcare systems. Cohen (2019a) writes that managing security risks is a ballooning, high-value industry necessary with our increasing reliance upon digital platforms, mobile devices, and the Internet of Things. Its market is forecast to climb from $120 billion in 2017 to $300 billion by 2024. It remains imperative that this persistent and pervasive risk in health care be addressed, but little regulatory scrutiny is on the horizon.

A *New York Times* piece on ransomware led off with the concept that hackers can lock us out of our computers unless we pay a ransom (usually in bitcoin). These types of attacks are becoming more widespread and damaging by day (Popper, 2020).

Most data attacks are likely underreported because victims are quietly paying off without notifying authorities. Nevertheless, 205,280 organized attributed files had been hacked in 2019, a 41% annual increase. Newsworthy among hacks have included the City of New Orleans, Baltimore, many other municipalities, a growing number of smaller businesses, physician practices, and hospitals. According to the FBI, ransomware attacks are increasing and ongoing (Bennett, 2020). Smaller organizations (like health providers) are considered to be more vulnerable (Boulton, 2020). A single health system could lose as many as 80,000 EHRs to hacking. In April 2020, providers, insurers, and their business associates reported 38 breaches alone, affecting 446,000 patients (Cohen, 2020a). More than 570 data breaches occurred in 2019 (Cohen, 2020b).

A hack, and the demand for ransomware, can easily cripple a business, even after it searches out any alternative than to just pay the extortion money, which can be very high. Unless the healthcare organization routinely backs up its information on back-up servers, they are stuck paying the ransom to regain access of their data. For providers, health care is the fourth most common target for ransomware. When a hospital is hit, business operations essentially close down, the EHR system is dismantled, and Internet-connected medical devices are compromised. If the EHRs are inoperable, the question is where did the provider store its old patient forms to still continue patient care? Tens of thousands of medical records have been hacked over the last decade. Thus, patients must be diverted to other hospitals immediately for care. Often the server of the company is shut down by some malware; the entire data files can be stolen, so the demands for ransomware are attempted to be met, usually paid in cryptocurrency, such as bitcoin, to avoid any tracing of the crime.

The upsurge in cyberattacks has hit healthcare organizations and insurers hard, mostly when they have failed to upgrade their security software, which tends to be a dynamic required process. Sometimes foreign and otherwise domestic sources can be found to be the culprits, but malware can easily be obtained for hacking (Bennett, 2020). This author states that while anyone can launch one of these attacks, more of them are directed at tech companies than health care which makes one wonder why IT firms don't have better security and gives one pause to trust them with our security (Cohen, 2020c).

As the Internet privacy landscape hopefully evolves toward greater transparency and some accountability, how will AI impact medical malpractice and its liability. Already EHRs are being seen more easily assisting plaintiff lawyers for filing suits. How to tell patients that AI and cloud-computing are part of their care will impact informed consent; practitioners must address many patient perceptions of computers and AI and relate to documenting potential medical errors (Knowles, 2019). Additionally, the liability exposure to AI product designers and manufacturers has begun to escalate (Howze, 2018). This is a completely new frontier in medical malpractice liability.

Minimal structures provide roadmaps for Big Data in health care (Adamson, 2015). IoT will be an unprecedented generation of incessant streams of disparate data from diagnostic devices, plus new sensors and wearables, along with attempts at social determinants, all data sent to cloud computing to pass through sophisticated tools to protect it. Not brushing aside the prime concern for security, *Medical Economics* enthusiastically reported that IT brings the promise of better and cheaper oversight of chronic diseases by both patients and providers (Hurt, 2019, p. 33).

The volume, velocity, and variety in streams coming into Big Data clusters may enable real-time alerting, predictive analytics of "flight paths" of a patient, with genomics coming into play for futuristic assessments. Adamson (2015) expands in detail on where Big Data in health may be headed, though it is very complicated, and generally not easily understood. Enterprise Data Warehouse (EDW) architecture will transition from relational databases to work with unstructured Big Data, including IoT, and watch personal information. *And in the end*, the large IT firms will be solving the most data analysis problems in health care, so we can hope they will act differently than they have to date.

After the Cambridge Analytica fiasco, there were many calls for users to leave social media outright, and due to the revelations of the inherent manipulation and lack of user consent on personal data, many people did drop out. Twitter, best known as the Trump propaganda arm, as a platform works differently than Facebook. A Twitter user follows an overall network for trends in varying spheres they choose and to communicate with consumers of key influencers on issues of their interest, no friending, just following. Facebook has a more complicated business model, diversified to obtain realms of personal data for microtargeting ads to its users. The number of users on Facebook, plus their staying longer on the site, and growth of users is important, so therefore issues of privacy and censorship may differ.

Surely what Facebook does in the "cloak and dagger realm" of social media is not something the firm wants public. Nevertheless, greater sales revenues depend upon manipulation that measures interests, anticipates desires, and modifies behaviors, all in the purpose of discovering chances for advertisers to sell. Dependency by users is key so that users come back, including promoting key drivers of more engagement: fear of missing out, loathing, anxiety, and outrage. Facebook is extraordinary rich in the two hundred million monthly users, or about 3/5 of the American population (Gramlich, 2019); these folk do not seem necessarily to feel that Facebook is misusing or abusing their data (Waters, 2018a, 2018b, 2018c, 2018d; LaForgia, Confessore, 2018).

Much press has been given to detail the Cambridge Analytica scandal, but it should be noted that it had quite an impact on the bottom line with the series of mishaps Facebook underwent from 2018 on (Frenkel, 2018; Nicolaou & Edgecliffe-Johnson, 2018). Did Facebook learn its lesson about securing users data? Tech stocks face their ups and downs in the market, but it greatly disturbs Wall Street traders and investors when they do not gain (Phillips, 2018). Losing capitalization after all is not good for any business, but especially the social media titans. After the Cambridge Analytica newsbreak, the numbers on the Facebook platform flatlined for a while (Confessore, 2018). The total number of users determines ad revenues, plus how much time they hang out digitally, how many ads they see, and the price of the ads.

Facebook has applied for patents to use smartphone cameras and microphones as spy tools to study user behavior and assess personality (Zetlin, 2018). Such surveillance is the mainstay of several Internet technology firms, and they are staking out the healthcare system for greater opportunities, as well as across the globe (Staley, 2018). Isaac (2020) details how Big Tech firms are seizing the moment with their huge cash bundles. This could be particularly ominous since AI capabilities are moving forward at such great speed (Metz & Lohr, 2018).

Foroohar (2020) in "Facebook and the Creation of a U.S. Oligarch" in the *Financial Times* notes that Twitter and Snapchat notably perform fact checking and now curbing the power of Trump, yet Zuckerberg chose to refuse removal of his inaccurate and inflammatory posts. What should be the proper balance between free speech and disinformation remains a heightened debate in any given democratic society. Foroohar (2020) in "Facebook and the Creation of a U.S. Oligarch" in the Financial Times notes that Twitter and Snapchat notably perform fact checking, yet Facebook chose to not remove any of President Trump's inaccurate and inflammatory posts. Does Zuckerberg with Facebook start to be defined as an oligarchy in America? Or is he merely engaged in a desperate search to remain relevant in American life and social media as people discover new ways to interact that may make Facebook a relic of the past?

Summary

It is far from certain what the entry and implications of Amazon, Apple, IBM, and other IT firms will mean to the existing playing field in the healthcare sector. As we examine the cooperation of Warren *B*uffett, *A*mazon, (Jeff Bezos), and Jaime *D*imon (Morgan Stanley Chase)—now to be referred to as *"BAD"*—for their employees, it is further unclear whether such direct contracting moves may portend a *nascent beginning for a new wave of corporate class reorganization of the American healthcare system*, as seen when Carnegie and Rockefeller Foundations reorganized medical education in the 1920s (Berliner, 1977; Brown, 1975). (See Chap. 1.)

It should be remembered that technology costs a lot in terms of software and hardware purchases, but many organizations find that implementation costs, often unforeseen, so mistakes pile up along the way. Thus, managements remain more intent on not wanting to lose control as processes move forward. Contracted vendor dynamics often reveal this as such. The health sector has a track record of uncertain outcomes from sales pitches to create efficiencies and make it better.

Medical practices may just be realizing how much change in ownership is on the horizon. Their interface with the new organizational powers will reshape physicians' lives in the dramatic turbulence. The implications for scrutiny over doctor decision-making are extant (Feinglass & Salmon, 1990).

From the above descriptions, one can witness a succession of unique situations that may lead to a broader grasp of the overall corporate direction for the healthcare sector. A popular perspective may react from the exceptional confusion of individual mergers and acquisitions. As new ventures get underway, confusion and shifting patterns in the medical marketplace, perhaps over the decade, may portend a future of continued disarray. Nevertheless, large swatches of the population's personal data portend potential for social control over the population, as well as crucial privacy issues over one's health data, both becoming critical issues over this decade.

The reader may notice that the Trump era is filled with mammoth uncertainties for health industry situations, along with a propensity of intolerance and the rise of blatant social injustice, with government paramilitary occupations threatening our democracy. This condition makes functioning of the traditional health system quite different, as we witness several urban systems collapsing due to the coronavirus outbreak. It also is disillusioning while pressuring for change in human and professional values. There is a greater need for formulating alternatives clearly and for a more precise sense of what needs to be done to resist most aspects of this expanding medical marketplace.

The profiteers display a decadent neglect of the true nature of people's health and health care, with their substitution of making money being prime. Republican ideological support for all things in the medical marketplace and their opposition to more oversight and governmental regulation over health services will allow the incursion of IT firms into health care becoming more problematic than it needs to be.

References

Adamson, D. (2015). Big data in healthcare made simple: Where it stands today and where it's going. *Health Catalyst*. Available via DIALOG. https://catalyst.nejm.org/ai-means-doctors-doctoring/. Accessed 4 Sept 2019.

Alderman, L., & Satariano, A. (2020). *Amazon's showdown in France tests its ability to sidestep labor*. Available at: https://www.nytimes.com/2020/05/14/technology/amazon-unions-france-coronavirus.html. Accessed 12 Oct 2020.

Alexander, D., & Tindera, M. (2020). *The five billionaires who have gained the most since Trump became president*. Available at: https://www.forbes.com/sites/danalexander/2020/01/21/the-five-billionaires-who-have-gained-the-most-since-trump-becamepresident/#4022db342ded. Accessed 12 Oct 2020.

Allen, M. (2018). *Health insurers are vacuuming up details about you – and it could raise your rates*. Available at: https://www.propublica.org/article/health-insurers-are-vacuuming-up-details-about-you-and-it-could-raise-your-rates. Accessed 12 Oct 2020.

Allen, M. (2020). Axios AM. *Axios*. Available via DIALOG. https://www.axios.com/newsletters/axios-am-4f4dedec-e4b9-49d7-a119-a65306f2e3a9.html. Accessed 27 Feb 2020.

Al-Siddiq, W. (2019). Next generation wearables: Achieving a value-based care system. *Medical Economics*. Available via DIALOG. https://www.medicaleconomics.com/article/next-genera-tion-wearables-achieving-value-based-care-system. Accessed 19 Nov 2019.

Anderson, J., & Rainie, L. (2018). *Artificial intelligence and the future of humans*. Available at: https://www.pewresearch.org/internet/2018/12/10/artificial-intelligence-and-the-future-of-humans/. Accessed 12 Oct 2020.

Armstrong, R., & Megaw, N. (2020). Payments groups join forces to survive. *Financial Times*. Available via DIALOG. https://www.ft.com/content/e9966946-486e-11ea-aee2-9ddb-dc86190d. Accessed 17 Mar 2020.

Arndt, R. Z. (2018a). Apple vs. Epic: Appraising the apps. *Modern Healthcare*. Available via DIALOG. http://www.modernhealthcare.com/article/20180414/NEWS/180419952. Accessed 6 Aug 2018.

Arndt, R. Z. (2018b). The internet of things to hack into it. *Modern Healthcare*, p. 20.

Associated Press. (2020). *Netflix adds 8.8 million subscribers in Q4 2019 despite Disney Plus challenge.* Available at: https://tech.hindustantimes.com/tech/news/netflix-adds-8-8-million-subscribers-in-q4-2019-despite-disney-plus-challenge-story-JoRP3WVhQIiiBVbVli4W8I. html. Accessed 12 Oct 2020.

Axios. (2020). Stat du joir: Amazon prime passes Netflix. *Axios*. Available via DIALOG. https://www. axios.com/newsletters/axios-am-3aaf7de3-6ce2-4c5e-a9a9-4918208d832f.html?chunk=6&utm_term=twsocialshare#story6. Accessed 18 Mar 2020.

Bagnara, G. (2020). *Does the U.S. need a national digital currency?* Available at: https://www. wsj.com/articles/does-the-u-s-need-a-national-digital-currency-11582513201. Accessed 12 Oct 2020.

Bambrough, B. (2018). iPhone maker Apple is eyeing the healthcare market with employee clinics. *Verdict*. Available via DIALOG. https://www.verdict.co.uk/iphone-maker-apple-eyeing-healthcare-market-employee-clinics/. Accessed 27 July 2018.

Barnes, B. (2019). Disney is new to streaming, but its marketing is unmatched. Available at: https://www.nytimes.com/2019/10/27/business/media/disney-plus-marketing.html. Accessed 12 Oct 2020.

Barnes, B., & Sperling, N. (2019). Streaming services make a big splash. *The New York Times*. Available via DIALOG. https://www.nytimes.com/2019/12/09/movies/golden-globes-nominations.html?searchResultPosition=5. Accessed 17 Mar 2020.

Barnes, B., & Sperling, N. (2020). Netflix is spending big, but can it crash the Oscars party? *Chicago Tribune*. Available via DIALOG. https://www.chicagotribune.com/featured/sns-nyt-netflix-oscars-nominations-20200206-kw63ndvhyjg6tlffbliln3pchm-story.html. Accessed 27 Feb 2020.

Barney, C. (2020). Coronavirus: Streaming platforms see big surge during pandemic. *The Mercury News*. Available via DIALOG. https://www.mercurynews.com/2020/04/07/coronavirus-streaming-platforms-see-big-surge-during-pandemic/. Accessed 23 July 2020.

Bass, D. (2018). Microsoft looks to lure Health-Care companies to its cloud with new tools. *Bloomberg*. Available via DIALOG. https://www.bloomberg.com/news/articles/2018-02-28/microsoft-looks-to-lure-health-care-companies-to-its-cloud-with-new-tools. Accessed 24 Aug 2018.

BBC. (2018). *Facebook admits it was used to "incite offline violence" in Myanmar.* Available at: https://www.bbc.com/news/world-asia-46105934. Accessed 13 Oct 2020.

Behar, Y. (2018). Five Artificial intelligence insiders in their own words. *The New York Times*. Available via DIALOG. https://www.nytimes.com/2018/10/19/business/five-Artificial -intelligence-insiders-in-their-own-words.html. Accessed 19 Nov 2019.

Benner, K., & Kang, C. (2019). How a top antitrust official helped T-Mobile and Sprint merge. *The New York Times*. Available via DIALOG. https://www.nytimes.com/2019/12/19/technology/sprint-t-mobile-merger-antitrust-official.html. Accessed 25 Dec 2019.

Bennett, D. (2020). *I Used Dark Web Ransomware to Sabotage My Boss.* Available via DIALOG. https://www.bloomberg.com/features/2020-dark-web-ransomware/. Accessed 24 July 2020.

Berger, B., & Cho, H. (2019). *Emerging technologies towards enhancing privacy in genomic data sharing.* Available at: https://genomebiology.biomedcentral.com/articles/10.1186/s13059-019-1741-0. Accessed 12 Oct 2020.

Berliner, H. S. (1977). Emerging ideologies in medicine. *Review of Radical Political Economics, 9*(1), 116–124.

Biddle, S. (2018). *Facebook uses artificial intelligence to predict your future actions for advertisers, says confidential document.* Available at: https://theintercept.com/2018/04/13/facebook-advertising-data-artificial-intelligence-ai/. Accessed 12 Oct 2020.

Binham, C., Giles, C., & Keohane, D. (2019). *Facebook's Libra currency draws instant response from regulators.* Available at: https://app.ft.com/content/5535fb3a-91ea-11e9-b7ea-60e35ef678d2. Accessed 12 Oct 2020.

Bond, S. (2018). *Amazon's ever-increasing power unnerves vendors*. Available via DIALOG. https://www.ft.com/content/c82ce968-bc8a-11e8-94b2-17176fbf93f5. Accessed 23 July 2020.

Boulton, G. (2020). Ransomware scams aim small. *USA Today-Press Reader*. Available via DIALOG. https://www.pressreader.com/usa/usa-today-us-edition/20200130/281784221071972. Accessed 17 Mar 2020.

Bowles, N., & Conger, K. (2019). Where are the Tech Zillionaires? San Francisco faces the I.P.O. Fizzle. *The New York Times*. Available via DIALOG. https://www.nytimes.com/2019/12/19/technology/tech-IPO-san-francisco.html. Accessed 25 Dec 2019.

Bradshaw, T. (2018a). Apple hopes older buyers will strap on watch for health benefits. The Financial Times. Available via DIALOG. https://www.ft.com/content/83e17d1a-b77a-11e8-b3ef-799c8613f4a1. Accessed 4 Mar 2020.

Bradshaw, T. (2018b) Apple to beat its own record for 'biggest quarter ever' after iPhone X launch. Financial Times. Available via DIALOG. https://www.ft.com/content/f3ce6f0c-c040-11e7-b8a3-38a6e068f464. Accessed 6 Aug 2018.

Bradshaw, T. (2018c). China court bans sales of some iPhones. *Financial Times*. Available via DIALOG. https://www.ft.com/content/4d9f48a4-fc85-11e8-ac00-57a2a826423e. Accessed 5 Nov 2019.

Bradshaw, T. (2018d). Services arm helps push Apple towards $1tn. *Financial Times*.

Bradshaw, T., & Lewis, L. (2019). Sony and Microsoft join forces in battle for video games market. *Financial Times*. Available via DIALOG. https://www.ft.com/content/c8b3b27a-789d-11e9-be7d-6d846537acab. Accessed 17 Oct 2019.

Bresnick, J. (2018a). AI, Big data IoT bring growth to multiple healthcare markets. *Health Analytics*. Available via DIALOG. https://healthitanalytics.com/news/ai-big-data-iot-bring-growth-to-multiple-healthcare-markets. Accessed 28 Sept 2018.

Brody, B., & Simon, Z. (2018). *Facebook comes under renewed fire for how it handled misinformation*. Available at: https://www.savannahnow.com/news/20181115/facebook-comes-under-renewed-fire-for-how-it-handled-misinformation. Accessed 12 Oct 2020.

Brown, E. R. (1975). Public health in imperialism: Early Rockefeller programs at home and abroad. *American Journal of Public Health, J66*, 897–903.

Brustein, J., & Bergen, M. (2019). *Google wants to do business with the military—many of its employees don't*. Available at: https://www.bloomberg.com/features/2019-google-military-contract-dilemma/. Accessed 12 Oct 2020.

Bughin, J., & Woetzel, J. (2019). *Navigating a world of disruption*. McKinsey Global Institute. Available via DIALOG. https://www.mckinsey.com/featured-insights/innovation-and-growth/navigating-a-world-of-disruption#. Accessed 23 July 2020.

Castellucci, M. (2020). Health systems try to trim waste to reduce healthcare spending. *Modern Healthcare*. Available via DIALOG https://www.modernhealthcare.com/safety-quality/health-systems-try-trim-waste-reduce-healthcare-spending. Accessed 22 July 2020.

Celi, L., & Stone, D. (2018). The challenge of medical Artificial intelligence. *AIMED The Inaugural Issue*, pp. 12–19.

Chen, B. X. (2019). Devices that will invade your life in 2019 (and what's overhyped). *The New York Times*. Available via DIALOG. https://www.nytimes.com/2019/01/03/technology/personaltech/tech-2019-overhyped.html. Accessed 19 Nov 2019.

Chen, B. X. (2020a). Oohs, aahs and Alexa in your car. *The New York Times*. Available via DIALOG. https://www.nytimes.com/2020/01/10/technology/ces-2020.html. Accessed 17 Mar 2020.

Chen, B. X. (2020b). The costly trap of subscription overload. *The New York Times*. Available via DIALOG. https://www.nytimes.com/2020/01/29/technology/personaltech/paying-subscription-services.html. Accessed 4 Feb 2020.

Chettipally, U. (2018). *Case in point: Predicting sepsis in hospitalized patients*. AIMED the Inaugural Issue, pp. 28–29.

Chicago Tribune Editorial Board. (2018). Can Bezos, Buffet and Dimon Revolutionize American Health Care? *Chicago Tribune*, February 8, 2018. Available via DIALOG. https://www.chicagotribune.com/opinion/editorials/ct-edit-dimon-amazon-health-care-20180205-story.html. Accessed 24 July 2020.

Chmielewski, D. (2019). *Netflix shrugs off its new, bigger competitors – Apple and Disney*. Available at: https://www.forbes.com/sites/dawnchmielewski/2019/04/16/netflix-shrugs-off-its-new-bigger-competitors%2D%2Dapple-and-disney/#631b1e93ab48. Accessed 12 Oct 2020.

Cohen, J. (2018). Amazon could still disrupt the prescription drug market. *Forbes*. Available via DIALOG. https://www.forbes.com/sites/joshuacohen/2018/06/08/amazon-could-still-disrupt-the-prescription-drug-market/#14b9e4be2035. Accessed 27 July 2018.

Cohen, J. K. (2018a). Apple's app store turns 10 – Here are 4 ways it's tackled healthcare. *Becker's Hospital Review*. Available via DIALOG. https://www.beckershospitalreview.com/healthcare-information-technology/apple-s-app-store-turns-10-here-are-4-ways-it-s-tackled-healthcare.html. Accessed 6 Aug 2018.

Cohen, J. K. (2018b). Are smartphones and tablets the next frontier for EHRs? Why this IT expert says yes. *Becker's Hospital Review*. Available via DIALOG. https://www.beckershospitalreview.com/ehrs/are-smartphones-and-tablets-the-next-frontier-for-ehrs-why-this-it-expert-says-yes.html. Accessed 4 Mar 2020.

Cohen, J. K. (2018c). Microsoft rolls out genomics service on Azure cloud. *Becker's Health IT & CIO Report*. Available via DIALOG. https://www.beckershospitalreview.com/data-analytics-precision-medicine/microsoft-rolls-out-genomics-service-on-azure-cloud.html. Accessed 24 Aug 2018.

Cohen, J. K. (2018d). Why health IT experts think Apple will succeed where Google failed with medical records. *Becker's Hospital Review*. Available via DIALOG. https://www.beckershospitalreview.com/healthcare-information-technology/why-health-it-experts-think-apple-will-succeed-where-google-failed-with-medical-records.html. Accessed 6 Aug 2018.

Cohen, J. K. (2019a). Apple rolls out iPhone health records feature to veterans. *Becker's Hospital Review*. Available via DIALOG. https://www.beckershospitalreview.com/ehrs/apple-rolls-out-iphone-health-records-feature-to-veterans.html. Accessed 4 Mar 2020.

Cohen, J. K. (2019b). Beth Israel deaconess teams with Amazon to boost efficiency. *Press Reader*. Available via DIALOG. https://www.pressreader.com/usa/modern-healthcare/20190311/281625306615611. Accessed 4 Mar 2020.

Cohen, J. K. (2020a). Lawmakers press VA officials on app privacy. *Modern Healthcare*. Available via DIALOG. https://www.modernhealthcare.com/information-technology/lawmakers-press-va-officials-app-privacy. Accessed 27 Feb 2020.

Cohen, J. K. (2020b). Ransomware targeting health systems in more "sophisticated" ways. *Modern Healthcare*. Available via DIALOG. https://www.modernhealthcare.com/cybersecurity/ransomware-targeting-health-systems-more-sophisticated-ways. Accessed 27 Feb 2020.

Cohen, J. K. (2020c). Hospitals question FDA plan for clinical-decision software oversight. *Modern Healthcare*. Available via DIALOG. https://www.modernhealthcare.com/information-technology/hospitals-vendors-question-fdas-plan-oversee-decision-support-software. Accessed 4 Mar 2020.

Colvin, G. (2019). What's behind the great billionaire backlash? *Fortune*. Available via DIALOG. https://fortune.com/2019/12/19/billionaire-backlash-2020-economic-fairness/. Accessed 23 July 2020.

Condliffe, J. (2019). *The week in tech: What not to expect from big tech's antitrust showdown*. Available at: https://www.nytimes.com/2019/06/07/technology/big-tech-antitrust.html. Accessed 12 Oct 2020.

Confessore, N. (2018). Cambridge Analytica and Facebook: The scandal and the fallout so far. *The New York Times*. Available via DIALOG. https://www.nytimes.com/2018/04/04/us/politics/cambridge-analytica-scandal-fallout.html. Accessed 24 July 2020.

Contreras, B. (2019). *The digital transformation of healthcare*. Available via DIALOG. https://www.managedhealthcareexecutive.com/news/digital-transformation-healthcare. Accessed 17 Oct 2019.

Davenport, T. H., & Bean, R. (2019). *Sharing employee health data at the health transformation alliance*. Available at: https://www.forbes.com/sites/tomdavenport/2019/05/02/sharing-employee-health-data-at-the-health-transformation-alliance/#72016a983b1e. Accessed 12 Oct 2020.

Davis, B. (2019). The Future of Health: Unlocking the Value of Digital Health Data. *Deloitte Consulting*. Available   https://www2.deloitte.com/content/dam/Deloitte/us/Documents/life-sciences-health-care/us-cons-aws-data-exchange.pdf. Accessed 2 June 2020.

Davis, J. (2019). Microsoft, Hill-Rom team to bring medical device data to EHRs. *EHR Intelligence*. Available via DIALOG. https://ehrintelligence.com/news/microsoft-hill-rom-team-to-bring-medical-device-data-to-ehrs. Accessed 5 Nov 2019.

DeVynck, G., & Baker, L. (2019). Google's Fitbit acquisition gets instant antitrust scrutiny. *Bloomberg Law*. Available via DIALOG. https://news.bloomberglaw.com/tech-and-telecom-law/googles-fitbit-acquisition-likely-to-face-antitrust-scrutiny. Accessed 25 Dec 2019.

Diakantonis, D. (2019). Why Walmart and other retailers are buying Artificial intelligence start-ups. *The Middle Market*. Available via DIALOG. https://www.themiddlemarket.com/news/Artificial -intelligence-helps-retailers-anticipate-customer-needs. Accessed 5 Dec 2019.

Diakantonis, D. (2020). How Amazon is using M&A to revolutionize healthcare. *The Middle Market*. Available via DIALOG. https://www.themiddlemarket.com/news/how-amazon-is-using-m-a-to-revolutionize-healthcare. Accessed 23 July 2020.

Diamond, D. (2019). *Walmart pushing for bigger health care role*. Accessed at: https://www.politico.com/newsletters/politico-pulse/2019/09/30/walmart-pushing-for-bigger-health-care-role-763063. Accessed 12 Oct 2020.

Dorsey, E. R., & Topol, E. J. (2016). State of telehealth. *NEJM, 375*, 154–161.

Duhigg, C. (2018). The case against Google. *The New York Times*. Available via DIALOG. https://www.nytimes.com/2018/02/20/magazine/the-case-against-google.html. Accessed 24 Aug 2018.

Duhigg, C. (2019). *Is Amazon unstoppable?* Available at: https://www.newyorker.com/magazine/2019/10/21/is-amazon-unstoppable. Accessed 12 Oct 2020.

Eavis, P. (2018). What Wall Street missed at Facebook. *The New York Times*. Available via DIALOG.   https://www.nytimes.com/2018/07/26/business/dealbook/facebook-wall-street.html. Accessed 25 Dec 2019.

Edwards, H., & Edwards, D. (2018). With these patents, Apple could win the next major platform war. *Quartz*. Available via DIALOG. https://qz.com/1225997/with-these-patents-apple-could-win-the-next-major-platform-war/. Accessed 27 July 2018.

Ellison, A. (2018). Amazon expands prime day deals to whole foods. *Becker's Hospital Review*. Available via DIALOG. https://www.beckershospitalreview.com/business/amazon-expands-prime-day-deals-to-whole-foods.html. Accessed 6 Aug 2018.

Epstein, A. (2019). Disney is betting its entire future on streaming. *Quartz*. Available via DIALOG.   https://qz.com/1744149/disney-is-betting-everything-on-its-disney-streaming-service/. Accessed 19 Nov 2019.

Espinoza, J., & Murgia, M. (2020). *Sundar Pichai supports calls for moratorium on facial recognition*. Available via DIALOG. https://www.ft.com/content/0e19e81c-3b98-11ea-a01a-bae547046735. Accessed 24 July 2020.

Evans, J. (2018). Apple's next big idea: Private healthcare. *Computer World*. Available via DIALOG.   https://www.computerworld.com/article/3258806/apple-ios/apples-next-big-idea-private-healthcare.html. Accessed 27 July 2018.

Evans, W. (2019). Ruthless quotas at Amazon are maiming employees. *The Atlantic*. https://www.theatlantic.com/technology/archive/2019/11/amazon-warehouse-reports-show-worker-injuries/602530/. Accessed 28 May 2020.

Faber, J. (2020). *Gamers get virtual access to high fashion and accessories*. Available at: https://www.ft.com/content/59cb4152-1bf9-11ea-81f0-0c253907d3e0. Accessed 12 Oct 2020.

Farr, C. (2017). Apple explored buying a medical-clinic start up as part of a bigger push into health care. *CNBC*. Available via DIALOG. https://www.cnbc.com/2017/10/16/apple-considered-acquisition-of-crossover-health-part-of-health-push.html. Accessed 6 Aug 2018.

Farr, C. (2018a). Apple CEO: We can make a 'significant contribution' in health care. *CNBC*. Available via DIALOG. https://www.cnbc.com/2018/02/13/apple-ceo-tim-cook-can-make-significant-contribution-in-health-care.html. Accessed 27 July 2018.

Farr, C. (2018b). Apple is launching medical clinics to deliver the 'world's best health care experience' to its employees. *CNBC*. Available via DIALOG. https://www.cnbc.com/2018/02/27/apple-launching-medical-clinics-for-employees.html. Accessed 27 July 2018.

Farr, C. (2019). *The inside story of why Amazon bought PillPack in its effort to crack the $500 billion prescription market.* Available at: https://www.cnbc.com/2019/05/10/why-amazon-bought-pillpack-for-753-million-and-what-happens-next.html. Accessed on October 12, 2020

Feibus, M. (2019). Data privacy: How much are your intimate details worth? More than a happy meal? *USA Today.* Available via DIALOG. https://www.usatoday.com/story/tech/columnist/2019/07/30/data-value-amazon-facebook-grows-but-consumers-get-short-shrift/1837854001/. Accessed 23 July 2020.

Feinglass, J., & Salmon, J. (1990). Corporatization of medicine: The use of medical management information systems to increase the clinical productivity of physicians. *International Journal of Health Services, 20*(2), 233–252.

Fernando, J. (2020). *FAANG stocks.* Available at: https://www.investopedia.com/terms/f/faang-stocks.asp#:~:text=FAANG%20is%20an%20acronym%20referring,(formerly%20known%20as%20Google). Accessed 13 Oct 2020.

Financial Times. (2020c). Reasons to beware the growing $1tn tech club. *Financial Times.* Available via DIALOG. https://www.ft.com/content/a8dade28-392d-11ea-a6d3-9a26f8c3cba4. Accessed 17 Mar 2020.

Five Artificial Intelligence Insiders in Their Own Words. (2018). Available at: https://www.nytimes.com/2018/10/19/business/five-artificial-intelligence-insiders-in-their-own-words.html. Accessed 12 Oct 2020.

Foer, F. (2019). Jeff Bezos's Master Plan. *The Atlantic.* Available via DIALOG. https://www.theatlantic.com/magazine/archive/2019/11/what-jeff-bezos-wants/598363/?gclid=EAIaIQobChMI_r7-8Juj6wIV1ZFbCh1RKQcwEAAYASAAEgKvn_D_BwE. Accessed 17 Aug 2020.

Foroohar, R. (2018). Apple sows seeds of next market swing. *Financial Times.* Available via DIALOG. https://www.ft.com/content/fb864306-54ff-11e8-b24e-cad6aa67e23e. Accessed 6 Aug 2018.

Foroohar, R. (2020). Facebook and the creation of a US oligarch. *Financial Times.* Available via DIALOG. https://www.ft.com/content/0f2c8952-a719-11ea-92e2-cbd9b7e28ee6. Accessed 24 July 2020.

Fortune. (2019). Tech does K street: Yearly lobbying amounts for selected tech companies. *Fortune.com.*

Fowler, G. A. (2019). *It's the middle of the night. Do you know who your iPhone is talking to?* Available at: https://www.washingtonpost.com/technology/2019/05/28/its-middle-night-do-you-know-who-your-iphone-is-talking/. Accessed 12 Oct 2020.

Frakt, A. (2019). *The huge waste in the U.S. health system.* Available at: https://www.nytimes.com/2019/10/07/upshot/health-care-waste-study.html. Accessed 12 Oct 2020.

Frellick, M. (2018). AI speeds diabetic retinopathy diagnosis without specialist. *Medscape.* Available via DIALOG. https://www.medscape.com/viewarticle/901297. Accessed 28 Sept 2018.

Frenkel, S. (2018). Microsoft employees question C.E.O over company's contract with ICE. *The New York Times.* Available via DIALOG. https://www.nytimes.com/2018/07/26/technology/microsoft-ice-immigration.html. Accessed 17 Oct 2019.

Frenkel, S., & Barnes, J. E. (2020). *Russians again targeting Americans with disinformation, Facebook and Twitter say.* Available at: https://www.nytimes.com/2020/09/01/technology/facebook-russia-disinformation-election.html. Accessed 12 Oct 2020.

Frenkel, S., Confessore, N., Kang, N., Rosenberg, M., & Nicas, J. (2018). *Delay, deny and deflect: How Facebook's leaders fought through crisis.* Available at: https://www.nytimes.com/2018/11/14/technology/facebook-data-russia-election-racism.html. Accessed 12 Oct 2020.

Frenkel, S., Isaac, M., Kang, C., & Dance, G. J. X. (2020). *Facebook employees stage virtual walkout to protest Trump posts.* Available at: https://www.nytimes.com/2020/06/01/technology/facebook-employee-protest-trump.html. Accessed 13 Oct 2020.

Fried, I. (2020). *Nationalism and authoritarianism threaten the internet's universality.* Available at: https://www.axios.com/internet-freedom-nationalism-authoritarianism-767da13b-b6bf-4aac-8f05-78f0a6353f08.html. Accessed 12 Oct 2020.

Funahashi, T., Borgo, L., & Joshi, N. (2019). Saving lives with virtual cardiac rehabilitation. *NEJM Catalyst*. Available via DIALOG. https://catalyst.nejm.org/saving-lives-virtual-cardiac-rehab/. Accessed 4 Sept 2019.

Fung, B. (2020) *With new coronavirus tracker, Apple and Google may finally get their big break in health care*. Available at: https://www.cnn.com/2020/04/30/tech/apple-google-contact-tracing/index.html. Accessed 12 Oct 2020.

Gal, A. (2019). *The cutting edge of IoT*. Available at: https://www.forbes.com/sites/forbestech-council/2019/07/15/the-cutting-edge-of-iot/#147039da4499. Accessed 12 Oct 2020.

Galvin, J., Han, F., Hynes, S., Qu, J., Rajgopal, K., & Shek, A. (2018). *Synergy and disruption: Ten trends shaping Fintech*. Available via DIALOG https://www.mckinsey.com/industries/financial-services/our-insights/synergy-and-disruption-ten-trends-shaping-fintech. Accessed 23 July 2020.

Gandolf, S. (2018). *Social media is changing healthcare*. Available at: https://healthcaresuccess.com/blog/doctor-marketing/social-media-is-changing-healthcare.html. Accessed 12 Oct 2020.

Gerlis, M. (2020). *Art markets find high-tech ways to reach buyers*. Available at: https://www.ft.com/content/7481e2d4-6e02-11ea-89df-41bea055720b. Accessed 12 Oct 2020.

Glazer, E., Tracy, R., & Horwitz, J. (2019). *FTC approves roughly $5 billion Facebook settlement*. Available at: https://www.wsj.com/articles/ftc-approves-roughly-5-billion-facebook-settle-ment-11562960538. Accessed 13 Oct 2020.

Glorikian, H., & Branca, M. A. (2017). *MoneyBall medicine: Thriving in the new data-driven healthcare market*. New York, NY: Productivity Press.

Goldmacher, S. (2020). *Biden pours millions into Facebook ads, blowing past Trump's record*. Available at: https://www.nytimes.com/2020/06/08/us/politics/biden-trump-facebook-ads.html. Accessed 12 Oct 2020.

Goodman, J. D. (2019). *Amazon pulls out of planned New York City headquarters*. Available at: https://www.nytimes.com/2019/02/14/nyregion/amazon-hq2-queens.html. Accessed 12 Oct 2020.

Google Mission Statement. (2020). Available at https://www.google.com/search/howsearchworks/mission/. Accessed 24 July 2020.

Goold, S. D., & Lipkin, M. (1999). The doctor-patient relationship. *Journal of General Internal Medicine, 14*, S26–S33.

Gramlich, J. (2019). *10 facts about Americans and Facebook*. Available at: https://www.pewre-search.org/fact-tank/2019/05/16/facts-about-americans-and-facebook/. Accessed 12 Oct 2020.

Grind, K., Schechner, S., McMillan, R., & West, J. (2019). *How Google interferes with its search algorithms and changes your results*. Available via DIALOG. https://www.wsj.com/articles/how-google-interferes-with-its-search-algorithms-and-changes-your-results-11573823753. Accessed 24 July 2020.

Grissinger, M. (2019). Understanding human over-reliance on technology. *Medication Errors, 6*(44), 320.

Guastella, J. (2020). *Emerging opportunities for financial services companies in China*. Available via DIALOG. https://www2.deloitte.com/us/en/pages/dbriefs-webcasts/events/march/2020/dbriefs-emerging-opportunities-financial-services-companies-in-china.html. Accessed 23 July 2020.

Gurman, M. (2018). Apple resorts to promo deals, trade-ins to boost iPhone sales. *Bloomberg*. Available via DIALOG. https://www.bloomberg.com/news/articles/2018-12-04/apple-is-said-to-reassign-marketing-staff-to-boost-iphone-sales. Accessed 4 Mar 2020.

Gurman, M., & Wittenstein, J. (2020). Apple shares top $300 amid optimism about holiday sales. *Bloomberg*. Available via DIALOG. https://finance.yahoo.com/news/apple-tops-300-first-time-205618658.html. Accessed 4 Mar 2020.

Haefner, M. (2017). Aetna CEO: Talking on Apple's business model a 'real deal'. *Becker's Hospital Review*. Available via DIALOG. https://www.beckershospitalreview.com/payer-issues/aetna-ceo-taking-on-apple-s-business-model-a-real-deal.html. Accessed 6 Aug 2018.

Haenssle, H. A., Fink, C., Schneiderbauer, R., Toberer, F., Buhl, T., Blum, A., … Zalaudek, I. (2018). Man against machine: Diagnostic performance of a deep learning convolutional neural network for dermoscopic melanoma recognition in comparison to 58 dermatologists. *Annals of Oncology, 29*(8), 1836–1842.

Hailu, R. (2019). Fitbits and other wearables may not accurately track heart rates in people of color. *Stat News*. Available via DIALOG. https://www.statnews.com/2019/07/24/fitbit-accuracy-dark-skin/. Accessed 19 Nov 2019.

Harper, J. (2018). *2019 trends in natural language processing*. Available at: https://aibusiness.com/document.asp?doc_id=760714. Accessed 13 Oct 2020.

Harwell, D. (2020). *Ring and Nest helped normalize American surveillance and turned us into a nation of voyeurs*. Available at: https://www.washingtonpost.com/technology/2020/02/18/ring-nest-surveillance-doorbell-camera/. Accessed 12 Oct 2020.

Heath, T., & Bogage, J. (2020). *Dow pops nearly 700 points as Wall Street nears the end of a historically bad quarter*. Available at: https://www.washingtonpost.com/business/2020/03/30/stocks-markets-economy-coronavirus/. Accessed 13 Oct 2020.

Hoffower, H. (2020). Americans have more credit-card debt than ever, and millennials are really struggling to pay theirs off. *Business Insider*. Available via DIALOG. https://www.businessinsider.com/us-credit-card-debt-record-high-millennials-delinquency-rates-2020-2. Accessed 23 July 2020.

Hollander, J. E., & Carr, B. G. (2020). Virtually perfect? Telemedicine for Covid-19. *NEJM, 382*, 1679–1681.

Horowitz, J. (2020). *Here's what could really sink the global economy: $19 trillion in risky corporate debt*. Available at: https://portside.org/2020-03-15/heres-what-could-really-sink-global-economy-19-trillion-risky-corporate-debt. Accessed 12 Oct 2020.

Howze, Y. T. (2018). *Strategies to unlock AI's potential in health care, part 5: Product liability prevention for AI product designers- and their lawyers*. Available via DIALOG. https://www.mintz.com/insights-center/viewpoints/2146/2018-11-strategies-unlock-ais-potential-health-care-part-5-product. Accessed 4 Sept 2019.

Hsu. (2019). 500 billion prescription market. Available at: https://www.cnbc.com/2019/05/10/why-amazon-bought-pillpack-for-753-million-and-what-happens-next.html. Accessed 12 Oct 2020.

Huber, N. (2020). Internet of things: Smart cities pick up the pace. *Financial Times*. Available via DIALOG. https://www.ft.com/content/140ae3f0-1b6f-11ea-81f0-0c253907d3e0. Accessed 17 Mar 2020.

Hurt, A. (2019). *What the internet of medical things means to your practice*. Available at: https://www.medicaleconomics.com/view/what-internet-medical-things-means-your-practice. Accessed 12 Oct 2020.

Ibrahim. (2018). *Five Artificial Intelligence Insiders in Their Own Words*. Available at: https://www.nytimes.com/2018/10/19/business/five-artificial-intelligence-insiders-in-their-own-words.html. Accessed October 12, 2020

Inserro, A. (2019). Restoring the doctor-patient relationship with artificial intelligence. *AJMC*. Available via DIALOG. https://www.ajmc.com/focus-of-the-week/restoring-the-doctorndashpatient-relationship-with-Artificial-intelligence. Accessed 4 Sept 2019.

IOM (2013), Kaiser Health Network. (2012) *IOM Report: Estimated $750B Wasted Annually In Health Care System*. Available at: https://khn.org/morning-breakout/iom-report/. Accessed on October 12, 2020

Isaac, M. (2020). *The economy is reeling. The tech giants spy opportunity*. Available at: https://www.nytimes.com/2020/06/13/technology/facebook-amazon-apple-google-microsoft-tech-pandemic-opportunity.html. Accessed 12 Oct 2020.

Isaac, M., & Frenkel, S. (2018). *Facebook removes Iranian network that was spreading disinformation*. Available at: https://www.nytimes.com/2018/10/26/technology/facebook-removes-iranian-network-that-was-spreading-disinformation.html. Accessed 12 Oct 2020.

Ives, M. (2019). A.I vs. the Tree Thieves. *The New York Times*. Available via DIALOG. https://www.nytimes.com/2019/10/15/climate/indonesia-logging-deforestation.html. Accessed 17 Oct 2019.

Janakiram, M. S. V. (2018) *IBM wants to make artificial intelligence fair and transparent with AI OpenScale*. Available at: https://www.forbes.com/sites/janakirammsv/2018/10/21/ibm-wants-to-make-artificial-intelligence-fair-and-transparent-with-ai-openscale/#cf71f1251cc2. Accessed 13 Oct 2020.

Japsen, B. (2016). Pfizer partners with IBM Watson to advance cancer drug discovery. *Forbes*. Available via DIALOG. https://www.forbes.com/sites/brucejapsen/2016/12/01/pfizer-partners-with-ibm-watson-to-advance-cancer-drug-discovery/#364fb0221b1e. Accessed 17 Oct 2019.

Japsen, B. (2019). *As CVS rolls out health hubs, Walmart prepares clinic expansion*. Available at: https://www.forbes.com/sites/brucejapsen/2019/09/03/as-cvs-rolls-out-health-hubs-walmart-prepares-clinic-expansion/#6cd13f1f61b2. Accessed 12 Oct 2020.

Jha, M. R. (2019). *Protecting intellectual property in media and broadcasting*. Available at: https://www.worldtrademarkreview.com/protecting-intellectual-property-media-and-broadcasting. Accessed 13 Oct 2020.

Kacik, A. (2018). Amazon primed to streamline healthcare supply chain. *Modern Healthcare*. Available via DIALOG. https://www.modernhealthcare.com/article/20180929/NEWS/180929919/amazon-primed-to-streamline-healthcare-supply-chain. Accessed 4 Mar 2020.

Karlgaard, R. (2018). *Why technology prophet George Gilder predicts big tech's disruption*. Available at: https://www.forbes.com/sites/richkarlgaard/2018/02/09/why-technology-prophet-george-gilder-predicts-big-techs-disruption/#26d14bc32d21. Accessed 12 Oct 2020.

Kauflin, J. (2020). Why visa is buying Fintech startup plaid for $5.3 billion. *Forbes*. Available via DIALOG https://www.forbes.com/sites/jeffkauflin/2020/01/13/why-visa-is-buying-fintech-startup-plaid-for-53-billion/#4c9e92612a8b. Accessed 23 July 2020.

Kendall-Taylor, A., Frantz, E., & Wright, J. (2020). The digital dictators. *Foreign Affairs*. Available via DIALOG. https://www.foreignaffairs.com/articles/china/2020-02-06/digital-dictators. Accessed 14 Feb 2020.

Kent, J. (2019). Over 95% of healthcare CFOs doubt their data analytics abilities. *Health IT Analytics*. Available via DIALOG. https://healthitanalytics.com/news/over-95-of-healthcare-cfos-doubt-their-data-analytics-abilities. Accessed 4 Sept 2019.

Kent, J. (2020). *Applying artificial intelligence to chronic disease management*. Available at: https://healthitanalytics.com/features/applying-artificial-intelligence-to-chronic-disease-man-agement. Accessed 12 Oct 2020.

Khalid, A. (2020). *What hand sanitizer shortages on Amazon reveal about global supply*. Available at: https://qz.com/1812216/what-hand-sanitizer-shortages-on-amazon-say-about-global-sup-ply/. Accessed 12 Oct 2020.

Killingsworth, S. (2019). *What we got right (and wrong) in 2019*. Available via DIALOG. https://www.bloomberg.com/news/articles/2019-10-25/what-businessweek-got-right-and-wrong-in-2019. Accessed 24 July 2020.

Kim, T. (2018). *Walgreens, CVS and Rite-Aid lose 100 billion cloud market*. Available at: https://www.statista.com/chart/18819/worldwide-market-share-of-leading-cloud-infrastructure-ser-vice-providers/. Accessed 12 Oct 2020.

Kirlin, C. (2020). *Google burns the cookies (and what it means for healthcare marketing)*. Available at: https://www.mmm-online.com/home/opinion/google-burns-the-cookies-and-what-it-means-for-healthcare-marketing/. Accessed 12 Oct 2020.

Kissinger, H. (2018). *How the enlightenment ends. Philosophically, intellectually—in every way—human society is unprepared for the rise of artificial intelligence*. Available via https://www.theatlantic.com/magazine/archive/2018/06/henry-kissinger-ai-could-mean-the-end-of-human-history/559124/. Accessed 20 May 2020.

Klebnikov, S. (2019). *Netflix and Disney shares fall after Apple unveils $4.99 streaming service*. Available at: https://www.forbes.com/sites/sergeiklebnikov/2019/09/10/netflix-and-disney-shares-fall-after-apple-unveils-499-streaming-service/#6cfb27e54b66. Accessed 12 Oct 2020.

Knowles, M. (2019). Viewpoint: How to tell patients AI is part of their care. *Becker's Hospital Review*. Available via DIALOG. https://www.beckershospitalreview.com/quality/viewpoint-how-to-tell-patients-ai-is-part-of-their-care.html. Accessed 4 Sept 2019.

Kolko, G. (1963). *The triumph of conservatism. A reinterpretation of American history, 1900-1916*. New York, NY: Free Press.

Krotoski, A. (2020). Alexa, where do you get your news from? *Financial Times*. Available via DIALOG. https://www.ft.com/content/eea6df18-fcbc-11e9-a354-36acbbb0d9b6. Accessed 17 Mar 2020.

Kuchler, H. (2019). Amazon to call its joint healthcare venture Haven. *Financial Times*. Available via DIALOG. https://www.ft.com/content/76943368-4056-11e9-9bee-efab61506f44. Accessed 27 Feb 2020.

Larson, M. (2018). *Overhyped growth Turkeys get plucked … while "safe money" stocks surge!* Available at: https://greyhouse.weissratings.com/overhyped-growth-turkeys-get-plucked-while-safe-money-stocks-surge. Accessed 12 Oct 2020.

Lee, E. (2020). *Everyone you know just signed up for Netflix*. Available at: https://www.nytimes.com/2020/04/21/business/media/netflix-q1-2020-earnings-nflx.html. Accessed 12 Oct 2020.

Lee, P. (2018). *Microsoft's focus on transforming healthcare: Intelligent health through AI and the cloud*. Microsoft. Available via DIALOG. https://blogs.microsoft.com/blog/2018/02/28/microsofts-focus-transforming-healthcare-intelligent-health-ai-cloud/. Accessed 24 Aug 2018.

Lewin, J., & Balser, J. (2019). Healthcare leaders must embrace, advance AI to shape the next transformation in care. *Modern Healthcare*. Available via DIALOG. https://www.modern-healthcare.com/opinion-editorial/commentary-healthcare-leaders-must-embrace-advance-ai. Accessed 4 Sept 2019.

Lewis, L. (2020). *China app downloads surge due to coronavirus outbreak*. Available at: https://www.ft.com/content/f1704f82-5238-11ea-8841-482eed0038b1. Accessed 12 Oct 2020.

Liao, S. (2020). Gaming's biggest names are ditching twitch for $10 million contracts. *CNN*. Available via DIALOG. https://www.cnn.com/2020/01/26/tech/video-game-streaming-wars/index.html. Accessed 14 Feb 2020.

Livingston (2019) 7.5bn GitHub bet. Available via DIALOG. https://article.wn.com/view/2018/06/04/Microsoft_paying_75bn_in_stock_for_popular_coder_hangout_Git/. Accessed 24 August 2018

Lohr, S. (2020). Ginni Rometty to step down as C.E.O of IBM. *The New York Times*. Available via DIALOG. https://www.nytimes.com/2020/01/30/technology/ginni-rometty-ibm-ceo.html. Accessed 4 Feb 2020.

Luthi, S. (2019). CMS to launch new direct-contracting pay models in 2020. *Modern Healthcare*. Accessed via DIALOG. https://www.modernhealthcare.com/payment/cms-launch-new-direct-contracting-pay-models-2020. Accessed 23 July 2020.

Lynch, D. (2019). *Corporate debt nears a record $10 trillion, and borrowing binge poses new risk*. Available via DIALOG. https://www.washingtonpost.com/business/economy/corporate-debt-nears-a-record-10-trillion-and-borrowing-binge-poses-new-risks/2019/11/29/1f86ba3e-114b-11ea-bf62-eadd5d11f559_story.html+&cd=1&hl=en&ct=clnk&gl=us. Accessed 23 July 2020.

Madrigal, A. C. (2018) *When the tech mythology collapses*. Available at: https://www.theatlantic.com/technology/archive/2018/11/facebook-google-amazon-and-collapse-tech-mythology/575989/. Accessed 12 Oct 2020.

Manjoo, F. (2018). *What stays on Facebook and what goes? The social network cannot answer*. Available at: https://www.nytimes.com/2018/07/19/technology/facebook-misinformation.html. Accessed 12 Oct 2020.

Marcus, G., & Davis, E. (2019). Build A.I. we can trust. *The New York Times*. Available via DIALOG. https://www.nytimes.com/2019/09/06/opinion/ai-explainability.html. Accessed 4 Sept 2019.

Mazzolini, C. (2019). 9 things ruining medicine for physicians. *Medical Economics*. Available via DIALOG. https://www.medicaleconomics.com/news/9-things-ruining-medicine-physicians. Accessed 4 Sept 2019.

McGee, J. (2019). *Amazon, unfazed by New York reversal, vows commitment to Nashville*. Available at: https://www.tennessean.com/story/money/tech/2019/03/04/amazon-nashville-commitment-new-york-city-rejection/3028733002/. Accessed 13 Oct 2020.

McGee, P. (2020a). Apple shuts 42 China retail stores due to coronavirus. *Financial Times*. Available via DIALOG. https://www.ft.com/content/b8027b84-4514-11ea-aeb3-955839e06441. Accessed 4 Feb 2020.

McGee, P. (2020b). Five things to watch out for in Apple's earnings. *Financial Times*. Available via DIALOG. https://www.ft.com/content/9518e03e-3ea9-11ea-a01a-bae547046735. Accessed 4 Mar 2020.

McGee, P., Murphy, H., & Bradshaw, T. (2020). *Coronavirus apps: The risk of slipping into a surveillance state*. Available at: https://www.ft.com/content/d2609e26-8875-11ea-a01c-a28a3e3fbd33. Accessed 13 Oct 2020.

Metz, C., & Lohr, S. (2018). IBM's new program would like to have a debate with you. *The New York Times*. Available via DIALOG. https://www.nytimes.com/2018/06/18/technology/ibm-debater-artificial-intelligence.html. Accessed 24 Aug 2018.

Miller, C. (2017). Report: Apple entered deep acquisition talks with health clinic startup as it mulls into primary care. *9 to 5 Mac*. Available via DIALOG. https://9to5mac.com/2017/10/16/report-apple-primary-care-deal/. Accessed 6 Aug 2018.

Mirtskulava, L. (2018). Monitoring brain attacks using AI diagnosis. *AIMED The Inaugural Issue*, pp. 30–35.

Moise, F. (2019). *The 'Amazoning' of healthcare will bring challenges and opportunities for health plans*. Available via DIALOG: https://www.dhitglobal.org/the-amazoning-of-healthcare-will-bring-challenges-and-opportunities-for-health-plans/. Accessed 24 July 2020.

Moreau, Y. (2019). *Crack down on genomic surveillance*. Available at: https://www.nature.com/articles/d41586-019-03687-x?proof=trueInJun. Accessed 12 Oct 2020.

Muchmore, S., Howland, D., & Byers, J. (2018). *How Amazon, JPM, Berkshire could disrupt healthcare (or not)*. Available via DIALOG. https://www.healthcaredive.com/news/how-amazon-jpm-and-berkshire-could-disrupt-healthcare-or-not/516003/. Accessed 17 August 2020.

Murgia, M. (2019). *AI's new workforce: The data-labelling industry spread globally*. Available at: https://www.ft.com/content/56dde36c-aa40-11e9-984c-fac8325aaa04. Accessed 12 Oct 2020.

Murphy, H. (2018). *Facebook's Libra overhauls core parts of its digital currency vision*. Available at: https://www.ft.com/content/23a33fcb-1342-4a18-be39-504e8507f752. Accessed 12 Oct 2020.

Murphy, M. (2019). Apple pay is a sleeper hit. *Quartz*. Available via DIALOG. https://qz.com/co/1389679/apple-pay-is-a-sleeper-hit//. Accessed 19 Nov 2019.

Murray, A. (2019). *The 2019 Fortune 500 CEO survey results are in*. Available at: https://fortune.com/2019/05/16/fortune-500-2019-ceo-survey/. Accessed 12 Oct 2020.

Murtha, J. (2018). The numbers behind the first FDA-approved autonomous AI diagnostic system. *Healthcare Analytic News*. Available via DIALOG. https://www.hcanews.com/news/the-numbers-behind-the-first-fdaapproved-autonomous-ai-diagnostic-system. Accessed 28 Sept 2018.

Needleman, S. E. (2019). Google Stadia, Microsoft xCloud, Apple arcade: So many ways to play…and pay. *The Wall Street Journal*. Available via DIALOG. https://www.wsj.com/articles/google-stadia-microsoft-xcloud-apple-arcade-so-many-ways-to-playand-pay-11574168580. Accessed 25 Dec 2019.

Neville, S., & Atkins, R. (2018). *Novartis weighs reinsurance tie-up to fund ultra-expensive drugs*. Available at: https://www.ft.com/content/d9685d58-f6db-11e8-8b7c-6fa24bd5409c. Accessed 13 Oct 2020.

Newton, C. (2020). *Snap will stop promoting Trump's account after concluding his tweets incited violence*. Available on: https://www.theverge.com/2020/6/3/21279280/snapchat-snap-remove-trump-account-discover-promotion-incite-violence-twitter. Accessed 12 Oct 2020.

Nicas, J. (2018) Hit by $5.1 billion fine, but still Google surges. The New York Times. Available via DIALOG. https://www.nytimes.com/2018/07/23/technology/google-earnings-alphabet.html. Accessed 24 Aug 2018.

Nicolaou, A. (2020a). Amazon streaming passes 55m user mark. *Financial Times*. Available via DIALOG. https://www.ft.com/content/8acedb52-3be2-11ea-a01a-bae547046735. Accessed 4 Feb 2020.

Nicolaou, A. (2020b). Amazon music subscriber numbers close in on Apple. *Financial Times*. Available via DIALOG. https://app.ft.com/cms/s/8acedb52-3be2-11ea-a01a-bae547046735.html. Accessed 17 Mar 2020.

Nicolaou, A. (2020c). Netflix's US subscriber growth slows amid heightened sector competition. *Financial Times*. Available via DIALOG. https://www.ft.com/content/93f2b922-3c7f-11ea-a01a-bae547046735. Accessed 27 Feb 2020.

Nicolaou, A., & Edgecliffe-Johnson, A. (2018). *Facebook "caught flat-footed" by data leak scandal, news chief says*. Available at: https://app.ft.com/content/99911950-2de5-11e8-a34a-7e7563b0b0f4. Accessed 13 Oct 2020.

NPR. (2018). *Stock market gyrations making you dizzy? Get used to it, analysts say*. Available at: https://www.cpr.org/2018/12/31/stock-market-gyrations-making-you-dizzy-get-used-to-it-analysts-say/. Accessed 13 Oct 2020.

O'Brien, M. (2019). Do we need grocery- Toting robots? *AP News*. Available via DIALOG. https://apnews.com/57a4bd0719a1481ab234a01be45c42cc. Accessed 25 Dec 2019.

O'Brien, T. (2020). Trump holds postal service hostage to settle Amazon score. *Bloomberg Opinion*. https://www.bloomberg.com/opinion/articles/2020-04-27/coronavirus-trump-s-postal-service-war-is-with-amazon-and-bezos. Accessed 28 May 2020.

O'Connor, A. (2019). A.I. is likely to transform medicine. *The New York Times*. Available via DIALOG. https://www.nytimes.com/2019/03/11/well/live/how-Artificial -intelligence-could-transform-medicine.html. Accessed 4 Sept 2019.

Osnos, E. (2018). *Can Mark Zuckerberg fix Facebook before it breaks democracy*. Available via DIALOG: https://www.newyorker.com/magazine/2018/09/17/can-mark-zuckerberg-fix-face-book-before-it-breaks-democracy. Accessed 24 July 2020.

Ovide, S. (2019). Amazon wakes up to the Tecklash on privacy. *Bloomberg*. Available via DIALOG. https://www.bloomberg.com/opinion/articles/2019-09-26/amazon-wakes-up-to-the-techlash-on-privacy. Accessed 23 July 2020.

Park, A. (2019). Here's how well the Apple watch can detect heart problems. *Time*. Available via DIALOG. https://time.com/5727608/apple-watch-heart-study/. Accessed 19 Nov 2019.

Paulson, H. (2018). *We are living in an age of unprecedented risks*. Available via DIALOG. https://www.ft.com/content/a55e705e-dcfc-11e8-b173-ebef6ab1374a. Accessed 24 July 2020.

PBS.org. (2020). *Amazon empire, the rise and reign of Jeff Bezos*. Ep. 12. Available at https://www.pbs.org/wgbh/frontline/film/amazon-empire/. Accessed 23 July 2020.

Perez, S. (2019). Apple partners with VA health records to veterans. *Techcrunch*. Available via DIALOG. https://techcrunch.com/2019/02/11/apple-partners-with-va-to-bring-health-records-to-veterans/?guccounter=1&guce_referrer=aHR0cHM6Ly93d3cuZ29vZ2xlLmNvbS8&guce_referrer_sig=AQAAANga224scPHV7nTLx5kaoNNQbG_5zsiPyOU4z9pOir_rFsO-cE6Dl6lLCvQ5NaxcO8t9sVj7RpT-O281qkuUrRh4YhFlG1YnOG-FCPzreFpVQ8eI2Urg-zkN6dx8SrmqI0pwIIqxZckfZ8BH_T6BdPMQpZgo3e_D1yGq7iL69BmDj1. Accessed 4 Mar 2020.

Perrigo, B. (2019). *Facebook says it's removing more hate speech than ever before. But there's a catch*. Available at: https://time.com/5739688/facebook-hate-speech-languages/. Accessed 13 Oct 2020.

Phillips, A. (2018). *The very public problem of privacy*. Available at: https://medium.com/@alis-saphillips/the-very-public-problem-of-privacy-f54f400c4681. Accessed 13 Oct 2020.

Pifer, R. (2019). Amazon launches virtual medical clinic for Seattle employees. *Healthcare Drive*. Available via DIALOG. https://www.healthcaredive.com/news/amazon-launches-virtual-med-ical-clinic-for-seattle-employees/563629/. Accessed 4 Mar 2020.

Piketty, T. (2014). *Capital in the twenty first century*. Cambridge, MA: Harvard University Press.

Poniewozik, J. (2019). The great streaming space-time warp is coming. *The New York Times*. Available via DIALOG. https://www.nytimes.com/2019/11/01/arts/television/apple-tv-plus-disney-plus.html. Accessed 25 Dec 2019.

Poon, S. J., Schuur, J. D., & Mehrotra, A. (2018). Trends in visits to acute care venues for treatment of low-acuity conditions in the United States from 2008 to 2015. *JAMA Internal Medicine, 178*, 1342–1349.

Popken, B. (2018). *Google sells the future, powered by your personal data*. Available at: https://www.nbcnews.com/tech/tech-news/google-sells-future-powered-your-personal-data-n870501. Accessed 12 Oct 2020.

Popper, N. (2020). *Ransomware attacks grow, crippling cities and businesses*. Available at: https://www.nytimes.com/2020/02/09/technology/ransomware-attacks.html. Accessed 13 Oct 2020.

Reints, R. (2018). *Alphabet invests 375 million in healthcare startup Oscar*. Available at: https://fortune.com/2018/08/14/alphabet-oscar-health-investment/. Accessed 13 Oct 2020.

Richter, F. (2020). *Amazon leads billion cloud market*. Available at: https://www.statista.com/chart/18819/worldwide-market-share-of-leading-cloud-infrastructure-service-providers/. Accessed 12 Oct 2020.

Rizzo, L., Flint, J., & Haggin, P. (2020). *Fox, Comcast pursue takeovers of ad-supported video services*. Available at: https://www.wsj.com/articles/nbcuniversal-in-talks-to-acquire-streaming-service-vudu-from-walmart-11582320612. Accessed 13 Oct 2020.

Robbins, R. (2019). Apple launching studies testing whether Apple Watch can monitor hearing, mobility, and women's health. *Stat News*. Available via DIALOG. https://www.statnews.com/2019/09/10/apple-watch-new-health-studies/. Accessed 19 Nov 2019.

Robbins, R., & Herper, M. (2019). 5 burning questions about Google Fitbit acquisition- and its implications for health and privacy. *Stat News*. Available via DIALOG. https://www.statnews.com/2019/11/01/google-fitbit-acquisition-5-burning-questions/. Accessed 19 Nov 2019.

Rocco, M. (2018). Snip Snip: Morgan Stanley latest to cut Apple target on China woes. *Financial Times*. Available via DIALOG. https://www.ft.com/content/cc64bbcc-fa2f-11e8-8b7c-6fa24bd5409c. Accessed 23 Oct 2019.

Rogers, L. (2015). *Should companies remain politically neutral on social media?* Available at https://www.socialmediatoday.com/social-networks/leeyen-rogers/2015-07-01/should-companies-remain-politically-neutral-social-media. Accessed 24 July 2020.

Romm, T., Stanley-Becker, I., & Timberg, C. (2020). *Facebook won't limit political ad targeting or stop false claims under new ad rules*. Available at: https://www.washingtonpost.com/technology/2020/01/09/facebook-wont-limit-political-ad-targeting-or-stop-pols-lying/. Accessed 12 Oct 2020.

Rosenberg, S., & Fried, I. (2020a). Ginni Rometty out as IBM CEO. *Axios*. Available via DIALOG. https://www.axios.com/ginni-rometty-out-as-ibm-ceo-47abf685-7d75-49b6-b68b-3806d590ee2c.html. Accessed 4 Feb 2020.

Rosenberg, S., & Fried, I. (2020b). Tech can't remember what to do in a down market. *Axios*. Available via DIALOG. https://www.axios.com/tech-cant-remember-what-to-do-in-a-down-market-ca1e8750-f9f9-4461-97c4-710b9de0e9cc.html. Accessed 27 Feb 2020.

Rosenfeld, J. (2019). Can AI help prevent physician burnout? *Medical Economics*. Available via DIALOG. https://www.medicaleconomics.com/medical-economics-blog/can-Artificial-intelligence-help-prevent-physician-burnout. Accessed 4 Sept 2019.

Ross, C. (2019). FDA clarifies how it will regulate digital health and Artificial intelligence. *Stat News*. Available via DIALOG. https://www.statnews.com/2019/09/26/fda-Artificial -intelligence-digital-health-rules/. Accessed 19 Nov 2019.

Ross, C., & Swetlitz, I. (2017a). IBM pitched its Watson supercomputers as a revolution in cancer care its nowhere close. *Stat News*. Available via DIALOG. https://www.statnews.com/2017/09/05/watson-ibm-cancer/. Accessed 17 Oct 2019.

Ross, C., & Swetlitz, I. (2017b). IBM to Congress: Watson will transform health care, so keep your hands off our supercomputer. *Boston Globe*. Available via DIALOG. https://www.bostonglobe.com/business/2017/10/05/statwatson/VH0E7lRwyZIWWYnHnuUSlN/story.html. Accessed 17 Oct 2019.

Salmon, J., & Dedhiya, S. (1998). The vital role of pharmacy benefit management firms in health services research. *Journal of Managed Care Pharmacy, 4*(1), 23–28.

Satariano, A. (2018). *G.D.P.R., a new privacy law, makes Europe world's leading tech watchdog*. Available at: https://eproofing.springer.com/books_v3/mainpage.php?token=5GXt1bGuld3aErrwLK1ZpDaBgGbi_1Cr5BYP-6Nk4wUFzprSPvkZ-1UqXWyWR6M8. Accessed 13 Oct 2020.

Schleifer, T., & Molla, R. (2020). *Big Tech opponent Bernie Sanders raises more money from Big Tech employees than anyone else*. Available at: https://www.vox.com/recode/2020/2/6/21125684/bernie-sanders-tech-employees-donations-andrew-yang-amazon-googlefacebook-apple. Accessed 13 Oct 2020.

Schulte, F., & Fry, E. (2020). *New federal rules allow patients to access medical records via smartphone*. Available at: https://fortune.com/2020/03/09/medical-records-smartphones-ehrs-2020/. Accessed 13 Oct 2020.

Scott, D. (2018). *Why Apple, Amazon, and Google are making big health care moves – Silicon Valley big health care moves*. https://www.vox.com/technology/2018/3/6/17071750/amazon-health-care-apple-google-uber. Accessed 22 July 2020.

SenGupta, R. (2019). The great integration of data, technology and services. *The Financial Times*. Available via DIALOG. https://www.ft.com/content/99f6f334-eab7-11e9-85f4-d00e5018f061. Accessed 23 Oct 2019.

Shah, A. (2020). Smartwatch project cuts health costs. *The Wall Street Journal*. Available via DIALOG. https://www.wsj.com/articles/kaiser-permanente-bets-on-smartwatches-to-lower-costs-11578565801. Accessed 4 Feb 2020.

Shah, N. R., & Lee, T. H. (2019). What AI means for doctors and doctoring. *NEJM Catalyst*. Available via DIALOG. https://catalyst.nejm.org/ai-means-doctors-doctoring/. Accessed 4 Sept 2019.

Sheikh, K., Watkins, D., Wu, J., & Grondahl, M. (2020). How bad will the crisis get? *The New York Times*. Available via DIALOG. https://www.nytimes.com/interactive/2020/world/asia/china-coronavirus-contain.html. Accessed 4 Feb 2020.

Shrank, W. H., Rogstad, T. L., & Parekh, N. (2019). Waste in the US health care system – estimated costs and potential for savings. *JAMA, 322*(15), 1501–1509. Available via DIALOG. https://jamanetwork.com/journals/jama/articleabstract/2752664. Accessed 25 Dec 2019.

Siegele, L. (2018). How to fix what's wrong with the internet. *The Economist*. Available via DIALOG. https://www.economist.com/special-report/2018/06/28/how-to-fix-what-has-gone-wrong-with-the-internet. Accessed 22 July 2020.

Silver, V., & Frier, S. (2018). *Terrorists are still recruiting on Facebook, despite Zuckerberg's reassurances*. Available at: https://www.bloomberg.com/news/articles/2018-05-10/terrorists-creep-onto-facebook-as-fast-as-it-can-shut-them-down. Accessed 13 Oct 2020.

Sim, I. (2019). Mobile devices and health. *The New England Journal of Medicine, 381*, 956–968.

Singer, N. (2019a). Battle brews over moving health records to the cloud. *App News*. Available via DIALOG. https://app.newsoveraudio.com/articles/a-battle-brews-over-moving-medical-records-to-your-smartphone-751129. Accessed 14 Feb 2020.

Singer, N. (2019b). When apps get your medical data, your privacy may go with it. *The New York Times*. Available via DIALOG. https://www.nytimes.com/2019/09/03/technology/smartphone-medical-records.html. Accessed 24 July 2020.

Sink, J., Egkolfopoulou, M., & Fabian, J. (2020). *Twitter-Trump clash escalates after he signs social media order*. Accessed via DIALOG. https://www.bloomberg.com/news/articles/2020-05-28/trump-says-he-ll-sign-order-to-limit-twitter-s-legal-protections. Accessed 24 July 2020.

Smith, A. (2018). *Public attitudes toward technology companies*. Available at: https://www.pewresearch.org/internet/2018/06/28/public-attitudes-toward-technology-companies/. Accessed 12 Oct 2020.

Sommer, J. (2018). Tech stocks should not move together. *The New York Times*. Available via DIALOG. https://www.nytimes.com/2018/12/13/business/tech-stocks-together.html. Accessed 17 Mar 2020.

Spitzer, J. (2018a). Apple adds medical records to its health app. *Becker's Hospital Review*. Available via DIALOG. https://www.beckershospitalreview.com/healthcare-information-technology/apple-adds-medical-records-to-its-health-app.html. Accessed 27 July 2018.

Spitzer, J. (2018b). Apple's health records beta feature now available at 39 health systems. *Becker's Hospital Review*. Available via DIALOG. https://www.beckershospitalreview.com/healthcare-information-technology/apple-s-health-records-beta-feature-now-available-at-39-health-systems.html. Accessed 6 Aug 2018.

Stacey, K., & Shubber, K. (2019). Which antitrust investigations should Big Tech worry about? *Financial Times*. Available at https://www.ft.com/content/abcc5070-f68f-11e9-a79c-bc9a-cae3b654. Accessed 22 July 2020.

Stacey, K., Shubber, K., & Murphy, H. (2019). *Which antitrust investigations should Big Tech worry about?* Available at: https://www.ft.com/content/abcc5070-f68f-11e9-a79c-bc9a-cae3b654. Accessed 13 Oct 2020.

Staley, O. (2018). *Our system is so broken, we're turning to billionaires like Bezos to save us.* Available via DIALOG. https://www.yahoo.com/news/m/09558729-1894-3f49-af78-16e854b5f3f0/our-system-is-so-broken%2C.html. Accessed 23 July 2020.

Steinmetz, K. (2018). *Google's biggest problem? It can never be as transparent as we need it to be.* Accessed via DIALOG. https://news.yahoo.com/google-apos-biggest-problem-never-213707586.html. Accessed 24 July 2020.

Stern, J. (2019). First, the smartphone changed. Then, over a decade, it changed us. *The Wall Street Journal.* Available via DIALOG. https://www.wsj.com/articles/first-the-smartphone-changed-then-over-a-decade-it-changed-us-11576618873. Accessed 14 Feb 2020.

Stoller, M. (2019). *Why U.S. businesses want trustbusting.* Available at: https://www.wsj.com/articles/why-u-s-businesses-want-trustbusting-11570803088. Accessed 13 Oct 2020.

Streitfeld, D. (2020). *As Amazon rises, so does the opposition.* Available at: https://www.nytimes.com/2020/04/18/technology/athena-mitchell-amazon.html. Accessed 12 Oct 2020.

Swartz, J. (2020). *Alphabet shares decline on revenue miss; YouTube ad, cloud revenues finally revealed.* Available at: https://www.marketwatch.com/story/alphabet-shares-rise-on-earnings-beat-2020-02-03. Accessed 13 Oct 2020.

Sweeney, E. (2018). *Bolstered by FDA's policy shift, 'digiceuticals' could soon carve out a bigger role in healthcare.* Available via DIALOG https://www.fiercehealthcare.com/mobile/digital-therapeutics-digiceuticals-fda-pear-therapeutics-mobile-apps-substance-abuse. Accessed 22 July 2020.

Swisher, K. (2018). Introducing the internet bill of rights. *The New York Times.* Available via DIALOG. https://www.nytimes.com/2018/10/04/opinion/ro-khanna-internet-bill-of-rights.html. Accessed 22 July 2020.

The Economist. (2014). The AI will see you now. *The Economist.* Available via DIALOG. https://www.economist.com/science-and-technology/2014/08/20/the-computer-will-see-you-now. Accessed 4 Sept 2019.

The Economist. (2018). *Google's Android fine is not enough to change its behaviour.* Available via DIALOG. https://www.economist.com/leaders/2018/07/19/googles-android-fine-is-not-enough-to-change-its-behaviour. Accessed 24 July 2020.

Thompson, S., & Warzel, C. (2019). Twelve million phones, one dataset, zero privacy. *The New York Times.* Available via DIALOG. https://www.nytimes.com/interactive/2019/12/19/opinion/location-tracking-cell-phone.html. Accessed 24 July 2020.

Torchia, M., & Shirer, M. (2018). *Worldwide spending on augmented and virtual reality expected to surpass $20 billion in 2019, according to IDC.* https://www.businesswire.com/news/home/20181206005037/en/Worldwide-Spending-Augmented-Virtual-Reality-Expected-Surpass. Accessed 22 July 2020.

Towers-Clark, C. (2019). *The cutting-edge of AI cancer detection.* Available at: https://www.forbes.com/sites/charlestowersclark/2019/04/30/the-cutting-edge-of-ai-cancer-detection/#518eaea17336. Accessed 12 Oct 2020.

Tsukayama, H. (2012). *Facebook users can add organ donor status.* Available at: https://www.washingtonpost.com/business/technology/facebook-users-can-add-organ-donor-status/2012/05/01/gIQA9tmwtT_story.html. Accessed 12 Oct 2020.

Valentino-DeVries. (2019). 200 Million Fine for Not Protecting Location Data. Available at: https://www.nytimes.com/2020/02/28/technology/fcc-cellphones-location-data-fines.html. Accessed on October 13, 2020.

Vigna, P. (2019). Brace for the digital-money wars. *The Wall Street Journal.* Available via DIALOG. https://www.wsj.com/articles/brace-for-the-digital-money-wars-11575694806. Accessed 25 Dec 2019.

Vivero, D. (2019). Views why Amazon accepting HSA dollars is a big deal. *Healthcare Dive.* Available via DIALOG. https://www.healthcaredive.com/news/amazon-launches-virtual-medical-clinic-for-seattle-employees/563629/. Accessed 4 Mar 2020.

Wakabayashi, D. (2020). *Google takes aim at Amazon. Again.* Available at: https://www.nytimes.com/2020/07/23/technology/google-ecommerce-amazon.html. Accessed 13 Oct 2020.

Wakabayashi, D., & Phillips, M. (2020). As tech giants grow, smallest are squeezed. *The New York Times*. Available via DIALOG. https://www.nytimes.com/2018/05/02/technology/china-xi-jinping-technology-innovation.html. Accessed 27 Feb 2020.

Waters, R., Kuchler, H., & Massoudi, A. (2018). *Microsoft changes tune on open software with $7.5bn GitHub bet. Available via DIALOG.* https://article.wn.com/view/2018/06/04/Microsoft_paying_75bn_in_stock_for_popular_coder_hangout_Git/. Accessed 24 Aug 2018.

Waters, R. (2018a). Microsoft gets ahead in the cloud. *Financial Times*. Available via DIALOG. https://www.ft.com/content/320d606c-5c3a-11e8-9334-2218e7146b04. Accessed 24 Aug 2018.

Waters, R. (2018b). Microsoft in $7.5bn group hug with GitHub. *Financial Times*. Accessed 24 Aug 2018.

Waters, R. (2018c). Microsoft on track for strongest annual growth in over a decade. *Financial Times*. Available via DIALOG. https://www.ft.com/content/6add94ac-49a7-11e8-8ee8-cae73aab7ccb. Accessed 17 Oct 2019.

Waters, R. (2018d). Microsoft's tussle for top spot highlights its transformation. *Financial Times*. Available via DIALOG. https://www.ft.com/content/619d0834-f1ed-11e8-ae55-df4bf40f9d0d. Accessed 17 Oct 2019.

Waters, R. (2020a). Apple pays $200m for AI start-up Xnor in machine learning race. *Financial Times*. Available via DIALOG. https://www.ft.com/content/8ea5f6b2-37e0-11ea-a6d3-9a26f8c3cba4. Accessed 4 Mar 2020.

Waters, R. (2020b). IBM turns to veteran technology for edge in cloud computing battle. *Financial Times*. https://app.ft.com/content/15f6f69a-43d8-11ea-a43a-c4b328d9061c?sectionid=tech;

Nicas, J. (2018). Hit by $5.1 billion fine, But still Google surges. *The New York Times*. Available via DIALOG. https://www.nytimes.com/2018/07/23/technology/google-earnings-alphabet.html. Accessed 24 Aug 2018.

Watson, A. (2020). *SVoD service multiple subscriptions in the US 2020*. Available at: https://www.statista.com/statistics/778912/video-streaming-service-multiple-subscriptions/. Accessed 12 Oct 2020.

Weise, K. (2020a). *Ahead of the pack, how Microsoft told workers to stay home*. Available at: https://www.nytimes.com/2020/03/15/technology/microsoft-coronavirus-response.html. Accessed 13 Oct 2020.

Weise, K. (2020b). Jeff Bezos, Tabloid Man. *The New York Times*. Available via DIALOG. https://www.nytimes.com/2020/01/23/technology/jeff-bezos-tabloids.html. Accessed 17 Mar 2020.

Weise, K., & Conger, K. (2020). Gaps in Amazon's response as virus spreads to more than 50 warehouses. *The New York Times*. Available via DIALOG. https://www.nytimes.com/2020/04/05/technology/coronavirus-amazon-workers.html. Accessed 23 July 2020.

Wheatley, M. (2019). *Oracle's stock drops after it misses revenue targets*. Available at: https://siliconangle.com/2019/12/12/oracles-stock-drops-misses-revenue-targets/. Accessed 12 Oct 2020.

White, E. (2019). Samsung eyes slice of Apple's $50bn-a-year service model. *Financial Times*. Available via DIALOG. https://www.ft.com/content/a15feece-052d-11ea-9afa-d9e2401fa7ca. Accessed 17 Mar 2020.

Wigglesworth, R. (2018). Facebook sheds $120bn in value as 'bombshells' spark record sell-off. *Financial Times*.

Wigglesworth, R. (2020). *How America's 1% came to dominate equity ownership*. Available at: https://www.ft.com/content/2501e154-4789-11ea-aeb3-955839e06441. Accessed 13 Oct 2020.

Wilson, L. (2019). Machine learning: Will it revolutionize healthcare? *Medical Economics*, pp. 36–37.

Wince, R. (2018). Pragmatic AI in pharma. *Pharmaceutical Executive*. Available via DIALOG. http://www.pharmexec.com/pragmatic-ai-pharma. Accessed 28 Sept 2018.

Wingfield, N. (2018). *Inside Amazon Go, a store of the future*. Available at: https://www.nytimes.com/2018/01/21/technology/inside-amazon-go-a-store-of-the-future.html. Accessed 12 Oct 2020.

Wise, J. (2018). AI system interprets eye scans as accurately as top specialists. *The BMJ*. Available via DIALOG. https://www.bmj.com/content/362/bmj.k3484. Accessed 28 Sept 2018.

Zetlin, M. (2018). *Facebook is patenting technology to spy on you through your smartphone camera and microphone*. Available at: https://www.inc.com/minda-zetlin/facebook-patents-spying-smartphone-camera-microphone-privacy.html. Accessed 13 Oct 2020.

Zhong, R. (2019). *Huawei's sales jump despite Trump's blacklisting*. Available at: https://www.nytimes.com/2019/07/30/technology/huawei-trump.html. Accessed 13 Oct 2020.

Zuboff, S. (2019). *The age of surveillance Capitalism: The fight for a human future at the new frontier of power*. New York, NY: Public Affairs.

Chapter 6
Physician Employment Status: Collective Bargaining and Strikes

Throughout medical history, physicians have rarely formed unions and/or carried out strikes. Today, the medical profession worldwide seems in a heightened state of discontent, but their chosen directions to fight back over their conditions of labor appear blurry and ineffective. As mentioned in previous chapters of this book, the profession of medicine has been facing ongoing threats to their professional practice for many years now. It was Carr-Saunders and Wilson who are credited with describing the transition of occupations into professions (Carr-Saunders & Wilson, 1933). The concept of a professional was defined as possessing the following traits:

- Specialized skill and training
- Minimum fees and salaries
- Formation of professional associations
- Code of ethics

The professional as defined above is supposed to act in the best interest of their client/patient, and they (along with their fellow professionals) determine what is good or bad, and the client/patient has no choice but to acquiesce to that judgment (Greenwood, 1957). Scott states that professionals participate in two systems, the profession and the organization they work in. The professional association place limits on what the organization the professional works in may or may not ask that member to do in carrying out its missions and goals (Scott W. R., 1966).

With the continual increase in corporatization schemes, physicians continue to be drawn into the role of employee of ever-larger organizations which leave the independent physician-run practice behind; it has become financially more and more difficult to maintain a practice while procuring sufficient reimbursement from insurance companies and patients (Rosenthal, 2014). As a result, they are not able to maintain their professional independence which would allow them to act as their patient's agent in determining what would be done and where it would be done. Because they now have to obey the corporate mandate of cost cutting and revenue enhancement, they no longer have free rein to do as they wish in their professional practice.

© Springer Nature Switzerland AG 2021
J. W. Salmon, S. L. Thompson, *The Corporatization of American Health Care*,
https://doi.org/10.1007/978-3-030-60667-1_6

Braverman describes the separation of "intellectual work from the work of execution" which he describes as a "technical condition" used by hierarchical organizations that controls "both the hand and brain worker," improves profitability, and naturally serves everyone but the "needs of the people" (Braverman, Labor and Monopoly Capital, 1974). Thompson (1983) expands on that concept by enunciating the capitalist labor process as having the following tendencies:

- Deskilling
- Fragmentation of tasks
- Hierarchical organization
- Division between manual and mental work
- Struggle to establish the most effective means to control labor

The change of social form of labor from self-employed to employment within an organization is an inevitable outgrowth of corporate capitalism. As more and more physicians went from self-employment and loose associations through admitting privileges to actual employees of those organizations, such transitions completed the process of capturing all means of healthcare production within the organization itself. Krause describes the decline of medicine as a professional guild particularly as the profession lost the ability to control the numbers entering the profession with the federal government-enforced expansion in the 1960s (Krause, 1996). The leverage was primarily over federal research dollars that institutions would lose grant monies unless they increased the size of their graduating classes. Once they lost control of how many could enter the profession, they began to lose their uniqueness and regulation, so standardization became paramount subject to the bureaucratic machinery (Weber, 1978). Waitzkin further described the proletarianization of physicians that occurred in the 1980s (Waitzkin, 2016). He states that physicians were free to choose their working hours, the staff who supported that work, how much time and effort to spend on patients, and most importantly what they could charge for those services. Since doctors now mainly work for corporations, all of those decisions are made by their corporate bosses, which has led to loss of autonomy as well as satisfaction with the profession.

Freeman underscores this concept by pointing out that Marxists believe that the highly educated workforce will be "locked out of participation and decision making that they constitute the new working class" (Freeman, 1979). And as increasing uncertainty over changes occurring in health care accelerates more, more physicians are opting for salaried positions within organizations with its attendant loss of control over the conception of their work (Rosenthal, 2014). They find their bargaining power continually undermined and diminished by both the healthcare organizations in which they practice and insurance companies they must bargain reimbursement rates. In addition, as employees of organizations, they find themselves in "at-will" employment, which means they can be hired and fired at will, for good reasons, bad reasons, or no reason at all. Given organizational metrics performance often imposed without professional input, it is certainly *not* a stretch to believe that physicians may find themselves having to meet productivity measures to maximize revenue often at the expense of patient care quality. The pressure to see more patients in a given day will increase as productivity pressures are pressed. Physicians will face removal from practice panels with interference in physician/patient relationships and then be subject to economic credentialing by hospitals (Black, 2012). The problem with economic credentialing is that it substitutes economic criteria over quality concerns and can remove physicians from practice for criteria that has little to do with a physician's clinical competency (Dallet, 1994).

Given these ongoing threats to the profession of medicine, one wonders whether collective bargaining and striking would grant physicians leverage in dealing with their employers and whether they would be able to reconcile that choice with their oath to "do no harm." A 2010 Physicians Foundation Report remarked that "most physicians will be compelled to consolidate with other practitioners, become hospital employees, or align with large hospitals" (Miller, 2010). Since that time, little has improved in the morale of physicians in employment practice. In a more recent report, it has been noted that 78% of physicians, surveyed sometimes, often or always feel burned out, while only 12% rarely or never feel burned out (The Physicians Foundation, 2018). The increasing time spent on paperwork vs. patient care is taking its toll with an increasing dislike of electronic health records, one of the primary causes of increasing dissatisfaction (Guwande, 2018).

But would unions and collective bargaining truly help physicians regain some measure of control over their work life? Malinowski, Minkler, and Stock believe that union membership "can help in defining health-related problems and solutions, reaching out to affected workers, disseminating research findings, and advocating needed changes" (Malinowski, Minkler, & Stock, 2015). Hagedorn et al. elaborate that concept in that "labor union contracts create higher wage and benefit standards, working hours' limits, workplace hazards protections, and other factors. Unions also promote well-being by encouraging democratic participation and a sense of community among workers" (Hagedorn, Paras, Greenwich, & Hagopian, 2016). Their findings suggest that while health practitioners have not typically looked to labor organizations for promoting the public's health, unions can address and improve the social determinants of health of their membership through better income, more job security, and a better work-life balance. For example, the National Union of Healthcare Workers (NUHW) went on strike at Salinas Valley Memorial Hospital in California to protest plans to cut more than 100 staff, while at the same time, the hospital was planning large payments to a departing CEO and outside consultants. Also at the same time, the hospital was cutting patient care staffing to increase operating surplus, which put the hospital's patients at increased risk of an adverse event (Brenner, 2011). The daylong strike was followed by a 2-day lockout by the employer in what was deemed retaliation for union activity. These hard cores tactics by employers have increased over time with outright refusals to recognize duly authorized bargaining representatives happening.

In 2016, when Advocate Health System in Chicago took over 56 Walgreens in-store clinics, the 160 nurse practitioners sent a demand to Advocate to bargain, but was met with a refusal to meet and recognize the union. Unfair labor practices were filed with the National Labor Relations Board (NLRB) after which the Board found sufficient evidence to file a complaint to the Federal District Court. Advocate's response is typical of employers who value a "direct" relationship with their employees rather than have to meet with a third party union to negotiate terms and conditions of employment (Sweeney, 2017).

Barbash (1984) describes conditions that create worker proneness to unions, which are:

- Their bargaining power as individuals
- The threat which cost discipline presents to them
- The work groups' ability to mount an effective response
- The employer's ability to counter that response
- The ways in which the external economy and society abet or discourage the forces of cost discipline and protectivism
- Worker's personal characteristics

But since 1979, national union membership, especially in the overall private sector, has declined significantly. On bread-and-butter issues, it appears that the decline in the labor movement has led to several phenomena that are not good news for labor itself (Rosenfeld, Denice, & Laird, 2016). Among the findings were:

- An annual wage loss of $2704 per worker which spread out over 40.2 million nonunion private sector men comes to $2.1 billion fewer dollars.
- An increase in weekly wages of about 2–3% for working women if union density had remained at 1979 levels.
- An estimated 8% higher wage for non-college graduate workers if union density had remained at 1979 levels (vs. 2015 levels) which meant $3016 less annually.
- Last, "union decline has exacerbated wage inequality in the United States by dampening the pay of nonunion workers as well as by eroding the share of workers directly benefitting from unionization" (Rosenfeld et al., 2016).

These findings support the notion that a strong union presence can set pay and benefit levels that nonunion employees tend to follow. One study found that unions can offer black workers "higher wages, and better access to health insurance and retirement benefits than their non-union peers" (Bucknor, 2016). An earlier study found that "unionization raised service-sector workers' wages by 10.1% -- about $2.00 per hour -- compared to non-union service-sector workers with similar characteristics" (Schmitt, 2009). The report goes on to state that "service-sector workers who are able to bargain collectively earn more and are more likely to have benefits associated with good jobs. The data, therefore, suggest that better protection of workers' right to unionize would have a substantial positive impact on the pay and benefits of service-sector workers."

The Origins of Unionization and Collective Bargaining

The erosion of individual liberties in employment can be traced back to the Industrial Revolution, in which individuals became less self-sufficient and more beholden to others to earn a living. For the purposes of this chapter, we won't include indentured servitude or slavery in this discussion but rather focus on that point in time in which free individuals routinely engaged in working for others, whereby they traded autonomy for a more consistent way to make a living. As industrialization grew, administration of an ever-complex workforce and economy became necessary (Dulles, 1966). Initially skilled workers formed craft guilds which allowed them to separate themselves from their overseers and the vagaries of the market (Krause, *Death Of the Guilds: Professions, States, and the Advance of Capitalism, 1930 to Present*, 1996). As differences between capital and labor became greater, workers responded by attempting to band together to protect themselves. Many of these attempts were doomed to failure primarily because of either legal action taken against them by employers (such as criminal conspiracies and restraints of trade and workers organizations became enjoined from their activities). A secondary reason for their failure was that they attempted to do too much, that is, they attempted to unify a workforce that had different needs and desires, not to mention different skills (Rayback, 1966).

Unions act as a hedge against economic insecurity caused by "part-time work and unpaid internships to the exploitation of student athletes to increasing number of Uber drivers and other "gig economy workers" (Bivens et al., 2017). Younger workers seemed to be more amenable to labor unions than their older colleagues primarily because they entered the workforce when these labor issues were becoming entrenched in the workplace (Breunig, 2015).

As previously mentioned, unionization and collective bargaining appear to be waning movements in the United States especially in the private sector. With the latest decision by the Supreme Court, they could be on the wane in the public sector as well (Janus v. American Federation of State, County and Municipal Employees, 2018). However, since that ruling in June 2018, it appears that public sector unions have not lost as many members as predicted and some have increased their membership (DiSalvo, 2019). Current union membership in 2018 is around 10.5% of workers, down from 35–40% in 1983 (Rho & Brown, 2019).

But it was noted in this report that the group with the largest growth in the private sector unionization was professional and related occupations, leading one to believe that unions and collective bargaining may be useful in gaining back power in the workplace to better control pay and conditions of work. Data from 2019 shows that the rate of unionization for private sector workers is 6.2% while public sector unionization rates are at 33.6% (Bureau of Labor Statistics, 2020).

So what about physicians? Could unions and collective bargaining be an answer to the ongoing threats of corporatization to their profession? It is clear that large numbers of physicians have never sought out unionization in the United States, primarily because of the individualistic nature of American physicians, but also the result of antitrust concerns caused by individual and independent practitioners banding together to set prices and restrain trade. As physicians have evolved from independent practitioners to employees of large group practices, faculty foundations, and/or healthcare systems, this legal barrier to organizing has evaporated. However, the belief that a pursuit of collective solutions to what many consider an infringement of their individual rights and professional prerogatives continues to confront physicians.

Magali (1977) states that the very idea of an independent professional who is used to going it alone would join a union is a contradiction because it would cause one to surrender that autonomy which is at the heart of a professional endeavor. But to this point, professionals can and do join together to protect their professional autonomy against the "collective colossus" (Magali, 1977). It's an odd conundrum in that physicians and their professional associations were hugely concerned with threats to their autonomy and the profession from the government so they never saw the corporate takeover of medicine and health care while at the same time rejecting collective bargaining, the one hedge that could effectively combat that corporate takeover, they rejected outright.

For those physicians who do consider collective action and the organizations who would represent them, Aronowitz warns that professionals demand more than dealing with the usual salary and working conditions issues; they also expect a union to act as a professional association to address the issues of knowledge as well (Aronowitz, 1998). Page states that collective bargaining, unions, and strikes can be helpful for employed physicians who have lost control of their workplace and profession; what remains unclear is who would avail themselves of the opportunity to participate and join these organizations (Page, 2016). Page suggests that the future of physician unions would likely involve more interest in control over the profession rather than pay raises and other bread-and-butter issues.

What Exactly Do Unions Do?

In a seminal text from 1970, Hirschman (1970) describes how an employer finds out about its shortcomings. The first way is through exit, either customers stop buying their product or employees leave the firm. Management is compelled to find out why revenues declined and how to fix the problems that exit represents. The second is through voice, that is, direct expression of dissatisfaction by customers and employees to management with the expectation that dissatisfaction will be actually addressed because customers and employees have sufficient leverage to get employers to listen and act.

In 1970 there were limited forums that one could articulate voice, but in 2019 there are multiple platforms in which to express one's displeasure (e.g., using Yelp, Facebook, and Twitter to express displeasure with doctors online). It is through this second mechanism of voice that unions can become an effective tool in both enunciating employee's collective voice not only over wages and conditions of employment but, in the case before us, to the type of care a physician might provide to an organization's patients (Freeman & Medoff, *What Do Unions Do?*, 1984). This enhanced voice function that a union could provide would reduce exit, which would consequently reduce turnover costs, training costs, and work disruptions. They found that the presence of a union enhanced loyalty, which coincidentally increased the employer's incentive to invest in their employees, which can in turn lead to increased productivity (Freeman & Medoff, *What Do Unions Do?*, 1984). When voice and loyalty were not present in sufficient quantities, then exit became an increasingly viable solution. As Harmon pointed out in his article on the history of resident and intern unions, "Intern and resident organizations were responsible in part for persuading organized, medicine and medical education to listen to its younger colleagues" (Harmon, 1978). He goes on to predict that "As with teachers, nurses, and airline pilot, doctors persist in seeking a strong voice in decision-making through negotiated contracts. This outcome seems to become inevitable as institutions in our society continue to be larger and more complex." Scheffler reinforces the notion of voice "if physicians are to have an effective seat at the table with the corporate executives and bean counters of today's managed care world, and warrant widespread public support in the process, their collective voice must be backed by economic power and legal standing. As physicians are increasingly coming to understand about the managed care market, where there is *no exit* [emphasis added], a wise and disciplined voice is not only the best course of action, but also the only viable one" (Scheffler, 1999).

Through the 1980s and 1990s with the growth of health maintenance organizations (HMOs) and preferred provider organizations (PPOs), it became clear that discontent was building from physicians (Hadley & Mitchell, 1997). Physicians in self-employed private practice were not able to organize for the purpose of collective bargaining since it would indicate an illegal restraint of trade because they are not in a defined employer-employee relationship so there is no one employer with whom they can theoretically bargain. Nevertheless, there were numerous incidents of HMOs bullying practitioners, removing them from the practice panel, stealing their patients, and telling them what decisions had to be made for economic purposes by the management. Physicians increasingly saw their future delimited as issues of professional autonomy because this historically was the rallying cry of the bulk of the conservative profession. Yet there was no apparent strike activity related to the managed care movement, and physicians had little alternative but to complain in their periodicals and at their professional meetings (Berenson, 1991).

One professional group in the healthcare arena that has taken to unions and collective bargaining is nursing. Nursing has been able to make great strides in improving their practice situations and their economic remuneration as a result of embracing collective bargaining as a solution to what ailed them. This included a judicious use of the strike weapon to enforce their positions at the bargaining table. It is the subject of this chapter to highlight why and how medicine and physicians might do well to follow suit. Physicians as a rule have difficulties with the strike weapon primarily because they see withholding services of any kind for any reason as appearing unethical. In order for physicians to get past this ethical issue, they might need to understand that striking could be an ethical response to protest organizational imperatives that violate their professional practices and norms, such that longer-term goals in patient care can be met and improved upon. For some on the academic side of nursing, unionization "conjures up not the image of Rosie the Riveter but rather that of a Handmaiden gone strident" (Gorman & Westing, 2013).

The question is: Would these nursing findings translate to the much higher paid profession of medicine? Other highly paid professions who are unionized may yield some clues on how that may work. For example, the Chicago Symphony Orchestra is a unionized orchestra that recently went on strike to protest a change in the retirement plan that would have shifted from a defined benefit plan to a direct contribution plan. Also at issue was salary as it relates to how comparable orchestras across the country were paid (Reich, 2019). The strike was settled after 7 weeks with the help of Chicago Mayor Rahm Emanuel, which included a 13.25% increase in base salary over 5 years, as well as maintenance of the defined benefit plan, but a shift to a defined contribution plan for those members hired after July 2020 (Johnson, 2019). University professors at the University of Illinois at Chicago have unionized in the past few years. As Janet Smith, a University of Illinois at Chicago professor and head of the union stated, while professionals do different kinds of work, they still remain laborers and thus have to resort to tools that laborers use to gain voice in the workplace (Rhodes, 2019). But Thompson cautions that "unions will be required to move off their traditional terrain if they are to challenge capital on its own terms of planning, investment, and resources, even to provide adequate forms of resistance to issues of jobs, skills, and living standards" (Thompson, 1983). Dobkin makes clear that "Unorganized physicians have had little influence on the public policies affecting patient care, hospital conditions, medical training, or working conditions. Although potentially powerful as agents of change in health care, most physicians typically have remained passive about social, political and economic matters in health, thus contributing greatly to the trend toward control of health services by business or by managerial or political interests" (Dobkin, 1975). While that was written roughly 45 years ago, it was prescient in describing the trend toward proletarianization of the profession of medicine and how physicians would acquiesce to that movement by remaining unorganized while unable to define their collective interest.

One such situation occurred in 2015 when a group of physicians of a non-profit parent health system that oversaw the hospital where they worked were being forced to spend less time with each patient so that they could see more patients or "speed up" (Scheiber, 2016). In 2012 a group of hospitalists were told that the corporation was considering outsourcing their practice because of what the system could get paid vs. what the care actually costs. The group decided to seek representation for purposes of fighting back. About a third of the group of 36 doctors said no thanks and left. Those that remained voted overwhelmingly to join an affiliate of the American Federation of Teachers who also happened to represent the nurses at the hospital. The hospital eventually backed down from their outsourcing threat but continued to try and squeeze more productivity and concessions out of the physician group.

Brewbaker strikes a note of caution in that "Even if one agrees that consumers are in significant need of protection from their health plans, it does not follow that physicians are the one to protect them" (Brewbaker III, 2000). Mondore and Trivisonmo found that unions in hospitals tended to lower both engagement and satisfaction because of "restrictive work rules, low employee morale, and unions activities such as contract campaigns, grievances and job actions that are designed to disparage organizations and drive a wedge between leaders and employees" (Mondore & Tivisonmo, 2015)

There are fine lines between employees who use unions to protect their voice and position within the hierarchy to make sure that their views are heard and considered in the process of improving organizational outcomes and objectives and those who use unions as a cudgel to increase positions of self interest in terms of salary and benefits. Unions can be useful tools to obtain both, but the former must never be sacrificed for the latter. This distinction must be made unequivocally when using the strike weapon effectively to enforce one's bargaining position.

Physician Strikes

Traditionally, unions utilize the strike weapon or work stoppages to enforce their bargaining positions with management. Thus, employers face industrial actions, refusals of certain duties, or slowdowns to provoke management into yielding to worker demands. Strikes usually are the last alternative after negotiations fail to seek the desired progress when parties have reached an impasse. Often times, strikes occur for one of several reasons, such as supporting another union who is out on strike, protesting an unfair labor practice of the employer (as defined in either the NLRA or various state statues, depending on the jurisdiction), forcing the recognition of the union as the employees' exclusive bargaining agent, or causing economic harm to the employer organization and in today's corporate market to their profit margins.

Strikes can be carried out for a variety of reasons, from using them to force an employer to recognize the union as the bargaining agent for its employees to a means to enforce a collective bargaining position to obtain concessions from an employer. Strikes or work stoppages are tactics that unions employ to extract concessions during the collective bargaining process. Strikes are often viewed as a failure of the process, but are used for a variety of reasons. Those reasons include sympathy for another striking union, protesting unfair employment practices, or forcing an employer to recognize the union as the employee's exclusive bargaining agent. Strikes can also be used to cause economic harm to the employer being struck. It is that harm that can cause reservations on the part of physicians who may wish to strike as it may cause harm to the very population they wish to serve.

It is the patient who may be harmed by any employment action, and it is their interests that the parties to any labor dispute use to support their positions (Loewy, *Of Healthcare Professionals, Ethics And Strikes*, 2000). As Chima points out, "the right to strike is so important to the functioning of modern democratic societies that its suppression would be unjustified. The right to strike is now accepted as an indispensable component of collective bargaining and perhaps a fundamental human right" (Chima, 2013).

Overall, union membership has declined from a high of 40 percent in the mid-1950s to roughly 11% today of the US workforce (U.S. Bureau Of Labor Statistics, 2013). Of that 12%, 6.6% of the private sector is unionized, while 36% of the public sector is unionized. Consequently, industrial worker strikes in the United States are few and far between with strikes among physicians even more so. The number of strikes over the past 40 years has shown an even steeper drop-off as evidenced by the data represented in Fig. 6.1.

As the number of strikes among workers has diminished since 1960, it might be suggested that the more recent strikes by unions were for unions choosing to strike under desperate conditions and/or as a form of protest. As Yates points out, strikes may have substantially decreased because of the constraints under which unions and workers work in the current economy; there have been increases in striking seen in areas such as health and education (Yates, 2009). Unfortunately for union members, strikes recently have led to permanent unemployment and replacement of the strikers at the workplace as Reagan's action against the air traffic controllers (PATCO) in the early 1980s indicated. Corporate entities, including those in health care, pushed back against workers and their unions in emboldened ways with little in the way of a response from the state and federal agencies designed to protect union members'

Fig. 6.1 Work stoppages in the United States: 1947–2018 (Source: Bureau of Labor Statistics, United States Department of Labor, 2019)

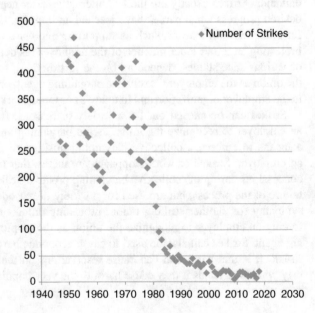

rights to collectively bargain. As a result, strikes had become less and less common, but they do happen; however, in 2019 there appeared to be an uptick in strike activity in the educational service industry with teachers in Los Angeles, Chicago, Denver, and Oakland walking off the job (Demanuelle-Hall & DiMaggio, 2019). This was in addition to the UAW at General Motors strike that involved 46,000 workers that lasted 29 days (Statistics, 2020). The surge was believed to have been caused by a low unemployment rate in that fired strikers could more easily find another job plus low unemployment (<4%) can give employees more leverage in pressing demands because employers don't have a ready supply or replacements lined up (Shierholz & Poydock, 2020). The major reason that the authors found for the increase in strikes is the lag in wage growth that should have occurred as result of low unemployment. Teachers, in particular, have been willing to walk out, not just over pay and working conditions but also the very way in which public education is delivered including health and safety issues within the schools as well as how those schools should be staffed (Dampier, 2019). The high employment rate is said to allow workers to feel more secure in their jobs and thus more able to engage in strikes and job actions simply because there are not many options for employers to hire replacements (Castellucci, 2019).

For physicians the issue of striking is one of the largest reasons that they would never consider a union because of the ethical conflict between withholding labor and a commitment to treat all patients in need of medical care regardless of how they themselves are treated. As Brunton and Sayers point out in their study of a junior doctors strike in New Zealand, that "anti-strike ethical rhetoric is Kantian in its characteristics, while the pro-strike ethical rhetoric is Utilitarian in its characteristics" (Brunton & Sayers, 2011). What is a strike and why do unions withhold labor?

So while physician strikes are pretty rare, where can we look for guidance as to the use of the strike weapon in health care? Nurses provide many more examples of the use of the strike weapon in health care as nursing unionization has become more commonplace. For example, one such strike in Minnesota in 2010 saw 12,000 nurses walk out over nurse-to-patient ratios that were deemed too low to provide for safe and effective quality health care (Albers, 2010). Six years later roughly 4800 nurses went on strike at the Minneapolis-based Allina Health System (Gooch, 2016). The primary issues for the strike were over the usual issues of health benefits, staffing, and safety. The strike lasted 7 days and nurses returned to work under the terms of their previous contract. Several unfair labor practices were lodged against Allina (Olson, 2016). In April of 2019 10,000 nurses in New York City threatened to strike at three of New York City's biggest hospital systems (McGeehan, *New York Hospitals Reach a Landmark Deal on Nurse Staffing*, 2019). The threat appeared to have worked as the union reached agreement with the hospitals that would lead to the hiring of 1450 more nurses as well as establish minimum ratios of nurses to patients.

A grocery store strike offers an important lesson on the power of strikes, and that is "After years and years where the number of strikes dwindled to a pitifully small number, accompanied by a barrage of negativity from media and political elites, workers are beginning to see that it is one of the most effective ways to fight back. That's true of teachers, nurses and other healthcare workers…" (Piascik, 2019). Nurses have gone on strike in many other places as well. At roughly the same time, nurses at Stanford Health Care in California voted to authorize a strike because contract talks had not been resolved over the issues of wages, workplace safety, and others (Ho, 2019). In September 2019, 2200 nurses went on a 1-day strike at the University of Chicago Hospitals which turned into a lockout for several more days due to the hospital contracting with outside sources to provide staffing for a set number of days (Schencker, 2019). The primary issue was over what the nurses' union described as overtime and safe staffing ratios at the hospital. The strike itself caused no issues with patient safety or care as the hospital had gone on bypass as well as curtailed services for a few days until the nurse had returned to work. As the COVID-19 pandemic continues on, it seems that we can expect to see more job actions related to patient as well as practitioner safety with dire shortages of equipment, testing, and personal protective equipment becoming a greater and greater issue (Stockman & Baker, 2020).

Moreover, what other healthcare professionals do in the use of the strike weapon is important. Nursing usually has little say about their practice and is beholden not only to physicians but also to the administrators of the organizations which employ them. Nursing lacks autonomy and power due to gender problems in the culture of many societies, and in most nations, nurses are considered the "handmaidens" to the higher status, much higher paid physician staff. Outside of the United States where the profession comes from generally middle-class families, nursing internationally (even in Europe) has working-class origins and not university prepared so not appearing to be a "profession" but, as Friedson has noted, a "semiprofession" (Friedson, 1980).

Yet, from a number of case studies, nursing militancy usually has resulted from the administrative milieu that provides the conditions of their labor. In their employed wage-contract status, nurses (perhaps also by gender) find solidarity that differs from that among physicians (Muysken, 1982). There is a tendency among certain nurse groups for union membership, and the job actions normally include clear concerns for patient care that are ethically justified by the striking nurses based upon poor quality resulting from heavy patient loads, overcrowding, poor working conditions, and lack of material and psychological support by managers in the respective organizations (Breda, 1997). Hibberd and Norris found that "to strike places nurses in the dilemma of having to choose between loyalty to patients in providing uninterrupted services, and loyalty to peers in collectively pursuing improvements in working conditions and socio-economic status. Although nurses caring for seriously ill patients may prefer not to strike, there are certain circumstances, including the fear of peer alienation, which might compel them to take strike action" (Hibberd & Norris, 1991). Historically, collective bargaining and strikes has begun to level the playing field between nurses and their stronger adversaries in the healthcare system hierarchy (Kravitz, Leake, & Zawacki, 1992). In juxtaposition, pharmacists subject to corporate chain drugstores and pharmacy benefit managements firms have been reluctant to organize; there are few strikes over wages and speedups and the conditions of pharmacy labor (Zgarrick, McHugh, & Droege, 2006).

So why would physicians ever consider collective bargaining and striking as a solution to what ails the profession? In the United States, corporate and governmental cost containment strategies; overall marketplace schemes in health care, coupled with increasing clinical scrutiny and administrative dominance imposed under privatization by the insurance industry, managed care firms, governments, and now the Accountable Care Organizations; are rattling physicians who seem bewildered by the administrative obfuscation amidst rapid change.

This discontent across various countries has led to the consideration of strikes, amidst carrying out other job actions in opposition to the private and public control exerted upon physician autonomy (Thompson & Salmon, 2014). Braverman (1974) described these conditions almost 40 years ago as a continuous change in the labor process such that the unity of conception and execution is dissolved.

While the formation of labor unions and the threat of strikes might be a natural response to this process of rationalization in the medical field, both issues arouse intense debate from inside the health professions, as well as with the public and policymakers. Nevertheless, as physicians increasingly experience their wage-contract employment within healthcare organizations, they realize that their work is becoming more highly controlled by nonphysician administrators detached from long-standing professional ethics. As Thompson and Salmon have previously pointed out, physicians are losing their status as independent practitioners and are finding themselves in a traditional employer-employee relationship which further reinforces the imposed production norms of health care (Thompson & Salmon, 2003).

The question then becomes how do physicians utilize a strike weapon within the collective bargaining relationship to improve patient care and working conditions? Given the exacerbation of labor strife across national health systems across the world, it is important to explore the issue of what constitutes an ethical physician strike as we observe the trajectory of the profession's discontent with the conditions of medical practice.

Second, theorists have posed descriptions of the forces of corporatization, proletarianization, and/or deprofessionalization of physicians (Salmon, 1990). These are not phenomena unique to the United States (Scarpaci, 1990); nevertheless, our for-profit delivery system (not-for-profit in name only) renders administrative control over escalating costs and dubious quality as an immediate imperative. Collective bargaining by physicians has arisen under many situations, but most efforts did not advance, or these instances were quelled in various ways (Thompson & Salmon, 2003). Of the over 900,000 American physicians dedicated to patient care, roughly 50,000 may belong to unions, and another 200,000 may be eligible to join unions due to their employment status. It is important to point out that there has to be a defined employer-employee role for a physician to join a union and have that union represent that physician as well as others vs. their employer. Nowadays, the growth of contract work by physicians, whether this be in hospitals, managed care organizations, or as junior partners in large group practices and/or academic faculty foundations, is becoming the dominant employment paradigm (Rama, 2019).

Physicians in labor organizations face an ethical dilemma over their wish to withdraw their labor in furtherance of their collective bargaining objectives. This ethical dilemma is directly in conflict with the state oath of providing for patient care to those in need. It is also highlighted in the American Medical Association (AMA) policy opinion E-9.025 on Collective Action and Patient Advocacy. This policy clearly states that "Whenever engaging in advocacy efforts, physicians must ensure that the health of patients is not jeopardized and that patient care is not compromised" (The Council on Ethical and Judicial Affairs of the American Medical Association, 2004). The report further states that "Physicians should refrain from the use of the strike as a bargaining tactic. In rare circumstances, individual or grassroots actions, such as brief limitations of personal availability, may be appropriate as a means of calling attention to needed changes in patient care. Physicians are cautioned that some actions may put them or their organizations at risk of violating antitrust laws" (The Council on Ethical and Judicial Affairs of the American Medical Association, 2004). But as 15 years have passed since this AMA edict, more and more physicians have been pulled into corporate employment and become just another cog in the healthcare machine.

However a prevalent physician strikes may become, can they be justified in light of the profession's oath to "do no harm?" Sixty-three percent of physicians indicated in 1979 that they were in favor or physicians organizing, though only 55% thought they should be allowed to strike and less a number (46%) said that they would participate in a strike if they all agreed with the issues that led to the strike (Wassertheil-Smoller, Croen, & Siegel, 1979). In 2003 under hotly debated ethical issues, most physicians accepted that if he/she were going to join a union, the union needed the strike weapon for success in the collective bargaining process (Thompson & Salmon, 2003). It would seem that given the current state of the practice, it might be reasonable to infer that those percentages listed above have not decreased over time and that militancy might be on the increase as a result of the issues previously described. A study that asked medical students in Israel gives a slightly different finding in that 97% believe that striking is a legitimate tool for physicians and 43% said the suffering of patients caused by the strike was totally or near totally justified (Lachter, Lachter, & Beiran, 2007). Su-Ting explores how professional attitudes are formed in training on the concept of strikes that "create an ethical tension between an obligation to care for current patients (e.g., to provide care and avoid abandonment) and obligation to better care for future patients by seeking system improvements (e.g., improvement in safety, to access, and in the composition and strength of the health care workforce)" (Su-Ting, Srinvasan, Der-Martirosian, Kravitz, & Wilkes, 2011).

The provocation of physician militancy to consider striking seems to be an attempt to halt the ever-increasing encroachment of management prerogatives over their medical practice. Dissatisfaction with immediate supervision, outrage over the extent of corporate profiteering, and other imposed performance standards to enhance profitability and remove or lessen autonomous practice are aggravating conditions to the medical profession today (Loewy, *Of Healthcare Professionals, Ethics and Strikes*, 2000). This militancy takes place within an extremely complex and often misunderstood set of policies that befuddle even the experts in the field who devote their lives to untangling these policy issues. For example, in the heavily unionized professional sector of public school teachers, militant attitudes occurred most often if they were dissatisfied with their supervisor and if they felt little control over their jobs (McClendon & Klaas, 1993). Studies examining reasons behind strikes by both physicians and other healthcare workers point out that the strikes occur over concerns for the practitioner's own welfare; secondly professionals may strike because of concerns for their patients. Couple these concerns with dissatisfaction over the current state of the practice of medicine and the loss of autonomy and control over the profession and their patients and the stage is set for increased militancy of physicians. As more and more physicians enter employer-employee positions, it becomes even more imperative for them to be the "champions" of their patients' interests, especially when confronted with corporate bottom line mandates to the point of risking their livelihoods when patients are put at risk from those mandates (Manthous, 2012).

But unlike school teachers who inconvenience students and their parents by going out on strike, it would seem the stakes for causing greater harm would occur if physicians and other healthcare practitioners went out on strike. Concern for patient welfare raises the question of whether the striking can be permissible under certain circumstances. This contradiction between professional self-interest and patients' welfare can vary depending upon the point of view. "When physicians within an organization are treated badly, it is clearly understood that this treatment might lead to substandard patient care. Strikes that bring about higher pay and better treatment of professionals might conceivably yield improved morale and thus better patient care" (Thompson & Salmon, 2014). Wolfe seems to support the notion that "if the rights and health of patients and the public are preserved, strikes can serve as an important catalyst in converting a rigid and conservative health system into a more flexible democratic organization for all its workers" (Wolfe, 1979). Most documented strikes by attending physicians were provided by economic concerns, yet mindful of public reaction; patient care concerns become touted as the reason for the job action. Nevertheless, the ethical issue over whether physicians should strike or not centers on doing harm to patients as a result. Our concern here is to examine professional job actions to distill their reasons and general outcomes: The United States and several examples internationally can bring these issues into better focus.

In the United States, it has consistently been deemed legal for physicians to strike, though the climate seems against eligibility of most physicians to collectively bargain because of restrictive interpretations of law by courts. In 1935, the Wagner Act (National Labor Relations Act) guaranteed most workers the right to unionize and bargain collectively, not excluding healthcare workers. Amended in 1947 by the Taft-Hartley Act, healthcare workers of non-profit hospitals were prohibited from forming unions and engaging in collective bargaining. By 1974 this exclusion was repealed, but a 10-day advanced written notice was required prior to any strike action (National Labor Relations Act, 2013).

Over the past 50 years, physicians' strikes have arisen most commonly over wages, hours, malpractice insurance issues, as well as health insurance administrative and financial controls. Each national health system operates within a different context, and these should be examined in order to understand the degree of self-interest versus concerns for patient welfare.

Strikes by physicians have been in evidence on the North American continent since 1962 when the Saskatchewan Medical Care Insurance Act became law. Badgley and Wolfe's Doctors' Strike diagnosed the Saskatchewan physician strike as a "medical profession, accustomed to not exercising its prerogatives without external constraint, [that] opposed legislation enacted by a government elected by its people." What started out as an intent to protect patient rights resulted in a contest of wills between physicians and the provincial government over implementation of a single-payer insurance model that became the basis of Canada's national health insurance program. Misjudging the mood of the public which favored the government and party in power was the downfall of this physician strike. The popularity of the provincial government and its Medicare program stood against the "lack of care" anecdotes, so the job action ended after a mere 23 days. It is instructive to recognize again the disunity among private practitioners and the difficulty in assessing where the public and patients end up in defining their professional interests (Badgley & Wolfe, 1967).

In 1966, approximately 1500 physicians, dentists, and optometrists in the Doctor's Association in New York City went on strike to protest wages (Keith, 1984). Four years later in 1970, specialists in Quebec walked out in protest of the public insurance program in a similar way to the doctors actions in Saskatchewan (Baer, 1997).

In 1974 the house staff officers at Howard University went on strike for 12 days primarily over excessive hours and poor working conditions and thus gained a salary increase following a 12-hour strike. Management provided improved laboratory facilities and nursing coverage and a better fringe benefit package for the house staff (paying for malpractice insurance coverage) (The New Physician, 1975). In 1975 the Council for Interns and Residents went on strike against 15 voluntary hospitals and 6 affiliated public hospitals in New York City for over 3 days. Their complaints included excessive hours and performing out of title work. Significant public support including the New York Press and the American Medical Association and the public came for the CIR when the hospitals refused binding arbitration (Harmon, 1978).

In Chicago in 1975, Cook County Hospital had 500 house officers walk out for 18 days leading to the longest physician strike in US history. Their concern was the quality of patient care and working conditions, and their demands centered on patient care improvements and decreased working hours. The union defied a temporary restraining order issued by the courts and the final settlement provided for oversight of patient care improvements, such as more IV teams, faster lab and x-ray request processing, reduction of house staff work week, and Spanish language interpreters. Subsequently a Cook Country judge put seven strike leaders in jail and fined the union $10,000 (Harmon, 1978).

In 1976 Los Angeles County saw physicians partly withdraw services over medical malpractice insurance; 75% of Los Angeles County's physicians went on strike for 35 days, beginning with just surgeons and anesthesiologists, but later joined by primary care physicians. Their objective was to pressure the state legislature for effective malpractice insurance reform. Most of the major issues remained unresolved, but some minor reform proposals occurred in the legislature. This incident is important to understand since the James study examined outcomes due to the withdrawal of services and found "no evidence of a significant impact on the general public in finding medical care" (James, 1979, p. 437).

Again in 1976, interns and residents in New York City conducted two strikes at two separate hospitals. Some 30 strikers were fired but eventually rehired, and the house staff was successful in obtaining a considerable increase in their salaries. They graciously turned 50% of that amount back into a patient care fund controlled by the house staff in order to buy equipment and hire essential healthcare staff (Harmon, 1978).

In 1980, physicians in Quebec protested government control of medicine by staging a 1-day strike. Specialists wanted to be able to opt out of the Canadian national health insurance scheme or to extra bill patients over and beyond the fee schedule. General practitioners did not support specialist demands, so the strike failed (Budrys, 1997).

In 1986 physicians in Ontario went on strike again over extra billing prohibition by the health ministry. This province had previously allowed them to opt out of the NHI plan and extra bill, but in 1984 this practice was ceased by the provincial health plan on direction of the federal government. The ban on extra billing was considered to be an impingement on their autonomy and on the doctor-patient relationship. Like the strike in Quebec, the Ontario physicians did not receive popular support, and the action failed. The public and the government did not want to compromise the Canadian right to health care even if physicians were not (on their terms) compensated adequately (Kravitz, Shapiro, Linn, & Froelicher, 1989).

In 1996 again in Canada, the 9-year-old practice of subsidizing physicians' malpractice insurance was ended in Ontario province. Obstetricians and orthopedic surgeons stopped taking new patients, and general surgeons and family practitioners later supported them. There was a short withdrawal of services, but the government backed down and partially restored the malpractice insurance subsidy (Baer, 1997).

In 2000, physicians in New Brunswick, Canada, went on strike for 3 days after bargaining to gain equity with other provinces' pay rates. The New Brunswick Province offered a lucrative increase, and the physicians returned to work reluctantly when the provincial offer was not increased as they asked (Walker, 2001).

In 2003, the United States saw several physician work stoppages over malpractice insurance premiums that were spiraling upward (Charatan, 2003). Jury awards in malpractice suits are usually blamed by physicians for increased premiums, yet trial lawyers correctly point to malpractice insurance companies raising premiums due to what are termed "hard markets" and falling investments in hard economic times, as most people realize these premiums for certain categories of physicians are extremely high and present an economic burden on practices (Baker, 2005). These work stoppages often included not holding office hours, protesting at state capitals, and not performing elective surgeries from time to time. Jones notes that these physicians usually do not garner public sympathy particularly in states where physician incomes greatly exceed local residents' incomes. Backlashes against physicians occur where there is resentment over highly paid professionals seeking to further their self-interest and not necessarily their patients' benefit. This would be a failure of the strategy in conducting a work stoppage but not necessarily a condemnation of the tactic itself Jones (2003).

Since the early 2000s, there has been little activity in the area of physician strikes in North America. One *Advocacy Blog* on the American College of Physicians website reaffirmed the ACPs code of ethics in that "strikes, boycotts, and other collective actions to deny care to patients or to inconvenience them are flat out unethical" (Doherty, 2012). Interestingly there has been recent activity overseas, but it appears that did not have its intended effect. The British Medical Association in the United Kingdom went on strike over pensions. While the strike did appear to have about a third of the population behind it, most physicians apparently were not. Most physicians did not stop seeing patients which negated the effect of holding a strike in the first place as no one appeared inconvenienced (Praities, *Low Turnout Blunts Protest*, 2012). Physicians went on strike in Estonia for 2 weeks over poor working conditions. The government had taken the offensive to publish physician salaries in an attempt to paint physicians as greedy and out of touch. The two sides eventually settled with a decrease in physicians' workload by 20% in outpatient clinics and 16% in inpatient settings. Minimum salaries also increased (Ermel, 2012).

In Korea, it was noted that striking by "hard to replace" physicians did have the ability to alter the trajectory of certain health reforms related to financing, pharmaceuticals, and provider payments. All of these attempted changes threatened physicians' livelihood, and while they were unable to completely block all of the reforms, they were able to place themselves as an interest to be considered in future policy changes (Kwon & Reich, 2005).

In Ireland, doctors went on strike for 1 day, which resulted in the cancellation of 15,000 hospital appointments, but covered emergencies (Quinn, 2013). The strike was caused by austerity measures implemented by the European Union in response to the global economic crisis and involved a dispute over long working hours (100 hours per week), which violated EU employment laws and more importantly put patients' lives at risk.

In sum, the above details of physician protests, job actions, and strikes indicate a common theme that is a fundamental discontent with the conditions over medical practice in both the United States and Canada, as well as overseas. Actions are taken as a result of the loss of physician welfare and autonomy *against both government and corporate constraints* as the impositions brought on by administrators.

As highlighted in Chap. 4 on malpractice insurance concerns, malpractice liability continues to be a significant concern for medical professionals. As described in that chapter, insurance carriers rebuild profit margins that lessen when their underperforming investments pass through tough economic times (Baker, 2005). The bulk of malpractice suits by patients is usually found to be attributable to a small group of physicians, and state medical boards seem to lack the ability for more effective disciplining of so-called bad doctors by the profession itself (Levine, Oshel, & Wolfe, 2011). But one medical ethicist believes that striking over malpractice insurance rates cannot be justified primarily because of the perceived harm that would come to patients (Fiester, 2004).

It is important to recognize that across the globe, the health professions have various roles and relationships and different characteristics from what we see in the United States. The discontent that propels the situational factors in unionization that lead to job actions must be differentiated across national health systems, just as where corporate for-profit health care in the United States used to be differentiated from what we see in the "not-for-profit" sphere. Younger professionals struggling over what they deem to be inadequate remuneration, fewer hours and workloads of exploitation of their labor, and deleterious and declining working conditions that impinge on quality are important to consider. In most nations, disparities in physician ranks are significant, not just by specialty but also by age.

Essential to the investigation of the physician strike phenomena is the patient and population impacts. In short, what have been the effects of physician strikes on patient morbidity and mortality? Few studies examine the morbidity and mortality rates and how they changed pre- and post-strike, that being the 1976 Los Angeles County physician strike. James examined the period where elective surgery was abandoned with only emergency surgery continuing. He found that 55 to 154 deaths did *not* occur when elective surgery was postponed due to the strike.

This study ponders the question that physician strikes are inherently harmful to the population, and, if so, should they be avoided by all means? (James, 1979). Health workers have carried out short strikes in Kenya in both 2010 and 2016, and there were no discernable effects on overall mortality in the area covered by these workers (Ong'ayo et al., 2019). A junior doctor strike elicited similar results in that there was no appreciable increase in mortality during the strike, but they did find that the strike caused significant reduction in the provision of health care with 9% fewer admissions, 7% reduction in accident and emergency visits, and a 6% reduction in outpatient visits (Furnivall, Bottle, & Aylin, 2018). Naturally there are always anecdotal reports of a strike leading to increased mortality, and in one case where a strike was blamed for a patient's death, it merited a brief report in *The Lancet* (Chapman, *Doctors' Strike Blamed For Patient's Death in Germany*, 2006). Cunningham, Mitchell, Venkat Narayan, and Yusuf (2008) describe this as a paradoxical pattern in that when health workers strike, the mortality level either stays level or decreases. While it's difficult to know for sure if the strike was the cause, publicity such as this cannot help physicians make their case for striking for a future of better and safer health care.

In contrast an Israeli physician strike in 1983 led to greater involuntary admissions to psychiatric services since community interventions on behalf of striking doctors lessened during the strike. Increased hospitalizations resulted when community resources were diminished. No data on mortality was collected (Scholsber, Zielber, & Avraham, 1989). Thus, the lack of decent health services research that may be advisable to be in place when medical professionals consider job actions would be a worthwhile policy consideration.

In the United States, the general public and many health professionals have noted that marketplace medicine as health policy has created conditions that are majorly behind the rising professional discontent. It should be noted that both the Clinton and Obama health reforms relied upon corporate and entrepreneurial entities to seek profit opportunities in health care as a way of bringing about "reform." Historically we have witnessed the neglect of the uninsured and the underinsured populations who do not yield sufficient returns on investments for profit-maximizing providers. Austerity measures taken by state governments in response to lower tax receipts and less support from the federal government create constraints upon reimbursement levels, growing patient "out-of-pocket" payments, and public sector provider cuts, with consumers suffering as a result. It is not clear that the mandated health insurance exchanges in states under Obamacare, along with the formation of Accountable Care Organizations that are supposed to contain costs and improve quality, are going to be able to solve the worsening practice situations that many healthcare professionals in the United States confront.

Privatization schemes have been promulgated across the globe in many national healthcare systems, mainly led by American ideology that marketplace medicine is more "efficient" and can find solutions better than the historical public sector medicine that serve many countries. Exporting the US system with its high-cost inflation, administrative dominance, and concentration of high-tech tertiary care (including costly supplies, equipment, information technology, and pharmaceuticals purchased by US and European firms) is not necessarily the best solution for the world's citizens (Salmon, 1990). Increasing problems with access in these international settings and again growing administrative overhead and diminished funding of traditional public health services are not likely to yield improved population health in these respective nations. Marketplace reforms in essence have redirected health care from its social purpose away from improving overall population health and well-being and toward maximizing profits and increasing market share, under the guise of cost and quality improvement.

Ethical Issues Across the Future

Begun in the late 1960s, the increasing corporatization of medicine has changed the character of medical practice in profound ways. This transformation of the delivery systems of care altered working conditions, not only adversely affecting doctors' job satisfaction in these enlarging corporate entities but, in effect, profoundly eroding past physician prerogatives (McKinlay & Stoeckle, 1988). With Obamacare's continuance of the bureaucratization of health care with health insurance exchanges, Accountable Care Organizations, and the strength and role of both the centers for Medicare and Medicaid and large commercial insurance companies, physicians may find unionization as a way to fight back against what they perceive as the harmful alteration of the practice of medicine, with the ongoing transformation of the delivery system. The purpose of any strike actions would be to create discomfort to employers who are eroding professional autonomy and prerogatives. The obvious impact on employer organizations through strikes will be reduced revenues and less profit. What remains unclear is how will patient morbidity and mortality be affected.

The profession's ethical foundation in the Oath of Hippocrates fundamentally represents the core of the profession's ethics. With the edict to do no harm, it gives rise to question whether unionization and strike actions may benefit patients in certain ways. Much discussion over ethics in medicine these days leads to polarized opinions. It can be generally stated that a number of recent activities involving physicians have been embarrassments (participating in torture, executions, certain clinical trials, promotion of pharmaceuticals after huge kickbacks, etc.). Linn highlights this moral dilemma of opposing positions with a quote from a physician (in Israel) who stated, "We are very strong when we talk about the patients, but when we face them alone, we just do the work. The government knows this is our weak point and all the years it took advantage of our conscience" (Linn, 1987).

Stepping back to view the issue of unions and strikes requires broader analysis concerning the long-term benefits to populations' health and whether they may outweigh short-term losses to present patient populations. In other words, is a short-term disruption in care necessary to countervail corporate power in a for-profit healthcare system? The mere threat of a strike can be a potent weapon as Badgley and Wolfe (1965) surmised in their study of the Saskatchewan physician strike of 1962. They noted that unless the public is fully behind professionals, and their case is clearly portrayed as improving patient care, utilization of the strike may inevitably backfire and cause more harm than good. Thomasma and Hurley suggest criteria for the conduct of ethical strikes: provide a1 0-day notice under the National Labor Relations Act, and demonstrate this to the larger public; maintain that improving patient care is the primary motive for the strike action; report that all other avenues have been exhausted; provide that emergency patient conditions will be cared for and not abandoned; assure that all current patients hospitalized will be cared for and also not abandoned; and relay that the terms for ending the strike will be subject to public scrutiny and further discussion (Thomasma & Hurley, 1988). It should be remembered that never was there a policy debate over whether the American people (or physicians) wanted a profit-based delivery system, nor whether such a corporate-controlled system was the best way to organize finance and delivery of health care to the American people.

The American Medical Association supports collective bargaining but opposes striking for any reason. They continue to defend the private practice of medicine which has fragmented its members and been found to be unresponsive of the new realities in health care and in particular medicine. Many physicians who work for organizations increasingly on a wage-contract basis are not as involved in AMA membership and politics. Up until AFSCME and SEIU began organizing physicians, the AMA opposed unionization; now it supports the Physicians for Responsible Negotiation, an unaffiliated organization that opposes striking for any reason; members of this union do not have leverage to support their positions through the collective bargaining process, and the AMA has since ceased support of this entity.

In contrast to the AMA, the British Medical Association (BMA) does support striking and has the force behind it with its right to strike and ability to do so to win demands from the British National Health Service. This has been exercised when government policy has changed conditions for maintaining the quantity and quality of health care in that nation, although recent history suggests a significant physician apathy toward the use of the strike weapon (Praities, 2012). Ultimately, it is the public who uses health care that determines the success or failure of any job action including a strike. Any strike action should be carefully considered to include gauging the level of public support for such an action. Without it, any strike is doomed to failure.

Conclusion

While few policymakers and observers predict that physician unions will be the wave of the future, nevertheless it is imperative that physicians consider the option of organizing that may help them regain their ability to speak for their patients and their quality of care within corporate structures that have different priorities. And while it becomes obvious to some observers that physicians will be rendered powerless to defend their professional values in the face of the corporate onslaught, no wave of unionization has ever materialized in response.

While physicians in the United States remain distrustful of government interference in their affairs, they did not appear to notice the encroachment of the corporate sector which was doing much more to undermine their professional well-being. Physicians still rant against payments they receive from Medicare and Medicaid, but a substantial number have now noticed that commercial insurance companies have followed Medicare's lead in delaying and reducing reimbursements; several insurers have higher denial of care and prior authorization, which makes it difficult for maintaining their standard of living. Organized medicine's resistance against Medicare-for-All proposals is a case in point. A majority of physicians do favor a single payer, Medicare-for-All system; the AMA continues to oppose a more simplified reimbursement system that would eliminate many reimbursement issues they face (Scott, 2019). Even if they could back a single-payer system in the United States, it will not, however, resolve their organizational woes as employees within healthcare organizations as more and more pressure would be put upon them to increase efficiency and decrease costs at the expense of patient care. Corporate domination in the US healthcare system may actually go for the increasing funding with little regulatory restraints as with Obamacare.

Collective bargaining could help in making sure their voice is heard. Perceived abuses of medical malpractice insurance companies, health maintenance organizations, preferred provider organizations, pharmacy benefit managers, and other corporate employers are additional encroachments on professional autonomy and heighten physician's dissatisfaction with the practice of medicine. As the quest for cost control and quality utilization monitoring under Obamacare and whenever

Trumpcare moves forward, it is likely that discontent will rise even further. All payers are poised to reduce professional fees, demand care justifications, withhold payments, and apply punitive actions if clinical standards that *they set* are not met by practicing physicians. Attempts to "bend" the healthcare cost curve will most likely be borne by providers and in particular physicians and patients, some of which may actually be quality improvements (reduction of never events, low value procedures, churning, and other excess utilization). This is the prescribed direction of the federal government, by most state governments and by corporate employers who are trying to wrangle a much reduced outlay for benefits as health reform progresses.

Besides the bureaucratic interference with professional decision-making, it is noteworthy to look at physician practice patterns and physician salaries. Policymakers talk about rewarding high-quality primary care since newly enrolled patients under federal, state, and private health insurances need to be served. Attracting medical school graduates away from the high-earning specialties to primary care will be achieved if incomes in primary care medicine can be enhanced, as there remain significant discrepancies between specialty salaries and those in family medicine, internal medicine, psychiatry, and pediatrics. Substitution is happening now for nurse practitioners, physician assistants, and other health practitioners in retail and community practices.

What is the response of the medical profession which is besieged by the turmoil of all of this change coming down upon them to their professional lives and lifestyles? Will physicians resort to unionization for collective bargaining and the use of a strike to fight back against the array of corporate and government changes involved in the corporate transformation of the American healthcare system? Employment trends for physicians point toward less private practice and more opportunities housed within organizations, such as faculty foundations within an academic medical center. The future is quite uncertain as much of this shakes out in this mixtures of Obama health reform and the dynamics of marketplace medicine. Whither goes the profession and how attune it is to public sentiment will be key. If the American public shares the same dissatisfactions with the corporate healthcare system, their access, quality, cost, and accountability issues, it is likely that physicians might gain sufficient power. Will they then look to fight back with that unity of patients and population groups behind them? Ultimately, the use of collective bargaining and the strike tool is really a choice between potential harm to patient clienteles in the immediate term and longer-term improvement in patient care quality over the future. When this trade-off becomes acceptable to physicians, striking becomes a possible tool to use in supporting one's interest in collective bargaining and changing the nature of the US profit-based delivery system.

Most practicing physicians are too busy with patient care, and, generally speaking, many are disgruntled since they are relatively unschooled in policy analysis and trends in medical care organization. The latter macro-analysis is normally difficult to achieve when one's education and life in practice keeps one oriented to the micro-level, one patient at a time. Most doctors missed the changing auspice of corporate involvement in health policy planning and the actual delivery of services. This lack of clarity into what has been happening, how it came to be, and what are the implications of the corporate transformation delimits the individual doctors' range of actions. It also makes it precarious as to where factions of the overall profession may lead.

Will strategies to oppose overall conditions lead more physicians to consider collective bargaining and the use of strikes to protect their interests? As more and more physicians become employees within organizations, their status and ability to collectively bargain may become clearer. This leads to the more difficult decision on whether to unionize (if possible) and whether or not to threaten the strike weapon to further their collective bargaining goals. As this literature review reveals, there has been ample discussion of the surrounding issues for physicians to delve into the debate and choose directions that they as individual practitioners and the profession may consider.

Glick states that "health workers, and particularly physicians, are in a special class because they deal with human lives and because, upon joining the profession or accepting their job, they have *voluntarily* [emphasis added] undertaken a commitment to those they serve" (Glick, 1986). Fiester (2004) supports this rather dated stand, stating that "Because physician strikes intend to harm to patients, challenge the obligations of the physician to her patient, and risk decreasing the public's esteem for the profession." Perhaps the issue of protection of patient care in the face of corporate fealty to the bottom line is a case in point of why these two views should be considered quaint relics of the past.

Effectiveness of strikes is often determined by disruption to another party. Either the healthcare organization or its patients would be the disrupted party in a physician strike. It's important that the disruption to the organization is maximized while minimizing the disruption to the patients themselves as long as provisions are made to take care of patient emergencies (Metcalfe, Chowdhury, & Salim, 2015). One of the issues that commonly comes up in relation to the role of strikes for physicians is that patients will die if physicians walk off the job. Several studies have proven that not to be the case. They concluded that strikes may reduce mortality in several ways, including a reduction in elective surgeries and the reassignment of available resources to emergency care, and the strikes themselves didn't last long enough to get a good read on whether or not this effect could be maintained over a longer period of time. In the United Kingdom, junior doctors went on strike in 2016 that was about the deeper dissatisfactions among professionals who feel "devalued and denigrated" (Penfield, 2018).

Physician strikes over demands for extra billing or reimbursement issues have *not* been successful because it is much more difficult to argue that the public's health may be improved with higher doctor pay and the moral trade-off of little or no care for improved care later doesn't seem to persuade the public of the righteousness of the action (Breslin, 1987). As Mechanic points out, "Doctors remain highly privileged professionals in our society, however, and they have much to lose by using the strike weapon capriciously and in a way that alienates the public. The large support and respect that patients give to their doctors—despite some erosion in recent years—is still one of the major assets physicians hold" (Mechanic, 1989). To be more specific, patients tend to highly regard their personal physicians, but respect for the general profession has waned over time.

The notion of one ethical value (improvement of patient care) taking precedence over another (provide care no matter what) is at the heart of a decision to strike. The object is to improve the first without seriously compromising the second (Smith, 1980). This notion was used to justify a physician strike in Israel in 1983 (Grosskopf, Buckman, & Garty, 1985). Over 30 years ago, Wolinsky stated that he believed that the loss of professional dominance in medicine "will accrue from the benign neglect of maintain the public's imputation of medicine's original avowed promise" (Wolinsky, 1988). To the extent that he was correct that lost professionalism did occur, his take on their regaining self-regulation among physicians by a "return to stewardship and their role as fiduciary agency" to successfully combat intervention by the federal government seemed to understate the role of private insurance as well as healthcare organizations as employers of physicians. It also doesn't recognize current reality of the administrative superstructure in health care provided by MBA-trained leaders.

Some useful guidance on how professionals can strike in the face of what might be termed a hostile environment for labor is the recent spate of teacher strikes, particularly in states that there is no collective bargaining for public employees. Even more important after the Janus decision, which limited public sector unions' ability to collect fair share fees, the issue of union survival becomes paramount so that they can effectively represent their members' interests at the bargaining table and the political arena. Teachers have been faced with decline in classroom conditions, pay and working conditions, as well as outright attacks on public education by anti-union advocates. In October of 2019, Chicago teachers went on strike not so much over issues of pay, but rather to put in contract language that specifies the hiring and staffing levels of counselors, health aids, and librarians (Goldstein, 2019). In Los Angeles teachers went on strike because they realized that without the inconvenience and disruption caused by a strike, change would never occur (Wong, 2019). As Wong points out, there appears to be increasing support for labor unions and strikes to get them higher pay as well as funding increases for schools (Wong, 2019). Further job actions in Oklahoma and West Virginia (nonunion strongholds) have proven effective in getting concessions in terms of wages and conditions of employment improved. These "general" strikes were quite effective in highlighting how bad things were in the schools of those states.

It was noted by Gallup in 2019 that 64% of Americans approve of labor unions, which is the highest approval rating since 1999, up 16% from this nadir in 2009 (Jones, 2019). Perhaps the teachers and nurses can lead the way on the use of collective bargaining and striking to help physicians understand that major disruption may be necessary to regain professional power. This is a necessity for physicians to gain the ability to sufficiently advocate for their patients and the quality of care they and their healthcare organizations provide.

References

Albers, J. (2010, July 13). Minnesota nurses strike advances debate on hospital safety, quality fundamental health care system change needed. *Twin Cities Daily Planet*.

Aronowitz, S. (1998). *From the ashes of the old - American labor and America's future*. Boston, MA: Houghton-Mifflin.

Badgley, R. F., & Wolfe, S. M. (1965). Medical care and conflict in Saskatchewan. *Milbank Memorial Fund Quarterly, 43*, 463–479.

Badgley, R. F., & Wolfe, S. M. (1967). *Doctors' strike - medical care and conflict in Saskatchewan*. Toronto, ON: Macmillan of Canada.

Baer, N. (1997). Despite some PR fallout, proponents say MD walkouts increase awareness and may improve health care. *Canadian Medical Association Journal, 157*, 1268–1271.

Baker, T. (2005). *Medical malpractice myth*. Chicago, IL: University Of Chicago Press.

Barbash, J. (1984). *The elements of industrial relations*. Madison, WI: University of Wisconsin Press.

Berenson, R. A. (1991). A physician's view of managed care. *Health Affairs, 10*, 106–119.

Bivens, J., Engdahl, L., Gould, E., Kroeger, T., McNicholas, C., Mishel, L., . . . Zipperer, B. (2017, August 24). *How today's unions help working people*. Retrieved from Economic Policy Institute. https://www.epi.org/publication/how-todays-unions-help-working-people-giving-workers-the-power-to-improve-their-jobs-and-unrig-the-economy/

Black, S. E. (2012). Economic credentialing of physicians by insurance companies and headache medicine. *Headache, 52*, 1073–1040.

Braverman, H. (1974). *Labor and monopoly capital*. New York, NY: Monthly Review Press.

Breda, K. L. (1997). Professional nurses in unions: Working together pays off. *Journal of Professional Nursing, 13*, 99–109.

Brenner, M. (2011, June 24). *California strike highlights hospital's skewed priorities*. Retrieved from Labor Notes. http://labornotes.org/2011/06/california-strike-highlights-hospitals-skewed-priorities

Breslin, E. M. (1987, August). The moral costs of the Ontario physicians' strike. *Hastings Center Report*, 11–14.

Breunig, E. (2015, May 1). Even conservative millennials support unions. *The New Republic*. Retrieved from https://newrepublic.com/article/121688/pew-releases-new-labor-survey-millennials-supports-unions

Brewbaker, W. S., III. (2000). Physician unions and the future of competition in the health care sector. *UC Davis Law Journal, 33*, 545–600.

Brunton, M., & Sayers, J. G. (2011). Jostling for the ethical high ground during a junior doctors' strike. *Australian Journal of Communication, 38*, 69–87.

Bucknor, C. (2016, August). *Black workers, unions, and inequality*. Retrieved from Center for Economic and Policy Research. http://cepr.net/images/stories/reports/black-workers-unions-2016-08.pdf?v=2

Budrys, G. (1997). *When doctors join unions*. Ithaca, NY: Cornell University Press.

Bureau of Labor Statistics. (2020, January 22). *Union members - 2019*. Retrieved from Bureau of Labor Statistics. https://www.bls.gov/news.release/union2.nr0.htm

Bureau of Labor Statistics. (2020). Annual work stoppages involving 1,000 or more workers, 1947 – 2019. Available at: https://www.bls.gov/web/wkstp/annual-listing.htm. Accessed on December 2, 2020.

Bureau of Labor Statistics, United States Department of Labor. (2019, July 29). *Annual work stoppages involving 1,000 or more workers, 1947–2018*. Retrieved from Bureau of Labor Statistics. https://www.bls.gov/web/wkstp/annual-listing.htm

Carr-Saunders, A. M., & Wilson, P. A. (1933). *The Professions*. Oxford, UK: Clarendon Press.

Castellucci, M. (2019, September 28). Low unemployment emboldening healthcare workers to strike. *Modern Healthcare*. Retrieved from https://www.modernhealthcare.com/labor/low-unemployment-emboldening-healthcare-workers-strike?utm_source=modern-healthcare-am&utm_medi%E2%80%A6.

Chapman, C. (2006). Doctors' strike blamed for patient's death in Germany. *The Lancet, 368*(9531), 189.

Charatan, F. (2003). U.S. medical liability crisis spurs doctors' walkouts and rallies. *British Medical Journal, 326*, 126.

Chima, S. C. (2013). Global medicine: Is it ethical or morally justifiable for doctors and other healthcare workers to go on strike? *BMC Medical Ethics, 14*, S5–S15.

Cunningham, S. A., Mitchell, K., Venkat Narayan, K. M., & Yusuf, S. (2008). Doctors' strike and mortality: A review. *Social Science & Medicine, 67*, 1784–1788.

Dallet, B. (1994). Economic credentialing: Your money or your life! *Health Matrix: Journal of Law-Medicine, 4*, 325–363.

Dampier, C. (2019, October 25). Chicago's striking teachers helped spark a new wave of teacher activists. Here's why teacher activism is on the rise. *Chicago Tribune*.

DeManuelle-Hall, J., DiMaggio, D. (2019). 2019 Year in Review: Workers Strike Back. Available at: https://www.labornotes.org/2019/12/2019-year-review-workers-strike-back. Accessed on December 2, 2020.

DiSalvo, D. (2019, February 14). *Public-sector unions after Janus: An update.* Retrieved from Manhattan Institute. https://www.manhattan-institute.org/public-sector-unions-after-janus

Dobkin, J. (1975). Housestaff strike - immoral or inevitable? *New York State Journal of Medicine, 75*(10), 1785–1786.

Doherty, B. (2012, January 6). *The ACP advocate blog.* Retrieved from American College of Physicians. http://advocacyblog.acponline.org/2012/01/physician-strikes-cant-be-justified-to.html

Dulles, F. (1966). *Labor in America - A history.* New York, NY: Thomas Y. Crowell.

Ermel, R. (2012, October 16). Estonian physician on strike. *World Medical Journal*, pp. 200–201.

Fiester, A. (2004). Physicians and strikes: Can a walkout over the malpractice crisis be ethically justified? *The American Journal of Bioethics, 4*, W12–W16.

Freeman, R. B. (1979). *Labor economics.* Englewood Cliffs, NJ: Prentice-Hall.

Freeman, R. B., & Medoff, J. L. (1984). *What do unions do?* New York City, NY: Basic Books.

Friedson, E. (1980). Patterns of practice in the hospital. In A. Etzioni & E. W. Lehman (Eds.), *A sociological reader on complex organizations.* New York, NY: Hold, Rinheart and Winston.

Furnivall, D., Bottle, A., & Aylin, P. (2018, February 8). *Retrospective analysis of the national impact of industrial action by english junior doctors in 2016.* Retrieved from BMJ Open. https://bmjopen.bmj.com/content/bmjopen/8/1/e019319.full.pdf

Glick, S. M. (1986). Health workers' strikes: A further rejoinder. *Journal of Medical Ethics, 12*, 43–44.

Goldstein, D. (2019, October 25). It's more than pay: Striking teachers demand counselors and nurses. *New York Times*, p. A12.

Gooch, K. (2016, September 6). *8 Latest developments on Allina health's dispute with nurses.* Retrieved from Becker's Hospital Review. http://www.beckershospitalreview.com/human-cap-ital-and-risk/8-latest-developments-on-the-allina-health-nurse-dispute.html

Gorman, G., & Westing, C. (2013). Nursing, unionization, and caste: The lessons of local 6456. *Advances in Nursing Science, 36*, 258–264.

Greenwood, E. (1957). Attributes of a profession. *Social Work, 2*, 44–55.

Grosskopf, I., Buckman, G., & Garty, M. (1985). Ethical dilemmas of the doctors' strike in Israel. *Journal of Medical Ethics, 11*, 70–71.

Guwande, A. (2018, November 5). *Why doctors hate their computers.* Retrieved from The New Yorker. https://www.newyorker.com/magazine/2018/11/12/why-doctors-hate-their-computers

Hadley, J., & Mitchell, J. M. (1997). Effects of HMO market penetration on physicians' work effort and satisfaction. *Health Affairs, 16*, 99–111.

Hagedorn, J., Paras, C. A., Greenwich, H., & Hagopian, A. (2016). The role of labor unions in creating working conditions that promote public health. *American Journal of Public Health, 106*, 989–995.

Harmon, RG. (1978). Intern and resident organizations in the United States: 1937–1977. Milbank Memorial Fund Quarterly, 500–30.

Hibberd, J. M., & Norris, J. (1991). Strikes by nurses: Perceptions of colleagues coping with fall-out. *The Canadian Journal of Nursing Research, 23*, 43–54.

Hirschman, A. O. (1970). *Exit, voice and loyalty - Response to decline in firms, organizations, and states*. Cambridge, MA: Harvard University Press.

Ho, C. (2019, April 11). *Nurses authorize strike at Stanford, Lucile Packard Children's Hospital*. Retrieved from San Francisco Chronicle. https://www.sfchronicle.com/business/article/Nurses-authorize-strike-at-Stanford-Lucile-13760829.php?psid=frG5a

James, J. J. (1979). Impacts of the medical malpractice slowdown in Los Angeles County: January 1976. *American Journal of Public Health, 69*, 437–334.

Janus v. American Federation of State, County and Municipal Employees, 16–1466 (US Supreme Court June 27, 2018).

Johnson, L. A. (2019, April 27). *CSO strike is over as trustees and musicians approve new five-year contract*. Retrieved from Chicago Classical Review. https://chicagoclassicalreview.com/2019/04/trustees-approve-new-five-year-contract-cso-strike-is-over/

Jones, J. M. (2019, August 28). *As labor day turns 125, union approval near 50-year high*. Retrieved from Gallup. https://news.gallup.com/poll/265916/labor-day-turns-125-union-approval-near-year-high.aspx

Jones, T. (2003, January 4). Surgeons' strike over insurance splits W. Va. *Chicago Tribune*.

Keith, S. N. (1984). Collective bargaining and strikes among physicians. *Journal of the National Medical Association, 76*, 1117–1121.

Krause, E. A. (1996). *Death of the guilds: Professions, states, and the advance of capitalism, 1930 to present*. New Haven, CT: Yale University Press.

Kravitz, R. L., Leake, B., & Zawacki, B. E. (1992). Nurses' views of a public hospital nurses' strike. *Western Journal of Nursing Research, 14*, 645–661.

Kravitz, R., Shapiro, M. F., Linn, L. S., & Froelicher, E. S. (1989). Risk factors associated with participation in the Ontario, Canada doctors' strike. *American Journal of Public Health, 79*, 1227–1233.

Kwon, S., & Reich, M. R. (2005). The changing process and politics of health policy in Korea. *Journal of Health Politics, 30*, 1003–1025.

Lachter, J., Lachter, L., & Beiran, I. (2007). Attitudes of medical students to a physicians' strike. *Medical Teacher, 29*, 411.

Levine, A., Oshel, R., & Wolfe, S. (2011). *State medical boards fail to discipline doctors with hospital actions against them*. Washington, D.C.: Public Citizen. Retrieved from http://www.citizen.org/documents/1937.pdf

Linn, R. (1987). Moral reasoning and behavior of striking physicians in Israel. *Psychological Reports, 60*, 443–453.

Loewy, E. H. (2000). Of healthcare professionals, ethics and strikes. *Cambridge Quarterly of Healthcare Ethics, 9*, 513–520.

Magali, L. (1977). *The rise of professionalism*. Berkeley & Los Angeles, CA: University of California Press.

Malinowski, B., Minkler, M., & Stock, L. (2015). Labor unions: A public health institution. *American Journal of Public Health, 105*, 261–271.

Manthous, C. A. (2012). Hippocrates as hospital employee: Balancing beneficence and contractual duty. *American Journal of Critical Care, 21*, 60–66.

McClendon, J. A., & Klaas, B. (1993). An analysis of a university faculty strike. *Industrial and Labor Relations Review, 46*, 560–573.

McGeehan, P. (2019, April 10). New York hospitals reach a landmark deal on nurse staffing. *New York Times*, p. A25.

McKinlay, J. B., & Stoeckle, J. D. (1988). Corporatization and the social transformation of doctoring. *International Journal of Health Services, 18*, 191–205.

Mechanic, D. (1989). Doctor strikes and other signs of discontent. *American Journal of Public Health, 79*, 1218–1219.

Metcalfe, D., Chowdhury, R., & Salim, A. (2015, November 25). *What are the consequences when doctors strike?* Retrieved from BMJ. https://www.bmj.com/content/351/bmj.h6231

Miller, P. (2010, October 23). *Health reform and the decline of physician private practice.* Retrieved from The Physicians Foundation. https://physiciansfoundation.org/research-insights/health-reform-and-the-decline-of-physician-private-practice-2010/

Mondore, S., & Tivisonmo, J. G. (2015, July 9). *The new costs of unionization in healthcare union elections and representation: Lower HCAHPS scores and increase readmission rates.* Retrieved from IRI Analytics. http://www.fha.org/files/education/acrobat/2015Feb_LaborTrends_WhitePaper.pdf

Muysken, J. (1982). Collective responsibility and the strike weapon. *The Journal of Medicine and Philosophy, 7,* 101–112.

National Labor Relations Act. (2013, June 12). Retrieved from National Labor Relations Board. http://www.nlrb.gov/national-labor-relations-act

Olson, J. (2016, June 26). *Twin cities nurses' strike is over; Dispute with Allina is not.* Retrieved from Minneapolis Star-Tribune. http://www.startribune.com/twin-cities-nurses-strike-is-over-but-not-their-dispute-with-allina/384401821/

Ong'ayo, G., Wang'ondu, R., Bottomley, C., Nyaguara, A., Tsofa, B. K., Williams, T. N., . . . Etyang, A. O. (2019, May 22). *Effect of strikes by health workers on mortality between 2010 and 2016 in Kilifi, Kenya: A population-based cohort analysis.* Retrieved from The Lancet Global Health. https://www.thelancet.com/journals/langlo/article/PIIS2214-109X(19)30188-3/fulltext

Page, L. (2016, August 17). *Would unions really help doctors get what they want?* Retrieved from Medscape.com. https://www.medscape.com/viewarticle/866869

Penfield, R. (2018). Why junior doctors need more autonomy. *British Medical Journal, 363,* k4525.

Piascik, A. (2019, April 22). *Grocery store workers take on billion dollar multinational.* Retrieved from Counterpunch. https://www.counterpunch.org/2019/04/22/grocery-store-workers-take-on-billion-dollar-multinational/

Praities, N. (2012, June 27). Low turnout blunts protest. *Pulsetoday.co.uk,* p. 9.

Quinn, E. (2013, October 8). *Irish doctors strike to protest work hours amid austerity.* Retrieved from Wall Street Journal. https://www.wsj.com/articles/no-headline-available-1381217911?tesla=y

Rama, A. (2019). *Physician practice benchmark survey.* Chicago, IL: American Medical Association. Retrieved from https://www.ama-assn.org/system/files/2019-09/prp-care-delivery-payment-models-2018.pdf

Rayback, J. G. (1966). *A history of American labor.* New York, NY: The Free Press.

Reich, H. (2019, March 11). *CSO musicians picket in front of Orchestra Hall after announcing strike.* Retrieved from Chicago Tribune. https://www.chicagotribune.com/entertainment/music/howard-reich/ct-ent-cso-musicians-union-0311-story.html#nws=true

Rho, H. J., & Brown, H. (2019, March 6). *Union Membership Byte 2019.* Retrieved from Center for Economic and Policy Research. http://cepr.net/data-bytes/union-membership-bytes/union-byte-2019-01

Rhodes, D. (2019, May 28). *'Because we know strikes work': College unions leverage publicity in touch contract battles.* Retrieved from Chicago Tribune. https://www.chicagotribune.com/news/breaking/ct-met-college-university-labor-unions-strikes-20190523-story.html

Rosenfeld, J., Denice, P., & Laird, J. (2016, August 30). *Union decline lowers wages of nonunion workers.* Retrieved from Economic Policy Institute. https://www.epi.org/publication/union-decline-lowers-wages-of-nonunion-workers-the-overlooked-reason-why-wages-are-stuck-and-inequality-is-growing/

Rosenthal, E. (2014, February 13). Apprehensive, many doctors shift to jobs with salaries. Retrieved from New York Times. http://www.nytimes.com/2014/02/14/us/salaried-doctors-may-not-lead-to-cheaper-health-care.html?emc=eta1&_r=0

Salmon, J. W. (1990). *"The corporate transformation of health care" Part I, issues and directions.* Amityville, NY: Baywood.

Scarpaci, J. L. (1990). Physician proletarianization and medical care restructuring in Argentina and Uruguay. *Economic Geography, 66,* 362–277.

Scheffler, R. M. (1999). Physician collective bargaining: A turning point in U.S. medicine. *Journal of Health Politics, Policy and Law, 24*, 1071–1076.

Scheiber, N. (2016, January 9). Doctors unionize to resist the medical machine. *New York Times*, p. BU 1.

Schencker, L. (2019, September 20). Hospital strike: 2,200 University of Chicago Medical Center nurses walk off the job. *Chicago Tribune*. Retrieved from https://www.chicagotribune.com/business/ct-biz-university-of-chicago-hospital-nurse-strike-20190920-7ddk2jacgbgsxea47k-qwp6delu-story.html

Schmitt, J. (2009, April). *Unions and upward mobility for service-sector workers*. Retrieved from Center for Economic and Policy Research. http://cepr.net/documents/publications/unions-service-2009-04.pdf

Scholsber, A., Zielber, N., & Avraham, F. (1989). Effects of a psychiatrists strike on emergency psychiatric referral and admissions. *Social Psychology and Psychiatric Epidemiology, 24*, 84–87.

Scott, D. (2019, June 12). *The Nation's most prominent doctors group almost dropped its opposition to medicare-for-all*. Retrieved from Vox. https://www.vox.com/policy-and-politics/2019/6/12/18662722/ama-medicare-for-all-single-payer-vote-2020

Scott, W. R. (1966). In H. M. Vollmer & D. L. Mills (Eds.), *Professionalization*. Englewood Cliffs, NJ: Prentice-Hall.

Smith, K. (1980). Competing ethical values in medicine. *New England Journal of Medicine, 303*, 1482.

Stockman, F., & Baker, M. (2020, March 6). Nurses battling coronavirus beg for protective gear and better planning. *New York Times*, p. A10.

Su-Ting, L. T., Srinvasan, M., Der-Martirosian, C., Kravitz, R. L., & Wilkes, M. S. (2011). Developing personal values: Trainees' attitudes toward strikes by health care providers. *Academic Medicine, 86*, 580–585.

Sweeney, B. (2017, March 1). *Can the national labor relations board drag advocate to the bargaining table*. Retrieved from Crain's Chicago Business. https://www.chicagobusiness.com/article/20170301/NEWS03/170309978/can-the-national-labor-relations-board-drag-advocate-health-care-to-the-bargaining-table#utm_medium=email&utm%E2%80%A6

The Council on Ethical and Judicial Affairs of the American Medical Association. (2004). *Amendment to opinion E-9.025, "Collective action and patient advocacy"*. Chicago, IL: American Medical Association.

The New Physician. (1975). Housestaff Win Patient Care Improvements. *The New Physician, 24*, 75.

The Physicians Foundation. (2018, September 18). *2018 survey of America's physicians - Practice patterns & perspectives*. Retrieved from The Physicians Foundation. https://physiciansfoundation.org/wp-content/uploads/2018/09/physicians-survey-results-final-2018.pdf

Thomasma, D. C., & Hurley, R. M. (1988). The ethics of health professional strikes. In J. M. Moanagle & D. C. Thomasma (Eds.), *Medical ethics - A guide for health professionals*. Rockville, MD: Aspen.

Thompson, P. (1983). *The nature of work - An introduction to debates on the labour process*. London, UK: MacMilen Press.

Thompson, S. L., & Salmon, J. W. (2003). Physician collective bargaining In a U.S. Public Hospital. *International Journal of Health Services, 33*, 55–76.

Thompson, S. L., & Salmon, J. W. (2014). Physician strikes. *Chest, 146*, 1369–1374.

U.S. Bureau Of Labor Statistics. (2013). *Union Members in 2012*. Washington, D.C.: U.S. Bureau Of Labor Statistics. Retrieved from http://www.bls.gov/news.release/union2.toc.htm

Waitzkin, H. (2016, May 20). *Doctor-Workers: Unite!* Retrieved from Medscape.com. https://www.medscape.com/viewarticle/863297

Walker, A. (2001, January 23). East Coast doctors stronger after strike. *Medical Post, 37*.

Wassertheil-Smoller, S., Croen, L., & Siegel, B. (1979). Physicians' changing attitudes about striking. *Medical Care, 17*(1), 79–85.

Weber, M. (1978). In G. Roth & K. Wittich (Eds.), *Economy and society*. Berkeley, CA: University of California Press.

Wolfe, S. (1979). Strikes by health workers: A look at the concept, ethics, and impacts. *American Journal of Public Health, 69*, 431–433.

Wolinsky, F. D. (1988). The professional dominance perspective, revisited. *The Milbank Quarterly, 66*, 33–47.

Wong, A. (2019, January 22). *America's teachers are furious*. Retrieved from The Atlantic. https://www.theatlantic.com/education/archive/2019/01/teachers-are-launching-a-rebellion/580975/

Yates, C. A. (2009). In defence of the right to strike. *University of New Brunswick Law Journal, 59*, 128–137.

Zgarrick, D. P., McHugh, P. P., & Droege, M. (2006). Prevalence of and interest in unionization among staff pharmacists. *Research in Social and Administrative Pharmacy, 2*, 329–246.

Chapter 7
Conclusion: Progressive Directions

Ideas, concepts, and strategies can be found among American progressive health voices dating back to Henry Sigerist (Fee & Brown, 1997; Sigerist, 1960) and before, in Germany, Rudolph Virchow (McNeely, 2002). Such broader perspectives that embody health and health care for all citizens represent an idealism that never seemed to take hold firmly in the American healthcare system.

Many cultural and economic forces stand against a collective sense of popular health, partly due to the episodic piecemeal reimbursement for medical practitioners but more to the focusing on high-margin activities (e.g., elective procedures and surgeries). The social medicine perspective that recognizes that individual health lies in social groupings was *not* persuasive under American individualism (Waitzkin & Waterman, 1974; Waitzkin, 2000). Social epidemiologists repeatedly have demonstrated that people do get sick in groups; they share many clinical and social demographic characteristics in common (Cwikel, 2006; Salmon, 2008). Therefore, it makes imminent sense to address disease patterns in targeted population groups through community-based interventions and *not* as individuals unrelated to the people and places they interact with on a regular basis (McKeown, 1965; Roemer, 1956).

Biomedicine's grip remains doctor-centered, symptomatic- and disease-focused, episodic, and hospital-based with its technology fetish. In brief, it has made lots of money for providers and the medical industrial complex. Preventive medicine never took hold, and health promotion for populations never was developed. Moreover, there was not much money to be made in it, either.

Nevertheless, in certain academic medical centers, particularly beginning with the War on Poverty and Great Society policies, discussions in public health circles led to several designs and implementations from a social medicine perspective. Examples implemented were Neighborhood Health Centers, Comprehensive Health Planning, Regional Medical Programs, and a few more from when Public Health Service Commission Corps members were socially minded. These more forward-looking beginning attempts, unfortunately, did not advance widely due to prevailing forces of capitalism and subsequent Republican dismantling, as well as

© Springer Nature Switzerland AG 2021
J. W. Salmon, S. L. Thompson, *The Corporatization of American Health Care*,
https://doi.org/10.1007/978-3-030-60667-1_7

complacency within the House of American medicine. The dominance of the structural payment arrangement of fee-for-service medicine and cost-reimbursed hospital care was profoundly influential in defeating alternative visions of healthcare delivery.

Observations Elsewhere

Thus, the United States never experienced a collective sense of health like what began in Europe, neither at the time of Bismarck's Social Insurance Sickness Funds after 1890 nor the establishment of the National Health Service in post-World War Britain following the Beveridge Report of 1947. Social democratic policies have allowed Europe's universalist health systems to do better on access and cost, even as every citizen gets coverage. America has ignored the social epidemiological lens except by some determined scholars (Berkman et al., 2014; Braveman & Gottlieb, 2014).

Clearly, American capitalist development provided plenty of empirical observations of the social, occupational, and ecological causations of disease patterns and its failure to address much causations except the most grievous and publicized one. Business was constantly externalizing their production costs to workers, and to the environment, but always sought to deny or cover it up. Even with Nixon's establishment of the Occupational Safety and Health Administration (OSHA) and the Environmental Protection Agency (EPA), huge potential advances in developing a social epidemiological lens were neglected to examine broader health (Diez-Roux, 1998; Krieger, 2001).

Yet, investigations were branded as lackluster or "nonscientific" endeavors, and they were politically squashed (Daum, 1973; Stellman, 1973). Fringe progressive elements within medicine were noted academicians and those in public service at each level of government, but they never received enough attention, funding, nor broad support to effectuate remedial actions on the scale needed, nor much system even philosophical reorientation to attune to the fuller context of health.

Earlier on, certain prepaid group practices held a few potentialities in its *managed care principles for population health* (Roemer, 1978), yet organized medicine vilified the idea as anti-American "socialism" and unnecessary interference in the sacrosanct physician-patient relationship. As time progressed, more corporate influences were drawn into the medical industrial complex by the increased federal backing, with the *practices of managed* care corrupted with the Nixon-type profit-seeking HMOs (Salmon, 1978). Meanwhile, Medicaid for the states' indigent was never developed from a social medicine perspective, nor even much of a community medicine thrust; each program was a revenue stream for providers (Brown, 1983):

Additionally, social medicine successes from overseas never broke through the American arrogance that "the USA has the best healthcare system in the world" misbelief. Amazingly, at each point of national health reform debate in America from Democrats Bill Clinton through Barack Obama, few analyses of elsewhere internationally ever entered our domestic debates. In general, when considering changes in our own healthcare system, there is little examination of other nations that may suggest new ideas, programmatic approaches, and/or even mistakes to enlighten our national public policy formulation. This would be so crucial as implementations result in significant stumbling blocks, as clearly seen in Obamacare with plan cancellations in the Fall of 2013. Republicans have also misread the strong public concerns against narrower networks and for pre-existing conditions being held sacrosanct. The obvious rebuke to Republicans as the Party of no ideas on health (just repeal but no replace) was the 2018 election where the House flipped to the Democrats and voters in four states favored expansion of their Medicaid programs under the ACA (Armour, 2018).

Marketplace Medicine Dominates

Marketplace medicine has achieved such a strong ideological grip on our national consciousness, especially within the ranks of the health professions. Vested interests have been very persuasive in their propaganda against systems in other nations. Canada's universal national health insurance model is maligned continually as unworkable here in the United States, even though our own Medicare system borrowed both its name and some structure from the Canadian national system—just without becoming universal for everyone!

Americans do not realize how much of their money is wasted in this corporate healthcare system on overly priced, tax-supported care, coupled with such climbing out-of-pocket personal payments for their families for this corporate healthcare system. Especially compared to other nations, the United States is spending twice per capita than the universal plans in Canada and Germany with the next highest national outlays. Only lately have Democratic presidential candidates Bernie Sanders and Elizabeth Warren brought to light the huge profits in the insurance and pharmaceutical industries (Martin, 2019), when advocating a Medicare-for-All solution to deal with them. Given the near death of the Trump "repeal and replace," Medicaid expansion referendums in 2016 indicated public favor in states where Republican governors and legislatures had turned down the ACA generous support (Mulvihill & Alonso-Zaldivar, 2018).

For too long, many citizens have faced dire financial stress over their health care. Private insurance has indentured workers to depend upon jobs they may not like; they may lose family coverage if they leave a job or as ongoing reality reveals lose health coverage with the huge unemployment. Before the ongoing massive unemployment and loss of insurance caused by the COVID-19 Pandemic, some polls seemed to indicate many people were satisfied with their private coverage, a reality surely not guaranteed now in 2020. Hospitals sue patients for unpaid medical bills and garnish their wages; unpaid bills even before became the single greatest cause of bankruptcies for American families. The American Hospital Association takes no official position on this issue, but instead funneled millions of dollars worth of ads opposing single-payer insurance. The American Medical Association dropped out of the Partnership for America's Health Care Future, begun by the pharmaceutical industry and the for-profit hospital group (Diamond & Cancryn, 2019). Nevertheless, forces for corporatization that prefer the status quo of marketplace medicine continue to resist progressive thinking and any changes except that which benefits them.

What Direction Now?

To regain a moral compass in health policy, there needs to be much greater clarity over, and charity for, the plight of the uninsured and medically underserved; health professionals witness the unnecessary suffering of these minions who have lacked access over decades; without access, they do not get better, but just suffer needlessly and then cost much more to treat downstream for their chronic illnesses when they usually end up in the public sector. Surely, the high death rate of minorities from COVID-19 has revealed the long-standing inequities embedded in our health system structure (Dean, 2020); their health status emanates from underlying social conditions (Case & Deaton, 2020). Historically, the US Surgeon General's reports have annually delineated populations and disease conditions that, in a socially just and humane society, should have been significantly targeted to reduce the widespread health inequities in this richest nation of the world. Richardson (2017) has argued that Democrats must seize a historic opportunity *not* to make the rich richer. Yet Democrats must dislodge Mitch McConnell's Senate grip in service to Donald Trump so legislation can be passed (Editorial: Burns & Martin, 2017).

Completely absent of any compassion, the Trump Administration considers compassion in health as a sorrowfully nonexistent commodity. In the COVID-19 outbreak, testing was restrained and not widely available to the high-risk groups of elderly, prisoners, or detainees, though a few states and counties later targeted minority communities and began to address, though tragically late, nursing homes. Supply chain arrangements over essential testing supplies, personal protective equipment (PPE), ventilators, etc. were poorly coordinated and corrupt (McSwane, 2020). Witness his May 2020 trip to Michigan extolling his made-up "man of the year award" while never mentioning the folks harmed by two power dam breaks that flooded many Michiganders' homes and businesses a few days right before (Karni, 2020). Nor has Trump himself sadly shown much knowledge of the plight of minorities, immigrants, protestors, or anyone criticizing him. His attacks on opponents have been said to disgrace the Office of the Presidency and proven to embarrass our nation on the world stage. Thus, despite campaign promises on expanded health coverage, lower drug prices, and almost all healthcare reform ideas, there has been nothing! (Hamblin, 2019).

Unpreparedness on Several Counts

The "repeal and replace" cry lessened most emphasis in health care, even as Title X funding was cut from Planned Parenthood amidst Trump's remaking of women's health policy (Alonzo-Zaldivar & Crary, 2018; Luthi, 2018). The GOP healthcare bill in 2017 sliced the Centers for Disease Control and Prevention's budget (Facher, 2017), as well as closed down the White House's National Security Council Directorate for Global Health Security and Biodefense (Cameron, 2020), two ominous actions that left the nation less prepared for the COVID-19 pandemic. How terrible present health and economic conditions became for the working and middle class was displayed in Trump's incompetent handling of the supply chain distribution, given urban health systems collapsing and the resultant massive societal unemployment, reaching 42 million by June 2020 (Cox, 2020). For employers, outlays for health coverage shrunk, so bottom lines benefited some, despite slacking production. The unemployed—now expanding Medicaid roles by 20% to 30%—will bring greater profits to drug store chains and pharmacy benefit managers (PBMs), though at the expense of their losing more lucrative employer-sponsored participants (Fein, 2020). Whether under fee-for-service or managed care, volume dispensing is key to these pharmacy players.

In today's economy, the question to ask now is: Do the 170 some million Americans really like their employment-based private insurance, versus what Medicare single payer could be for them as a needed shield in these bad times? Republicans have recently proffered short-term, limited duration plans during the epidemic to compete with the Obama exchange plans; insurers may deny based on preexisting conditions, which the ACA had made illegal (Cohrs, 2020).

Depictions in the news media often present human-interest stories, but without further notice or indictment of those who perpetuate perverse conditions. In general, the establishment and corporate media downplayed both Sanders and Warren's universal Medicare and their outright criticisms of the insurance and pharmaceutical industries while favoring Centrist Democrats' criticisms of Medicare for All (Pedersen, 2019). Greater depth of analyses must forcefully be put forward for restructuring strategies for change and to help rid profit-taking from the healthcare system.

The pandemic has been said to present a turning point in health care due to its unprecedented impact domestically and worldwide; however, it is not just a need for data science conducted under the auspice of Silicon Valley (Aitken, 2020). It was surely a wake-up call on unpreparedness and inequalities. Several advocacy groups have remarked that out the ashes of COVID-19, a Medicare-for-All movement should arise (Abrams, 2020). To achieve such a national policy, its proponents must lead the public to see and understand how much the broader context of corporate health has to do with system corruption that created the mass vulnerability to the virus (PNHP, 2020). As progressives should readily realize, a financing solution alone is clearly insufficient, even if providers acknowledge and try to address social determinants of diseases. Overhauling the dominant players, restraining egregious profits, and restructuring care patterns across the system must be at the forefront of progressive policymaking. Greatly increased funding for new enrollees would be welcomed by the forces of greed, but without regulatory restraint to strive for ethical efficiencies, a newly constructed healthcare system may be unlikely.

Broad structural reorganization must be planned in phases to move toward equity in health and to gradually rid corporate profit-taking throughout health care (Eyer, 1984). Greater numbers of individual patients and families themselves now ponder the overall post-COVID-19 condition, when they face vastly delimited quality care—and cannot afford it. Folks may realize how much single-payer ideas are now worthy of consideration for benefiting themselves and everyone. Notwithstanding, Americans should never settle for a stripped down Medicaid-for-All mechanism that compromises care benefits. For those who are able purchase add-on private coverage, will it be enough to revitalize the medical industrial complex?

So, messages for positive progressive principles must be shared to fend off Centrist Democrats spouting their similar corporate/Republican talking points to preserve the status quo or at best merely tinker on the margins of reform like a state-by-state public option. Thinking about how to reorganize the overall delivery system and to advocate for a new equitable public policy for all of the American people may have to reach beyond the average person's grasp; as Trump himself once said, "Nobody knew health care could be so complicated." Such an educational strategy necessitates clear articulation of what visionary reforms might concretely mean for families, communities, and the entire population—so necessary during the 2020 election campaign beyond merely "building on the ACA."

Republican health policies historically have been so focused on special interests at the expense of the public's health, that it was worth the review in Chaps. 1 and 2 to see how vested interests benefitted from past administrations, notwithstanding the Democrats who also failed to enact more progressive policies, instead merely feeding the corporate monster. Even with the Affordable Care Act decreasing George W. Bush's number of uninsured by 41% in 2017, some 20+ million still were kept out of insurance coverage after 6 years of its passage—a legacy that prevailed into Trump's rule.

Remember again that giving someone an insurance card is *not* in reality guaranteeing access to care. Access means assuring timely availability of affordable, comprehensive, quality care that is continuous by lowering social and cultural barriers to that care for a given population (Gulliford et al., 2002). This means guaranteeing substantial infrastructural improvement so that *physicians are there in all communities for relationships with patients and families.* The ACA did not do this!

The Current Crisis

Minorities and the poor have borne the greatest burden with class and race mostly accounting for the structural discrimination over why universal care has not been established here. News accounts demonstrate that minorities, the homeless, the aged in nursing homes and homes for the disabled, prisoners, and the poor have been most gravely stricken by COVID-19; these are groups that right-wing factions may consider as Charles Dickens's "surplus population" of the unproductive. To some degree, knowing much earlier these people were most at risk for infection, it may be assumed that a planned biological and economic genocide might have been orchestrated, since too little, too late, or no federal policies were enacted.

Ongoing, this may demonstrate systemic social injustice and just may account for Trump's sinister delay in rolling out faster widespread virus testing with a supply chain to ensure adequate distribution (Callahan & Botella, 2020; McSwane & Gabrielson, 2020). Incompetence in managing supply lines might have been overcome had the Administration been dedicated to different values and concerns for clearly those groups who were forgotten in the outbreak.

For sure, a persistent ongoing financial crisis in health care is ahead for providers (Barnett, Mehrotra, & Landon, 2020). Value-based care will require reconceptualization with telemedicine taking hold: Will the finance powers that be provoke a "renaissance" for value-based insurance? (Olmstead, 2020). Many agree the pandemic will not preserve much of the same (The pandemic will recast the health-care industrial complex, 2020).

It remains certain that corporate domination over the American healthcare system will never cease with both the Democratic and Republican parties still under sway of the corporate grip; business lobbies were able to direct legislative and executive actions before the coronavirus outbreak and are gearing up for more federal largess post-COVID-19. Apple and Google have proceeded with their tracking devices under government subsidization and medical record advances during the epidemic, even with skeptics and concerns over privacy (Apple, Google debut major effort to help people track if they've come in contact with coronavirus, 2020; The pandemic has spawned a new way to study medical records, 2020; The Economist, 2020a). Dumaine (2020) claims Amazon was built for the pandemic, becoming bigger and stronger. If the politicians and public swallow the belief in Big Data, greater largess will flow into their coffers as they forge further control over policymaking. Adding to the persuasiveness of this line of thinking is that clinicians and most citizens now recognize strengthening the public health infrastructure must come in preparedness for the next disease disaster. IT firms see large steady profit streams and improved public popularity for solving the COVID-19 crisis as well as future epidemics, in addition to their already addressing health system dysfunctions.

The *New England Journal of Medicine Catalyst* (Barnett et al., 2020) surveyed clinicians to uncover:

1. Many providers will be financially devastated, with perhaps significant staffing shortages.
2. Feelings of expendability may be sensed "when being directed by ignorant administrators with little clinical understanding" (Barnett et al., 2020).
3. Inventory management with proper logistical coordination will be better maintained, especially for personal protective equipment (PPE), ventilators and drug supplies, etc.
4. Should the coronavirus remain endemic, or its curve flattened, or cases diminish, cross-training may become a routine.
5. Telemedicine will grow with enhanced technologies.
6. Burnout will likely be better understood with more interventions commonplace.
7. Delivery of services will become more diverse and efficient.
8. Independent rural hospital closings, plus clinics.
9. Hopefully increased understandings of population needs.
10. Clinical leadership roles will be strengthened.

11. At point of inflection, will systems learn from the lessons of the pandemic?

Many hospitals face a precarious future given the coronavirus impact: margins will shrink, strategies and restructuring will come, staff may leave or die as was the case in hotspot areas, closings will be likely concentrated in red states, and unless financing can be assured, amalgamations will decline.

The CARES Act of 2020

The Congressional bailout paid billions to the wealthiest hospital chains, just as big hospitals got richer off Obamacare, forsaking many struggling health providers (Drucker et al., 2020). Last year, the pharmaceutical industry spent $295 million on lobbying, more than any other industry (Accountable.US, 2020). This industry seems to be trying to redeem itself (Gordon, 2020) in the public's mind with high-speed coronavirus treatments and a vaccine (Thomas & Grady, 2020). The IT industry already has numerous inroads in health care as discussed earlier, and many big firms are planning their "solutions" to the present system chaos, without privacy controls or other oversight. The pandemic will likely recast the entire healthcare industrial complex (The Economist, 2020b); McKinsey claims the virus recovery will be digital as IT firms beef up their growing extensions into health care (McKinsey & Company, 2020).

Infrastructural development and added federal economic stimulus will likely flow mainly into corporate coffers (as was seen with the Boeing bailout, airline subsidization, and channeling Small Business Administration loans through the biggest banks). Unless strong popular resistance is mounted and the Trump Administration is brought to justice, Democrats must take much different stands on the economic recovery, or the more powerful will win in negotiations for future subsidizations. Historians, beyond the scathing flow of media reviews to Trump's response to the COVID-19 epidemic, will have much to pour through.

In the midst of Trump's first 3 years of uncertainty and policy confusion, the insurance industry seemed to do fine (Luthi & Dickson, 2017), particularly on Medicare advantage plans (Livingston, 2018). In 2019, health profits boosted CEO salaries by 15.7%, with the head of CVS pocketing $36.5 million. Articles in the trade magazines tried to explain the impact of COVID-19, which was that with healthcare organizations cancelling all elective procedures because of the huge increase in pandemic patients entering their hospitals, their outlay for these procedures is way down (Liss, 2020; Livingston, 2020). And insurance companies were given a boost when the Supreme Court upheld the ACA's "risk corridors" extra payments to insurers if sicker patients had signed up on their roles—a $12 billion infusion of cash that Republicans in Congress had unfunded in their continuing repeal of the ACA (Liptak, 2020).

Note that the massive decrease in elective procedures and surgeries, and an epidemic of diagnoses and their too often cascade iatrogenesis (Welch et al., 2007), can present phenomenal outlays for insurers; unemployed workers are not having premiums paid for them anymore, but at best Medicaid may be picking up the tab for the costly repair work now during the layoff. In the second Congressional Heroes Act appropriations bill under consideration, House Speaker Nancy Pelosi favored health insurers by providing subsidized 9 months' coverage for furloughed workers and the unemployed using COBRA for continued insurance coverage (Lacy & Walker, 2020). It is key to note that not all health care is hurting; health insurers are thriving with the diminished utilization (Johnson, 2020), but will they cut premiums and co-pays as some auto insurers have? Not much hope resides for insurers to step up to demonstrate their commitment to the nation's health (Navathe & Emanuel, 2020).

The booming federal deficit in trillions, and the tendency by Trump and the Republicans to distribute funding in their way to business, may leave fewer funds for health and social spending over several coming years. Schneider in the *New England Journal of Medicine* points out the tragic data gap that continues to undermine the US response even as this country tallies the most cases and deaths in the world (Schneider, 2020), yet with little clarity, as the nation watches second and third waves of the virus after Trump's churches returning and rallies beginning in the "reopening of the economy." Lack of faith in Washington given the handling of the COVID-19 crisis (Tavernise, 2020), as well as the state and local conduct toward the summer protests, may cement negative views toward politicians and public policy that may delimit progressive possibilities. Atkins (2020) argues we need a renewed Party that tells the truth and represents working Americans. It remains to be seen even under a winning Democratic Administration whether regulatory regress will return to the political environment as before 2016. As Lilla wrote in *The New York Times*, a state of radical uncertainty awaits the nation and world: Does anyone really know what's going to happen? (Lilla, 2020). Given the Minneapolis cop killing George Floyd and the subsequent protests and rioting across the nation, profound clouds may hang over our nation's future up until the election.

Future Role of Labor Unions

One must recognize that the history of American medical care is intricately intertwined with the American Labor Movement, which was highly instrumental in bringing out positive changes in health coverage and in public policy. Union membership has substantially lessened, though since the Reagan years, will under current circumstances, lead unions to re-emerge as a stronger voice in national policymaking. After the Second World War, unions embraced employment-based coverage but tended to abandon broader population advocacy. Yet today with new organizing campaigns, issues look different since the working class has growing minority representation, and they are truly hurting and vocal. Employment-based coverage has been presented by Centrist Democrats as a huge obstacle against the adoption of single-payer health insurance for all—nevertheless, with up to 60 million jobs lost and no coverage solutions for them in 2020, people may now feel much differently, especially about the role of private insurance.

American unions had earlier on sought to address the very conditions of life, including health insurance as a benefit for families, workers' compensation, occupational health, child and maternal health care, and more benefit additions over time. Labor must now get behind such policy concerns and fight hard for universalist social democratic policy changes (Atkins, 2020).

An Expanded Corporatization?

Nevertheless, the interests, objectives, and behaviors of corporate entities that were centralizing in health care fought against Labor's efforts and supported the shift to private ownership in the healthcare system. This different healthcare power structure brought along changes in traditions, philosophies, and the way history is being interpreted. The greater complexity and increased size of the health sector led to changes in the relative size of its different components (pharmaceuticals and hospitals vs. physicians) and the change in the position of the health sector in society in general (both parties' administrations have recognized health services as boosting economic growth). It was under these circumstances that proprietary health services took root both in the medical care sector (HMOs, ambulatory care, etc.) and in hospitals, along with the rise of powerful administrators replacing physicians in command. Will the American Labor movement get behind our critique of corporate health care? Given these developments, the position of "the physician" is subject to alteration. Will the profession be granted the evidence and relative power to meet clinical and financial goals? How will Labor respond to Medicine's current quandary?

Clearly, information technology can and will make substantial contributions to help solve the data dilemmas in health care; however, such directions should proceed with oversight and multiple cautions. Understanding the origins of the American healthcare system before and after the viral outbreak will be more illuminating to rebuild it for more equitable distribution of services to all our citizenry. The trillion dollar IT behemoths are positioned to seize new opening opportunities with their huge cash buckets (McKinsey & Company, 2020) under the seemingly prevailing mood that they can "solve" our healthcare problems. Most of their activity stays under the public radar; meanwhile, their corporate public affair offices maintain vigil over popular favor for most of what they do, despite critics more dismayed by notable specific unsavory business behaviors. The well-cited discussion in Chap. 5 should provoke caution in addition to worries.

Public policy has never truly addressed the issue of what should be the nature of the relationship between health services within a profit-based economy: What is the proper role for profit-oriented firms in the supply, provider functions, and insurance segment? How should their roles be assessed and at what costs and control are they permitted? What safeguards should be instituted to preserve a more appropriate and popularly desired balance? What is the necessary regulatory oversight for maintaining accountability?

More importantly, is the structure and control over what we have now the *best and the only way to organize healthcare services for the benefit of the American people* and for their health promotion and well-being in the whole population? Do we want a system designed and run by those with huge financial interests in the system?

References

Abrams, A. (2020). *For organizer Ady Barkan, COVID-19 is yet another reason to pass medicare for all*. Available at: https://time.com/5810489/medicare-for-allcoronavirus-2/. Accessed on October 13, 2020.

Accountable.US. (2020). *Lobbying spending in 2019 nears all-time high as health sector smashes records*. Available at: https://www.accountable.us/news/bigpharma-earnings-season-record-profits-from-patients-being-poured-into-windfall-earnings-for-lobbyists/. Accessed 13 Oct 2020.

Aitken, M. (2020). *COVID-19 as a positive turning point in healthcare*. https://www.iqvia.com/insights/the-iqvia-institute/covid-19/covid-19-as-a-positive-turning-point-in-healthcare. Accessed July 25, 2020.

Alonzo-Zaldivar, R., & Crary, D. (2018). *Trump remaking federal policy on women's reproductive health*. Available at: https://apnews.com/article/0a165e54c0a94600871539472ba82ba1. Accessed 13 Oct 2020.

Armour, S. (2018, October 22). Votes in red states to test support for Medicaid expansion. *Wall Street Journal*. p. A3.

Atkins, J. B. (2020). We need a party that tells the truth and represents workers. *Portside*. Available via DIALOG. https://portside.org/2020-05-26/we-need-party-tells-truth-and-represents-workers. Accessed June 2, 2020.

Barnett, M. L., Mehrotra, A., & Landon, B. E. (2020). COVID-19 and the upcoming financial crisis in healthcare. *NEJM Catalyst*. Available via DIALOG. https://catalyst.nejm.org/doi/full/10.1056/CAT.20.0153. Accessed June 4, 2020.

Berkman, L. F., Kawachi, I., & Glymour, M. M. (2014). *Social epidemiology*. Oxford, UK: Oxford University Press.

Braveman, P., & Gottlieb, L. (2014). The social determinants of health: It's time to consider the causes of the causes. *Public Health Reports (Washington, D.C.: 1974), 129*(Suppl 2), 19–31.

Brown, E. R. (1983). Medicare and medicaid: The process, value, and limits of health care reforms. *Journal of Health Policy, 4*(3), 335–366.

Burns, A., & Martin, J. (2017). *McConnell, in private, doubts if Trump can save presidency*. Available at: https://www.nytimes.com/2017/08/22/us/politics/mitchmcconnell-trump.html. Accessed 13 Oct 2020.

Callahan, P., & Botella, S. (2020, August 7). The White House paid up to $500 million Too Much for these ventilators, Congressional Investigators say. *ProPublica*.

Cameron, B. (2020). I ran the White House pandemic office. Trump closed it. *The Washington Post*. Available via DIALOG. https://www.washingtonpost.com/outlook/nsc-pandemic-office-trump-closed/2020/03/13/a70de09c-6491-11ea-acca-80c22bbee96f_story.html. Accessed June 11, 2020.

Case, A., & Deaton, A. (2020). *America can afford a world-class health system. Why don't we have one?* Available on: https://www.nytimes.com/2020/04/14/opinion/sunday/covid-inequality-health-care.html. Accessed 13 Oct 2020.

Cohrs, R. (2020). Appeals court weighs legality of limited health plans amid COVID-19 crisis. *Modern Healthcare*. Available via DIALOG. https://www.modernhealthcare.com/legal/appeals-court-weighs-legality-junk-insurance-plans-amid-covid-19-outbreak. Accessed June 3, 2020.

Cox, J. (2020). *Coronavirus job losses could total 47 million, unemployment rate may hit 32%, Fed estimates*. Available at: https://www.cnbc.com/2020/03/30/coronavirus-job-losses-could-total-47-million-unemployment-rate-of-32percent-fed-says.html. Accessed 13 Oct 2020.

Cwikel, J. G. (2006). *Social epidemiology: Strategies for public health activism*. New York, NY: Columbia University Press.

Daum, S. (1973). *Work is dangerous to your health*. New York, NY: Vintage.

Dean, L. (2020). The pandemic has exposed health disparities; we need to act on these painful lessons. *Modern Healthcare*. Available via DIALOG. https://www.modernhealthcare.com/opinion-editorial/pandemic-has-exposed-health-disparities-we-need-act-these-painful-lessons. Accessed June 3, 2020.

Diamond, D., & Cancryn, A. (2019). AMA drops out of industry coalition opposed to Medicare expansion. *Politico*. Available via DIALOG. https://www.politico.com/story/2019/08/15/ama-drops-out-of-industry-coalition-opposed-to-medicare-expansion-1664604. Accessed June 3, 2020.

Diez-Roux, A. V. (1998). Bringing context back into epidemiology: Variables and fallacies in multilevel analysis. *American Journal of Public Health, 88*(2), 216–222.

Drucker, J., Silver-Greenberg, J., & Kliff, S. (2020). *Wealthiest hospitals got billions in bailout for struggling health providers*. Available at: https://www.nytimes.com/2020/05/25/business/coronavirus-hospitals-bailout.html. Accessed 11 Oct 2020.

Dumaine, B. (2020). *Amazon was built for the pandemic—and will likely emerge from it stronger than ever*. Available at: https://fortune.com/2020/05/18/amazonbusiness-jeff-bezos-amzn-sales-revenue-coronavirus-pandemic/. Accessed 13 Oct 2020.

Eyer, J. (1984). Capital, health, and illness. In J. McKinlay (Ed.), *Issues in the political economy of health*. New York, NY: Tavistock.

Facher, L. (2017). Obamacare repeal and Trump's spending plan put CDC budget in peril. *STAT News*. Available via DIALOG. https://www.statnews.com/2017/03/07/cdc-budget-obamacare-repeal/. Accessed June 11, 2020.

Fein, A. J. (2020). *Four unexpected ways that the COVID-19 medicaid boom will affect PMB and pharmacy profits*. Available at: https://www.drugchannels.net/2020/04/four-unexpected-ways-that-covid-19.html; for Single-Payer Health Care Reform. Available at: https://pnhp.org/what-is-single-payer/physicians-proposal/. Accessed 13 Oct 2020.

Gordon, J. (2020). 'After Covid pharma no longer looks like a big oil or tobacco.' *City Wire*. Available via DIALOG. https://citywire.co.uk/investment-trust-insider/news/after-covid-pharma-no-longer-looks-like-big-oil-or-tobacco/a1357550. Accessed June 2, 2020.

Gulliford, M., Figueroa, J. I., Morgan, M., Hughes, D., Gibson, B., Beech, R., & Hudson, M. (2002). What does "access to health care" mean? *Journal of Health Services Research & Policy, 7*(3), 186–188.

Hamblin, J. (2019). Has Trump actually done anything about drug prices? *The Atlantic*. Available via DIALOG: https://www.theatlantic.com/health/archive/2019/05/trump-actually-decreasing-drug-prices/589096/. Accessed July 25, 2020.

Johnson, J. (2020). Thriving during a pandemic: UnitedHealth group posts surge in profits as millions lose insurance and thousands die. *Common Dreams*. Available via DIALOG. https://www.commondreams.org/news/2020/04/16/thriving-during-pandemic-unitedhealth-group-posts-surge-profits-millions-lose. Accessed June 4, 2020.

Karni, A. (2020). *In Michigan visit, Trump forgoes criticism and talks about the economy and the flood*. Available at: https://www.nytimes.com/2020/05/21/us/politics/trump-michigan-visit.html. Accessed 13 Oct 2020.

Krieger, N. (2001). The ostrich, the albatross, and public health: An ecosocial perspective--or why an explicit focus on health consequences of discrimination and deprivation is vital for good science and public health practice. *Public Health Reports (Washington, D.C.: 1974), 116*(5), 419–423.

Lacy, A., & Walker, J. (2020). Heroes act delivers a win to the health insurance industry. *The Intercept*. Available via DIALOG. https://theintercept.com/2020/05/12/heroes-act-coronavirus-health-insurance-industry/. Accessed June 4, 2020.

Lilla, M. (2020). No one knows what's going to happen. *The New York Times*. Available via DIALOG. https://www.nytimes.com/2020/05/22/opinion/sunday/coronavirus-prediction-future.html. Accessed June 4, 2020.

Liptak, A. (2020). Supreme Court rules for insurers in $12 billion Obamacare case. *New York Times*. Available via DIALOG: https://www.nytimes.com/2020/04/27/us/supreme-court-obamacare-insurance.html. Accessed July 25, 2020.

Liss, S. (2020). Despite the pandemic, insurers seem cautiously optimistic about 2020. *Here's why*. Available via DIALOG: https://www.healthcaredive.com/news/despite-the-pandemic-insurers-seem-cautiously-optimistic-about-2020-here/577511/. Accessed July 25, 2020.

Livingston, S. (2018). Insurers profit from Medicare Advantage's incentive to add coding that boots reimbursement. *Modern Healthcare*. Available via DIALOG. https://www.modernhealthcare.com/article/20180901/NEWS/180839977/insurers-profit-from-medicare-advantage-s-incentive-to-add-coding-that-boosts-reimbursement. Accessed June 4, 2020.

Livingston, S. (2020). Large Health Insurers Appear Immune to COVID-19. *Modern Healthcare*. Available via DIALOG. https://www.modernhealthcare.com/insurance/large-health-insurers-appear-immune-covid-19. Accessed July 25, 2020.

Luthi, S. (2018). *Trump could ban Title X funding for Planned Parenthood*. Available at: https://www.modernhealthcare.com/article/20180426/NEWS/180429923/trump-could-ban-title-x-funding-for-planned-parenthood. Accessed 13 Oct 2020.

Luthi, S., & Dickson, V. (2017). *2018 Outlook on politics and policy: Insurers will come out ahead*. Available at: https://www.modernhealthcare.com/article/20171230/NEWS/171239990/2018-outlook-on-politics-and-policy-insurers-will-come-out-ahead. Accessed 13 Oct 2020.

Martin, J. (2019). *Elizabeth Warren and Bernie Sanders have a problem: Each other*. Available on: https://www.nytimes.com/2019/12/16/us/politics/elizabethwarren-bernie-sanders-democrats-2020.html. Accessed 13 Oct 2020.

McKeown, T. (1965). *Medicine in modern society*. London, UK: George, Allen and Unwin.

McKinsey & Company. (2020). *The next normal: The recovery will be digital*. Available at: https://www.mckinsey.com/~/media/McKinsey/Business%20Functions/McKinsey%20Digital/Our%20Insights/How%20six%20companies%20are%20using%20technology%20and%20data%20to%20transform%20themselves/The-next-normal-the-recovery-will-be-digital.pdf. Accessed 13 Oct 2020.

McSwane, J. D. (2020). *The secret, absurd world of coronavirus mask traders and middlemen trying to get rich off government money*. Available at: https://www.propublica.org/article/the-secret-absurd-world-of-coronavirus-mask-traders-and-middlemen-trying-to-get-rich-off-government-money. Accessed 13 Oct 2020.

McSwane, J. D., & Gabrielson, R. (2020, June 18). The Trump administration paid millions for test tubes—and got unusable mini soda bottles. *ProPublica*.

Mulvihill, G., & Alonso-Zaldivar, R. (2018). ACA big issue on voter agenda. *Chicago Tribune*. 11 October. Sec 2 p. 1.

Navathe, A. S., & Emanuel, E. J. (2020). Health insurers as heroes? *The New York Times*. Available via DIALOG. https://www.nytimes.com/2020/05/06/opinion/coronavirus-insurance.html. Accessed June 4, 2020.

Olmstead, R. (2020). Is a value-based insurance design experiencing a renaissance? *Employee Benefit Adviser*. Available via DIALOG. https://www.employeebenefitadviser.com/opinion/is-value-based-insurance-design-experiencing-a-renaissance. Accessed June 4, 2020.

Pedersen, B. (2019). Medicare for all: Promise and perils. Incremental reforms are more likely than a complete overhaul. *Kiplinger's Personal Finance*. Available via DIALOG. https://www.kiplinger.com/article/insurance/T027-C000-S002-medicare-for-all-promise-and-perils.html. Accessed June 11, 2020.

PNHP. (2020). Physicians' Proposal - Beyond the Affordable Care Act: A Physicians' Proposal for Single-Payer Health Care Reform. Available at: https://pnhp.org/what-is-single-payer/physicians-proposal/. Accessed on October 13, 2020.

Richardson, H. C. (2017). *Democrats have a historic opportunity. They must not make the rich richer.* Available at: https://www.theguardian.com/commentisfree/2017/aug/03/democrats-trump-better-deal-income-inequality. Accessed 13 Oct 2020.

Roemer, M. I. (1956). *Medical care in relation to public health: A study of relationships between preventive and curative health services throughout the world.* Geneva, Switzerland: World Health Organization.

Roemer, M. I. (1978). Social medicine: The advance of organized health services in America. *Springer Series on Health Care and Society, 3,* 1–560.

Salmon, J. W. (1978). *Corporate attempts to reorganize the American health care system.* Unpublished thesis at Cornell University, Ithaca, NY.

Salmon, J. W. (2008). Review essay: Cwikel, J. G. Social epidemiology: Strategies for public health activism. *International Journal of Global Social Work Practice,* (1), Fall.

Schneider, E. C. (2020). Failing the test- The tragic data gap undermining the U.S. pandemic response. *The New England Journal of Medicine.* Available via DIALOG. https://www.nejm.org/doi/full/10.1056/NEJMp2014836. Accessed June 4, 2020.

Stellman, J. M. (1973). *Work is dangerous to your health: A handbook of health hazards in the workplace and what you can do about them.* New York, NY: Pantheon Books.

Tavernise, S. (2020). Will this crisis cement Americans' lack of faith in Washington? *The New York Times.* Available via DIALOG. https://www.nytimes.com/2020/05/23/us/coronavirus-government-trust.html. Accessed June 4, 2020.

The Economist. (2020a). *The pandemic has spawned a new way to study medical records.* Available at: https://www.economist.com/science-andtechnology/2020/05/14/the-pandemic-has-spawned-a-new-way-to-study-medical-records. Accessed 13 Oct 2020.

The Economist. (2020b). The pandemic will recast America's health-care industrial complex. *The Economist.* Available via DIALOG. https://www.economist.com/business/2020/05/09/the-pandemic-will-recast-americas-health-care-industrial-complex. Accessed June 4, 2020.

Thomas, K., & Grady, D. (2020). *How upbeat vaccine news fueled a stock surge, and an uproar.* Available at: https://www.nytimes.com/2020/05/23/health/coronavirus-vaccine-moderna.html. Accessed 13 Oct 2020.

Waitzkin, H. (2000). The second sickness: Contradictions of capitalist healthcare. Lanham, MD: Rowman & Littlefield Publishers, Inc.

Waitzkin, H., & Waterman, B. (1974). The exploitation of illness in capitalist society. Indianapolis, IN: MacMillan.

Index

© Springer Nature Switzerland AG 2021
J. W. Salmon, S. L. Thompson, *The Corporatization of American Health Care*,
https://doi.org/10.1007/978-3-030-60667-1

Printed in the United States
by Baker & Taylor Publisher Services